CONTENTS

CONTENTS (Continued)

Proceedings Of The
Second AIAA Symposium
On

Aerodynamics Of Sports
& Competition Automobiles

Edited By Bernard Pershing

May 11, 1974

Los Angeles, California

Volume 16

American Institute Of Aeronautics & Astronautics
Lecture Series

American Institute Of Aeronautics & Astronautics

9841 Airport Boulevard • Suite 800 • Los Angeles, California 90045

Publisher and Library Distributor

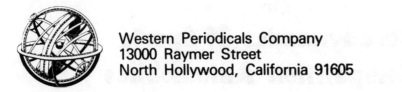

Western Periodicals Company
13000 Raymer Street
North Hollywood, California 91605

Trade Distributor

3501 Hennepin Avenue South
Minneapolis, Minnesota 55408

ISBN 0-87938-028-4

FORWARD

In April 1968, the Los Angeles Section of the American Institute of Aeronautics and Astronautics presented the symposium, The Aerodynamics of Sports and Competition Automobiles. In response to the continued interest in automotive aerodynamics and the progress achieved in this field in recent years, a second symposium was organized and presented May 11, 1974. The symposium was devoted to an examination of the role of aerodynamics in the design, development and operation of high performance land-borne vehicles.

In their continued striving for greater performance, designers of sports cars, dragsters and land speed record cars have placed themselves at the forefront of automotive technology. This symposium has provided a platform for presentation of the newest developments in automotive aerodynamics and has given automotive enthusiasts of all ages and all ranges of technical background an opportunity to gather and exchange information and ideas.

The collection of papers presented is unique in its range of subject matter. In the five meeting sessions, motorcycles and trucks as well as high performance cars were discussed from both the technical and the historical viewpoint. In the first session, System Design, Bernard Pershing presented a general survey of those areas in which aerodynamics exhibit first order effects on the performance and handling qualities of land-borne vehicles while E. Eugene Larrabee gave a comprehensive review of analytic methods for assessing aerodynamic effects on road vehicle performance, stability and control. A series of compact sedan and sports car designs configured to control the flow about and beneath their contours was described by Walter Korff. Lynn Yakel reviewed the development and operation of a series of his two and four-wheel streamliner designs which achieved National and World records at the Bonneville Salt Flats while Peter Bryant discussed methods for developing and measuring aerodynamic downforce on race cars.

The second session, Flow Field Analysis, was particularly rich in the originality and quality of material presented. The wake properties of various vehicle types at zero and non-zero angle of yaw were investigated in wind tunnel tests reported by Jeffrey Howell and some dramatic flow visualization studies of trapped vortex flows on general bluff bodies and automobiles was presented by J. J. Cornish III. A detailed description of the airflow and pressure distribution about an isolated road tire was given by J. E. Fackrell and J. K. Harvey. This work is of particular interest since by using a rotating tire on a moving ground plane correctly modeled data was obtained on a fundamental problem of road vehicle aerodynamics. Glen Brown reviewed the various methods for the aerodynamic testing of road vehicles and described an effective low cost technique based on the concept of absolute and relative data accuracy.

Dean Batchelor's historical survey of Bonneville record cars was a comprehensive and sensitive narration of past achievements on the Salt by one who, when he wasn't setting records himself, was documenting them in his capacity as automotive writer and magazine editor.

In the third session, Vehicle Dynamics and Handling Qualities, Hans-Hermann Braess and co-authors described the full scale wind tunnel and road tests they performed in the aerodynamic development of the Porsche Model 911 Carrera and discussed the effects of aerodynamics on handling and performance. The effects of aerodynamic download on stability, steady state steering, path response and cornering performance, were analytically examined by Roger Hawks.

In the fourth session, Motorcycles, Kevin Cooper utilized the test data obtained in the National Aeronautical Establishment wind tunnel to analyse the effects of aerodynamics on the performance, stability, and dynamic response of motorcycles and to identify the performance penalties and dynamic unstabilities which can result from improper aerodynamic design. In one of the more original papers of the meeting, Douglas Malewicki reviewed the technical aspects of the motorcycle long distance jump maneuver and examined the critical factors governing safe and consistant performance. The last paper of the session by Jon McKibben described the two year development program of the Honda Hawk which culminated in the record speed of 287 mph and discussed the chassis and aerodynamic related stability functions peculiar to two-wheel vehicles.

In the fifth session, Aerodynamic Drag, Bain Dayman in his analytic examination of roll-down test techniques quantified the effects on the inferred aerodynamic drag coefficient introduced by the assumption of constant tire rolling resistance and presented an approach which substantially reduces these errors. A discussion of the basic elements of bluff body drag as it relates to truck air resistance was given by Peter Lissaman while Jeffrey Kirsch presented the results of a full scale vehicle road test conducted to evaluate the use of front mounted vanes to reduce the aerodynamic drag of bluff bodies.

The discussion periods following the papers provided platforms for a lively exchange of ideas and an airing of opinions. As they were an integral part of the symposium, every effort was expended in transcribing these remarks from the tape recordings for inclusion in the transactions. Because of less-than-perfect acoustics, we were not always successful. Where it was not possible to identify the audience speakers, their comments are preceded by "AUD. QUESTION".

I would like to express my personal thanks and appreciation to the speakers and to many others who contributed to the symposium. A special note of thanks to Richard Scherrer who helped chair the day's sessions, to David Wier and Henry Jex who served as proxy speakers and to Dean Batchelor whose memorable talk I am honored to document in these transactions. I would also like to acknowledge the outstanding contributions of William A. Moore who designed the meeting announcement and transaction cover, Strother MacMinn who helped set the tone of the meeting with wall hangings of his students, Alex Tremulis who provided the model display of his automotive designs, Fred Timson who provided photographic coverage, and committee members Roberta Nichols and Donald Seiveno. Thanks to those who assisted in the preparation of the transactions; Stephanie Johnson, Kathy Hodge, Ava Norman, Linda Weber, and Liza and Marlane Pershing. A personal thanks to my wife Beverly for her council, assistance, and eternal patience.

Bernard Pershing
Program Chairman and Editor

The papers in this volume were contributed by people with a deep and personal involvement in automotive aerodynamics. So that you may know them as something more than a printed name under a title, we take this opportunity to introduce...

THE AUTHORS

BERNARD PERSHING ("Automotive Aerodynamics - A Simple Survey") is a Member of the Technical Staff of the Fluid Dynamics Department, The Aerospace Corporation, El Segundo, California. After receiving a B.S. in Mechanical Engineering from the University of Wisconsin in 1952, he joined Lockheed Aircraft Corporation, Burbank, California, as a design engineer. In 1956 he received an M.S. in Aeronautical Engineering from the University of Southern California and transferred to the Aerodynamics Section of Lockheed's Preliminary Design Department where he performed configuration, performance, stability, and control analysis of projects ranging from helicopters to reentry vehicles. Since joining The Aerospace Corporation in 1963, he has conducted studies on the aerodynamics of slender delta wings, and a variety of other projects ranging from manned and unmanned reentry systems to long endurance aircraft and dirigibles. He is presently involved in the technical support of Air Force advanced ballistic reentry vehicle research and development programs.

Bernard Pershing first became involved with automobiles in 1962, when he served as aerodynamics consultant on Craig Breedlove's jet-powered Spirit of America World Land Speed Record Project which in 1963 captured the record for America at a speed of 407.45 mph. Prior to this adventure he had been totally involved with airplanes but the "Spirit of America" project kindled his interest in automotive aerodynamics and since then his efforts have been devoted to the application of this technology to dragsters, Group 7 sports cars and other forms of high performance land vehicles.

Recognizing a need for greater communication in this technical area, in 1968 he organized, co-chaired and edited the transactions of the AIAA Symposium, "The Aerodynamics of Sports and Competition Automobiles," at which he also presented a paper summarizing his studies on dragster aerodynamics. In 1974 he organized, co-chaired and edited the transactions of the Second Symposium and presented a review paper on automotive aerodynamics. His most recent project has been the design and development of a low drag wing-canard system for the Vels-Parnelli Jones Formula 1 and Formula 5000 cars driven by Mario Andretti.

Bernard Pershing is an Associate Fellow of the AIAA, a member of SAE and American Helicopter Society and a Registered Professional Engineer in California. Among his outside interests he lists Chinese cooking, model aviation, classical guitar music and kite building and flying. He is a member in good standing of the American Kiteflyers Association.

E. EUGENE LARRABEE ("Road Vehicle Aerodynamics - or - Aerodynamics as an Annoyance") is Associate Professor of Aeronautics
and Astronautics, Massachusetts Institute of
Technology. A native of Massachusetts, Professor Larrabee received his undergraduate
training at Worcester Polytechnic Institute.
After graduating in 1942, he worked as an airplane aerodynamicist for the Curtiss-Wright
Corporation in Buffalo, New York. He earned
an M.S. from the Massachusetts Institute of
Technology in 1948, and since then has been a
member of their faculty teaching courses in
applied aerodynamics, aircraft dynamics, and
automobile design. He has held summer positions with Cornell Aeronautical Laboratories
(now Calspan), Douglas Aircraft Corporation,
Systems Technology, Inc., FAA, Grumman and NACA and has served as a consultant to Autodynetics, Inc. and to Alden Self Transit Systems. His publications range in subject matter from automotive dynamics, aerodynamics and wind
tunnel testing to planetary entry vehicle trajectory analysis. He explains his
broad range of professional experience in a 1961 Road and Track article as
follows. "...like faculty members everywhere in this country I work summers
in order to enjoy my students' standard of living. "

WALTER H. KORFF ("Automotive Aerodynamics - Its Performance, Potentials and Dangers"), President of the Korff Corporation,
Burbank, California, does research, development and prototype construction of automotive
and motorcycle designs. He attended Evans-
ville College and Tri-State College in Indiana
and then worked six years with the Detroit
auto makers as an automotive body engineer.
In 1940, he joined Lockheed Aircraft Corporation, Burbank, California. While at Lockheed,
he was a designer, supervisor, and Research
Engineer assigned to Advanced Concepts. His
unique assignments included the design of a
monorail and a transportation study to the year
2000. In 1968 he formed his own company to
pursue his ideas on small vehicle design.

In 1962 Walter Korff wrote a series of articles on automotive streamlining for
Sports Car Graphic magazine. These articles sparked interest in Detroit and in
California. He was invited to present his findings to the SAE at their 1963 Auto-
motive Engineering Congress in Detroit and the Summers brothers of Ontario,
California asked him to provide support for the aerodynamic design of their
Goldenrod World Speed Record Car which brought the wheel driven record back
to this country in November 1965.

Walter Korff is a member of the SAE and an Associate Fellow of the AIAA. He is
presently involved in the development of a series of small vehicles for industrial
and street use and for club racing. Prototypes have been tested and the project
is now nearing the production stage.

LYNN YAKEL ("Some Aspects of the Design of Land Speed Record Vehicles") has been a Design Engineer with North American Rockwell, California, for the past twenty years. He graduated from the Northrop Institute of Technology, Inglewood, California, in 1954 and received a B.S. in Aeronautical Engineering from that institution in 1962. Automobile and racing have been his avocation for many years, having begun while still in high school. He was a regular participant in the time trials at the Southern California dry lakes in the late '40's and at the Bonneville Salt Flats in the '50's. His avid interest in high speed land-borne vehicles has resulted in the design of the worlds fastest three liter automobile and two contenders for the motorcycle world record. It is the development of these vehicles which is the subject of his paper. Currently, he drives a Mercedes Benz 300SL "Gullwing" which has itself made many trips down the black line of the Salt in the past ten years.

PETER BRYANT ("The Can-Am Car and Ground Effects") is Chief Engineer for Majestic Motor Homes of San Jacinto, California. His career in auto racing began in 1957 when he joined Lotus Cars in England. Stimulated by the innovative approach of Lotus designer Colin Chapman, Peter began to formulate his own ideas on race car design. By 1963, he became chief mechanic for a leading English Formula 1 race team.

The opportunity to test his experience came when he emigrated to America in 1964 and was hired by Mickey Thompson to sort out problems with his radical Indianapolis cars. Peter Bryant roamed around racing as mechanics must, until 1969 when he was commissioned by Ernest Kanzler, an avid racing enthusiast, to design a car for the Canadian-American Challenge Cup Races. His design featured a titanium and aluminum chassis and a body shaped to enhance the aerodynamic downforce. For the following four years, his was one of the handful of cars which remained competitive in Can-Am racing.

In 1971 he designed a new Can-Am car, the "Shadow" which had radically small wheels and tires and the lowest profile of any car on the circuit. The car was fast but due to tire development costs had to be abandoned. A second "Shadow" was designed in 1972 which had conventional tires. It proved to be extremely fast and competitive but it also turned out to be his last Can-Am design as the Shadow team moved their factory to England and he chose to remain with his family in California.

Peter Bryant still enjoys auto racing and continues to do consulting in that field. He has also given lectures to the American Metals Society and the SAE on race car design. For relaxation he says he enjoys playing golf, "but only with people who have a sense of humor."

JEFFREY HOWELL ("Wake Properties of Typical Road Vehicles") is Research Fellow at the University of Warwick, England. He obtained a B.S. in Aeronautical Engineering at Queen Mary College, University of London, in 1969. Following this he spent a year as a Wind Tunnel Engineer for the British Aircraft Corporation, Waybridge, testing the BAC 1-11 and 3-11 series aircraft in their low speed facility. In late 1970 he accepted the offer to conduct postgraduate research in road vehicle aerodynamics at the City University, London, under Mr. Scibor-Rylski. This research concentrated on wind tunnel wake studies of bluff bodies near the ground and explored such items as body geometry, ground proximity, and interference effects between vehicles.

At the University of Warwick, Jeffrey Howell is currently involved in the Magnetic Levitation Project, a program which is chartered to produce a man-carrying vehicle to demonstrate the feasibility of this high speed ground transportation concept.

While at the City University, Jeffrey Howell performed a series of wind tunnel tests on the IBEC P2 Clubmens racing car and was responsible for the body construction. To quote Jeffrey, "The car driven by Ian Bracey has occasionally produced good results in the European Hill Climb Championship. Outside of my wife and young son my only interest is in racing car aerodynamics, the developments of which I follow with both amusement and respect."

JOSEPH J. CORNISH III ("Trapped Vortex Flow Control for Automobiles") is Director of Engineering, Lockheed-Georgia Company, Marietta, Georgia. He received a B.S. in Mechanical Engineering from Louisiana State University in 1950, followed by advanced studies in boundary layer theory at Mississippi State University where he earned an M.S. in 1951 and a Ph.D. in 1960. From 1950 to 1952 he was an Aeronautical Research Scientist with NACA, Langley Field, Virginia, and then joined the faculty of Mississippi State University where from 1960 to 1964 he held the position of Head, Aerophysics Department. While at Mississippi he was involved in a number of diverse low speed aerodynamic research programs including the development and flight testing of boundary layer control systems for aircraft, high lift systems, shrouded propellers, low drag airships, and variable camber wings. During this period he also provided consulting services to a number of aircraft firms.

In 1964 Dr. Cornish joined the Lockheed-Georgia Company as Associate Director of Research, Aerospace Sciences, and in 1971 was appointed to his present position of Director of Engineering. He holds patents on a number of flow control devices and has written over 20 papers on boundary layer theory, flow visualization and testing techniques, computer techniques for airfoil analysis, and automobile aerodynamics. His work has appeared in Scientific American Magazine, McGraw-Hill Encyclopedia of Science and Technology and major technical journals of America, Europe and Canada.

Dr. Cornish is a Registered Professional Engineer in Mississippi and has served on the Aerodynamics Committee of the American Helicopter Society and the Fluid Dynamics Committee of the American Institute of Aeronautics and Astronautics.

J.E. FACKRELL and J.K. HARVEY ("The Aerodynamics of an Isolated Road Wheel") of the Imperial College of London, England, have, in their collaboration on this program, conducted a series of tests which is fundamental to a better understanding of automotive aerodynamics. Dr. Fackrell is a Donald Campbell Research Fellow in the Department of Aeronautics. A graduate in mathematics from London University, he obtained an M.S. degree in aeronautics at the Imperial College for flow visualization work on trailing vortex breakdown. The present paper forms part of the work done on wheel aerodynamics for a Ph.D. degree in aeronautics obtained in 1973. The Donald Campbell Research Fellowship which he holds at present was established to promote studies connected with high speed car aerodynamics. To this end he has been studying the effect of the ground on the flow about bluff bodies. He has also been involved in the testing of racing cars for commercial concerns.

Dr. Harvey is Senior Lecturer in the Department of Aeronautics. He is a graduate of London University in Aeronautical Engineering and obtained a Ph.D. in 1960 at the Imperial College studying the aerodynamics of slender delta wings the type of which were subsequently used for Concorde. He then visited Princeton University, studying rarified hypersonic flows, which, after his return to England, remained one of his chief research interests. In the area of low speed aerodynamics, he has investigated the instabilities of vortex flows and, in particular with Dr. Fackrell, has studied the breakdown of trailing vortices left by aircraft.

As an extension of his interest in bluff body flow, he has been actively engaged in many aspects of racing car aerodynamics, acting in an advisory capacity first with BRM and now with the UOP Shadow team who participate in Grand Prix and Can-Am competitions.

HENRY R. JEX who presented the paper of Drs. Fackrell and Harvey at the symposium is Principle Research Engineer at Systems Technology, Inc., Hawthorne, California. He received a B.S. degree in Engineering from the Massachusetts Institute of Technology in 1951, and an M.S. from the California Institute of Technology in 1953. While at CalTech he worked in their Co-op Wind Tunnel and in 1955 joined Radioplane where as an aerodynamicist he was involved in preliminary design studies of various weapons, target, and meteorological systems. Since joining STI in 1958, he has worked on projects relating to stability and control, performance, and dynamics of the man/machine system, both aerodynamic and automotive. The scope of his work in aerospace vehicles ranges from ground effect machines to reentry vehicles. His recent work has involved measuring and modeling the human operator response to biodynamic environments such as vibration, high "g", and ship motion. He has also worked on studies of driving performance impairment in heavy versus light drinkers.

Henry Jex is an aerodynamic enthusiast and maintains a close interest in all phases of low speed aerodynamics, particularly soaring. His broad aerodynamic background makes him an ideal proxy speaker, a function he also performed at the first AIAA Auto-Aero Symposium in 1968. For relaxation he builds models of all types and enjoys extended traveling vacations with his family.

GLEN J. BROWN ("Low Cost Aerodynamic Testing Techniques for Automotive Development") is Project Engineer with Developmental Sciences, Inc., City of Industry, California, where he is currently involved in a variety of aerodynamic and hydrodynamic test programs such as subway aerodynamics, surface effect ship components, and remotely piloted vehicles. He received a B.S. in Mechanical Engineering from the California Institute of Technology in 1969, and since then has been actively engaged in a number of automotive aerodynamic development projects including various Formula A cars, the 1972 Eagle USAC car where he directed the wind tunnel test program, and design of the body for the 1973 Can-Am Porsche of George Folmer. At DSI he designed and developed a unique moving model track highway aerodynamic test facility for the U.S. Department of Transportation. His leisure time is spent in flying hang gliders and sailplanes.

DEAN BATCHELOR ("An Historical Survey of Bonneville Record Cars") as head of db Publications is currently involved in turning out a five-volume series about Ferrari. For one so young, he must still be called "the grand old man" of automotive publications. From 1956 to 1958 he was Associate Editor of Motor Life, later merged with Sports Car Graphic. He then joined Road and Track as Associate Editor, moved up to Editor in 1959, and from 1965 to 1974 served as Editorial Director of Road and Track and Car Life.

Prior to World War II he had been interested in cars and planes, and owned both customized and modified cars but was strictly a spectator at events. After World War II, while completing a four-year Industrial Design course at Chouinard Art Institute in Los Angeles, California, he became involved in hot rodding with a '32 Ford roadster, then sold it in 1949 to go in with Alex Xydias in building the So-Cal Special Streamliner. It was the fastest car at Bonneville in 1949 and 1950. He drove it in 1949, but voluntarily terminated his driving career after rolling it at El Mirage while running in a stiff crosswind. In 1952 he designed the body for the Hill-Davis "City of Burbank" later called the "Bob Estes Mercury Special" and in 1953 he designed the frame and body for the Mal Hooper Shadoff Special. During the early years of the Bonneville Nationals he served on the technical committee to set up the sports car class rules.

As Dean Batchelor tells it, "I guess the highpoints of my working at R&T had to be driving the Mercedes Benz W 196 GP car (circa 1954 and 1955) at the Daimler Benz test track in 1961; and rides around Riverside with Bob Bondurant in a Cobra Daytona coupe and Richie Ginther in a Ford GT 40. And, I suppose, testing Bill Harrah's Ferrari Daytona on a deserted stretch of U.S. 80, at dawn, with the tach at 7,000 in fifth and the speedometer reading 180!"

Dean Batchelor is a part of automotive history. He is also a perceptive observer and from his paper on Bonneville record cars it is clear that he loves what he has seen.

HANS-HERMANN BRAESS, HERMANN E. BURST, LUDWIG HAMM and ROLF HANNES ("Improvement of Handling Characteristics of Automobiles by Reducing the Aerodynamic Lift") of h. c. F. Porsche Aktiengesellschaft, Stuttgart have been collaborating since 1970 in the aerodynamic development of the Porsche 911 Carrerra. The results of this effort are presented in their paper. Dr.-Ing.

Braess, who is Chief of the Fundamental Research and Development Section, studied Mechanical Engineering from 1956 to 1963 at the Technical University in Hanover. After graduation, he did chassis design for Ford-Werke Aktiengesellschaft in Cologne and from 1964 to 1970 served as Scientific Assistant at the Technical University in Munich. He has been with Porsche since 1970. Hermann Burst is Chief of the Bodywork Research Section. He studied Mechanical Engineering from 1959 to 1967 at the Technical University in Stuttgart. Prior to joining Porsche in 1969 he did wind tunnel research as a Scientific Member at the Technical University in Stuttgart. His early work at Porsche included the aerodynamic design of the Types 908 and 917 racing cars. Ludwig Hamm is a member of the Fundamental Research and Development Section. He studied Mechanical Engineering at the Technical University in Karlsruhe from 1968 to 1973 and has been affiliated with Porsche since early 1974. Rolf Hannes, who joined Porsche in 1959, is Chief of the Road-Test Evaluation Department. He studied Mechanical Engineering from 1953 to 1956 at the School of Engineering in Esslingen and from 1956 to 1959 worked at Robert Bosch GmbH Stuttgart as a Machine-Tool Design and Production Engineer.

DAVID H. WIER, who presented the paper of H. H. Braess and his colleagues at the symposium, is Principle Research Engineer at Systems Technology, Inc., Hawthorne, California. His Ph. D. in Engineering was earned at the University of California at Los Angeles. His professional activities in the past few years have centered on the areas of motor vehicle dynamics, handling, and driver control processes. He has directed a number of research programs which have involved driver/vehicle modeling and analyses, driving simulator experiments, model scale wind tunnel tests, and a variety of full scale tests to measure driver performance and vehicle handling properties. He is the author or coauthor of over 50 journal articles, papers, and published reports in the areas of dynamics and control. Dr. Wier is a Senior Member of IEEE, and a member of AIAA, the Human Factors Society, and the Road User Characteristics Committee of the Highway Research Board. His choice as proxy speaker is fitting as he has the ideal technical background and is himself a proud owner of a Porsche 911.

ROGER J. HAWKS ("The Effect of Aerodynamic Download on Automobile Handling") is an Assistant Professor in the Department of Mechanical and Industrial Engineering at the Clarkson College of Technology in Potsdam, New York. He received a B. S. in Aeronautical Engineering from the University of Cincinnati in 1965, an M. S. in Aeronautics and Astronautics from the Massachusetts Institute of Technology in 1967, and a Ph. D. in Mechanical Engineering in 1972 from the University of Maryland. While at MIT he was involved with computer simulation of automobile dynamics and aerodynamics and at Maryland he instructed courses in mechanical engineering. He worked as an Aerospace Engineer at the

Goddard Space Flight Center of NASA and as an Aeronautical Engineer with the Fairchild-Hiller Corporation. In both of these positions he was involved with aerodynamic and flight dynamic analysis of sounding rocket systems. Dr. Hawks has also served as a consultant in automobile dynamics to a number of Eastern concerns. Since joining the faculty of Clarkson in 1972, he has taught undergraduate courses in mechanics, dynamics of machines, machine design, aerodynamics and automotive transportation systems. His field of research interest is vehicle dynamics. He is particularly interested in aerodynamic effects on automobile motions and has written a number of papers on the subject.

KEVIN R. COOPER ("The Effect of Aerodynamics on the Performance and Stability of High Speed Motorcycles") is Research Officer at the National Aeronautical Establishment, National Research Council in Ottawa, Canada. He received a General Arts degree from the University of Western Ontario, London, Ontario, in 1964 and B.S. in Physics from the same institution in 1967. In 1968 he obtained an M.S. in the field of low speed aerodynamics from the University of Toronto Aerospace Institute. Since that time he has worked in the Low Speed Aerodynamics Laboratory of the National Aeronautical Establishment on the aerodynamic problems of surface structures. He has been involved in problems concerning the aerodynamic loads on and the aeroelastic stability of tall ground-based structures, power lines, and large bridges. In recent years he has become involved in a growing amount of work on surface vehicles including trains, motorcycles, and trucks. Currently, he is managing to keep involved in the hardware side of engineering by constructing a sports car of his own design. As to the future, "I would like to continue my work on road, road racing, and record motorcycles, as they offer the possibility of considerable performance improvement through aerodynamic refinement."

DOUGLAS J. MALEWICKI ("The Dynamics and Aerodynamics of Jump Motorcycles") is Manager of Advanced Research and Development at the L.M. Cox Manufacturing Company, Santa Ana, California. A native of Chicago, Illinois, he received a B.S. degree in Aeronautical Engineering from the University of Illinois in 1961. He then worked as Research Engineer on the Polaris project at Lockheed Missiles and Space Company in Sunnyvale, California, and in 1963 earned an M.S. in Aerospace Engineering from Stanford University. After periods with North American Rockwell in Downey and Douglas Aircraft Company in Long Beach, he became a Project Engineer at Philco-Ford's Space and Reentry Systems Division in Newport Beach. Prior to joining Cox in 1970, he worked one year with the Cessna Aircraft Company of Wichita, Kansas as Senior Flight Test Engineer.

His aerospace experience includes weapons systems vulnerability analyses, loads, dynamic analyses, and thermal stress analyses of space systems, and flutter analyses of commercial aircraft. He has also been active in the field of model rocketry, an interest which started in his college days. He has published extensively in this field and from 1969 to 1972 served as technical editor of Model Rocketry, the Journal of Miniature Astronautics. In 1972 he presented a paper at the 23rd International Astronautical Congress in Vienna, Austria, describing his use of model rocketry as a basis for aerospace educational curricula.

Douglas Malewicki is an active skier and enjoys camping, hiking, sports car racing, and flying, both powered aircraft and hang gliders. These interests, combined with his technical background and large resources of energy and imagination, lead him naturally to an involvement with jump motorcycles. Since 1968 he has been associated with such projects as the Evel Knievel Grand Canyon Skycycle jumper and the Super Joe Einhorn Rocket Motorcycle. He is currently developing and promoting his own "Flying Motorcycle" concept, a hybrid vehicle that is part motorcycle, part hang glider and which has already performed many jumps of several hundred feet. In his few spare moments he enjoys playing a few pieces on his classical guitar.

JON McKIBBEN ("Motorcycle Streamliner Dynamics - or - Low Drag is the Easy Part") is President of the McKibben Engineering Company, Irvine, California, which provides technical assistance in litigations involving motor vehicle collisions. He holds two B.S. degrees, one in Mathematics from Stetson University, Florida in 1960, and one in Mechanical Engineering from the University of Florida in 1962. He joined the Chrysler Corporation in Detroit, Michigan, as a Test Engineer in 1962, and while there, earned an M.S. in Automotive Engineering from Chrysler Institute of Engineering. He branched out into the literary field when in 1967 he became Engineering Editor of Car Life Magazine. In 1968 he accepted the position of Chief Engineer of the Automotive Research Division of Application Research Corporation in Los Angeles, California. Shortly thereafter, he joined Digitek Corporation, Marina del Rey, California, as General Manager of their Automotive Research Division and in 1972 he took a similar position with Agbabian Associates of El Segundo, California, where he remained until Spring of 1975, when he left to form his own company. Currently, he is also serving as part-time faculty member at the University of Southern California Safety Center.

Jon McKibben is a professional driver holding licenses for automobile and motorcycle racing. He has set a number of national speed records in drag racing, has achieved the highest speed ever recorded for a motorcycle (286.7 mph) and regularly manages to add 500 miles per week to his motorcycle odometer. His four children all ride motorcycles and he prides himself that his oldest, age 10, can outspeed him if the course is short and rough enough. As for future plans, he states, "I am anxious to apply the knowledge we gained with the Honda Hawk and become the first motorcyclist to exceed 300 mph."

BAIN DAYMAN, JR. ("Effects of Realistic Tire Rolling Resistance Upon the Determination of Aerodynamic Drag from Road-Vehicle Coast-Down Tests") is Manager of the Thermodynamics and Fluid Dynamics Section at the Jet Propulsion Laboratory in Pasadena, California. He received his B.S. in Mechanical Engineering in 1950 and a Professional degree in Aeronautical Engineering in 1953, both from the California Institute of Technology. While working on his advanced degree, he was involved in the aerodynamic design of a number of high-speed road-vehicle projects such as the GM Firebird and several "Salt" ventures. He joined JPL in 1953 where he has been associated with aerodynamic testing and facilities. His experience covers the range from low subsonic to Jupiter entry velocities; from ground structures and vehicles to airplanes, missiles, and planetary entry probes. For the past several years he has been studying the aerodynamics of ground vehicles such as high speed trains in tunnels. His paper on the extraction of aerodynamic data from road tests is a result of his current interest in drag reduction of road vehicles.

PETER B.S. LISSAMAN ("Research in Aerodynamic Drag Reduction of Trucks") is Director of Aerosciences at AeroVironment, Inc., Pasadena, California. After completing his undergraduate work in England, he worked with Hanley Page and Bristol as an aerodynamicist and structural designer. Emigrating to America, he worked for Douglas Aircraft Corporation, Bendix, the U.S. Navy, and CalTech's Jet Propulsion Laboratory. He received his Ph.D. from the California Institute of Technology where his major area of research was in jet flap theory. He remained as a member of the CalTech faculty until 1970, when he joined the Northrop Corporation, Hawthorne, California as Director, Continuum Mechanics Department. In 1972, he assumed his present position at AeroVironment, Inc., where he is involved in research and development programs related to air quality, noise, vehicle testing and pollution measuring instrumentation.

Dr. Lissaman's interests are as varied as his talents. He has published on such wide ranging aerodynamic subjects as bird flight (where he showed that the observed V formation of migrating birds is aerodynamically the most efficient), sailplanes, sailboats, and windmills. Motivated by his interest in sailboats, in 1969 he organized and chaired "The Ancient Interface", the AIAA L.A. Section Symposium on The Aero/Hydrodynamics of Sailboats. The meeting was so well received that it has since become an annual event. Dr. Lissaman is a part time thespian, having appeared in a number of roles with the Pasadena Playhouse and is a Distinguished Lecturer of the AIAA.

JEFFREY W. KIRSCH ("Drag Reduction of Trucks With S^3 Vanes") is Manager of the Low Speed Aerodynamics Section at Systems, Science, and Software (S^3) of La Jolla, California. His education has been in Aeronautical Engineering and Physics, receiving a B.S. from Princeton in 1962, and an M.S. in 1963 and a Ph.D. in 1969, both from the University of Southern California. He was involved in liquid propellant rocket research at Rocketdyne and boundary layer analysis at McDonnell-Douglas prior to joining S^3 in the fall of 1969 as a member of their Continuum Mechanics Division. At S^3 Dr. Kirsch has worked on a number of diverse problems including the calculation of dust storms created by nuclear detonations, the validation of S^3 computer models for off-highway air pollution, and the development of predictive techniques for stress wave propagation in geologic materials. He is currently involved in research and development of the S^3 airvane drag reduction concept for application to bluff ground vehicles.

Dr. Kirsch first became interested in problems associated with bluff body aerodynamics in 1970. The results of his latest effort in this area are presented in his paper.

AUTOMOTIVE AERODYNAMICS - A SIMPLE SURVEY

Bernard Pershing
Consulting Engineer
Manhattan Beach, California, U.S.A.

Abstract

An examination is made of those areas in which external aerodynamics exhibit first order effects on the performance and handling qualities of land borne vehicles. A survey is performed of the physical characteristics and operational range of a representative set of vehicle types and an assessment is obtained of the relative importance of the aerodynamic and tire force systems and of their complex interaction. This interaction is made more definitive by a detailed examination of passenger sedan handling qualities as defined by an understeer parameter which includes the effects of a vehicle five-degree-of-freedom aerodynamic force system. Similar evaluations are made of the competition sports and acceleration class of vehicles. Areas of aerodynamic influence are identified and the significance of this influence on future design trends is discussed.

NOMENCLATURE

a = distance from cg to front tire contact point, fraction of wheelbase, L

A,B,C = defined in Eq. (A-14)

AR = aspect ratio

b = distance from cg to rear tire contact point, fraction of wheelbase, L

c = wheel track, ft

C_x = F_{xa}/qS

C_y = F_{ya}/qS

C_z = F_{za}/qS

C_{my} = M_{ya}/qSL

C_{mz} = M_{za}/qSL

f_r = defined in Eq. (A-14)

F = force, lb

g = gravitational acceleration, ft/sec^2

G = $\rho gS(C_D + \mu C_L)/2W$, ft^{-1}

h = cg height, ft

HP = horsepower

k = tire cornering stiffness, lb/radian

K = understeer rate factor, [see Eq. (A-12)], sec^2/ft^2

L = wheelbase, ft

L/D = lift-to-drag ratio

m = mass, lb-sec^2/ft

M = moment, lb-ft

q = $1/2 \rho u^2$, lb/ft^2

R = radius of curvature, ft

s = aerodynamic reference area, LC, ft^2

S = projected planform area, ft^2

t = time, sec

T = thrust, lb

u = velocity, ft/sec

U = understeer parameter [see Eq. (A-11)]

W = Vehicle weight, lb

x,y,z = body fixed coordinate system (see Fig. 4)

X,Y,Z = inertial reference frame (see Fig. 4)

α = tire slip angle, radians

β = aerodynamic sideslip angle, radians

γ = defined in Eq. (A-14)

δ = angular deflection, radians

λ = fraction of weight on driving wheels

μ = tire coefficient of friction, F/F_z

μ_0 = tire friction coefficient as $F_z \to 0$

μ_1 = $\partial\mu/\partial F_z$, lb^{-1}

υ = angle between velocity vector and inertial reference (see Fig. 4), radians

ρ = mass density of air, $lb\text{-}sec^2/ft^4$

ψ = angle between x axis and inertial reference (see Fig. 4), radians

Superscript

$(\ )'$ = $\partial(\ )/\partial\beta$

$(\dot{\ })$ = $\partial(\ )/\partial t$

$(\ddot{\ })$ = $\partial^2(\ )/\partial t^2$

$\overline{(\ )}$ = $(\ )/WL$

Subscript

a = aerodynamic

F = front tires

H = horizontal

i = inside wheel

o = outside wheel

rr = rolling resistance

R = rear tires

s = steering wheel

T = tractive force

V = vertical

x, y, z = components along x, y, z axis, positive as shown in Fig. 2

Abbreviations

AA/FD = Competition Dragster, Fuel Powered

FIA = Federation Internationale de l'Automobile

HP = horsepower

NHRA = National Hot Rod Association

USAC = United States Auto Club

WLSR = World Land Speed Record

1. INTRODUCTION

In recent years automotive aerodynamics has been transformed from the ignored to the esteemed. This metamorphosis is most evident in the field of competition sports cars and dragsters where the use of wings in conjunction with body designs based primarily on aerodynamic considerations has produced major improvements in performance and handling. Similarly, current commercial and passenger car designs reflect the greater consideration given by the automotive industry to the reduction of drag and to the control of aerodynamic lift, fore-and-aft for improved high speed handling.

Fundamental research on the external aerodynamics of high performance land vehicles is limited and the interaction of aerodynamics with the total vehicle system is yet to be fully understood. As a result, it is not always obvious by what methods external aerodynamics influences the various operating characteristics of automotive vehicles nor is it always clear at what speeds this influence becomes important. In order to provide insight into these questions, a survey is presented in this paper of the operational domain of automotive vehicles and fundamental examples of vehicle interaction with the aerodynamic force system are examined.

2. PHYSICAL CHARACTERISTICS

The relative importance of aerodynamics on vehicle performance and handling is dependent on such physical characteristics as vehicle weight, size, and horsepower, and on operational requirements such as speed range and degree of maneuverability. A general survey of the physical characteristics and operational requirements of a broad range of vehicle types is presented in Figs. 1 through 3. The vehicle types included in the survey are summarized in Table I.

2.1 POWER AND THRUST LOADING

Power and thrust characteristics of this sample set are shown in Fig. 1 for each of the vehicle types and are supported by data representing vehicles which, unless otherwise noted, are of 1970-1974 vintage. The parameter W/HP can be viewed as the number of pounds each vehicle horsepower is required to accelerate and in this sense is a direct indication of the potential performance of the vehicle. Street and recreation vehicles form the most docile group. Mini-cars are typified by W~2000 lbs, W/HP~40; the small

Table I
Survey of Land-Borne Vehicle Types

Street and Recreation Vehicles

Passenger Sedan	A mass production vehicle for short and intermediate range transportation. Operated over surface streets and high speed freeways by a driver population with a broad statistical distribution in skill, temperament, and judgement.
Highway Camper	A class of recreation vehicle consisting of a large rectangular structure attached to the bed of a pick-up truck to form a compact mobile home for camping and touring.

Competition Sports Cars

Formula 1	A single seat competition vehicle built exclusively for speed races on closed irregularly shaped circuits. An open car with restrictions on weight and engine displacement. The body shell is not allowed to extend beyond the midpoint of the tires and fixed aerodynamic devices of limited extend and location are permitted.
Group 7	A two-seater competition vehicle built exclusively for speed races on closed irregularly shaped circuits. All mechanical components covered by the body shell with fixed aerodynamic devices of limited extent and location permitted. No maximum limit on engine displacement.
Indianapolis Racer	A single place racer of limited engine displacement designed to operate counterclockwise on a closed oval track. Is required to have exposed wheels. Fixed aerodynamic devices of limited extent and location are permitted.

Acceleration Vehicles

AA/FD Dragster	Operates on an alcohol-nitro methane mixture accelerating from a standing start a distance of 1320 ft in minimum time. Fixed aerodynamic devices are permitted.
World Land Speed Record Car	Two types of WLSR car, reaction propulsion and wheel driven. Must run a two-way course through a one mile timing trap to establish a record within its category.

sedan by $W \sim 2500$ lbs, $W/HP \sim 28$; and the luxury sedan and touring car by $W \sim 4000$ lbs, $W/HP \sim 16$. These data indicate the variation of weight with power is of the form $W \sim \sqrt{HP}$. The power range of campers is 4500 lbs to 9000 lbs with W/HP lying consistently above that for the sedan. This difference in W/HP represents the 2000-lb to 5000-lb camper unit which is added to the bed of a pick-up truck whose power characteristics are essentially the same as those of the sedan.

The competition sports cars form a single well-defined region with $W \sim 1600$ lbs and W/HP varying from 2 to 4. Logically, the three types within this group, F-1, Group 7, and Indy car, display similar trends as they have common operational requirements and design restrictions.

The acceleration vehicles form two distinct groups, AA/FD dragsters and WLSR cars. The AA/FD dragster weight is of the order 1400 lbs with

$W/HP \sim 1$ while the WLSR cars have weights of the order 6000 lbs to 9000 lbs with $W/HP \sim 4$ for wheel driven cars and $0.1 < W/T < 2$ for those which are jet and rocket propelled.

For purposes of comparison, the power loading characteristics for various aircraft types are shown as lightly shaded regions in Fig. 1. The W/HP range of propeller driven aircraft is 6 to 20 with the value for light aircraft ($W < 4000$ lbs) falling in the upper range and overlapping the large passenger sedan. The value of W/T for current jet fighters is of the order 1.5 to 2. At high subsonic flight speeds, this value corresponds to the W/HP of the AA/FD dragster. Some appreciation of the ominous power of the AA/FD dragster can be obtained by reflecting on this comparison.

With the exception of the reaction-propelled WLSR vehicles, all types are wheel-driven and are powered almost exclusively by reciprocating inter-

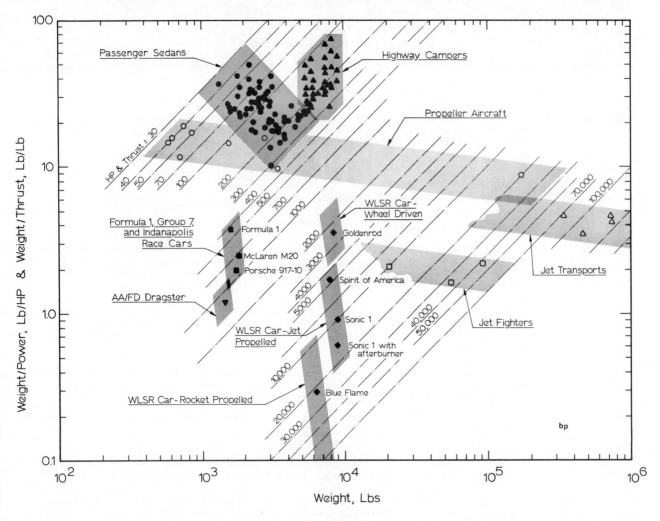

Figure 1. Power Loading Characteristics of Land-Borne Vehicles.

nal combustion engines. For these vehicles, increased power provides large improvements in performance up to that point where the tractive capability of the tires can be exceeded over the entire operating range of the vehicle. Beyond this point, increased power has a marginal effect on performance and in some cases can be detrimental due to secondary design factors such as increased vehicle weight. An approximate value for this limiting condition is given by the following expression.

$$(W/HP)_{min} \sim 550/\lambda\mu u_{max} \qquad (1)$$

Typical values of λ, μ and u_{max} are listed in Table II for wheel-driven vehicles and the resultant $(W/HP)_{min}$ is seen to correspond closely with the lower bound of the regions denoted in Fig. 1. The reaction-propelled WLSR vehicle

has no physically defined practical lower limit of (W/T) except that imposed by human factors such as driver control capability and "g" tolerance.

The power characteristics data for each vehicle type except the passenger sedan fall into bands of nearly constant weight. That is, within a vehicle type, major improvements in W/HP are made through increases in engine displacement

Table II
Minimum Useable Weight-to-Horsepower Ratio

Vehicle Type	u_{max} ft/sec	μ	λ	$(W/HP)_{min}$ lb/HP
Passenger Sedan	150	0.9	0.55	7.4
Formula 1 Car	320	1.4	0.65	1.88
Group 7 Car	340	1.4	0.65	1.78
Indy Car	340	1.4	0.65	1.78
AA/FD Dragster	340	2.0	1.00	0.89
WLSR Wheel-Driven	620	0.4	1.00	2.22

4

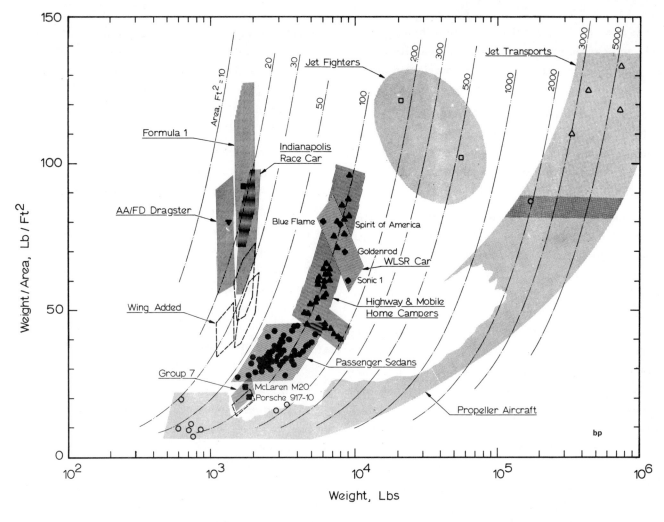

Figure 2. Area Loading Characteristics of Land-Borne Vehicles.

and/or power-displacement ratio, with only second order increases in vehicle weight. It is this characteristic which has made the power-plant the pivotal point in design and development of competition sports and WLSR vehicles.

2.2 Area Loading

The various automotive types are viewed in Fig. 2 as aerodynamic bodies or potential lifting surfaces. Area loading, W/S, is plotted versus vehicle gross weight, W. Regions denoting the basic vehicle without auxiliary aerodynamic surfaces are shown with solid borders; regions shown with broken lines denote the effect of added aerodynamic surfaces. The passenger sedan falls in the range, 27 lb/ft^2 < W/S < 46 lb/ft^2 while the camper reaches W/S as high as 100 lb/ft^2. The mobile home or integrally built camper has lower values of W/S, typically on the order

of 45 lb/ft^2. It is important to note that the camper, in contrast to the other vehicle types, is boxy in design and has a side area equal to or greater than its planform area. Therefore, lateral and longitudinal aerodynamic loads are expected to be more important for this type of vehicle.

Of particular interest is the large area loading of the Formula 1, Indy, and AA/FD cars, 55 lb/ft^2 < W/S < 140 lb/ft^2, and the reduction achieved by the addition of aerodynamic surfaces, 35 lb/ft^2 < W/S < 75 lb/ft^2. In some cases, this represents a reduction in W/S of 50%. The Group 7 car has the lowest area loading, 16 lb/ft^2 < W/S < 28 lb/ft^2, yet it is found in practice that the moderate reduction in W/S, typically 15%, achieved by the addition of an airfoil is mandatory in order to remain competitive. This results because the air-

5

foil is a more efficient lifting system than is the body and can be oriented to operate near its maximum capability. Therefore, its contribution per unit area far exceeds that of the basic body.

WLSR cars have relatively high W/S, 60 lb/ft^2 to 80 lb/ft^2. They are built slender to achieve minimum aerodynamic drag so that a well-designed WLSR car will invariably be volume-limited and high density.

A comparison of land vehicle W/S with that of aircraft, (denoted by the lightly shaded areas in Fig. 2) shows that propeller driven light aircraft have about the same W/S as Group 7 cars and one half that of passenger sedans. The W/S of WLSR cars and of Indy and Formula 1 cars and AA/FD dragsters unaugmented by airfoils are the same order as that of jet fighters and transports. With the addition of airfoils, the W/S of the latter three are reduced to about twice the value of the propeller driven light aircraft. From these comparisons, it is seen that the automotive types shown are not unlike aircraft in terms of their area loading. Yet, it is observed that land vehicles do not compare with aircraft as lifting systems. Clearly, this is because aircraft are designed to maximize aerodynamic efficiency, (high aspect ratio wings,

slender bodies, etc.), whereas land vehicles are not. Nevertheless, the similarities in W/S indicate the aerodynamic potential of the high speed land vehicle, a potential which is only now being seriously exploited.

2.3 Operational Range

The operational range of the vehicle types is shown in Fig. 3 in terms of velocity versus path curvature. The speed and maneuvering capability required of each vehicle type in the performance of its design tasks is denoted by the region to the left of its bounding curve. The speed envelope of the passenger sedan and camper extend from zero to the maximum practical or legal limit which may be less than terminal velocity. The sedan and camper must operate at values of path curvature, right and left, compatible with their cornering capabilities.

The Formula 1 and Group 7 cars are rarely required to operate at less than 70 ft/sec. They must maneuver right and left at their maximum cornering capability to negotiate turns some of which are separated by straights a mile or more in length. The Indy car operates continuously in the upper 30% of its speed envelope except for pit

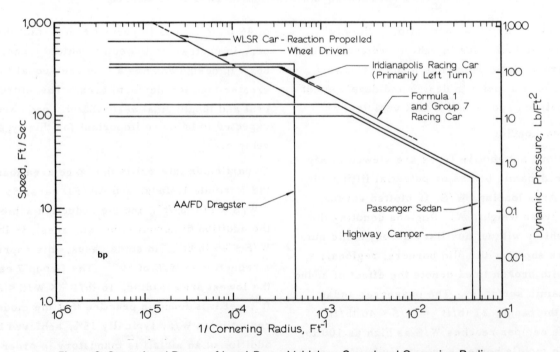

Figure 3. Operational Range of Land-Borne Vehicles - Speed and Cornering Radius.

Table III
Aerodynamic Force-to-Weight Characteristics

Vehicle Type	$(qS/W)_{max}$ Basic/ Basic + Airfoil	Aero Force-to-Weight Ratio		
		$(F_{xa}/W)_{max}$	$(F_{ya}/W)_{max}$	$(F_{za}/W)_{max}$
Passenger Sedan	0.725/---	0.15/---	± 0.20	-0.15/---
Highway Camper	0.268/---	0.25/---	± 0.20	-0.06/---
Formula 1 Car	1.69/2.65	0.35/0.45	± 0.15	-0.17/-1.50
Group 7 Car	8.37/9.56	0.45/0.58	± 0.25	-1.25/-2.50
Indy Car	2.44/3.62	0.40/0.52	± 0.20	-0.37/-1.60
AA/FD Dragster	2.44/3.96	0.60/0.80	± 0.10	-0.12/-2.00
WLSR-Wheel Driven	6.65/---	0.05/---	± 0.10	-0.10/---
WLSR - Reaction Propelled	16.25/---	1.20/---	± 0.10	-0.30/---

stops and operation under the yellow caution light. It is essentially unidirectional, but must possess good maneuvering capability to cope with traffic on the course. The AA/FD dragster and WLSR cars operate at maximum acceleration throughout their straight course runs. Sufficient maneuvering capability must be provided to maintain control against such disturbances as wind gusts, course irregularities, and asymmetric application of tire tractive force. All but the WLSR cars are truly subsonic. The wheel-driven WLSR car is currently at the threshold of compressibility while the reaction-propelled WLSR car is well into the low transonic range.

Some measure of the relative importance of aerodynamics to vehicle handling and performance is obtained by combining the data of Figs. 2 and 3 to form the parameter, qS/W. This parameter is indicative of the ratio of aerodynamic load to vehicle gross weight, F_a/W. The maximum value, $(qS/W)_{max}$, is listed in Table III for each basic vehicle type and for the basic vehicle plus airfoil, where applicable. Also presented are values of $(F_{xa}/W)_{max}$, $(F_{ya}/W)_{max}$, and $(F_{za}/W)_{max}$, based on estimates of the vehicle aerodynamic characteristics supported by test data where available. The aerodynamic sideforce is based on a 30 ft/sec crosswind at u_{max}. These data show the importance of vehicle geometry to (F_a/W). For example, because of the bluntness of the camper, its $(F_{xa}/W)_{max}$ is comparable with that of the passenger sedan though its $(qS/W)_{max}$ is three times less.

The conclusions drawn from this survey of vehicle physical characteristics and operational range are briefly summarized in Table IV. Of particular interest is the strong interaction displayed between the aerodynamic and tire force systems for all vehicle types.

3. DETAILED EXAMINATION OF VEHICLE AERODYNAMICS

3.1 Street and Recreation Vehicles

The primary characteristics important to safe operation and optimum performance of automotive vehicles are low drag, good acceleration, breaking and cornering capability and good handling qualities. The influence of aerodynamics on power requirements and fuel consumption is straightforward and has been treated in the literature (Refs. 1 and 2). Handling qualities, on the other hand, is a complex set of concepts. It is the subject of continued research (Refs. 3 through 8), and remains today in need of further study. Handling qualities are defined here as that set of objective and subjective measurements, taken over the operational range of the vehicle, which are associated with control, static and dynamic stability, and dynamic response of the machine and man-machine system. This definition is purposely general and is intended to include the two approaches currently under development, dynamic response analysis and performance task measurement.

The interaction of aerodynamics with vehicle handling is considered herein by the examination

7

Table IV
Summary of Aerodynamic Influence on Vehicle Performance and Handling

Aerodynamic Force System	Street and Recreation Vehicle	Competition Sports Car	Acceleration Vehicle
Longitudinal Lift, Pitching Moment	Important for sedans at freeway speeds. Has large influence on handling through modification of front and rear tire normal forces. This problem can be critical in combination with poorly maintained car (worn shock adsorbers, etc.) and/or unskilled driver. (F_{za}/W) of camper, small aero lift of secondary importance.	Important at intermediate and high speeds. Affects handling, cornering, and high speed braking through modification of front and rear tire normal forces. Vehicle always accelerating, braking and/or cornering. Airfoils which increase tire normal force and provide balance fore-and-aft are necessary for vehicle to be competitive.	Important at intermediate and high speeds. Affects handling of WLSR and AA/FD cars and traction of wheel-driven WLSR car and AA/FD dragster through modification of tire normal forces. Transonic variation of aero lift critical to control and structural integrity of reaction-propelled WLSR car.
Longitudinal Drag	Important at freeway speeds. Affects required engine size, acceleration for passing, fuel consumption, aerodynamic noise. High drag deteriorates handling of rear drive vehicle due to large tire tractive force requirements. Camper drag can cause large pitching moments seriously overloading rear wheels at high speed.	Important at intermediate and high speeds. Affects cornering power and handling through tractive force required of driving tires to overcome drag. High speed acceleration terminal velocity and fuel consumption also affected. Inefficient design (low effective L/D) of airfoil or other supplementary aero device deteriorates its contribution to vehicle handling and performance.	Important to WLSR cars at intermediate and high speeds; critical transonically. Affects power plant size, acceleration capability, required course length, fuel consumption (important for rockets), terminal velocity. Very important to wheel-driven reciprocating engine WLSR cars because of limited acceleration capability at high speeds. Moderate effect on AA/FD dragster trap speed, small effect on elapsed time.
Lateral/Directional Sideforce, Rolling Moment Yawing Moment	Important at freeway speeds. Affects vehicle response to gusts and sidewinds. Large side area of camper can cause coupling of lateral aero loads with vehicle suspension (roll steer, deflection steer, etc.) to deteriorate handling characteristics. Lateral aero has secondary effect on sedan lift distribution, fore-and-aft.	Moderately important at high speeds. Low profile and small lateral area preclude large lateral aero effects and/or strong coupling with suspension system. Primary source of directional stability provided by tire cornering stiffness characteristics which are enhanced by aero download.	Important at moderate and high speeds. Basic vehicle aerodynamically unstable without vertical tail. At WLSR speeds aero forces dominate tire forces. Stability and control must be provided aerodynamically. Vehicle flexibility can compound control problem at high q.

of the directional stability characteristics as defined by the understeer parameter, $U = 1 + Ku^2$, discussed by Ellis (Ref. 9) and Milner (Ref. 10). The parameter, U, is the rate of change of steering wheel deflection with respect to the vehicle path curvature, $[\partial \delta_s / \partial(1/R)]_u$, taken at constant velocity and normalized by the value at u = 0. The term, K is the understeer rate factor and is a convenient parameter for comparison of similar vehicles or the same vehicle with varying design characteristics. Understeer is defined as U > 1, neutral steer U = 1. For the case 0 < U < 1, the vehicle is considered to have stable oversteer, while U < 0 defines unstable oversteer. Alternate definitions for vehicle understeer may be chosen, $[\partial \delta_s / \partial u]_R$, for example, or vehicle response characteristics other than understeer may be selected for analysis. The parameter, U, is used herein as it is well suited to displaying the interaction of aerodynamics with other vehicle characteristics and the results obtained are easily interpreted.

The understeer characteristics of a typical front engine-rear drive compact passenger sedan are now examined by a numerical analysis employing

a formulation of the understeer rate factor, K which contains the effects of tractive and normal force on tire cornering stiffness and a five-degree-of-freedom aerodynamic force system. The derivation of K is given in Appendix A and is based on the coordinate system and idealized representation of the vehicle shown in Fig. 4 and the free body diagram of Fig. 5. The general layout and physical characteristics of the sedan employed in the analysis are shown in Fig. 6. The tire characteristics are based on the test data of Refs. 11 through 14. The aerodynamic characteristics are shown in Fig. 7 and are based on the wind tunnel data of Ref. 15 appropriately modified to account for differences in geometry between this vehicle and the test article of Ref. 15. The reference area, S, associated with the aerodynamic characteristics is the produce of wheelbase and wheel tread.

Two cases are considered. In Case I, the aerodynamic forces are omitted and K is computed using Eq. (A-15) of Appendix A. In Case II the aerodynamic characteristics of Fig. 7 are utilized in Eq. (A-14) of Appendix A to compute K. The results of these calculations are presented in

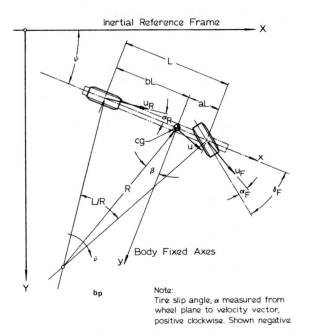

Figure 4. Coordinate System and Geometry.

Note:
Tire slip angle, α measured from wheel plane to velocity vector, positive clockwise. Shown negative.

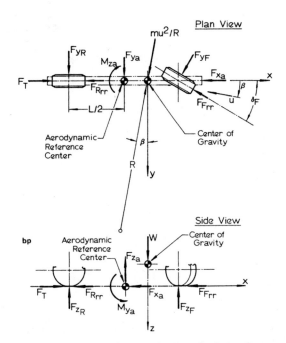

Figure 5. Force System in Steady-State Turn.

Figs. 8 and 9 as curves of U versus velocity for specified values of R. The characteristics of the curves are similar for both cases. U increases parabolically with velocity from its initial value of unity. The rate of increase diminishes and then becomes negative with continued increase in velocity until at sufficiently high values, U becomes negative. U deteriorates more rapidly at the smaller values of R, and in Case II, there is a marked degradation of U at high speeds due to the aerodynamic contribution. Lines of constant lateral acceleration, $\ddot{y}/g$, are also shown in

these plots, and the adverse effect of vehicle aerodynamics on U at constant $\ddot{y}/g$ is apparent.

The velocities for U_{max} and U = 0 are shown in Fig. 10 as a function of R, and comparison of Cases I and II clearly shows the adverse contribution of aerodynamics to vehicle understeer. These curves show that external aerodynamics has a first order effect on the understeer characteristics of a passenger sedan at speeds of the order 75 ft/sec and greater. This value corresponds to qS/w ≥ 0.1. The approximations employed do not compromise this conclusion as it

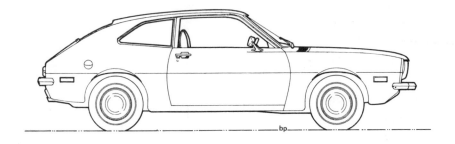

VEHICLE CHARACTERISTICS

Weight, W = 2,350 lbs.
Weight Distribution, front/rear = 55/45 %
Wheelbase, L = 7.84 ft.
Track, c = 4.58 ft.
Aerodynamic Reference Area, S = 35.9 ft²

TIRE CHARACTERISTICS

Zero-Load Friction Coefficient, μ_0, front/rear = 0.8/0.9
Friction Coefficient Lapse Rate, $\mu_1 = \partial\mu/\partial F_z$ = 0.0001 /lb.
Maximum Slip Angle, α_m, front/rear = -0.210/-0.174 rad.
Rolling Resistance/Normal Force, F_{rr}/F_z = 0.018

Figure 6. General Layout and Physical Characteristics of a Passenger Sedan.

9

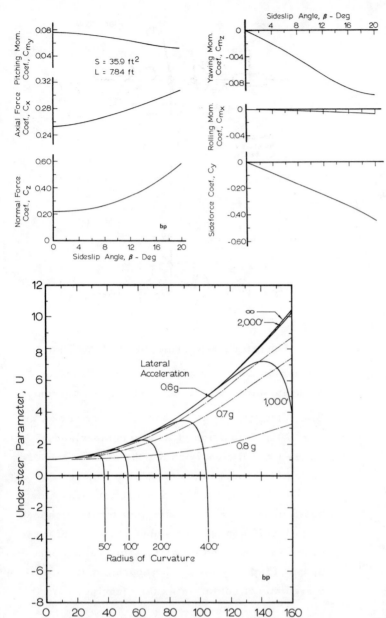

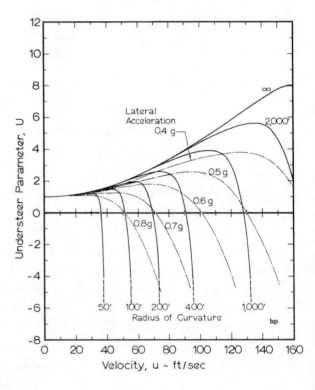

Figure 7, (Left). Aerodynamic Characteristics of a Passenger Sedan.

Figure 8, (Below Left). Understeer Characteristics of a Passenger Sedan - No Aerodynamics.

Figure 9, (Below Right). Understeer Characteristics of a Passenger Sedan - Aerodynamics Included.

Figure 10, (Bottom). Velocity and Radius of Curvature for U_{Max} and $U = 0$.

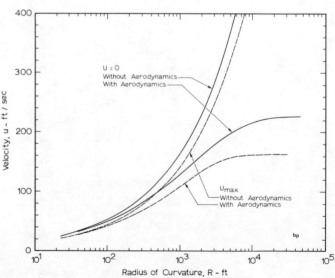

is probable that a more sophisticated analysis would show greater vehicle sensitivity due to the strong interaction between the aerodynamic force system and suspension geometry. For example, it is known that lift and pitching moment are strong functions of vehicle ground clearance, and in some road tests have shown an apparent variation as u^5 due to suspension deflection.

The relative sensitivity of U to variations in vehicle physical and aerodynamic characteristics is shown in Figs. 11 and 12. Curves of U for straight line operation at u = 140 ft/sec have been obtained by varying one parameter at a time, holding all

10

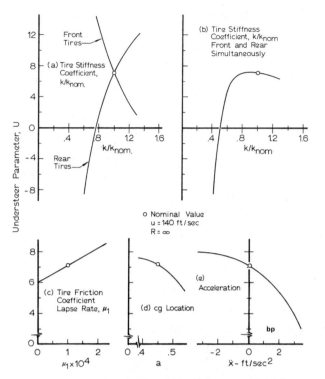

Figure 11. Sensitivity of Understeer to Vehicle Physical Characteristics.

to an increase in rear tire tractive force, F_T, and was computed assuming no fore-and-aft "weight transfer". As a result, the trend shown is somewhat conservative.

The effects of aerodynamic pitching and yawing moment are shown in Figs. 12a and 12b. Each contributes strongly to directional stability but through different mechanisms. The aerodynamic pitching moment works through the tires altering fore-and-aft normal force and cornering stiffness while the yawing moment works as in aircraft providing stability through the aerodynamic derivative $dC_{mz}/d\beta$. The aerodynamic lift and sideforce, Figs. 12c and 12d, have a secondary influence on U while large values of aerodynamic drag, Fig. 12e, seriously degrade directional stability at the speeds considered in this example.

Although a detailed discussion of the recreation vehicle is not intended, some remarks are warranted. Typically, the camper has five times the drag of a passenger sedan and a cg position 5% to 10% further aft. Unless compensated by an appropriate tire-suspension system, these effects

others constant at their nominal value. The sensitivity of U to tire cornering stiffness, k is presented in Fig. 11a. Since $k \sim \mu_0/\alpha_{max}$, the curves of Fig. 11a can be interpreted directly in terms of the tire friction coefficient, μ_0. U increases monotonically with a decrease in μ_{0F} and decreases monotonically with a decrease in μ_{0R}. Extremes in these conditions are obtained if, during hard braking, either front or rear wheels lock. With front wheel lock, the contribution of the front wheels is lost, $U \to +\infty$ and the vehicle will skid in a straight line unable to respond to steering command; with rear wheel lock, $U \to -\infty$ and the vehicle will spin out. A simultaneous reduction of μ_{0F} and μ_{0R}, Fig. 11b, has little effect on U until some critical value is reached, about 0.65 of nominal in the present example. Further reductions in μ_0 result in precipitous losses in U. This condition is representative of operation on wet roads where the tire friction coefficient is a fraction of its dry road value. The remaining curves show the relative increase in stability with μ_1, and loss in stability with aft cg location, and acceleration. This last effect is equivalent

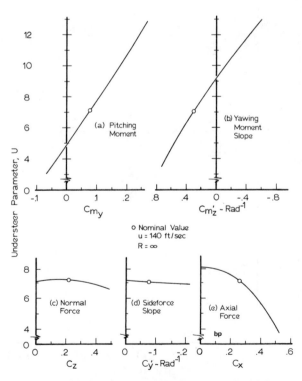

Figure 12. Sensitivity of Understeer to Vehicle Aerodynamic Characteristics.

11

can combine to seriously degrade understeer characteristics at freeway speeds. The box-like shape of the camper also produces large aerodynamic side forces and rolling moments in crosswinds which, in conjunction with adverse roll and deflection steer characteristics, can further degrade vehicle handling.

3.2 COMPETITION SPORTS CAR

3.2.1 Directional Stability

Handling qualities are important to the competition sports car in that they establish the ultimate level at which the man-machine system can operate consistently, and in so doing affect the safety of the overall operation. A poor handling car may be made to perform at its maximum capability for several laps by intense application of driver skill and effort, but over the length of the race, lap times will deteriorate. The complexity of the vehicle precludes accurate analytic prediction of understeer-oversteer characteristics; the final "set-up" is a master compromise arrived at by endless testing and adjusting. Typically, a road

racing car is set up to oversteer at low speeds to rapidly negotiate sharp corners and understeer at high speeds to provide stability when things happen quickly.

Major differences in physical characteristics exist between the passenger sedan and competition sports car. Nevertheless, the results of the previous section, in particular, the trends shown in Figs. 11 and 12, can, with appropriate interpretation, be applied here. For example, the contribution of the aerodynamic pitching moment to stability is made through the tire normal force; as the tire friction coefficient of the competition sports car is nearly twice that of the passenger sedan, it is seen that aerodynamics first become of interest at speeds of 50 to 60 ft/sec. This speed range also represents the lower limit of operation for the Formula 1 and Group 7 car. Accordingly, it is concluded that external aerodynamics is of interest over the entire operational range of this vehicle class.

The stability buildup for a Group 7 car is presented in Fig. 13. These data are in the form of curves of the derivative of yawing moment (normalized by vehicle weight and wheelbase) with respect to sideslip angle, $\partial \bar{M}_{z_{cg}} / \partial \beta$ and are obtained from Eq. (A-17) of Appendix A. Positive values of $\partial \bar{M}_{z_{cg}} / \partial \beta$ denote oversteer; negative values denote understeer. Unaccelerated straight line operation is assumed and the vehicle characteristics are noted on the figure. Without aerodynamic download the vehicle is unstable at all speeds becoming dangerously so in the upper speed range. With the addition of aerodynamic download over the rear wheels the ideal variation of $\bar{M}'_{z_{cg}}$ with u for a competition sports car is obtained. The low speed oversteer is relatively unaffected while a moderate amount of understeer is achieved at intermediate and high speeds.

These results demonstrate the vital contribution of aerodynamic download to vehicle stability. Further substantiation is obtained from driver evaluation. Although speeds in the 1972 Indianapolis 500 were 20 mph greater than the previous year, the drivers consistently stated that the cars

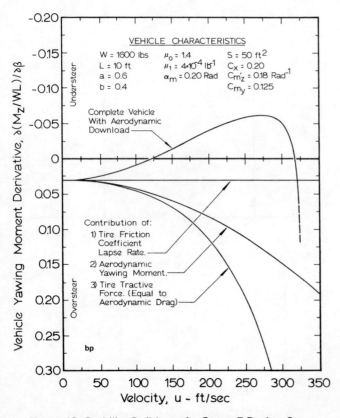

Figure 13. Stability Build up of a Group 7 Racing Car.

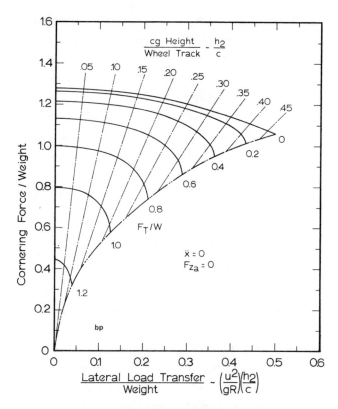

Figure 14. Cornering Power of a Group 7 Racing Car Without Aerodynamic Download.

handling and controllability are the governing factors in safe operation--at all speeds.

Further remarks on the application of aerodynamic devices to competition sports cars are offered in Appendix B wherein it is shown that an airfoil located horizontally over the rear wheels to generate download is 4 to 6 times more effective in providing directional stability than is a surface of equivalent area oriented vertically. It is further shown that the minimum acceptable aerodynamic efficiency or lift-to-drag ratio of such download devices is of the order 1.

3.2.2 Cornering

Fundamental to the performance of a closed circuit competition sports car is good cornering capability, particularly at high speed. The cornering power of a typical Group 7 car without aerodynamic download is presented in Fig. 14 and is obtained from Eqs. (B-3) and (B-4) of Appendix B. Curves of F_{yR}/W at constant F_T/W are shown versus lateral load transfer, $(u^2/gR)(h_2/c)$. Of interest are the adverse effects on F_{yR}/W of tractive force, particularly for $F_T/W > 0.3$, and of lateral load transfer. The latter is due to the degrading effect of μ_{1R} on the cornering stiffness of the outside rear tire.

felt more secure, "stuck to the road better" and were always under control due primarily to the download provided by the rear-mounted airfoils. These comments are significant as they show that speed per-se is not unsafe; rather vehicle

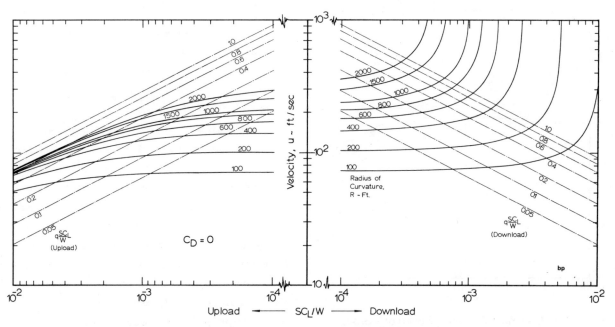

Figure 15a. Maximum Cornering Speed of a Group 7 Racing Car With Aerodynamic Download.

The influence of aerodynamic drag and download on maximum cornering speed is given by Eq. (B-6) of Appendix B. Two numerical examples of this relationship are presented in Fig. 15 for a Group 7 car. The first, Fig. 15a, shows curves of maximum cornering speed versus SC_L/W for a series of cornering radii and no aerodynamic drag. Lines of constant $(qS/W)C_L$ are superimposed from which it is seen that large benefits are obtained from download at intermediate and high speeds. The importance of download is most evident in Indy cars where typical values of $(qS/W)C_L$ range from 0.25 to 0.36. These values translate into potential speed increases of 18% to 25%. It has been observed that maximum cornering speeds have increased in the past several years from the 140 mph range to the 180 mph range, this increase being attributed in large part to the efficient utilization of fore-and-aft mounted airfoils.

The effect of aerodynamic drag on cornering speed is presented in Fig. 15b where it is seen that small values of drag do not significantly degrade cornering performance. This result is due to the tire friction ellipse model and zero acceleration assumptions employed. In practice, the vehicle does not maintain zero longitudinal acceleration through the turn, and as a result, the curves of

Fig. 15b are optimistic. From this consideration it is seen that low aerodynamic drag is desirable for optimum cornering performance. The arguments presented earlier for $(L/D)_{min}$ of aerodynamic devices also apply herein. That is, the minimum L/D of an aerodynamic modification which will not have a net adverse effect on cornering performance is given by Eq. (B-2) of Appendix B. Typically, this value is of the order 1 and is easily obtained by airfoils of the type currently in use.

3.3 ACCELERATION VEHICLE

3.3.1. Directional Stability

It is probable that the failures of the series of jet car WLSR contenders which appeared in the 1960-1962 era were, due in large part, to aerodynamic directional instability and/or loss of steering control due to nose lift. It was only after elimination of directional instability problems by the addition of a large vertical tail that the Breedlove "Spirit of America" was able to achieve the record speeds of 407.45 mph in 1963 and 526.28 mph in 1964. It is clear that the aerodynamic influence on stability and control characteristics of WLSR vehicles is of fundamental importance and in the opinion of the author is a more critical and challenging design problem than that of achieving low drag.

Results of the previous sections regarding directional stability and handling qualities are applicable to acceleration vehicles with one exception. At high speed, the tires of WLSR vehicles acting in conjunction with aerodynamic download are no longer capable of providing the necessary stabilizing forces because of the excessively large loads involved. This problem is compounded by the low tire friction coefficient of the Bonneville salt surface, of the order 0.4. Directional stability must be obtained aerodynamically by the use of adequate vertical tail area. The relative importance of vertical tail area and of aerodynamic download is obtained by an inspection of Eq. (B-1) of Appendix B, which, for $\mu_{1R} = 0$ and reaction propulsion, reduces to,

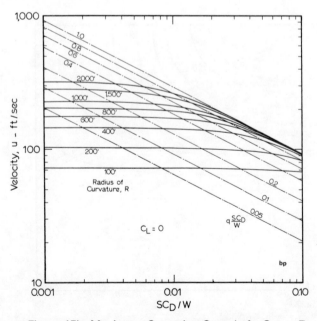

Figure 15b. Maximum Cornering Speed of a Group 7 Racing Car With Aerodynamic Drag.

14

$$\frac{(\partial M'_{zcg}/\partial S_H)}{(\partial M'_{zcg}/\partial S_V)} \sim \frac{\mu_{0R}}{\alpha_{mR}} \frac{C_{LH}}{C'_{LV}} > 1 \qquad (2)$$

The download required on the rear tires to overcome the aerodynamic destabilizing contribution of the body is of the order $F_{za} \sim -4 q S_\pi \alpha_{mR}/\mu_{0R}$ where S_π is the cross-sectional area of the body. At 600 mph, F_{za} is a download of the order 10,000 lb. As tire structural integrity is invariably the "Achilles Heel" of WLSR designs, loads of this magnitude are totally unacceptable. An equivalent level of directional stability can be provided by a vertical tail of area $S_V \sim 4 S_\pi/C_L$, or about 15 to 30 ft^2.

3.3.2 Performance

Dragster performance is given approximately by Eqs. (C-3) of Appendix C.

$$\dot{x} = \sqrt{2\mu g x}\left(1 - \frac{1}{2}Gx + \frac{5}{24}G^2x^2 - \ldots + \right) \qquad (3a)$$

$$t = \sqrt{\frac{2x}{\mu g}}\left(1 + \frac{1}{6}Gx - \frac{19}{24}G^2x^2 + \ldots - \right) \qquad (3b)$$

To first approximation, the performance is independent of the aerodynamic parameter, $G = \rho g S (C_D + \mu C_L)/2W$. The G enters as a second order correction having three times the effect on trap speed as on elapsed time. For typical values of $X = Gx$, say of the order 0.1, the corrections to trap speed and elapsed time are -5% and +1.7%, respectively. These effects, though small, are not negligible, as a 0.05 advantage in X represents a decisive 15-ft lead through the timing traps. The more detailed analysis of Ref. 16 confirms these trends and clearly establishes that significant improvements in performance can be obtained through drag reductions which are accompanied by little or no increase in vehicle weight. These results are summarized in the design trade-off curves shown in Fig. 16.

It is of interest to note that aerodynamic download acts as a negative drag in the parameter G. Download will improve performance over the speed

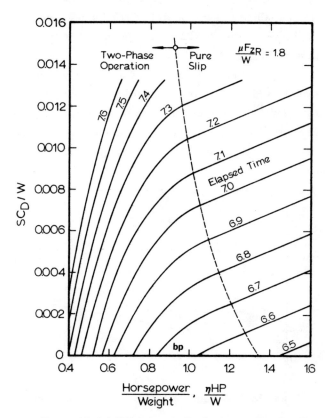

Figure 16. AA/FD Dragster Performance Trade-off Design Chart.

range in which power is sufficient to slip the driving wheels. Beyond this range, download in excess of that needed to prevent wheel spin is detrimental due to excess induced drag and tire rolling resistance.

WLSR runs are performed at the Bonneville Salt Flats or locations with equivalent surface characteristics. A length of about five miles is available for each of the two-way acceleration runs to the one mile timing trap. Trap speeds are determined

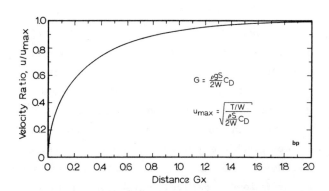

Figure 17. Generalized Performance Capability of a Constant Thrust WLSR Car.

by the limited acceleration distance and acceleration capability of the vehicle. This dependence is shown by Eq. (C-22) of Appendix C which is plotted in Fig. 17. Here, $C_L = 0$ and $\dot{X} = u/u_{max}$. To first order, the trap speed is directly proportional to $(T/W)^{1/2}$ and inversely proportional to $(SC_D/W)^{1/2}$. A numerical example for reaction-propelled vehicle operation at Bonneville is shown in Fig. 18. These data are based on Eq. (C-4)

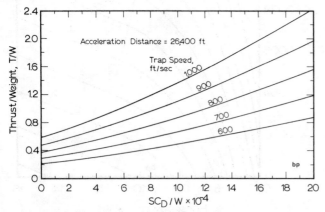

Figure 18. T/W Required for Specified Trap Speed.

of Appendix C. As speed requirements increase, greater attention must be paid to drag reduction, particularly transonically, lest the thrust requirements drive the system to unacceptable levels of size, weight, and cost. Minimum drag is also critical to the performance of the wheel-driven WLSR vehicle as its horsepower is relatively constant over the speed range. As a result, it becomes acceleration-limited well before entering the timing traps.

4. DISCUSSION

4.1 PASSENGER SEDAN

At present, passenger car design trends are dominated by the econimic and environmental aspects of energy consumption. Recent studies such as that of Ref. 17 show that significant gains can be made in reducing the pollution and increasing the fuel economy of passenger cars by reducing vehicle gross weight, engine size, and aerodynamic drag. These results are displayed by the following general expression for the required horsepower.

$$HP_{Req} = \frac{u}{550\eta}\left\{ W\left[\sin\gamma + C_1\cos\gamma + \left(1 + \frac{W'/W}{g}\right)\dot{u}\right] + \frac{1}{2}\rho(u + u_w)^2 S\left(C_D - C_1 C_L\right)\right\} \quad (4)$$

Here, η is the transmission efficiency, γ is the road inclination angle, C_1 is the rolling resistance, W' is the equivalent inertia of the rotating components, and u_w is the wind velocity. Eq. 4 states that the horsepower required to negotiate an incline, overcome rolling resistance, and accelerate, is proportional to vehicle gross weight whereas the horsepower required to overcome aerodynamic drag is proportional to the vehicle drag-area, SC_D. Some reduction in drag-area can be obtained by reducing vehicle size. However, the potential for size reduction is limited because of the fixed volume of the vehicle components and of the passenger compartment which is already near minimum volume. On the other hand, large reductions in C_D are possible through appropriate modifications of the vehicle shape.

It is concluded from these considerations that future trends in automotive design will be toward vehicles of light weight, low aerodynamic drag, small, efficient engines and good handling characteristics over the operational speed range. These trends mean higher values of qS/W and as a result external aerodynamics will assume new importance in determining both vehicle performance capability and handling characteristics. The determination of vehicle handling qualities in the design stage, already a complex procedure, will become even more so because of the strong aerodynamic input. It is anticipated that aerodynamic research, both analytic and experimental, will increase and out of it will evolve fundamental body shapes which will remain essentially invariant under the stylists transformation.

4.2 COMPETITION SPORTS AND ACCELERATION VEHICLES

In the field of competition sports cars and dragsters, vehicle aerodynamics are determined primarily by the rules imposed by the governing regulatory agencies rather than by a natural process of technical evolution. As a result, it is difficult to predict future design trends. A primary consideration in the formulation of these regulations is safety of operation. For example, several accidents involving the structural failure of airfoil installations in the initial period of their development prompted USAC and FIA to impose regulations restricting the type, size, and location of allowable aerodynamic devices. Subsequently, as a result of what were considered excessive speeds attained in the 1972 Indy 500, further restrictions were placed on the allowable span of airfoils.

The effectiveness of these regulations are questionable as they do not allow full utilization of the airfoils' stability augmentation capabilities. Nor can the issue of high speeds be used as a rationale for reducing airfoil effectiveness as there are other methods by which racing speeds can be surpressed. With regard to the structural integrity of airfoil installations, it is considered that there is, at present, sufficient understanding of this problem to establish technical specifications for the design, fabrication, and installation of various airfoil concepts which will preclude failure.

As a result of these considerations, it is believed that the present USAC and FIA regulations governing aerodynamic devices should be reexamined and, where necessary, revised to allow maximum utilization of the airfoils' stability augmentation capabilities so that, in truth, the regulations do assure maximum safety of vehicle operation.

APPENDIX A

VEHICLE DIRECTIONAL STABILITY: UNDERSTEER — OVERSTEER

A-1 THE UNDERSTEER RATE FACTOR, K

Consider an idealized vehicle performing a steady-state turn of radius R at a velocity u. The coordinate system and geometry are shown in Fig. 4. The external force system acting on the vehicle consists of the tire normal and friction forces and the aerodynamic force and moment system shown in the free body diagram of Fig. 5. With

the assumption that all angular deflections are small, the following set of dynamic equations are obtained.

$$F_{zF} = Wb - \frac{M_{ya}}{L} - \frac{F_{za}}{2} \qquad (A-1)$$

$$F_{zR} = Wa + \frac{M_{ya}}{L} - \frac{F_{za}}{2} \qquad (A-2)$$

$$F_T = -\frac{mu^2}{R}\beta + F_{yF}\delta_F + F_{xa} + F_{Frr} + F_{Rrr} \qquad (A-3)$$

$$F_{yF} = \frac{mu^2}{R}b + F_{xF}\delta_F - \frac{M_{za}}{L} - \frac{F_{ya}}{2} \qquad (A-4)$$

$$F_{yR} = \frac{mu^2 a}{R} + \frac{M_{za}}{L} - \frac{F_{ya}}{2} \qquad (A-5)$$

The tire rolling resistance terms are given by,

$$\left.\begin{array}{l} F_{Frr} = \left(\partial F_{Frr}/\partial F_{zF}\right)F_{zF} \\[2mm] F_{Rrr} = \left(\partial F_{Rrr}/\partial F_{zR}\right)F_{zR} \end{array}\right\} \qquad (A-6)$$

From the kinematics of Fig. 4,

$$\dot{v} = u/R \qquad (A-7)$$

$$\beta = a\alpha_R + b\left(\delta_F + \alpha_F\right) \qquad (A-8)$$

$$\delta_F = \dot{v}L/u - \left(\alpha_F - \alpha_R\right) \qquad (A-9)$$

The interaction of the tire cornering force and tractive force is accounted for by a form of the friction ellipse concept proposed by Ellis (Refs. 4 and 9), as follows.

$$F_{yF} = \frac{\alpha_F}{\alpha_{Fm}}\left(\mu_{0F} - \mu_{1F}F_{zF}\right)F_{zF} \qquad (A-10a)$$

$$F_{yR} = \frac{\alpha_R}{\alpha_{Rm}}\sqrt{\left(\mu_{0R} - \mu_{1R}F_{zR}\right)^2 F_{zR}^2 - F_T^2} \qquad (A-10b)$$

The terms α_{Rm} and α_{Fm} are the front and rear tire idealized maximum slip angles and are indicative of tire cornering stiffness.

The basic equation for the understeer parameter U is given by

$$U = 1 - \frac{U}{L} \frac{\partial\left(\alpha_F - \alpha_R\right)}{\partial \beta} \tag{A-11}$$

Eq. (A-11) can also be written

$$U = 1 + Ku^2 \tag{A-12}$$

where K, the understeer rate factor, is a convenient parameter for comparison of similar vehicles or the same vehicle with varying design characteristics. Combining Eqs. (A-1) through (A-12), an expression for K is obtained in the form,

$$K = \frac{\left\{ \begin{array}{c} \rho \dfrac{bS}{2W}\left(Bk_F - Ak_R\right) + \dfrac{b}{gL}\left(k_R + q\dfrac{SB}{W}\right) \\ - \dfrac{a}{gL}\left[1 + \dfrac{f_R\gamma}{a\left(F_{yF}/W\right)}\right]\left(\dfrac{qSA}{W} - k_F\right) \end{array} \right\}}{k_F\left(k_R - f_R{}' + q\dfrac{S}{W}B\right) - f_R\left(q\dfrac{S}{W}A - f_R\right)} \tag{A-13}$$

where

$$\gamma = \frac{b\delta_F}{R} - \beta + \frac{gL}{u^2}\left(F_{yF}/W\right)$$

$$A = \left(C_{my} + C_z/2\right)'\left(F_{zF}\mu_{1F}\alpha_F/\alpha_{Fm}\right.$$
$$\left. - F_{yF}/F_{zF}\right) + \left(C_{mz} + C_y/2\right)'$$

$$B = C\left(C_{my} - C_z/2\right)' - \left(C_{mz} - C_y/2\right)' \left.\right\} \tag{A-14a}$$
$$- \left[f_R/\left(F_{yF}/W\right)\right]\left[C_x' - \delta_F\left(C_{mz}\right.\right.$$
$$\left.\left. + C_y/2\right)' - 2m/\rho SR\right]$$

$$C = f_R\left(F_{yF}/W\right)\left(\mu_{0R} - \mu_{1R}F_{zR}\right)\left(\mu_{0R}\right.$$
$$\left. - 2\mu_{1R}F_{zR}\right)$$

and

$$f_R = \left(F_T/W\right)\left(F_{yR}/W\right)\left(F_{yF}/W\right)/k_R^2\alpha_{Rm}^2 \left.\right\}$$
$$k_F = F_{yF}/\alpha_F; \qquad k_R = F_{yR}/\alpha_R \left.\right\} \tag{A-14b}$$

With all aerodynamic forces set equal to zero, Eq. (A-13) reduces to

$$K = \frac{bk_R - ak_F\left[1 + f_R\left(b\delta_F - \beta\right)\big/a\left(F_{yF}/W\right)\right]}{gL\left[k_Rk_F + f_R\left(k_F a/b + f_R\right)\right]} \tag{A-15}$$

A-2 YAWING MOMENT DERIVATIVE, $\partial\overline{M}_{z_{cg}}/\partial\beta$

The static directional stability of an automobile is considered here from a viewpoint slightly different from that taken in the preceding section. Eqs. (A-1) through (A-10) are employed to obtain directly the vehicle yawing moment, M_z and its variation with sideslip angle, β. The vehicle is said to be stable (understeer) if the slope of the moment curve, $dM_{z_{cg}}/d\beta$, is such as to tend to reduce the absolute magnitude of β and is unstable (oversteer) if $\partial M_{z_{cg}}/\partial\beta$ tends to increase the absolute magnitude of β. This formulation is of interest as it more directly displays the effect of the relevant parameters on the magnitude of the vehicle lateral-directional force system.

Referring to Fig. 5, the yawing moment derivative normalized by vehicle weight and wheelbase is

$$\overline{M}_{z_{cg}}' = \frac{\partial\left(M_{zcg}/WL\right)}{\partial\beta}$$

$$= a\left(F_{yF}/W\right)' - b\left(F_{yR}/W\right)' + \overline{M}_{za}'$$
$$- \left(b - \frac{1}{2}\right)\left[\left(F_{ya}/W\right)' - \left(F_{xa}/W\right)\right.$$
$$\left. - \beta\left(F_{xa}/W\right)'\right] - a\delta_F\left(F_{Frr}/W\right)' \tag{A-16}$$

18

For $\beta = \delta_F = 0$, Eq. (A-16) reduces to

$$\overline{M}'_{zcg}{}_{\beta=\delta_F=0} = \frac{b}{\alpha_{mR}} \times$$

$$\sqrt{\left(\mu_{0R} - \mu_{1R} F_{zR}\right)^2 \left(F_{zR}/W\right)^2 - \left(F_T/W\right)^2}$$

$$- \frac{a}{\alpha_{mF}} \left(F_{zF}/W\right)\left(\mu_{0F} - \mu_{1F} F_{zF}\right)$$

$$+ (qS/W)\left[C'_{mz} - \left(b - \frac{1}{2}\right)C'_y\right] \quad \text{(A-17)}$$

APPENDIX B

GENERAL REMARKS ON THE UTILIZATION OF AERODYNAMIC DEVICES

B-1 DIRECTIONAL STABILITY

The most effective use of aerodynamics in providing vehicle stability may be assessed by first assuming an airfoil located horizontally over the rear wheels to generate a download and then oriented vertically to provide aerodynamic stability. The quantities $(\partial \overline{M}'_{zcg}/\partial S_H)$ and $(\partial \overline{M}'_{zcg}/\partial S_V)$ are obtained from Eq. (A-17) and their ratio takes the form

$$\frac{(\partial M'_{zcg}/\partial S_H)}{(\partial \overline{M}'_{zcg}/\partial S_V)} = \left(\frac{C_{LH}}{\alpha_{mR} C'_{LV}}\right) \times$$

$$\frac{\left(\mu_{0R} - \mu_{1R} F_{zR}\right)\left(\mu_{0R} - 2\mu_{1R} F_{zR}\right)\left(F_{zR}/W\right)}{\left(\mu_{0R} - \mu_{1R} F_{zR}\right)^2 \left(F_{zR}/W\right)^2 - \left(F_T/W\right)^2}$$

$$\text{(B-1)}$$

where C_{LH} and C'_{LV} are the lift coefficient and the lift curve slope, per radian of the airfoil. For a typical Group 7 car in unaccelerated operation, Eq. (B-1) yields values for $(\partial \overline{M}'_{zcg}/\partial S_H)/(\partial \overline{M}'_{zcg}/\partial S_V)$ of 4 to 6 indicating the superiority of aerodynamic download, at least in this speed regime.

There is great variation in aerodynamic efficiency among the devices used for generating download. As drag tends to degrade vehicle handling, it is appropriate to consider the minimum acceptable incremental lift-to-drag ratio, $(L/D)_{min}$, of these devices. From an inspection of Eqs. (A-13) and (A-17), it is seen that to first order, the handling

characteristics of the vehicle will remain unaltered if, as a result of aerodynamic modification, rear tire cornering stiffness remains invariant. Accordingly, $(L/D)_{min}$ satisfies the condition,

$$\partial k_R / \partial (L/D) = 0$$

from which is obtained,

$$(L/D)_{min} = \frac{(F_T/F_{zR})}{(\mu_{0R} - \mu_{1R} F_{zR})(\mu_{0R} - 2\mu_{1R} F_{zR})}$$

$$\text{(B-2)}$$

The most critical condition is obtained for $F_{Tmax} \sim (\mu_0 - \mu_1 F_{zR})F_{zR}$. For this case,

$$(L/D)_{min} \sim \frac{1}{(\mu_{0R} - 2\mu_{1R} F_{zR})} = 1 \sim 1$$

It is easily seen that all but the most inefficient of aerodynamic download devices will meet this criterion.

B-2 CORNERING

As a general rule, cornering capability is limited by the lateral force of the rear tires. At this condition, $\alpha_R \sim \alpha_{mR}$ and the maximum lateral force generated by the rear wheels is

$$F_{yR}/W = \left[\left(\mu_{0R} - \mu_{1R} F_{zR_i}\right)^2 \left(F_{zR_i}/W\right)^2 - \left(F_T/2W\right)^2\right]^{1/2}$$

$$+ \left[\left(\mu_{0R} - \mu_{1R} F_{zR_o}\right)^2 \left(F_{zR_o}/W\right)^2 - \left(T_T/2W\right)^2\right]^{1/2} \quad \text{(B-3)}$$

where

$$\left.\begin{aligned} F_{zR_i}/W &= \frac{1}{2}\left[a + M_{ya}/WL - F_{za}/2WL \right. \\ &\qquad\left. + h_1 \ddot{x}/Lg\right] - \frac{u^2}{gR}\frac{h_2}{c} \\[6pt] F_{zR_o}/W &= \frac{1}{2}\left[a + M_{ya}/WL - F_{za}/2WL \right. \\ &\qquad\left. + h_1 \ddot{x}/Lg\right] + \frac{u^2}{gR}\frac{h_2}{c} \end{aligned}\right\} \quad \text{(B-4)}$$

and the subscripts i and o refer to inside and out-side wheel. F_T/W is given by Eq. (A-3) with the term $\ddot{x}/g$ added and h_1 and h_2 are equivalent cg heights associated with longitudinal and lateral load transfer. Lateral load transfer is primarily a function of cg height, h, and rear tire track, c, but can be modified to some extent by adjustment of front and rear wheel roll stiffness.

The benefits of aerodynamic download to high speed cornering are apparent and can be quantita-tively evaluated by considering a simplified model in which $\mu_{1R} = 0$ and $F_T = F_{xa}$. For this case,

$$F_{yR}/W = \frac{au^2}{gR}$$

$$= \sqrt{\mu_{0R}^2 \left[a - (qS/W)C_L\right]^2 - (qS/W)^2 C_D^2}$$

$$(B-5)$$

and the maximum cornering speed is given by,

$$u_{max} = \left\{ \frac{a\mu_{0R}\left[\sqrt{\left(\frac{a}{gR}\right)^2 + \left(\frac{C_D}{2W/S}\right)^2} - \frac{\mu_{0R}}{2W/S}\frac{\rho C_L}{}\right]}{\left(\frac{a}{gR}\right)^2 - \left(\frac{\rho}{2W/S}\right)^2\left(\mu_{0R}^2 C_L^2 - C_D^2\right)} \right\}^{1/2}$$

$$(B-6)$$

APPENDIX C

ACCELERATION VEHICLE DYNAMICS

The entire acceleration run of the AA/FD dragster and about half the run of the wheel-driven WLSR car are performed under conditions of potential wheel slip. Therefore, the implications of aero-dynamics on the performance of these vehicles as well as the reaction-propelled WLSR car are ade-quately displayed by a constant-thrust model de-scribed by the following equation,

$$\ddot{x} + \frac{\rho gS}{2W}(C_D + \mu C_L)\dot{x}^2 - \mu g = 0 \quad (C-1)$$

For the wheel-driven vehicle, μ and C_L have their usual meaning, while for the reaction-propelled vehicle, $C_L = 0$ and μ is interpreted as the thrust-to-weight ratio, T/W. C_D is assumed constant over the acceleration run. This assumption as well as that of constant T/W are not strictly valid

in the high subsonic speed range, but are adequate for the present purpose. With the initial conditions $x = \dot{x} = 0$ at $t = 0$, Eq. (C-1) yields the following solutions.

$$\left.\begin{array}{l} \dot{X} = \tanh\tau = \sqrt{1 - e^{-2X}} \\ X = \ln\cosh\tau \end{array}\right\} (C_D + \mu C_L) > 0 \quad (C-2a)$$

$$\left.\begin{array}{l} \dot{X} = \mu gt \\ X = \frac{1}{2}\mu gt^2 \end{array}\right\} (C_D + \mu C_L) = 0 \quad (C-2b)$$

$$\left.\begin{array}{l} \dot{X} = \tan\tau = \sqrt{e^{2X} - 1} \\ X = -\ln\cos\tau \end{array}\right\} (C_D + \mu C_L) < 0 \quad (C-2c)$$

where $X = Gx$,

$\tau = \sqrt{\mu gG}\,t$,

and $G = \rho gS(C_D + \mu C_L)/2W$.

The acceleration distance of the AA/FD dragster is 1320 ft, yielding a value of X << 1 through the timing traps. This allows expansion of Eq. (C-2) as follows.

$$\dot{x} = \sqrt{2\mu gx}\left(1 - \frac{1}{2}Gx + \frac{5}{24}G^2x^2 - \ldots +\right) \quad (C-3a)$$

$$t = \sqrt{\frac{2x}{\mu g}}\left(1 + \frac{1}{6}Gx - \frac{19}{24}G^2x^2 + \ldots +\right) \quad (C-3b)$$

To the leading approximation, dragster perfor-mance is independent of the aerodynamic parame-ter, G which enters as a second order correction to both trap speed and elapsed time.

For WLSR operation, typified by the four-to-six mile run of the Bonneville Salt Flat, X is of the order 1 and Eq. (C-2) can be expanded as follows:

$$\dot{x} = \sqrt{\frac{T/W}{\frac{\rho S}{2W}C_D}}\left[1 - \frac{1}{2}\exp\left(-\rho g\frac{S}{W}C_Dx\right)\right.$$

$$\left. - \frac{1}{8}\exp\left(-2\rho g\frac{S}{W}C_Dx\right) - \ldots -\right] \quad (C-4)$$

To first order, the trap speed is determined by vehicle thrust-to-weight ratio and by the aerodyna-mic parameter, SC_D/W.

REFERENCES

(1) Schlichting, H.: "Aerodynamic Problems of Motor Cars". NATO AGARD Report 307. (October 1960).

(2) Romberg, G. F., Chianese, F., Jr., Lajoie, R. G.: "Aerodynamics of Race Cars in Drafting and Passing Situations". Paper 710213 presented at SAE Automotive Engineering Congress, Detroit, Michigan (January 1971).

(3) Milliken, W. F., et al.: "Research in Automobile Stability and Control and in Tyre Performance". Proc. Institution of Mechanical Engineers, Automotive Division, London, England (1956-57), No. 7.

(4) Ellis, J. R.: "The Dynamics of Vehicles During Braking". Proc. Symposium on Control of Vehicles During Braking and Cornering, Paper 4, Organized by Institution of Mechanical Engineers, Automobile Division. London, England. (June 1963).

(5) Dugoff, H., Fancher, P. S., and Segel, L.: Tire Performance Characteristics Affecting Vehicle Response to Steering and Braking Control Inputs". University of Michigan Report CST-460 (August 1969).

(6) McHenry, R. R.: "Research in Automobile Dynamics - A Computer Simulation of General Three-Dimensional Motions". Paper 710361 presented at SAE Mid-Year Meeting, Montreal, Que., Canada (June 1971).

(7) Belsdorf, M. R., Rice, R. S., and Bird, K. D.: "Performance Tasks as Measures of Vehicle Handling Qualities at the Limit of Performance". Paper 710081 presented at SAE Automotive Engineering Congress, Detroit, Michigan (January 1971).

(8) Milliken, W. F. and Dell'Amico, F.: "Standards for Safe Handling Characteristics of Automobiles". Proc. Joint Symposium on Vehicle and Road Design for Safety, Cranfield, England, (July 1968).

(9) Ellis, J. R.: "Understeer and Oversteer". Automobile Engineer, pp. 178-182 (May 1963).

(10) Milner, P. J.: Steady State Vehicle Handling". Automotive Engineer, 57, 11, pp. 430-435 (October 1967).

(11) Elliott, O. R., Klamp, W. K., and Kraemer, W. E.: "Passenger Tire Power Consumption". Paper 710575 presented at the SAE Mid-Year Meeting, Montreal, Que., Canada (June 1971).

(12) Floyd, C. W.: "Power Loss Testing of Passenger Tires". Paper 710576 presented at the SAE Mid-Year Meeting, Montreal, Que., Canada (June 1971).

(13) Bergman, W.: "Theoretical Prediction of the Effect of Friction on Cornering Force". SAE Transactions, pp. 614-634 (1961).

(14) Nordeen, D. L. and Cortese, A. D.: "Force and Moment Characteristics of Rolling Tires". SAE Paper 713A presented at the International Summer Meeting (June 1963).

(15) Turner, T. R.: Wind Tunnel Investigation of a 3/8-Scale Automobile Model Over a Moving-Belt Ground Plane". NASA TN D-4229 (November 1967).

(16) Pershing, B.: Dragster Aerodynamics - Streamlining Versus Weight". Proc. AIAA Symposium on the Aerodynamics of Sports and Competition Automobiles, pp. 39-51, Los Angeles, Calif. (April 20, 1968).

(17) Austin, Thomas C. and Hellman, Karl H., "Passenger Car Fuel Economy Trends and Influencing Factors". Paper 730790 presented at SAE Conference, Milwaukee, Wisconsin (September 1973).

AUD. QUESTION: Would you estimate approximately at what speeds aerodynamics start to play a part in the design of passenger cars?

PERSHING: I would use the phrase "freeway speeds". That is, at about 40 mph you might first notice aerodynamic effects on the handling; at higher speeds, say 55 to 65 mph, aerodynamic forces became significant. This is particularly true driving in windy or gusty weather, a factor people don't ordinarily think about until they get in their campers and try to cruise at high speeds in strong crosswinds. The point I wanted to make in the paper was that when you look into the future, the problems we now have with fuel shortages and with pollution will still be with us and these problems are now redirecting design trends towards cars which are lighter and more efficient but which have essentially the same utility, that is planform area. As this trend toward lighter weight and smaller engines continues, as I believe it will, the sensitivity to aerodynamic forces becomes greater. From the area loading plot, Figure 2, you see that such designs become more·like light airplanes rather than heavy bricks, and as this trend continues, a car which at today's weight might not respond to a gust at 40 mph will now have to be designed very carefully to minimize the adverse effects of crosswinds and interference from other vehicles.

AUD. QUESTION: To what extent is it possible to get a download on an automobile by designing the underside of the car in such a way as to get a Venturi effect?

PERSHING: That approach has been tried a number of times. Ford, in fact, tried it on some early configurations of their GT-40 race car and found, as most others have, that it didn't work. The venturi effect requires that the underpan near the center of the car be close to the ground but that as you move away from the center toward the front and back, the underpan slopes up to produce greater ground clearance at the nose and tail. In practice, the underpan upsweep at the nose invariably produces a strong upload on the nose and the large download which theory says should be generated by the low slung underpan at the center of the car just doesn't materialize. This is probably due to a combination of things, three-dimensional effects in the flow, tire interference, the interaction of the nose load with the suspension system.

There are other ways of getting download on a car. The most common method is to install a front-end spoiler to restrict the flow trying to go under the car. There is some wind tunnel test data which shows that these devices produce a negative pressure along the bottom of the car and force the stagnation point of the flow up on the hood where the large positive pressures can push the nose down. I would say this is the obvious way to go; any time you start lifting the nose you are going to get into a lot of trouble.

AERODYNAMICS OF ROAD VEHICLES, OR
AERODYNAMICS AS AN ANNOYANCE

E. Eugene Larrabee
Department of Aeronautics and Astronautics
Massachusetts Institute of Technology

ABSTRACT

Analytic methods are presented which facilitate the assessment of aerodynamic effects on road vehicle performance, stability, and control. Most of the phenomena described--e.g. aerodynamic drag, lift, side force, and moments--are at the annoyance level, and need to be discussed in the context of mathematical models where they can be incorporated at true value. Several of these models are presented which involve vehicle acceleration capability, chassis steering dynamics, tire mechanics, and driver lane holding strategies. Problems of experimental verification on the road or in wind tunnels are noted.

1. INTRODUCTION

The airplane and the automobile grew up together, both dependent on the internal combustion engine as a prime mover; but whereas the development of aerodynamic theory led to an understanding and exploitation of aerodynamic lift to sustain airplanes in flight, the same theory has yielded no corresponding benefit for automobiles; it predicts, instead, only an aerodynamic drag which resists forward motion. If automobile bodies do develop upward aerodynamic lift forces, these interfere with the action of the tires in providing lateral guidance; if cross winds produce horizontal aerodynamic lift forces, these also disturb lateral guidance; moreover, the engine combustion air

and cooling air requirements present an additional source of aerodynamic drag; and finally, the necessity of ventilating the passenger compartment may provide unwelcome noise. The aerodynamics of road vehicles, is, in short, the aerodynamics of annoyance.

This paper discusses analytical and experimental techniques for assessing these unfortunate aerodynamic tendencies and minimizing their impact. These techniques come from the author's experience in teaching a course in road vehicle design and dynamics at M.I.T. and in his activities as a consultant to a race car builder, a developer of personal rapid transit systems, and two research teams specializing in man-machine systems.

This paper is a revised and updated version of a seminar paper originally presented at the Cranfield Institute of Technology at Cranfield, England on 7 June 1973.

2. AERODYNAMIC EFFECTS ON STRAIGHT LINE PERFORMANCE

Practical considerations of overall length and component packaging make automobile bodies "bluff bodies" in the sense that their drag is dominated by the negative base pressure associated with separated flow about their after portions, a drag that is nearly proportional to the square of the airspeed. This suggests that its effect on straight line performance may be readily modeled and determined by road testing or accounted for in mathematical predictions of full throttle acceleration performance.

2.1 DRAG DETERMINATION BY COASTING DECELERATION

Consider an automobile coasting on a level road under calm air conditions. The equations of motion in terms of time spent or distance covered are:

$$m(dv/dt) = -\frac{\rho}{2} v^2 AC_D - \mu mg \qquad (1a)$$

$$mv(dv/ds) = -\frac{\rho}{2} v^2 AC_D - \mu mg \qquad (1b)$$

where C_D is the drag coefficient based on the reference area A (commonly the maximum cross sectional area of the body) and μ is the coefficient of rolling friction. If C_D and μ are considered constant, and if an "aerodynamic penetration", s_D is defined as

$$s_D \equiv \frac{2m}{\rho AC_D}$$

Then equation 1a and 1b may be rewritten in the dimensionless forms

$$\frac{dr}{1+r^2} = -\frac{v_r}{s_D} dt \qquad (1a')$$

$$\frac{rdr}{1+r^2} = -\frac{ds}{s_D} \qquad (1b')$$

where v_r is a speed at which air drag equals rolling friction

$$\frac{\rho}{2} v_r^2 AC_D \equiv \mu mg \qquad (3)$$

and r is a speed ratio defined as

$$r \equiv \frac{v}{v_r}$$

Equations (1a') and (1b') have simple analytic solutions (figure 1):

$$\frac{t_2 - t_1}{(s_D/v_r)} = \tan^{-1}(r_1) - \tan^{-1}(r_2) \qquad (2a)$$

$$\frac{s_2 - s_1}{s_D} = \frac{1}{2} \ln \frac{r_1^2 + 1}{r_2^2 + 1} \qquad (2b)$$

These solutions suggest procedures for determining air drag and rolling friction experimentally[1].

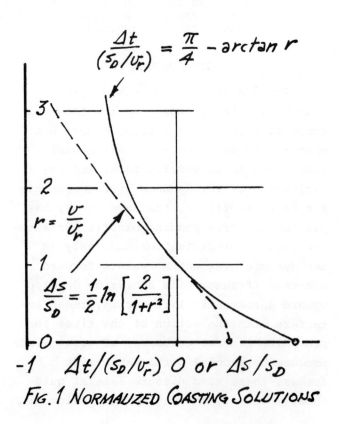

$$\frac{\Delta t}{(s_D/v_r)} = \frac{\pi}{4} - \arctan r$$

$$r = \frac{v}{v_r}$$

$$\frac{\Delta s}{s_D} = \frac{1}{2} \ln\left[\frac{2}{1+r^2}\right]$$

$$-1 \quad \Delta t/(s_D/v_r) \quad 0 \text{ or } \Delta s/s_D$$

FIG. 1 NORMALIZED COASTING SOLUTIONS

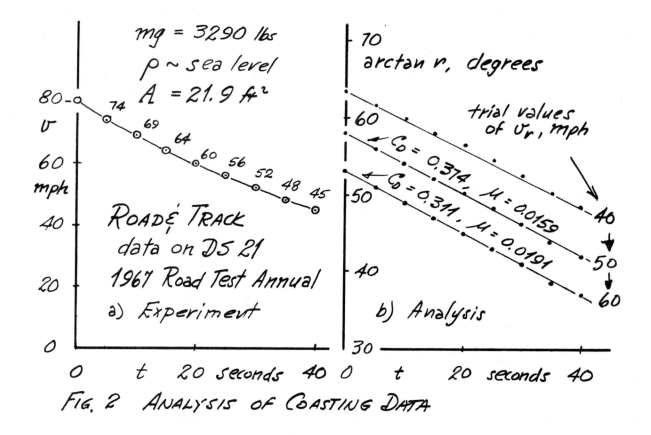

FIG. 2   ANALYSIS OF COASTING DATA

Figure 2 presents a time history of speed during a coasting deceleration test and its analytical treatment. One guesses the speed v_r which makes air drag equal to rolling friction and plots the corresponding trial values of arctangent of the speed ratio against time for several selected speeds, as shown. Too small a value of v_r will "overcompensate" the upward concave experimental data, providing an arctangent curve concave downwards; too large a value of v_r will "undercompensate" the data, leaving it concave upwards. The correct value of v_r will produce a straight line, corresponding to a deceleration process with a combination of constant and square law resistance which best fits the data.

To the extent that the rolling friction is constant the aerodynamic penetration is then determined from the slope of this line by the relation

$$s_D = \frac{v_r}{|\Delta \tan^{-1}(r)/\Delta t|} \quad (5)$$

The values of C_D and μ follow from the relations

$$C_D = \frac{2m}{\rho A\, s_D} \quad (6)$$

$$\mu = \frac{v_r^2}{g s_D}$$

If the rolling friction contains a component proportional to speed squared, this analysis will, of course, attribute it to "aerodynamic drag". The quality of of the data in Figure 2 does not permit a clear determination of v_r -- the arctangent curves for 50 and 60 mph being equally straight -- but the 50 mph results seem more plausible.

v_r	C_D	μ
50 mph	0.374	0.0159
60 mph	0.311	0.0191

Note that in any event the total energy loss is accounted for; the higher value of v_r leading to smaller aerodynamic (or square law) resistance and larger constant resistance.

2.2 PERFORMANCE PREDICTION

2.2.1 Analytical Estimation of Acceleration Through Gears

Figure 3 presents a set of representative "tractive effort" curves and an appropriate mathematical idealization. The tractive effort developed by the engine-transmission-driven wheel combination is modeled by a constant power hyperbola, truncated below a certain speed, v_i, at a constant value taken to be a fraction of the vehicle weight. The quantities η, λ, and γ are fitting constants, corresponding to the drive line efficiency, the fraction of weight on the driven wheels, and the limiting coefficient of friction at the driven wheels. The problem of calculating the acceleration through gears for a

vehicle modeled in this way appeared to have a simple analytic solution (which escaped the author); in typical academic style he assigned it as a home problem, and was delighted when one of his students, William V. Averre (pronounced "Avery") found the solution, which is described below:

In the traction (or torque) limited speed range, $0 < v < v_i$, the equation of motion is:

$$m\frac{dv}{dt} = mv\frac{dv}{ds} = (\lambda\gamma - \mu)mg - \frac{\rho}{2}v^2 AC_D \quad (8)$$

This can be cast in the form

$$\frac{d\xi}{1 - \xi^2} = \frac{d\delta}{s_D/v_f} \quad (9)$$

or

$$\frac{\xi d\xi}{1 - \xi^2} = \frac{d\sigma}{s_D} \quad (10)$$

depending on whether a time solution (Eq. 9) or a distance solution (Eq. 10) is sought. The dimensionless quantities in

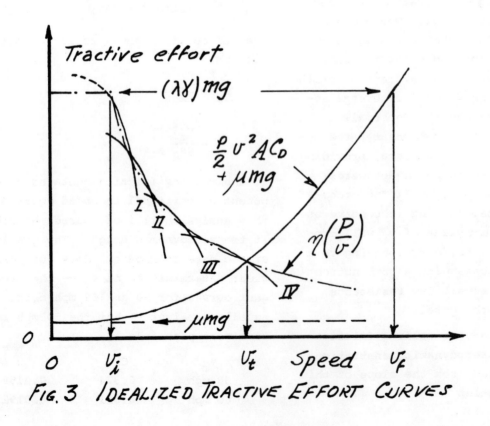

FIG. 3 IDEALIZED TRACTIVE EFFORT CURVES

26

equations 9 and 10 are:

$$\xi = v/v_f \qquad (11)$$

$$\delta = t/(s_D/v_f) \qquad (12)$$

$$\sigma = s/s_D \qquad (13)$$

which have been normalized with the reference quantities:

$$s_D = \frac{2m}{\rho AC_D} \qquad (Eq.\ 2) \qquad (14)$$

$$v_f^2 = (\lambda\gamma - \mu)g\ s_D \qquad (see\ figure\ 3)$$

Also,

$$v_i = \frac{\eta P}{\lambda\gamma mg} = \frac{\mathbb{P}}{\lambda\gamma g} ; \quad \mathbb{P} = \frac{\eta P}{m} \qquad (15)$$

In the power limited speed range, $(v_i < v < v_t)$ (see figure 3) the equation of motion is:

$$m\frac{dv}{dt} = mv\frac{dv}{ds} = \eta P\ (\frac{1}{v}) - \mu mg - \frac{\rho}{2}v^2 AC_D \qquad (16)$$

This can be cast in the form

$$\frac{rdr}{1 + \phi - \phi r - r^3} = \frac{d\tau}{(s_D/v_t)} \qquad (16)$$

or

$$\frac{r^2 dr}{1 + \phi - \phi r - r^3} = \frac{d\sigma}{s_D} \qquad (17)$$

depending again, on whether a time (Eq. 16) or distance solution (Eq. 17) is sought.

The dimensionless quantities are:

$$r = v/v_t \qquad (18)$$

$$\tau = t/(s_D/v_t) \qquad (19)$$

$$\phi = mg/(\frac{\rho}{2}v_t^2 AC_D) \qquad (20)$$

$$= \mu g\ s_D/(v_t^2) \qquad (20a)$$

= rolling friction/air drag at top speed

These are normalized with the top speed,

v_t, given by:

$$\frac{\rho}{2} AC_D\ v_t^3 + \mu mg\ v_t = \eta P \qquad (21)$$

or

$$v_t^3 + \mu g\ s_D\ v_t = \mathbb{P}s_D \qquad (21a)$$

Equations 9 and 10 are elementary integrals, but equations 16 and 17 are not; the third order denominator $1 + \phi - \phi r - r^3$ factors readily into $(1 - r)\ (1+\phi+\phi r+r^2)$ however, and the integrals are found by evaluating each of the terms in the resulting partial fraction expansion. The results are messy; the collected solutions are presented below:

Low speed $(0 < v < v_i)$ range:

$$\Delta\delta = \frac{1}{2}\ln\left\{\frac{1 + \xi_2}{1 - \xi_2}\right\}\left\{\frac{1 - \xi_1}{1 + \xi_1}\right\} \qquad (22)$$

$$\Delta\sigma = \frac{1}{2}\ln\left\{\frac{1 - \xi_1^2}{1 - \xi_2^2}\right\} \qquad (23)$$

High speed $(v_i < v < v_t)$ range:

$$\Delta\tau = \frac{1}{3 + \phi}\left[A + \frac{1}{2}(B) - \frac{3 + 2\phi}{3 + 4\phi}(C)\right] \qquad (24)$$

$$\Delta\sigma = \frac{1}{3 + \phi}\left[A - \frac{2 + \phi}{2}(B) - \frac{\phi}{3 + 4\phi}(C)\right] \qquad (25)$$

where

$$A = \ln\left[\frac{1 - r_3}{1 - r_4}\right] \qquad (26)$$

$$B = \ln\left[\frac{1 + \phi + r_4 + r_4^2}{1 + \phi + r_3 + r_3^2}\right] \qquad (27)$$

$$C = \tan^{-1}\left[\frac{1 + 2r_4}{3 + 4\phi}\right] - \tan^{-1}\left[\frac{1 + 2r_3}{3 + 4\phi}\right] \qquad (28)$$

The numerical evaluation of these integrals, particularly equations 24 and 25, presents difficulties. The log-log and tangent scales of a 10 inch slide rule lack sufficient precision for the calculation. Both Averre and Hawks have used a digital computer to evaluate four and five place tables for discrete increments of ξ, r, and φ, and these can then be plotted or otherwise interpolated, which is tedious; the availability of miniature computers, with log and trig functions, makes precise evalutation a simple process.

Figure 4 compares the result of such an evaluation with experimental data obtained on a DS-21 by the staff at <u>Road and Track</u> magazine (see also figure 2). In the evaluation, a low value of $\eta = 0.75$ was chosen to match the "observed" top speed; the values of $\lambda = 0.585$ and $\gamma = 0.8$ were chosen with regard to the weight distribution and typical tire properties; the values of μ and C_D (or s_D) were taken from the coasting deceleration test. The comparison of the calculated acceleration with the experimental acceleration shows that the DS-21

is torque rather than traction limited at low speeds, and that η should have been increased. Results of a subsequent evaluation with different values of η and γ are included to show the improvement.

2.2.2 Lift as a Factor in Straight Line Acceleration

Roger Hawks is another of my former students who has found stimulation in automotive problems. He and C.L. Sayre have written a paper[2] which shows how the "Averre Function" solutions can be adapted to the problem of calculating the acceleration of a vehicle acted on <u>both</u> by lift and drag, as shown in figure 5. Account is also taken of the change in normal loading on the driven wheels through the quantities

$$\lambda = \frac{a}{\ell - h\gamma} \qquad (29)$$

and

$$\Lambda = \frac{a - d}{\ell - h\gamma} \qquad (30)$$

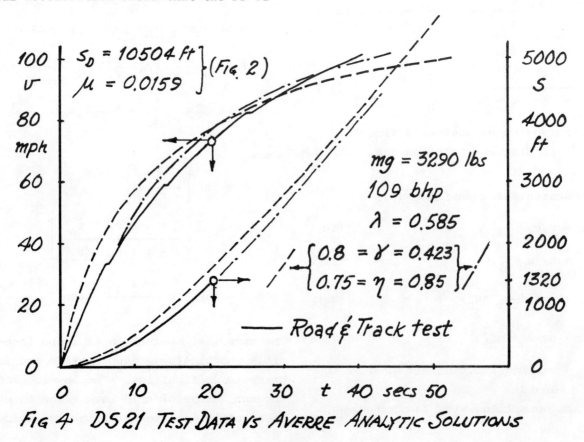

FIG 4 DS 21 TEST DATA VS AVERRE ANALYTIC SOLUTIONS

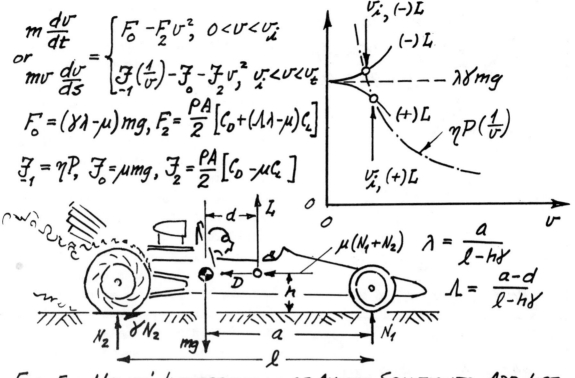

$$m \frac{dv}{dt}$$

$$\text{or} \quad mv \frac{dv}{ds} = \begin{cases} F_0 - F_2 v^2, & 0 < v < v_i \\ \mathcal{F}_{-1}\left(\frac{1}{v}\right) - \mathcal{F}_0 - \mathcal{F}_2 v^2, & v_i < v < v_t \end{cases}$$

$$F_0 = (\gamma\lambda - \mu)mg, \quad F_2 = \frac{\rho A}{2}\left[C_D + (\Lambda\lambda - \mu)C_L\right]$$

$$\mathcal{F}_{-1} = \eta P, \quad \mathcal{F}_0 = \mu mg, \quad \mathcal{F}_2 = \frac{\rho A}{2}\left[C_D - \mu C_L\right]$$

$$\lambda = \frac{a}{\ell - h\gamma}$$

$$\Lambda = \frac{a-d}{\ell - h\gamma}$$

FIG 5   HAWKS' INTERPRETATION OF AVERRE SOLUTION TO ADD LIFT

The $\frac{1}{m}\left(\frac{\rho}{2}v^2 AC_D\right) = \frac{v^2}{s_D}$ terms in equations 8 and 16 are replaced with v^2/ℓ_T and v^2/ℓ_p terms where

$$\ell_T = \frac{s_D s_L}{s_L + (\gamma\Lambda - \mu)s_D} \qquad (31)$$

$$\ell_p = \frac{s_D s_L}{s_L - \mu s_D} \qquad (32)$$

$$s_L = \frac{2m}{AC_L} \qquad (33)$$

depending on whether $v < v_i$ or $v > v_i$ respectively. The corresponding definition of v_f presents certain difficulties which are discussed in their paper. In any event, the equations of motion can be manipulated exactly into the form of equations 1, 10, 16, and 17.

Figure 6 presents some results from[2] which show how the elapsed times of class AA "fuel" dragsters might be improved by varying the drag coefficient (with envelope body work) and the L/D ratio (with external wings). I suspect some "cooking" of the vehicle parameters (note $\gamma = 1.9$ and $\eta P = 1500$ hp) to produce the agreement with measured performance at $C_D = 1$, $L/D = 0$, but something like this is going on - dragsters with down loading wings have now broached the six second "barrier".

2.3 WIND TUNNEL TESTING; SIMULATION OF THE GROUND PLANE

Aerodynamic testing of automobiles, trucks, buses and railroad trains is as old as the wind tunnel art; unlike the airplane, however, road vehicles generally present no problems amenable to wind tunnel research except drag and proper functioning of internal flow systems; e.g. is the pressure at the inlet location large enough compared to the pressure at the exit location to maintain the required volume of flow? Measurements of lift, cross wind force,

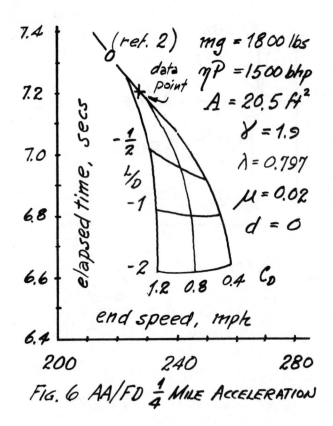

Fig. 6 AA/FD ¼ Mile Acceleration

$mg = 1800\ lbs$
$\eta P = 1500\ bhp$
$A = 20.5\ ft^2$
$\gamma = 1.9$
$\lambda = 0.797$
$\mu = 0.02$
$d = 0$

rolling moment, pitching moment, and yawing moment have also been made on a more or less routine basis, but little has been done with these piles of data for want of an adequate analytical framework to evaluate their importance. One of the central problems has been the simulation of the ground plane.

Figure 7 presents a collection of techniques for representing the ground plane in wind tunnels; it reflects also a history of wind tunnel balance development; see also [3]. In a day when wind tunnel models were held in the tunnel stream by a system of counter weighted wires passing vertically through the stream and attached to a mechanical balance above the test section, the only practical way of representing the ground plane was by an image model technique, which would supposedly produce a flat stream surface at the interface between model and image

wheels through symmetry. Practically, it was found that the viscous channel flow between the paired under bodies was unstable and tended to oscillate about the the symmetry plane. This motion could be suppressed by sandwiching an abbreviated plate between the wheels, which, however, produced its own upper and lower boundary layers, not present in the actual situation. The actual model and the image model were often connected rigidly together so that the experimental drag was considered to be half the drag of the combination; such an arrangement, of course, prevents the measurement of lift. To measure lift with an external balance and such an arrangement, the actual model must be attached to the balance, while the image model is attached to the floor.

A technique more in keeping with the mechanical balances and the bayonet type model mountings of tunnels built in the 1930's is the rigid ground board technique also shown in figure 7. The effect of the ground board boundary layer is minimized by flattening the underside of the model wheels so that they clear the board by something like the local displacement thickness, and sometimes suction is applied to the ground board, especially near the wheels, to help maintain a realistic flow field under the vehicle body. This technique can be used either with an external balance, or the model can be mounted on a sting which carries an internal balance.

Reference 4 discusses a series of tests which were performed with a moving ground board as shown in figure 7. Figure 8 shows the results of the tests, which were conducted at nearly full scale Reynolds number. The moving ground board is seen to affect mainly the lift; in the absence of ground board motion the flow velocities

30

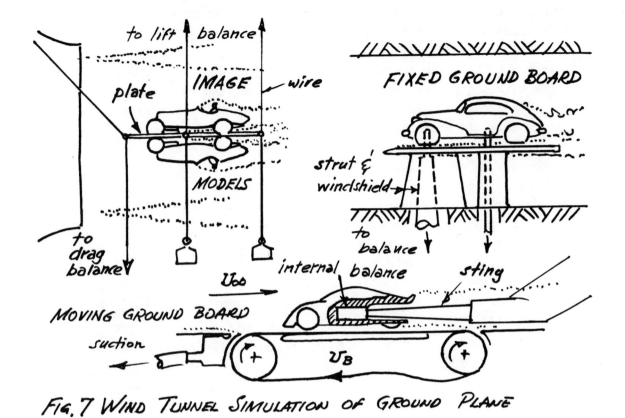

to lift balance

IMAGE — wire

plate

MODELS

to drag balance

FIXED GROUND BOARD

strut & windshield

to balance

U_∞

internal balance — sting

MOVING GROUND BOARD

suction

U_B

FIG. 7 WIND TUNNEL SIMULATION OF GROUND PLANE

pitching moment
C_m
0.2
0
-0.2

0.8

drag
C_D
0.4

0 0.8

lift
C_L
0.4

0

1	——
0.35	—·—	$\frac{U_B}{U_\infty}$
0	– – –

0   -5   -10   -15   -20 $\beta°$

rolling moment
C_ℓ
0.2
0

-0.2

Taken from NASA TN D-4225

yawing moment
C_m
0.2
0

-0.2
0.8

side force
C_y
0.4

sideslip angle

0   -5   -10   -15   -20 $\beta°$

FIG. 8 EFFECT OF GROUND BOARD MOVEMENT ON THE AERODYNAMIC
CHARACTERISTICS OF A 1965 FORD "GALAXIE"

under the vehicle are reduced, and the pressure is increased. Alternatively, according to the work of Fackrell and Harvey [5] it may be that the negative change in lift with the moving ground board is due to the circumstance that the powered model wheels did not actually touch it, and that strong negative pressures were produced in the venturi like flow between the bottoms of the wheels and the ground board. The intermediate belt speed results plotted are taken to represent the fixed ground board tests ordinarily conducted by the Ford Motor Company at the University of Maryland. It is reassuring to see that the other air loads are so little affected.

2.4 AERODYNAMIC LIFT

2.4.1 Estimation of Lift

One way of reducing the base drag of an automobile body, particularly a coupe or sedan, is to reduce its cross section gradually to zero at the tail. The simplest possible body of this type is an axissymmetric Rankine ovoid produced by the combination of a source, a sink, and a uniform stream aligned with the line connecting the singularities. A meridional plane through such a body might be taken to represent the ground plane, and the half of the body on one side of the plane an idealization of "aerodynamic" body work. In potential flow the pressure on such a body is largely negative except near the nose and the tail, and it might be supposed that the pressure distribution on such a half body, integrated over its planform on the ground plane, might give a reasonable estimate for the body lift, as suggested by figure 9.

Actually this calculation may be invalid; one is not allowed to specify an arbitrary pressure level, for example, undis-

turbed stream pressure, on the "underside" of such a body moving at vanishingly small clearances above the ground. A practical body has some kind of flow field under it, and in the absence of a hard corner of the lower side edge, or at the tail, there is no definite value of circulation and no definite value of lift. Cornish [6] suggests that the pressure under such a body can be made to take on any pressure available near the underside of the car by venting the underside to this pressure and preventing its contamination with other pressures (especially stagnation pressure!) by peripheral skirts extending to the road surface.

The lift on such a body depends critically on the nature of the flow beneath it, also as suggested by figure 9. The figure shows the flow for positive lift, but it might equally well be a negative lift if the underbody is bulged downward, and if appreciable separation does not occur as pressure recovery is attempted toward the tail. Generally, however, flat bottomed bodies with curved upper surfaces will develop positive lift. Alberto Morelli has given a useful technique for estimating this lift by the methods of slender wing theory in [7].

2.4.2 Miscellaneous Lift Sources and Cures

Figure 10 shows other sources of positive and negative lift which have been discussed and exploited recently. The lifting capacity of open wheels was unnoticed before the development of extremely wide rectangular section tires; it is caused by the ground plane induced flow symmetry between the real separated flow and the image separated flow: the real flow must then be symmetrical in such a way as to provide a lift. Opposite tendencies have been observed by Alberto Morelli on tires of more normal proportions, see [8], but Fackrell and Harvey [6] seem to have

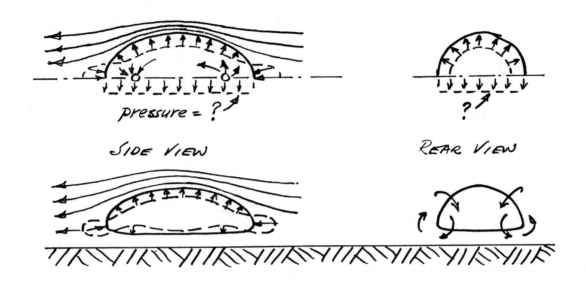

SIDE VIEW   REAR VIEW

Fig. 9 Lift on Half Bodies in Potential Flow

resolved this matter.

Sedan racing has produced a variety of fixes for the inherent lift "hot spots" of normal body work, which tend to be at the front of the engine compartment and at the wind shield header. These fixes include negative angle of attack (rake), duck tail spoilers which produce a positive pressure on the upper body near the tail, and chin spoilers, or skirts, which keep stagnation pressure from developing under the body.

Arched wheel houses, typical of competition sports car body work, have also proved to be troublesome sources of lift, particularly on Group 7 cars. Such wheel houses are now frequently constructed with ventilating holes, or louvres, which minimize the pressure differences between the interior and the exterior, and hence the lift producing negative pressures on the outside.

The development of airfoil and finite wing theory has led to an obvious application of wings to race cars in order to increase the radial load on the tires, and hence the cornering forces available on high speed turns. Indianapolis cars, for example, now maintain steady state lateral accelerations of 1.2 g's on the turns of an oval course. The first successful application of wings to road racing cars in the U.S. was made by Jim Hall, who attached wings directly to the wheel hub carriers of his cars. This system kept the downloads out of the suspension, but exposed the wing attachments to unending wheel hop mode accelerations of 40 to 50 g's. The wing attachments failed frequently by fatigue and earned such a bad reputation that most race car rules today require that wings be attached only to the body work.

The figure shows a typical Indianapolis car installation. In the past few years

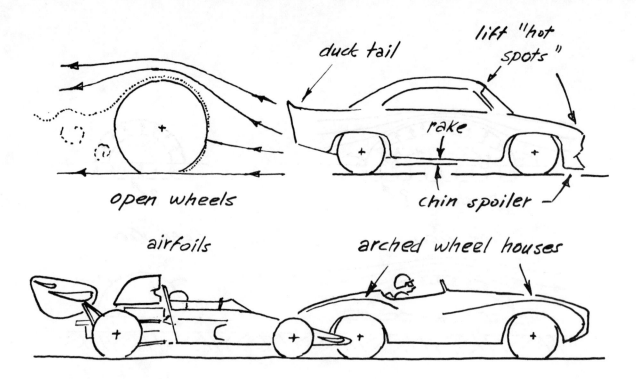

duck tail

lift "hot spots"

rake

chin spoiler

open wheels

airfoils

arched wheel houses

FIG 10   OTHER SOURCES OF LIFT - UP AND DOWN

it has gradually been appreciated that
the maximum lift coefficient of a wing is
best approached from the small angle of
attack side; that smooth upper body work
ahead of the wing greatly enhances its
effectiveness; and that, finally, the end
plates fitted to the wings to get the
most out of a span limited by the rules,
provide improved directional stability
when the wing is located as far aft as
the rules permit. Such an aft downloading
wing would lift the steered wheels from
the road at about 150 mph unless front
downloading wings were also provided.
Both wings together put the suspension on
the bump stops at about 200 mph, which
does not help rough track handling.

3.   AERODYNAMIC EFFECTS
ON VEHICLE LATERAL DYNAMICS

Although wind tunnel data on the aerodynamic characteristics of automobile
bodies in yaw has been routinely gathered
for many years, little use has been made
of it for want of an adequate analytical
treatment of the car-driver system. With-

out a mathematical model of the resistance
of the car-driver system to external disturbances, it is impossible to distinguish
between the various levels of annoyance or
danger which might correspond to different
levels of aerodynamic sensitivity to cross
winds, for example. The following sections describe such a model, aerodynamic
data relating to two kinds of disturbances,
and the practical significance of these
disturbances.

3.1 GOVERNING EQUATIONS OF MOTION

3.1.1 A Standard Form for the Equations
Describing Vehicle Lateral Dynamics

The axis system and choice of symbols for
state variables are shown in figure 11.
This convention, which has become the
standard of the U.S. Society of Automotive
Engineers, follows aeronautical practice
as closely as possible; not surprising
since it came from the Cornell Aeronautical Laboratory, now Calspan Inc.[9]. The
vehicle is considered (for simplicity) to
consist of two rigid bodies; an unsprung

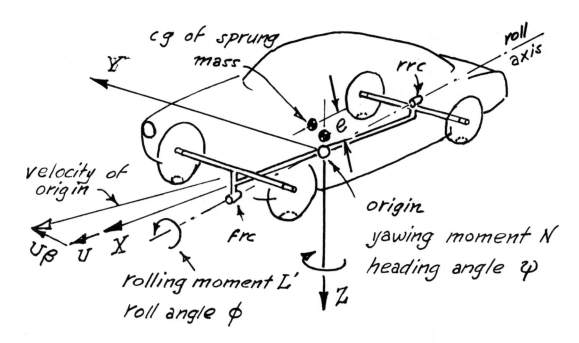

FIG. 11 TWO MASS, THREE DEGREE OF FREEDOM MODEL
OF VEHICLE LATERAL DYNAMICS

mass, which may be thought of as the wheels and an imaginary framework which keeps them all in alignment when seen from above, and a sprung mass, which is connected to the unsprung mass by an imaginary hinge whose axis connects the front and rear roll centres. The motion of the unsprung mass is completely specified by the X axis component, U, of the linear velocity of the origin, which is assumed constant; by the Y axis component, βU, of the linear velocity (β is the sideslip angle in radians if $\beta \ll 1$); and by the azimuth, or yaw angle, ψ, of the X axis. The X axis lies in the symmetry plane of the unsprung mass, which also contains the imaginary hinge line, or roll axis. The origin of the axis system is taken to be on the roll axis and directly below the centre of mass of the complete vehicle when the sprung mass has no roll angle, i.e. when the sprung mass plane of symmetry coincides with the

unsprung mass of plane of symmetry. The sprung mass has all of the motion of the unsprung mass implied by the quantities U, β, and ψ as well as the additional motion corresponding to a roll angle, ϕ, about the roll axis.

The equations of motion for this system were written down at least 20 years ago by Segel[9]. The inertial terms involved were given a precise derivation by Weir, Shortwell, and Johnson[10] about 15 years later. They are written here in a standard form adopted by the author for pedagogical reasons, using a notation similar to Segel's. The yawing moment, N, which acts on the vehicle as a whole, and the rolling moment, L', which acts only on the sprung mass, are made dimensionless by division with the product of the complete vehicle weight and the wheelbase, $mg\ell$; the side force, Y, which acts on the complete vehicle, is made dimensionless by division by the complete vehicle weight, mg. If the angles ϕ and β are small (ψ may sometimes be large), the equations may be written as sums of linearized perturbation terms, and become ($\lambda = d/dt$, the Laplace operator):

$$\frac{L'}{mg\ell} = \left[i_x \left(\frac{\ell}{g}\right) \lambda^2 - \ell_{\dot\phi}\lambda - \ell_\phi \right] \phi$$
$$+ \left[i_{xz} \left(\frac{\ell}{g}\right) \lambda^2 + \epsilon \left(\frac{U}{g}\right)\lambda \right] \psi$$
$$+ \epsilon \left(\frac{U}{g}\right) \lambda \beta \qquad (34)$$

$$\frac{N}{mg\ell} = \left[i_{xz} \left(\frac{\ell}{g}\right) \lambda^2 - n_\phi \right] \phi$$
$$+ \left[i_z \left(\frac{\ell}{g}\right) \lambda^2 - n_r \left(\frac{\ell}{U}\right)\lambda \right] \psi$$
$$- n_\beta \beta - n_\delta \delta \qquad (35)$$

$$\frac{Y}{mg} = \left[\epsilon \left(\frac{\ell}{g}\right) \lambda^2 - y_\phi \right] \phi$$
$$+ \left[\left(\frac{U}{g}\right) - y_r \left(\frac{\ell}{U}\right) \right] \lambda \psi$$
$$+ \left[\left(\frac{U}{g}\right) \lambda - y_\beta \right] \beta - y_\delta \delta \qquad (36)$$

The dimensionless inertial properties of this two mass system are contained in the four parameters:

$$i_x \equiv \frac{\text{sprung mass inertia in roll about roll axis}}{m\ell^2} \qquad (37)$$

$$i_z \equiv \frac{\text{complete vehicle inertia in yaw about Z axis}}{m\ell^2} \qquad (38)$$

$$i_{xz} \equiv \frac{\text{sprung mass product of inertia}}{m\ell^2} \qquad (39)$$

$$\epsilon = \frac{\text{(eccentricity of sprung mass about roll axis)}}{\text{(wheel base)}} \times \frac{\text{(sprung mass)}}{\text{(vehicle mass)}} \qquad (40)$$

$$= \frac{e}{\ell} \frac{m_s}{m}$$

In the experience of the author i_x, i_z, i_{xz}, and ϵ show little variation with vehicle size.

The quantities $\ell_{\dot\phi}$ and ℓ_ϕ are the corresponding measures of the suspension roll damping and stiffness;

$$\ell_{\dot\phi} \equiv \frac{1}{mg\,\ell} \frac{\partial L'}{\partial \left(\frac{d\phi}{dt}\right)} \qquad (41)$$

$$\ell_\phi \equiv \frac{1}{mg\,\ell} \frac{\partial L'}{\partial \phi} \qquad (42)$$

Note that although ℓ_ϕ is dimensionless (ϕ in radians is dimensionless) $\ell_{\dot\phi}$ is not; $\ell_{\dot\phi}$ has the dimensions of time. These quantities also show little variation with vehicle size.

Finally, the quantities n_ϕ, n_r, n_β, n_δ, y_ϕ, y_r, y_β, and y_δ are all dimensionless "stability derivatives" whose <u>values depend primarily on the vehicle tire characteristics</u> and secondarily on the vehicle suspension geometry. They are defined below:-

$$n_\phi \equiv \frac{1}{mg\ell} \frac{\partial N}{\partial \phi} \quad \binom{\text{roll}}{\text{steer}} \; (+) \text{ if understeer} \qquad (43)$$

$$n_r \equiv \frac{1}{mg\ell} \frac{\partial N}{\partial \left(\frac{\ell}{U}r\right)} \quad (\text{yaw damping, } r = \frac{d\psi}{dt}) \qquad (44)$$

$$n_\beta \equiv \frac{1}{mg\ell} \frac{\partial N}{\partial \beta} \quad \binom{\text{yaw due to}}{\text{sideslip.}} \; (+) \; \binom{\text{if}}{\text{understeer}} \qquad (45)$$

$$n_\delta \equiv \frac{1}{mg\ell} \frac{\partial N}{\partial \delta} \quad (\text{yaw due to steering angle}) \qquad (46)$$

$$y_\phi \equiv \frac{1}{mg} \frac{\partial Y}{\partial \phi} \quad (\text{side force due to roll}) \qquad (47)$$

$$y_r \equiv \frac{1}{mg} \quad \frac{\partial Y}{\partial \left(\frac{\ell}{U}r\right)} \quad \text{(side force due to yawing)} \qquad (48)$$

$$y_\beta \equiv \frac{1}{mg} \quad \frac{\partial Y}{\partial \beta} \quad \text{(side force due to sideslip)} \qquad (49)$$

$$y_\delta \equiv \frac{1}{mg} \quad \frac{\partial Y}{\partial \delta} \quad \text{(side force due to steering angle)} \qquad (50)$$

As a result of tire characteristics (discussed in the next section) all of the stability derivatives above tend to be independent of vehicle size and speed of operation; the effects of the latter are then explicitly indicated in equations 34-36 by the parameters ℓ (the wheelbase) and U (the speed). Eqs. 34-36 are thus a very suitable standard form, not only because most of the system parameters in it are dimensionless, which is particularly helpful in English speaking countries as we shift gears to metrification, but also because the time scaling properties of the system with size and speed are clearly indicated.

The author has written a short report (ref. 12) which compares the linearized automobile dynamics of Eqs. 40-42 with those of a more exact four-mass, ten degree of freedom non-linear simulation[11], and finds good agreement for lateral acceleration levels of less than (1/4) g.

3.1.2 The Central Role of Tire Mechanics

Except for the terms $\ell_\phi \frac{d\phi}{dt}$ and $\ell_\phi \phi$ in Eq. 34 all the other terms express an equilibrium between inertial reactions and forces due to tire loads, chiefly cornering forces due to tire slip angles; for example, the front tire slip angle due to yaw rate is $(a/U)d\psi/dt$; the front tire contribution to the yawing moment is $-2(a^2/U)CP_1 (d\psi/dt)$, where CP_1 is the "cornering power", or slope of the tire cornering force curve versus slip angle for an individual front tire; and the

yawing moment contribution of all tires due to yaw rate is given by:

$$\Delta N = mg\ell n_r \frac{\ell}{U} \quad \frac{d\psi}{df} \qquad (51)$$

where

$$n_r = -2 \left[\frac{CP_1}{mg} \left(\frac{a}{\ell}\right)^2 + \frac{CP_2}{mg} \left(\frac{b}{\ell}\right)^2 \right] \qquad (52)$$

Similar expressions may be derived for the other tire stability derivatives, but underlying them all are expressions for the "cornering power", $\partial Fy/\partial\alpha$, the camber thrust, $\partial Fy/\partial\phi$, and the aligning torque $\partial Mz/\partial\alpha$, for the individual tires as appropriate functions of the radial load, inflation pressure, and so on. The situation is analogous to aerodynamic stability derivatives for aircraft where wing and tail plane lift curve slopes are involved. What is needed is a theory of tire mechanics analogous to lifting line theory in the aerodynamics of wings.

Such a theory is available in an obscure report prepared by the late K.R. Thorson,[13] for the Boeing airplane company in 1951. Thorson's theory, Fig. 12, considers the lateral deflection of the tire to be like that of a continuous beam on an elastic foundation with a spring constant, k, per unit length along the neutral axis, and under a uniform tension, T. Its bending rigidity is EI, and the local lateral deflection, y, is given by:

$$EI \frac{d^4y}{dx^4} - T \frac{d^2y}{dx^2} + ky = \frac{dY}{dx} \qquad (53)$$

where dY/dx, the side loading per unit length of neutral axis, exists only in the footprint region of length $2\ell_f$ Thorson gives an approximate boundary value solution of Eq. 53 for the case of a small slip angle, α which shows that:

$$CP = \frac{\partial \left[\int_{-\ell}^{+\ell} \frac{dY}{dx} \, dx \right]}{\partial \alpha} \cong 2k(\ell_f + \sigma)^2 \qquad (54)$$

where σ, the "relaxation length", is

$$\sigma = \sqrt{2\sqrt{\frac{EI}{k}} + \frac{T}{k}} \qquad (55)$$

It is possible to show that for a tire of outer circumference, $2\pi R$, section width, b, and section height, h, inflated to a pressure p, that:

$$k \simeq p \, \frac{b}{h} \left(1 - \frac{h}{R}\right) \qquad (56)$$

$$T = p \, \frac{bh}{2} \qquad (57)$$

Values of EI are not readily calculated, but experiments with bias tires show that EI has such a value, that for nominal values of p, $\sigma \cong b$. The presence of circumferential steel belt plies notably increases the value of EI and σ. The footprint length $2\ell_f$ is a function of the tire radial load, F_r, given approximately by:

$$F_r = 2\ell_f b_t \, p \qquad (58)$$

where b_t is the tread width. Figure 12 shows how the experimental cornering force as a function of slip angle departs from the simple estimation given by equations 54-58. The author has expanded Thorson's results in ref. 14 to include the corresponding values of cornering force per unit inclination angle ("camber thrust") and aligning torque per unit slip angle. Comparison of these results with the appropriate experimental data shows that the approximate boundary conditions applied in the footprint region need to be critically examined. John Marshall II has done an SM Thesis at MIT (July 1973) under my supervision

showing how the elastic properties of the tread material between the carcass and the road surface affect the boundary conditions in the footprint region. A revised version of this thesis will soon be available in the proceedings of the Third International Conference on Vehicle System Dynamics held at Blacksburg, Virginia in August 1974

3.1.3 Aerodynamic Effects in Calm Air - Cross Wind Sensitivity

Equations 34-36 describe the lateral dynamics of a vehicle running in a vacuum; now we will consider the additional terms that must be added to the left hand side of the equations to represent the effect of moving through calm air and to the right hand side to represent the disturbance caused by cross winds of variable intensity. The technique employed follows that employed by Roger Hawks and the present author in (15).

Figure 13 shows typical wind tunnel data obtained on a complete automobile model when the "yaw" angle (more properly the sideslip angle) is varied. A side force is developed which is nearly a linear function of the sideslip angle β. The slope of this curve is roughly in agreement with slender body theory, assuming that the flow close to the body remains aligned with the body axis downstream of the maximum cross section axes by virtue of a lee side separation process. If the body had round cross sections $\partial Y/\partial \beta$ would be:

$$\frac{\partial Y}{\partial \beta} = -2 \left[\frac{\pi}{4} \, (\text{diameter})^2_{\text{max}} \right] \frac{\rho}{2} v^2$$

Assuming that the side force is mainly determined by the maximum body height, we have:

38

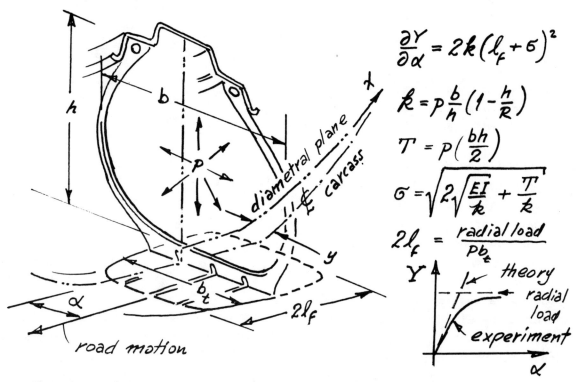

$$\frac{\partial Y}{\partial \alpha} = 2k(\ell_f + \sigma)^2$$

$$k = p\frac{b}{h}\left(1 - \frac{h}{R}\right)$$

$$T = p\left(\frac{bh}{2}\right)$$

$$\sigma = \sqrt{2\sqrt{\frac{EI}{k}} + \frac{T}{k}}$$

$$2\ell_f = \frac{radial\ load}{pb_t}$$

FIG. 12   ELEMENTS OF THORSON TIRE THEORY

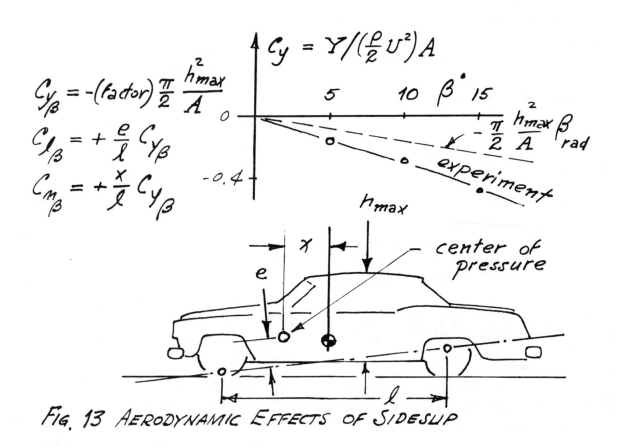

$$C_{Y_\beta} = -(factor)\frac{\pi}{2}\frac{h_{max}^2}{A}$$

$$C_{\ell_\beta} = +\frac{e}{\ell}C_{Y_\beta}$$

$$C_{m_\beta} = +\frac{x}{\ell}C_{Y_\beta}$$

$$C_y = Y/\left(\frac{\rho}{2}U^2\right)A$$

FIG. 13   AERODYNAMIC EFFECTS OF SIDESLIP

$$c_{Y_\beta} = \frac{1}{\frac{\rho}{2} v^2} \quad \frac{1}{A} \quad \frac{\partial Y}{\partial \beta} = -\frac{\pi}{2} \frac{(h)^2_{max}}{A} \quad .$$

Experimental data usually show that C_{Y_β} is larger than this value, especially for bodies with "hard" side edges. The experiments also show that the center of pressure of the side force due to sideslip is approximately at the centroid of the portion of side area which is <u>ahead</u> of the location of h_{max}, also in accord with slender body theory. C_{Y_β}, multiplied by the appropriate arm about either the Z axis or the roll axis, gives the corresponding values for C_{n_β} or C_{ℓ_β} when the arms are made dimensionless with the characteristic length, in this case the wheelbase. The value of C_{ℓ_β} needed for equation 34 should not contain the air loads on the wheels.

Figure 14 considers the question of a gradient of a cross wind structure which is defined in space fixed coordinates. If the vehicle has body work which has aerodynamic damping in yaw so that when moving through calm air at velocity U it develops a yawing moment given by

$$\Delta N = \left(\frac{\rho}{2} U^2\right) A \ell C_{n_r} \left(\frac{\ell}{U}\right) \frac{d\psi}{dt}$$

where C_{n_r} (if −) is a dimensionless aerodynamic yaw damping stability derivative, then the corresponding moment developed when the vehicle is enveloped in a cross wind with a gradient along X' (the space fixed axis) is:

$$\Delta N = \left(\frac{\rho}{2} U^2\right) A \ell \, C_{n_r} \left(\frac{\ell}{U}\right)\left(\frac{d\psi}{dt} - \frac{\partial v_w}{\partial X'}\right)$$

as shown by the figure. The gradient $\partial v_w / \partial X'$ is in fact implied by a cross wind that is an apparent time function of an observer moving with the vehicle velocity U:

$$\frac{\partial v_w}{\partial X'} = \frac{dv_w}{dt} \frac{dt}{dX'} = \frac{d(v_w)}{dt} \quad \frac{1}{U}$$

$$\cong \frac{d}{dt}\left(\frac{v_w}{U}\right) \tag{60}$$

The combined expression for yawing moment due to sideslip, yawing velocity, cross wind value, and cross wind gradient is therefore:

$$\Delta N = \frac{\rho}{2} U^2 A \ell \left[C_{n_\beta}\left(\beta - \frac{v_w}{U}\right) + C_{n_r}\left(\frac{\ell}{U}\right)\left(\frac{d\psi}{dt} - \frac{d}{dt}\left(\frac{v_w}{U}\right)\right)\right]$$

This can be put in dimensionless form by dividing through be $mg\ell$, following the example of equation 35:

$$\frac{\Delta N}{mg\ell} = Q\left[C_{n_\beta}\left(\beta - \frac{v_w}{U}\right) + C_{n_r}\left(\frac{\ell}{U}\right)\left(\frac{d\psi}{dt} - \frac{d}{dt}\left(\frac{v_w}{U}\right)\right)\right] \tag{61}$$

where

$$Q \equiv \frac{\left(\frac{\rho}{2} U^2\right) \ (A)}{mg} \tag{62}$$

In equation 61 the $C_{n_\beta}\beta$ term and the $C_{n_r}\left(\frac{\ell}{U}\right)\left(\frac{d\psi}{dt}\right)$ should be added to the left side of equation 35 to represent the combined effects of sideslip angle (β) and yaw rate ($d\psi/dt$) on the yawing moment of the vehicle in calm air; the terms $C_{n_\beta}\left(\frac{v_w}{U}\right)$ and $C_{n_r}\left(\frac{\ell}{U}\right)\left(\frac{d}{dt}\frac{v_w}{U}\right)$ should be added to the right hand side of equation 35 to represent the effects of the cross wind and its gradient with X' on the yawing moment. Similar expressions can be written down for the rolling moment and the side forces.

Figure 15 raises similar questions about the rolling velocity, the numerical value of the cross wind, and the gradient of the cross wind with altitude. All cross

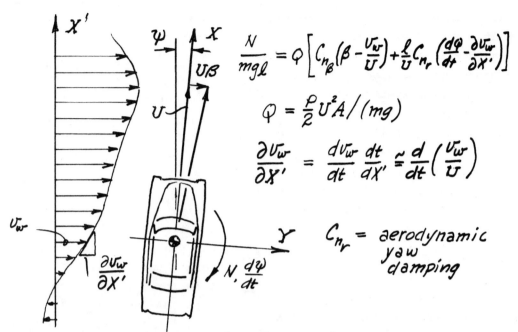

$$\frac{N}{mgl} = Q\left[C_{n_\beta}\left(\beta - \frac{v_{w}}{U}\right) + \frac{l}{U}C_{n_r}\left(\frac{d\psi}{dt} - \frac{\partial v_{w}}{\partial X'}\right)\right]$$

$$Q = \frac{\rho}{2}U^2 A / (mg)$$

$$\frac{\partial v_{w}}{\partial X'} = \frac{dv_{w}}{dt}\frac{dt}{dX'} \approx \frac{d}{dt}\left(\frac{v_{w}}{U}\right)$$

C_{n_r} = aerodynamic yaw damping

FIG. 14 EFFECTS OF SIDESLIP, YAW RATE, CROSS WIND AND CROSS WIND GRADIENT

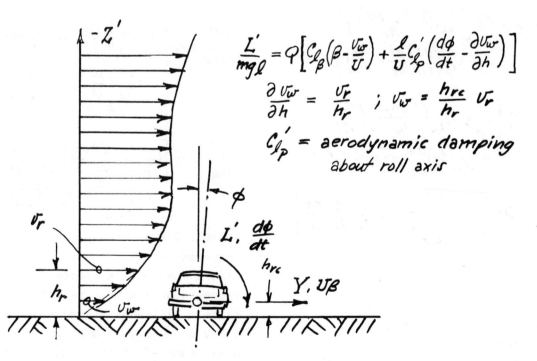

$$\frac{L'}{mgl} = Q\left[C_{l_\beta}\left(\beta - \frac{v_{w}}{U}\right) + \frac{l}{U}C_{l_p}'\left(\frac{d\phi}{dt} - \frac{\partial v_{w}}{\partial h}\right)\right]$$

$$\frac{\partial v_{w}}{\partial h} = \frac{v_r}{h_r} \quad ; \quad v_{w} = \frac{h_{rc}}{h_r}v_r$$

C_{l_p}' = aerodynamic damping about roll axis

FIG. 15 EFFECTS OF SIDESLIP, ROLL RATE, CROSS WIND AND CROSS WIND VERTICAL GRADIENT

41

winds are boundary layer flows and must vanish at the road surface. The form of equations 34-36 requires that the value of the cross wind be specified at the origin of the axis system, where a vertical line through the vehicle center of mass intersects the roll axis. Since this point may be rather low, it might be more appropriate to specify the cross wind v_r at a reference height h_r. The cross wind at the origin would then be:

$$v_w \cong v_r \frac{h_{origin}}{h_r} \tag{63}$$

If the vehicle has aerodynamic roll damping, the combined effects of sideslip, roll rate, cross wind strength, and cross wind gradient would be:

$$\Delta L' = \frac{\rho}{2} U^2 A l \left[C_{l_\beta} \left(\beta - \frac{v_w}{U} \right) + C_{l_p} \left(\frac{l}{U} \right) \left(\frac{d\phi}{dt} - \frac{\partial v_w}{\partial h} \right) \right]$$

$$\Delta L' = \frac{\rho}{2} U^2 A l \left[C_{l_\beta} \left(\beta - \frac{h_{origin}}{h_r} \right) \frac{v_r}{U} + C_{l_p} \left(\frac{l}{U} \right) \left(\frac{d\phi}{dt} - \frac{v_r}{h_r} \right) \right]$$

$$\frac{\Delta L'}{mgl} = Q \left[C_{l_\beta} \beta - C_{l_\beta} \left(\frac{h_{origin}}{h_r} \right) \left(\frac{v_r}{U} \right) + C_{l_p} \left(\frac{l}{U} \right) \frac{d\phi}{dt} - C_{l_p} \left(\frac{l}{U} \right) \frac{v_r}{h_r} \right]$$

$$\frac{\Delta L'}{mgl} = Q \left[C_{l_\beta} \beta - C_{l_\beta} \left(\frac{v_r}{U} \right) + C_{l_p} \left(\frac{l}{U} \right) \frac{d\phi}{dt} \right] \tag{64}$$

where

$$C_{l_{\beta_{eff}}} = C_{l_\beta} \left(\frac{h_{origin}}{h_r} \right) + \frac{l}{h_r} C_{l_p} \tag{65}$$

Similar expressions may be written to allow specification of the cross wind velocity at h_r for side forces and yawing moments, e.g.

$$C_{Y_{\beta_{eff}}} = C_{Y_\beta} \left(\frac{h_{origin}}{h_r} \right) + \frac{l}{h_r} C_{Y_p} \tag{66}$$

$$C_{n_{\beta_{eff}}} = C_{n\beta} \left(\frac{h_{origin}}{h_r} \right) + \frac{l}{h} C_{\eta p} \tag{67}$$

A great deal of uncertainty exists about the true values of C_{n_r}, C_{n_p}, C_{l_r}, C_{l_p}, C_{Y_r}, and C_{Y_p} which are required to implement equations 61, 65 and a similar equation for C_Y. The terms needed for equations 34-36 are:

$$\frac{\Delta L'}{mgl} = Q \left[C_{l_p} \left(\frac{l}{U} \right) \frac{d\phi}{dt} + C_{l_r} \left(\frac{l}{U} \right) \frac{d\psi}{dt} + C_{l_\beta} \beta - C_{l_{\beta_{eff}}} \left(\frac{v_r}{U} \right) - C_{l_r} \left(\frac{l}{U} \right) \frac{d}{dt} \left(\frac{v_r}{U} \right) \right] \tag{68}$$

$$\frac{\Delta N}{mgl} = Q \left[C_{n_p} \left(\frac{l}{U} \right) \frac{d\phi}{dt} + C_{n_r} \left(\frac{l}{U} \right) \frac{d\psi}{dt} + C_{n_\beta} \beta - C_{n_{\beta_{eff}}} \left(\frac{v_r}{U} \right) - C_{n_r} \left(\frac{l}{U} \right) \frac{d}{dt} \left(\frac{v_r}{U} \right) \right] \tag{69}$$

$$\frac{\Delta Y}{mg} = Q \left[C_{Y_p} \left(\frac{l}{U} \right) \frac{d\phi}{dt} + C_{Y_r} \left(\frac{l}{U} \right) \frac{d\psi}{dt} + C_{Y_\beta} \beta - C_{Y_{\beta_{eff}}} \left(\frac{v_r}{U} \right) - C_{Y_r} \left(\frac{l}{U} \right) \frac{d}{dt} \left(\frac{v_r}{U} \right) \right] \tag{70}$$

Roger Hawks and the present author have reconsidered this matter in (16) which uses a moving axis system centered in the sprung mass and less peculiar aerodynamic terms. Ellis has suggested that a similar formulation might be made in orthogonal axes centered on the center of mass of the complete vehicle with additional terms to represent kinematically constrained degrees of freedom for the suspension elements,

42

following the pattern of his pioneering text[17]. The knowledge of the aerodynamic rotary derivatives is not improved thereby, however.

4. STABILITY, CONTROL, AND DYNAMIC RESPONSE

4.1 A SIMPLE MATHEMATICAL MODEL OF DRIVER STEERING ACTIVITY

An automobile is under continuous manual control in consequence of the necessity for lane holding. The driving task has such short time constants, however, that it must be performed subconsciously, so that it is very difficult to examine one's strategy in accomplishing the task. We are forced to invent a strategy and then test it mathematically to see if it agrees with measurements of actual driver behavior.

The following section describes and examines such a strategy which appears to reproduce measured driver behavior.

Figure 16 shows a driver's eye view of what I call "Radiator Cap Steering Strategy". In this strategy the driver steers in such a way as to keep some distinctive feature of the forward silhouette of his vehicle aligned with a continuous aspect of the road ahead, in this case the radiator cap with the lane centerline a distance R ahead of the center of gravity of the vehicle. For a cab-over-engine truck I would have to say, he steers in such a way as to keep the extended plane of symmetry of his vehicle aligned with the lane centerline a distance R ahead of its center of gravity.

The figure shows how the error signal is made up of components corresponding to the lateral displacement of the lane centerline at the distance R ahead of the vehicle, the lateral displacement of the vehicle center of mass, y, and the heading angle of the vehicle, ψ, thus:

$$\varepsilon = \frac{Y_\ell - Y}{R} - \psi \tag{71}$$

This can also be expressed as:

$$\varepsilon = \frac{Y_\ell}{R} - \theta \tag{72}$$

where

$$\theta = \frac{Y}{R} + \psi \tag{73}$$

and the methods of servo mechanism analysis can be used to study the dynamics of the closed loop system where the forward loop transfer function contains the Laplace transform of the θ/δ open loop response.

The simplest possible forward loop transfer function corresponds to the case of a neutral steering car with the roll degree of freedom suppressed, a radius of gyration in yaw equal to half the wheelbase (a not unrepresentative value), and with no driver lag between perception of the error angle ε and application of a front wheel steering angle δ, i.e.

$$\delta = K\varepsilon \tag{74}$$

For such a simplified mathematical model, the open loop transfer function is:

$$\frac{\theta}{\delta} = \left[2A\left(\frac{g}{R}\right)\left\{1 + 2\left(\frac{R}{\ell}\right)\right\} \frac{\left[\lambda^2 + 4A\left(\frac{g}{U}\right)\lambda + \frac{8A\left(g/\ell\right)}{1 + 2\left(R/\ell\right)}\right]}{\left[\lambda^2\right]\left[\lambda + 4A\left(\frac{g}{U}\right)\right]^2} \right] \tag{75}$$

where A is the ratio of the cornering power of any of the four identical tires to the weight of the vehicle; $A \simeq 2$ for "undertired" vehicles such as large American sedans; $A \simeq 3$ for sports cars; and $A \simeq 4$ and above for "overtired" vehi-

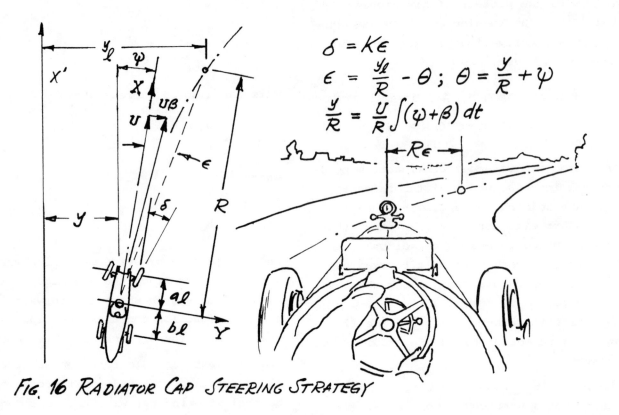

$$\delta = K\epsilon$$

$$\epsilon = \frac{y_\ell}{R} - \theta \; ; \; \theta = \frac{y}{R} + \psi$$

$$\frac{y}{R} = \frac{U}{R} \int (\psi + \beta) \, dt$$

FIG. 16 RADIATOR CAP STEERING STRATEGY

cles such as road racing cars.

Figure 17 presents a locus-of-roots diagram for an optimum version of the steering strategy in which the look ahead distance R is chosen so that the two zeros of the transfer function lie on the real axis midway between the double integration pole at the origin and the double vehicle pole at $\lambda = -4A(g/U)$. A forward loop gain is then chosen so that the closed loop roots lie at the branch points on the locus where the low gain circular locus meets the high gain asymptotes at the angles $\pm \pi/2$ springing from the pole-zero constellation centroid at $\lambda = -2A \, (g/U)$. This produces two identical complex closed loop roots with:

$$\omega_n = \sqrt{2} \; 2 \, A(g/U) \; \text{and a damping ratio} = \sqrt{2}/2$$

The corresponding look ahead distance is found to vary as the square of the speed

$$(R/\ell)_{opt} = (1/A) \left[(U^2/g\ell) \right] - 1/2 \tag{76}$$

The gain must be reduced with increasing speed nearly in direct proportion to the increase in R

$$(K)_{opt} = 2A(g\ell/U^2) \left[2 - A(\frac{g\ell}{U^2}) \right] \tag{77}$$

and the solution time for the closed loop system to a step lane change "command" is about $6/(\zeta\omega_n)$. Since no driver time lag is presumed, this solution really corresponds to "open loop", or better, "precognitive", steering behavior in which the driver practices the manoeuver to eliminate his own lag. To show the reasonableness of this description, consider a sports car for which:

U/g = 3 secs (U = 65.8 mph or 106 km/hr)
ℓ/g = (1/4)sec^2 (ℓ = 8.05 ft. or 2.45 m.)

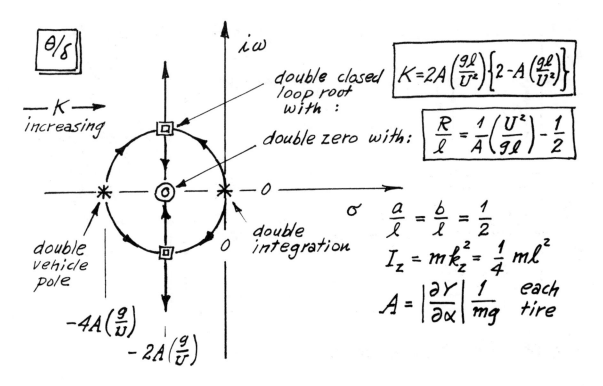

FIG. 17 LOCUS OF ROOTS FOR IDEALIZED STEERING STRATEGY

A = 3 (if mg = 3000 lbs,

   CP = 9000 $\frac{lbs}{rad}$ = 157 $\frac{lbs}{deg}$)

$(R/\ell)_{opt}$ = 23/2; R = 92.575 ft. or 28.2m

K_{opt} = 23/72 = 0.31944 ...

Solution time = 3 secs.

A former student was able to approach 3 second lane changes at 65 mph with his BMW 1600; I find that it takes me about 5 seconds with my Peugeot 504.

This strategy also works with driver lag considered and with the roll degree of freedom included. The driver lag may be modeled as four cascaded first order systems with equal time constants, and with first order lead compensation, thus:

$$\frac{\delta}{\delta c} = \frac{(\tau L \lambda + 1)}{(\tau \lambda + 1)^4} \tag{78}$$

No particular kind of physical plant is hereby assumed; the whole purpose of the 4th order lag is to make the first three derivatives of the driver response zero so that the modeled reaction will appear to include a perception process delay of τU seconds followed by a non-oscillatory output. A time constant $\tau = 1/10$ sec. appears to be a reasonable choice. To achieve satisfactory response with such a driver time lag function it is necessary to increase R over the value given by equation 76 by approximately 5-10 times U or to introduce first order lead compensation if R becomes unduly large. The size of τ_L needed to get good closed loop response with a "reasonable" value of R is a measure of driver compensation for inadequate vehicle dynamics.

Figure 18 compares the radiator cap steering strategy just described with a

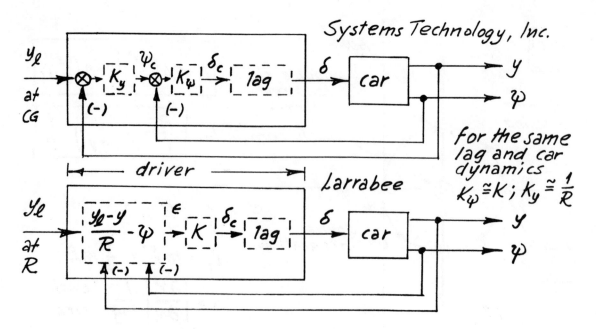

FIG. 18 TWO DRIVER MODELS

related strategy popular with my friends at Systems Technology, Inc.[18, 19]. In this strategy the driver compares the lateral position of his car with the lane centerline location under it and formulates an "internal" heading angle command which is proportional to the lateral position error:

$$\psi_c = K_y (y_\ell - y) \qquad (79)$$

This is then compared with the actual heading angle to produce a steering angle command

$$\delta_c = K_\psi (\psi_c - \psi) \qquad (80)$$

This steering angle command is then run through a convenient, different looking lag function to produce a steering angle

$$\delta = \delta_c (\tau_L \lambda + 1) \frac{(\tau \lambda - 1)^2}{(\tau \lambda + 1)^2} \qquad (81)$$

It has been found that this strategy produces essentially identical dynamics as that given by radiator cap steering strategy when:

$$K_y = 1/R$$

and

$$K_\psi = K$$

as might be expected. It is curious to note that the STI strategy arose from considerations of the limitations of the human operator in implementing an inner and outer loop strategy where the gains were set by considerations of driver lag, vehicle dynamics, and system stability; the hood ornament strategy arose from my efforts to generalize the mechanical guidance of the Alden-Boeing personal rapid transit vehicles at Morgantown where one of the principal limitations on vehicle speed lay in the fixed "look ahead" distance of its mechanical guide wheels. It seems to me that the look ahead distance R or the STI gain Ky ($\overset{\sim}{=}$ 1/R) are primarily determined by vehicle dynamics alone, while the value of K (or K_ψ) is determined by dynamics of the vehicle-driver combination.

4.2 EFFECT OF AERODYNAMICS ON THE LATERAL DYNAMICS OF A CAR AND ITS CROSS WIND RESPONSE

Having discussed a simplified model of vehicle dynamics, the appropriate aerodynamic terms to be added, and a model of driver lane holding activity, it now becomes possible to put the package together and test it, piece by piece. To do this I will use the example of a full size U.S. sedan, the 1963 Ford "Galaxie". It is the only car in the world whose inertias, tire characteristics, suspension characteristics and aerodynamic properties are in the public domain, thanks to the support of the U.S. Bureau of Public Roads, which paid Cornell Aeronautical Laboratories to produce a mathematical model of vehicle dynamics, which was validated with this vehicle[11] and to the work of Roger Hawks, who did much of his doctor's thesis in adding the appropriate aerodynamic terms to the Laboratory's mathematical model[16]. The vehicle in question was a used New York State Thruway police car; it was slightly damaged in a ramp jump and subsequently written off in an instrumented guard rail collision test.

Table I presents the collected inertial properties, suspension roll charateristics, the stability derivatives, aerodynamic derivatives, and driver model properties for this vehicle:

TABLE 1

1963 Ford "Galaxie" Lateral Characteristics

Inertial Properties
i_x = 0.0566 ϵ = 0.1235
i_z = 0.291 mg = 4780 lbs
i_{xz} = 0.0200 ℓ = 9.94 ft

Suspension roll characteristics
$\ell_{\dot\phi}$ = -0.00756 sec ℓ_ϕ = -1.230

Tire stability derivatives
$n_{\dot\phi}$ = +0.360 $y_{\dot\phi}$ = +0.231
n_r = -2.135 y_r = +0.183
n_β = +0.183 y_β = -8.52
n_δ = +2.04 y_δ = +4.30

Equilibrium conditions
U = 102.67 ft/sec   (70 mph)
U/g = 3.188 sec
ℓ/g = 0.0986 sec

Aerodynamic characteristics
A (body cross section area) = 24.6 ft^2
$Q = (\frac{\rho}{2}U^2)A/mg$ = 0.0645
C_{yp} = 0 C_{np} = 0 $C_{\ell p}$ = 0
C_{yr} = 0 C_{nr} = -2 $C_{\ell r}$ = 0
$C_{y\beta}$ = -1.65 $C_{n\beta}$ = -0.50 $C_{\ell\beta}$ = -0.11

Driver, or steering strategy
τ = 0.1 sec τ_i = 0
R = 205.33 ft K = 0.220

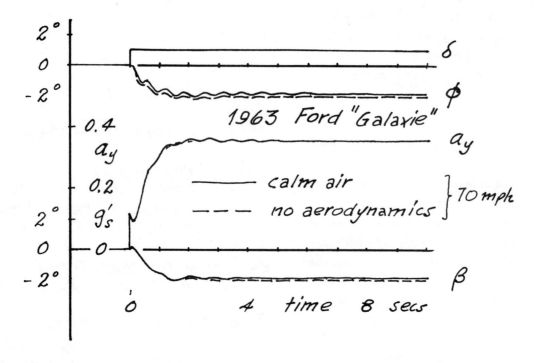

FIG. 19 BASIC VEHICLE DYNAMICS WITH AND WITHOUT AERODYNAMICS

Figure 19 presents the rather typical response of the example car to a step steering input with no aerodynamic terms included. The vehicle shows moderate understeering characteristics and a lightly damped high frequency roll mode. The lightly damped roll mode exists as a result of linearizing the damper resistance to roll velocity; in actuality the damper has considerable Coubomb friction which will "capture" the mode after a cycle or two.

Figure 19 also presents the same situation with left hand member aerodynamic terms included ($Q\, C_{\ell_\beta}\, \beta$, $Q\, C_{n_\beta}\, \beta$, $Q\, C_{n_r}\, \frac{\ell}{U}\, \frac{d\psi}{dt}$, $Q\, C_{Y_\beta}\, \beta$) to show the effect of aerodynamics in calm air at a vehicle speed of 70 mph. The effects are very small; the $C_{\ell_\beta}\beta$ term reduces the outward roll somewhat in the resulting steady turn.

Figure 20A and 20B show the operation of

the driver steering strategy, with calm air aerodynamic effects, when the driver is presented with a ramp function lane change command which extends over two seconds. The y/R response of the car driver combination should be compared with the (y_ℓ/R) input retarded in time by (R/U) since the input is specified a distance R ahead in space; when this is done it is seen that the (y/R) response agrees quite well with the clipped ramp function input; the vehicle is never more than about two feet off the commanded lane center line for a 12 foot centerline to centerline total change. The character of the driver's steering angle output, and the corresponding vehicle roll angle, heading angle, sideslip angle, and lateral acceleration are found to be smooth and well controlled. Note that the lightly damped roll mode of the vehicle is not perceptibly excited by the smooth steering

48

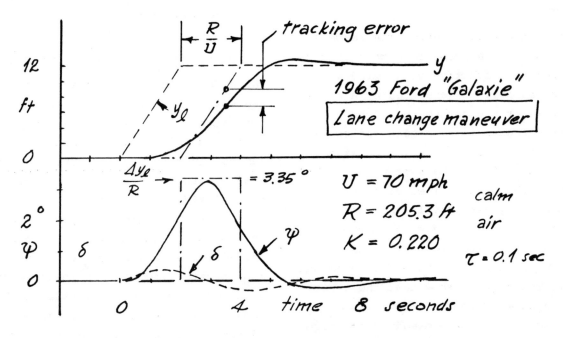

FIG. 20A DYNAMICS OF CAR-DRIVER COMBINATION

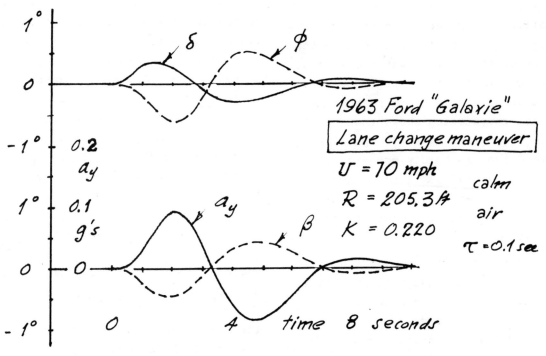

FIG. 20B DYNAMICS OF CAR-DRIVER COMBINATION

inputs associated with the steering strategy.

Figures 21A and 21B present the response of the same driver-vehicle combination to a clipped ramp function cross wind which might presumably be generated by a situation in which the car emerges from a sheltered region into an open region exposed to a prevailing wind. The wind velocity is taken to be 6 ft/sec at the height of the origin, i.e. at about 6 inches above ground level; this corresponds to quite a strong wind at the height of the center of gravity of the sprung mass, about 21 inches above ground level. The figures show that the vehicle is blown about 1 foot off course and stays there, because a steady state tire slip angle and front wheel steering angle are needed to balance the steady cross wind. With the simple steering strategy employed this displacement is needed in conjunction with the look ahead distance to generate the necessary error angle. In actuality the driver would "rezero" his error angle to regain the lane centerline after a time; it is felt that the initial offset is calculated correctly, however. The other details seem quite reasonable. The overall computation shows that a full size U.S. sedan running at 70 mph with an attentive driver is hardly bothered by strong cross winds; peak lateral acceleration of 0.01 g's are encountered, which are just perceptible, and which agree with experience.

Figure 22 shows the response of the same vehicle to the same cross wind when it is left uncontrolled. It is blown into the next lane in 8 seconds and develops a steady lateral acceleration; at the time of crossing the centerline of the adjacent lane it has acquired a heading angle of 2.5°, and this is increasing steadily;

the calculation verifies that driver control is required.

4.3 AERODYNAMIC DISTURBANCE OF AN AUTO-MOBILE BY A TRUCK IN AN ADJACENT LANE

The discussion in this session reports on the work of Systems Technology, Inc.[19] supported by the National Highway Traffic Safety Administration with the object (among other things) to define the potential hazard of increasing the permissible nominal width of buses and trucks on the U.S. interstate highway system from 96 inches to 102 inches (2438 mm to 2591 mm). This involved extensive wind tunnel testing to determine the air loads exerted on a car in close proximity to a truck as shown in figure 23. The longitudinal displacement of the truck relative to the car was systematically varied and the resulting yawing moment and side force acting on the car are plotted as functions of the relative displacement.

Although the tests were performed with successive fixed positions of the car and truck, the effect of differing relative velocities (as when overtaking) are readily taken into account. The aerodynamic disturbance acting on the car may be said to be due to local changes in sideslip angle caused by an equivalent source and sink velocity distribution, V_{ss}, caused by truck. The magnitude of this disturbance may be written as

$$\Delta N = (\frac{1}{2} \rho U^2_{car}) \ (A\ell) \ \Delta C_n \ (\frac{V_{ss}}{U_{car}}) \quad (82)$$

where $\Delta C_n (\frac{V_{ss}}{U_{car}})$ implies a linear relation of ΔC_n to (V_{ss}/U_{car}).

The magnitude of V_{ss}, however, is due to the speed of the truck:

$$V_{ss} \sim U_{truck} \qquad (83)$$

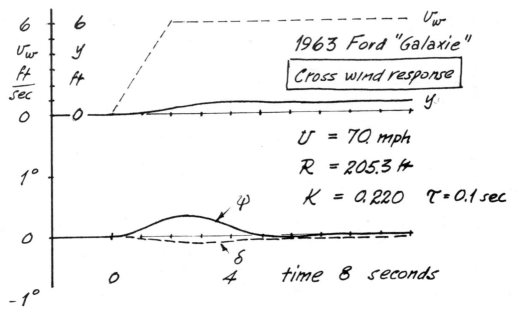

FIG. 21 A CROSS WIND RESPONSE OF CAR-DRIVER COMBINATION

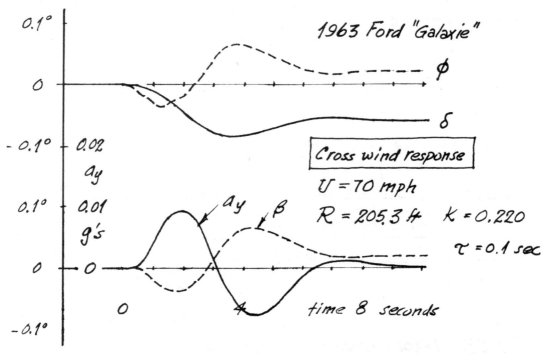

FIG. 21 B CROSS WIND RESPONSE OF A CAR-DRIVER COMBINATION

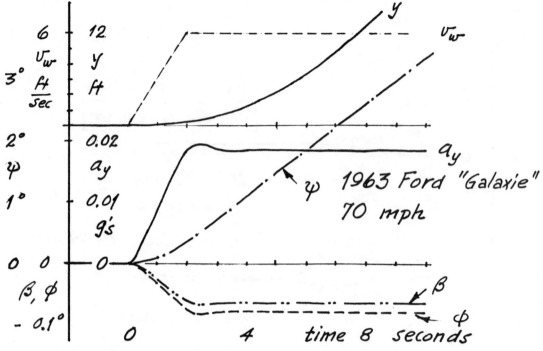

Fig. 22 Cross Wind Response of an Uncontrolled Vehicle

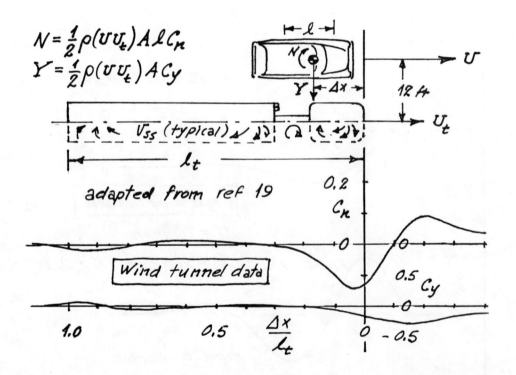

Fig. 23 Aerodynamics of Overtaking ~ Calm Air

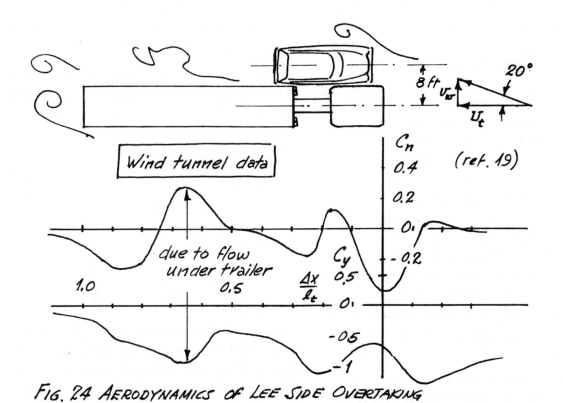

FIG. 24 AERODYNAMICS OF LEE SIDE OVERTAKING

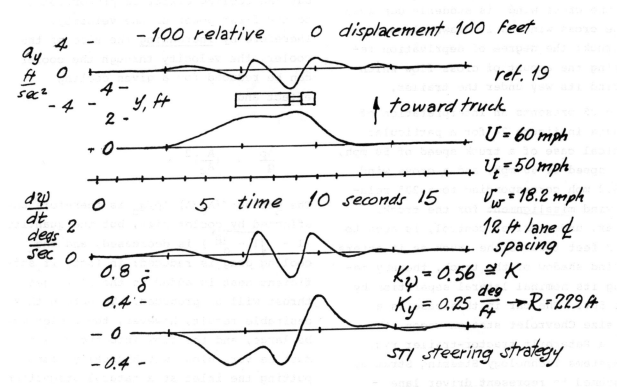

FIG. 25 CAR-DRIVER DYNAMICS - LEE SIDE OVERTAKING

From this it follows that:

$$\Delta N = \frac{1}{2} \rho \; (U_{car} \; U_{truck}) \; (A\ell) \Delta \; C_n \quad (84)$$

where ΔC_n is the dimensionless coefficient arising from static wind tunnel measurements normalized with the tunnel velocity. The author and one of his students, Mr. James Glowienka, confirmed the validity of this rule by performing moving model measurements in a small wind tunnel with a stationary car model restrained to the tunnel floor above a ground plane with a high frequency strain gauge balance, and a moving truck model propelled upstream by a giant rubber band catapult at velocities approaching 30% of the tunnel velocity.

Figure 24 represents a critical case uncovered in this investigation associated with lee side overtaking. The car-driver combination, previously in equilibrium with the cross wind, is suddenly deprived of the cross wind as it draws alongside the truck; the degree of deprivation reflecting the amount of cross flow which may find its way under the trailer.

Figure 25 presents an interpretation of the data in figure 24 for a particular practical case of a truck speed of 50 mph, a car speed of 60 mph, and a cross wind of 18.2 mph corresponding to a 20° relative wind misalignment for the truck. The car, under driver control, is seen to move 2 feet towards the truck as it enters the wind shadow of the truck, thereby reducing its nominal lateral separation by about 50%. The car in this case is a full size Chevrolet station wagon, the truck a Peterbilt tractor-trailer rig. The Systems Technology Steering Strategy is assumed to represent driver lane holding activity.

5. AERODYNAMICS OF AUTOMOTIVE COOLING AND VENTILATION SYSTEMS

Aeronautical research during the 30's and 40's established principles for low drag cooler installations which are summarized in figure 26. Assuming that the pressure loss Δp in the internal flow is confined to the cooler core itself, and that the mass flow through the cooler is proportional to the equivalent orifice area, A_c, then the increase of vehicle drag coefficient is:

$$\Delta C_D = 2 \frac{A_c}{A} \sqrt{\frac{\Delta p}{q_o}} \; (1 - \sqrt{1 - \frac{\Delta p}{q}}) \quad (85)$$

where A is the vehicle reference area for defining the drag coefficient, and $q_o = \frac{\rho}{2} V^2$ is the dynamic pressure based on vehicle velocity. The cooling pressure loss, Δp, is proportional to the square of the velocity through the cooler core but the cooling effect is proportional to the first power of the velocity. Therefore by _increasing_ the size of the cooler, the velocity through the cooler can be reduced for a given cooling effect and

$$\frac{\Delta p}{q} \sim (\frac{A}{A_c})^2$$

The product $(A_c/A) \; \Delta p/q_o$ is therefore unaffected by cooler size, but the quantity $(1 - \sqrt{1 - \frac{\Delta p}{q_o}})$ is decreased, and the cooling drag is reduced; in fact, if sufficient heat is added to the flow, jet thrust will be produced. To obtain this desirable result, however, the cooler must be large, and the flow into the cooler must be very slow, which usually means putting the inlet at a natural stagnation point of the flow over the body. Finally, a smooth nozzled passage must be provided

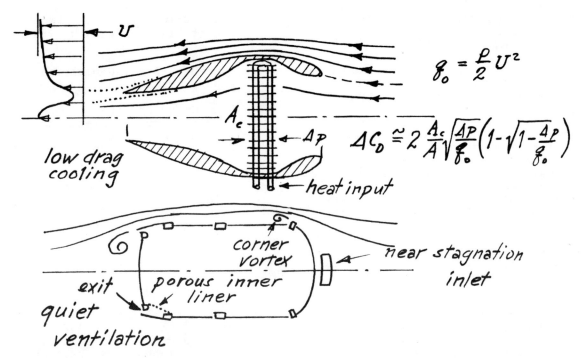

low drag cooling

$$q_0 = \frac{\rho}{2} U^2$$

heat input

$$\Delta C_D \cong 2 \frac{A_c}{A} \sqrt{\frac{\Delta p}{q_0}} \left(1 - \sqrt{1 - \frac{\Delta p}{q_0}}\right)$$

quiet ventilation

corner vortex

porous inner liner

exit

near stagnation inlet

FIG. 26 COOLING AND VENTILATION; DRAG AND NOISE

between the core and the exit gill to accelerate the exit flow to the highest velocity possible.

The author has yet to see anything like the low drag coolers installed in a World War II fighter aircraft on any race car; the most common failure is to provide a suitable nozzle between the core and the exit gill. NACA type "flush" inlets are also unsuitable for cooler and accessory inlet flows; they are intended to be high inlet velocity devices and were developed for jet engine inlets.

As for ventilation aerodynamics, figure 26 summarizes what has been learned by many automotive aerodynamicists: 1) sufficient pressure differential must exist between inlet and exit points to support the required volume of flow; 2) one must not listen to the windshield pillar vortices at high speeds; and 3) a pourous header lining makes a good grill diffuser to accept the exit flow.

THE END

REFERENCES

(1) "Measuring Car Drag", Larrabee, E.E. Road and Track magazine, vol. 12, No. 6, pp 24-28.

(2) "Aerodynamics and Automobile Performance", Hawks, R.J. and Sayre, C.L. Paper submitted to 2nd International Sym. on Road Vehicle Aerodynamics, 1971.

(3) "Aerodynamic Testing of High Performance Land-Borne Vehicles - a Critical Review", Bettes, William H. Paper published in the proceedings of the AIAA Sym. (Los Angles Section) on the Aerodynamics of Sports and Competition Cars, pp 89-113.

(4) "Wind Tunnel Investigation of a 3/8 Scale Automobile Model Over a Moving Belt Ground Plane", Turner, Thomas R., NASA Technical Note TN D-4229.

(5) "The Aerodynamics of an Isolated Road Wheel", Fackrell, D.E., and Harvey, J.K. Proceedings of the 2nd AIAA Symposium on the Aerodynamics of Sports & Competition Cars, 1974.

(6) "Trapped Vortex Flow Control for Automobiles", Cornish, J.J. 2nd AIAA Symposium on the Aerodynamics of Sports & Competition Cars, 1974.

(7) "Metodo Teorico per la Determinazione della Distribuzione di Portanza su di

un Veicolo", Morelli, Alberto, Associazione Tecnica dell' Automobile, Sept. 1964.

(8) "Azioni Aerodinamiche sulla Ruota d'Automobile", Morelli, Alberto, Associazione Tecnica dell' Automobile, June 1969.

(9) "Research in Automobile Stability and in Tire Performance", Milliken, W.F., Whitcomb, David W., Segel, Leonard, Close, William, Muzzey, Clifford, and Fonda, Albert, Reprint of 5 papers presented before the British Institute of Mechanical Engineers 1956.

(10) "Dynamics of the Automobile Related to Driver Control", Weir, D.H., Shortwell, C.P. and Johnson, W.A., Systems Technology Inc., Tech. Report 157-1, July 1968.

(11) "Vehicle Dynamics in Single Vehicle Accidents: Validation and Extensions of a Computer Simulation", McHenry, Raymond R., and DeLeys, Norman J., Cornell Aeronautical Laboratory Report, CAL No. VJ-2251-V-3, December 1968.

(12) "Automobile Dynamics - Comparisons of Cornering and Ride Response Predictions with Linear Theory and with a Non-Linear Computer Simulation", Larrabee, E.E., Cornell Aeronautical Laboratory Report CAL No. VJ-2251-V5.

(13) "A Rational Method for Predicting Tire Cornering Force and Lateral Stiffness", Thorson, K.R. Boeing Airplane Company, Internal Memorandum Report D11719, 22 March 1951.

(14) "Thorson Tire Theory Revisited", Larrabee, E.E., Unpublished Seminar Paper, October 1971.

(15) "The Calculated Effect of Cross Wind Gradients on the Disturbance of Automotive Vehicles", Hawks, R.J. and Larrabee, E.E., Proceedings of the AIAA Sym.*, pp 55-64.

(16) "The Effectiveness of Automatic Guidance in Reducing Automobile Cross Wind Response", Hawks, R.J. and Larrabee, E.E., Paper submitted to the 2nd International Sym. on Road Vehicle Aerodynamics 1971.

(17) "Vehicle Dynamics", Ellis, J.R., Business Books Ltd. 1969.

(18) "Conceptualization of Overtaking and Passing on Two-Lane Rural Road", Weir, David H. and McRuer, Duane, T., Systems Technology Inc. Report 1-193, December 1967.

(19) "Simulation Investigation of Driver/ Vehicle Performance in a Highway Gust Environment", Weir, P.H., Heffley, R.K., and Ringlard, R.F. Systems Technology Paper published in the proceedings at the 8th Annual Conference on Manual Control, 17th-19th May, 1972.

*From the Same symposium as Reference (3)

DISCUSSION

HENRY JEX: In your analysis of vehicle response in the lane change maneuver, did you perform these calculations both with and without aerodynamics and if so, what was the effect of aerodynamics on this maneuver as compared with the effect of aerodynamics on vehicle response in a crosswind?

LARRABEE: Yes, I did calculate the effect of vehicle aerodynamics on the lane change maneuver and found that there were essentially no effects, or at least the aerodynamic effects were just at the resolution level of the analog computer that was used in the study. On that particular heavy car running at moderate speeds, the aerodynamics do not affect the maneuvering ability at all but they do create a perceptible crosswind disturbance. If we had looked at a lighter automobile using the same modeling for the driver and vehicle, I believe the disturbance would have been quite a bit more.

PAUL LAMAR: In your predictions of the coast-down deceleration of the DS-21 (Figure 2) did you take into consideration the reduced transmission efficiency in the lower gears?

LARRABEE: No, I did not. In order to keep the math model simple, I assumed the driveline efficiency was constant. But you could of course construct a piece-wise solution by allowing the transmission efficiency to vary in a finite number of jumps at specified speeds.

FLOYD LEONARD: Would you say that the side force problem indicates the need for a vertical tail especially on the lighter weight cars that we may have in the future?

LARRABEE: I used to think so but I don't anymore. You can reduce the weathervane instability of a car by adding a vertical tail to it, but if you put on enough vertical tail to make the weathervane instability zero, then the sideforce generating capability of the automobile is monstrously increased. On balance, I don't think that is a good idea for conventional automobiles. However, on speed record cars that may take off and fly, a vertical tail is frequently necessary.

PERSHING: This is an important example of the integration of aerodynamics with the automobile. If you want to control weathervane effects, or more specifically, vehicle directional stability, it can be done more effectively by using aerodynamic download to make the tires work. This is true at least on roads and race courses where the tire friction coefficients are large. Forget about the vertical tail unless you are operating on the salt at very high speeds in which case tire traction is low and the aerodynamic forces become overwhelming.

BOB LIEBECK: In your equations for coast-down deceleration in terms of drag, isn't the assumption of a constant drag coefficient implicit? And if so, do you think that it is valid in the speed range you are considering?

LARRABEE: Yes, a constant drag coefficient is assumed. The automobile, typically, is a blunt body and its drag is not Reynolds number dependent over the speed range we are interested in. However, I believe that you could also design a vehicle shape for which this would not be true.

LEONARD: There seems to be a feeling that we can control problems by getting a high download aerodynamically, but doesn't this produce considerably increased drag that might be objectionable from a fuel consumption standpoint?

LARRABEE: It may. If the basic vehicle lifts very strongly without the aerodynamic download, say an aerodynamic coupe body shape, then sometimes canceling the lift of the basic body with a wing of about the same span as the body will result in a reduction of the induced drag which buys the skin friction of the wing and maybe also the increased base drag of the vehicle.

AUTOMOTIVE AERODYNAMICS

ITS PERFORMANCE, POTENTIALS AND DANGERS

Walter H. Korff
Korff Corporation
Burbank, CA 91506

Abstract

Benefits of aerodynamic streamlining for automobiles include improved acceleration at passing speeds, higher cruising and top speeds and much better fuel economy. These may be traded off for smaller engines and lower initial cost. Certain dangers become evident. Solutions require chassis redesign particularly as to center of gravity location along with body redesign. Design features are depicted.

1. INTRODUCTION

Most people think of aerodynamic streamlining for automobiles in terms of increased speed only. This is of course natural because aerodynamics originated in the development of fast aircraft and because its application to cars began in the racing field.

Aerodynamics as applied to automobiles of all types offers much more than increased speed as we can see in Figure 1.

```
┌─────────────────────────────────────────────────────────────┐
│      PRACTICAL AERODYNAMICALLY STREAMLINED CARS OFFER         │
│                                                              │
│  IMPROVED ACCELERATION:          FUEL ECONOMY IMPROVES BY:    │
│     2.4% at 40 mph.                 21% in city driving       │
│     8.1% at 60 mph.                 48% at a steady 60 mph.   │
│     20.0% at 80 mph                                           │
│                                  A reasonable overall estimate│
│  CRUISING AND TOP SPEED - UP 30%  may be 30 to 35% fuel savings│
│                                                              │
│  Equivalent performance permits a  Better stability and control│
│  smaller engine and a lighter     with less or no lift        │
│  chassis. - About 20% less weight                            │
│  with approx. 10% less cost       Less noise from wind buffeting│
│                                                              │
│          The above requires:                                 │
│          Reducing frontal area from 21 sq. ft. to 18 sq. ft. │
│          (low seats between frame rails)                     │
│          Drag coefficient (Cd) reduction from 0.52 to 0.21   │
│          This reduces air resistance to 34.4% as much as the │
│          "typical" compact sedan.                            │
└─────────────────────────────────────────────────────────────┘
```

Figure 1. Summary of Advantages to be Gained from Aerodynamic Streamlining.

2. PERFORMANCE POTENTIALS

To show what can be done we will compare a hypothetical modern compact sedan with a proposed compact sedan with an aerodynamic body and with the same horsepower and weight. It will be shown that acceleration is improved 2.4% at 40 mph; 8.1% at 60 mph; and 20% at 80 mph. Top speed moves up from 108 mph to 143 mph, a gain of 32%.

Depending on how we drive, fuel economy could improve by 48% at 60 mph steady speed. At full throttle acceleration (with a smaller engine for equivalent acceleration) the improvement drops to 21%. A reasonable overall estimate might be 35% improvement. Our present day fuel costs put automotive aerodynamics in a new, more important role for everybody.

Since less power is required for equivalent performance a smaller engine can be used along with its lighter chassis. This in turn can reduce weight and first cost. Cost, as much as 10% less, with the same performance and much better fuel economy, is possible.

It also seems that the electric car with its limited power, when it appears, will have a low drag shape to achieve acceptable performance.

Smooth airflow over, under, and around the aerodynamic car eliminates whistles, buffeting, and other strange sounds. A pleasant quietness adds to motoring enjoyment. Aerodynamic shapes can be exciting to look at also.

With such improvement potential we may wonder why aerodynamics haven't been applied more fully to cars before now. We do know that some efficient sports cars have accomplished noticeable improvements in this field. But it takes a lot of attention to details as well as a fresh look at overall vehicle design including major chassis changes to obtain the results we're talking about. Few manufacturers are prepared to go that far. And we might wonder if even fewer understand fully the problems involved.

3. DANGERS

Aerodynamics, if improperly applied to automobiles, can seriously, even dangerously, affect lift to the detriment of braking. It can also affect stability and directional control during passing and from side gusts. Even cornering can be affected.

These problems are due in part to the fact that the center of pressure moves further forward as a shape becomes more streamlined. However, the chassis designer wants the center of gravity further back to avoid wheel spin. Center of pressure should be behind the center of gravity for "weathercock" or directional stability and for stability in pitch. Wide rim tires can help but only to a point and not at all if momentarily airborne. A new look at center of gravity location and balance is needed as body shapes become more streamlined.

In recent years designers have just about given up on directing airflow under the car. They have relied instead on other devices (spoilers) to counteract lift. It is believed that a better approach is to see what can be done to activate

the flow underneath to gain the full benefits of aerodynamics.

A spoiler on the underside creates a low pressure wake behind it to reduce lift and adds but slight drag to a rough underside. However, if the underside is smooth with a good entry so that airflow remains strong it becomes an entirely different story. A spoiler, while creating a download, also spoils the flow of air, as its name implies, resulting in a large increase in drag. A fully streamlined car suffers far more when a spoiler is added. The Goldenrod record car's air drag increased 49% when a spoiler less than a half inch high was added to the nose to the 1/5th scale model in wind tunnel experiments.

4. DESIGN FEATURES

Figure 2 shows how a greater percentage of air can be directed to the underside by using a long smooth curve under the bumper. Note also that the body is set at a slight negative angle.

Figure 3 is a photo of the nose of this same body on our three wheel sports car. The aircooled engine is in the rear and gets its cooling from the underside. Runs on the hot dry lake last summer did not cause any overheating.

Figure 4 illustrates in plan view how underside airflow can be assisted. Note the fences (items 19 & 20) at each wheel. The radiator, item 16, is ducted and sealed so that hot, fast, outlet air

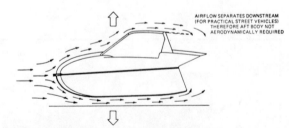

— UNDERSIDE CURVED — SMOOTH — BODY SET AT NEGATIVE ANGLE
   LIKE INVERTED WING SECTION

— MUCH FAST MOVING AIR GOES UNDER TO:
   — CREATE DOWNFORCE TO COUNTERACT LIFT OF TOPSIDE
   — INCREASES HIGHSPEED STABILITY — CONTROL — BRAKING
   — REDUCES WIND RESISTANCE — MORE EFFICIENT — LESS POWER REQUIRED

Figure 2. Airflow Over and Under a Faired Automotive Body Design.

is exited in a wide thin slot to speed up the boundary layer aft.

Figure 5 is a front view and Figure 6 a side view of the same car.

Figures 7 & 8 show an Indianapolis type racer. Radiator air flow exits to the sides rather than over the top. Fuel tanks of airfoil section are set at a negative angle for download. Fins at the rear wheels also reduce turbulence over the aft body.

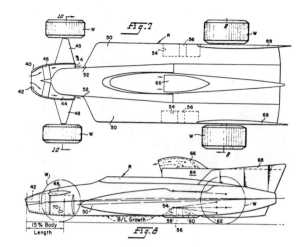

Figure 7 and 8. Indianapolis Type Racer.

Figure 3. Three Wheeled Vehicle With Faired Aerodynamic Body Design.

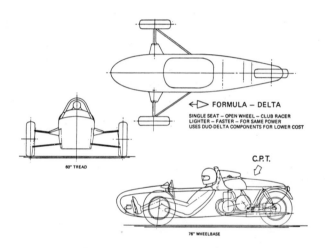

Figure 9. Formula Delta Single Seat Club Racer.

Figure 9 is a 3 view of our Formula Delta single seat club racer. The single rear wheel permits better aerodynamics for the aft body. But only if airflow is not restricted at the front suspension. Figure 10 is a photo of a model of the same machine.

5. CALCULATION OF PERFORMANCE

Let's compare the proposed streamlined compact sedan with the modern compact sedan. In one case the weight and horsepower will remain unchanged. This will show the gain in acceleration at 40, 60, and 80 mph and top speed by streamlining. In another case the weight and horsepower will be reduced to provide the same acceleration

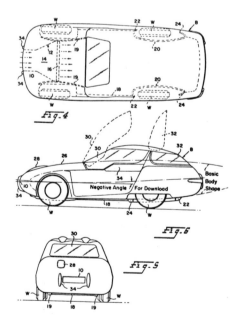

Figures 4, 5, and 6. General Arrangement of an Automobile with Flow Control Body Design.

Figure 10. Model of a Formula Delta Racer.

at 60 mph as for the modern compact sedan. This will show how much streamlining can reduce power requirements and weight while providing equivalent performance at the critical 60 mph passing speed. This also reduces the overall cost of the car and improves fuel economy.

The streamlined compact sedan has 18 sq ft of frontal area. This is the practical minimum by U.S. standards for three abreast seating and was achieved by utilizing a low seat and frame rails at the extreme sides (not under the seat) or integral frame and body. $C_d = 0.21$ can be achieved as itemized in Table 1. FAC_d (Frontal Area x C_d) becomes 3.78. Air resistance for the streamlined compact sedan then is only 34.4% as much as for the modern compact sedan as obtained by comparing FAC_d values. These values are tabulated for speeds up to 140 mph in Table 2.

With the same gross weight (3000 lb) and the same power (150 hp-SAE rated), the improvement in acceleration and top speed can be seen at the bottom of Table 3, when compared with Table 4.

SUMMARY

Acceleration at 40 mph is improved 0.1 mph/sec or 2.4%.
Acceleration at 60 mph is improved 0.3

Table I
Estimated Drag Buildup of a Passenger Sedan

Vehicle Component	Drag Coefficient, C_d		
	Pre-World War II Sedan	Modern Sedan	Proposed Streamline Sedan
Streamline body in free flow	0.04	0.04	0.04
Induced drag (due to lift)	0.04	0.03	0.00
Addition of wheels (bottom side only)	0.08 Lower "A" frame suspension and tie rod exposed	0.08 (Also exposed)	0.07 Smaller openings and blended edges of underpan
Grill, radiator, internal ducts	0.07 (Grillwork has high drag)	0.05 (Grill and forward duct)	0.01 (No grill--optimum slotted opening)
Windshield	0.09 Flat or "V" shaped	0.05 (Rounded sides)	0.04 (Smoother transition to top and sides)
Side window recesses and rain gutter	0.04	0.03	0.01 (No rain gutter-nearly flush side windows)
Blunt rear end	0.07	0.05	0.02 (50% of frontal area)
Underside	0.12 Exposed axles, frame-spring	0.08 Partially smooth under surface	0.00 Full smooth belly pan
Wheel openings (sides)	0.07 Wheel cutouts flush with wheels	0.04 Front wheel opening	0.00 Enclosed
Lights, head and turn signals	0.03 Exposed lens	0.03	0.00 Faired smooth
Exposed mirror, side trim, door handles, hinges, bumpers, license plates, antenna	0.08 (Considerable interference)	0.04	0.02 Best locations, faired or eliminated
Total C_d	0.73	0.52	0.21

Note: Above C_d values vary with specific designs

Table II
Horsepower Required to Overcome Wind Resistance

V_s mph	$FAC_d = 11$	$FAC_d = 3.78$
40	4.801	1.6766
60	16.204	5.5684
80	38.411	13.1994
100	75.021	25.780
120	128.000	44.548
140	205.858	70.740

Formula: Air drag in pounds,

$$\frac{FAC_d \times V_s^2}{391} = \text{lb drag at } V_s$$

Example: $\dfrac{11 \times 100^2}{391} = 281.3$ lb drag at 100 mph

Formula: hp required for air drag,

$$\frac{\text{lb drag} \times V_s}{375} = \text{hp required at } V_s$$

Example: $\dfrac{281.3 \times 100}{375} = 75.0$ hp at 100 mph

Table III
Horsepower Requirements of a Modern Compact Sedan With Power Options

Item	Horsepower Required and Available		
	At 40 mph	At 60 mph	At 80 mph
Wind resistance hp required	4.80	16.20	38.41
Rolling resistance hp required	5.10	9.00	14.40
Power required at wheel hubs	9.90	25.20	52.81
Power available at wheel hubs	120.00	120.00	120.00
Acceleration Power Available	110.10 hp	94.80 hp	77.19 hp
Lb/APA Ratio	27.25/1	31.6/1	38.8/1
Acceleration, mph/sec (Fig. 12)	4.2	3.7	3.0

Top Speed = 108.5 mph approx
Wind resistance	= 95.8 hp
Rolling resistance	= 24.6 hp
Total hp Required	= 120.4 hp

Frontal Area	= 21.15 sq ft
C_d	= 0.52
$FAC_d = F.A. \times C_d$	= 11.00
Gross Weight	= 3000 lb (with 2 people and 1/2 tank fuel)
SAE Rated hp	= 150 hp
hp At Wheel Hubs	= 120 hp (80% of Rated hp)
Weight/Power Ratio	= 20/1 lb/hp

mph/sec or 8.1%.
Acceleration at 80 mph is improved 0.6 mph/sec or 20.0%.

Top speed moves up from 108.5 mph to 143.6 mph--a gain of 35.1 mph or 32.4%.

If we decide that acceleration at 60 mph shall be the modern compact sedan performance to be equalled, not exceeded, we then achieve the following by streamlining.

Power can be reduced and a corresponding smaller and lighter engine and power train will be sufficient. Certain other chassis components may also be lightened. Five hundred pounds has arbitrarily been chosen as the weight saving, thus reducing the gross weight to 2500 lb for our proposed compact streamlined sedan.

We then make our lb/APA ratio (APA = Acceleration Power Available) at 60 mph equal to the same ratio for the modern compact sedan at that speed. This is 31.6/1. Backing up in the formula and using our new weight (2500 lb), we find that the hp for acceleration only should be 79.1 hp. By backing up further, we add the power required for rolling resistance and wind resistance to get

Table IV
Horsepower Requirements of Streamlined Compact Sedan

Item	Horsepower Required and Available		
	At 40 mph	At 60 mph	At 80 mph
Wind resistance hp required	1.68	5.57	13.20
Rolling resistance hp required	5.10	9.00	14.40
Power required at wheel hubs	6.78	14.57	27.60
Power available at wheel hubs	120.00	120.00	120.00
Acceleration Power Available	113.28	105.47	92.40
Lb/APA Ratio	26.50/1	28.51/1	32.48/1

Frontal Area	= 18 sq ft
C_d	= 0.21
$FAC_d = F.A. \times C_d$	= 3.78
Gross Weight	= 3000 lb (with 2 people and 1/2 tank fuel)
SAE Rated hp	= 150 hp
hp At Wheel Hubs	= 120 hp (80% of Rated hp)
Weight/Power Ratio	= 20/1 lb/hp

92.17 hp at the wheel hubs. The SAE rated hp then becomes 115.21 hp. This is a reduction of 34.8 hp (21%). This data is itemized in Table 5.

Actual power required at 60 mph drops from 25.2 hp to 13.07 hp at the wheel hubs. If the power train and other losses increase these values by 25%, then the SAE rated hp values become 31.5 hp and 16.3 hp. The saving is 15.2 hp or 48.2%. If engine efficiency is unchanged, then fuel economy should improve by 48.2% also at 60 mph steady speed. Improved fuel economy at full throttle acceleration would drop to 21% as a direct ratio of engine size. Overall fuel economy would vary between these two values depending on driving habits. A reasonable estimate might be, for most people, a gain in fuel economy of 35% that could be attributed to streamlining a compact sedan.

If the savings in size and weight for the engine, power train, and other chassis components affect only 50% of the cost of the vehicle then manufac-

turing cost drops by half of 21% or 10.5%. Since profits, dealer discounts, and other elements of the ultimate selling price are figured on a percentage basis, we can then assume that streamlining the compact sedan (with no change in 60 mph performance) can achieve a reduction in selling price of about 10%.

It should be noted that acceleration at 40 mph suffered by 0.2 mph/sec and improved at 80 mph by 0.1 mph/sec. Top speed moved up from 108.5 mph to 133.5 mph even though the horsepower was reduced by 21%.

Most people think of streamlining in terms of increased speed. This study illustrates the improve-

Table V
Horsepower Requirements of a Proposed Streamlined Compact Sedan

Hp and weight reduced for performance equivalent to modern compact sedan at 60 mph passing speed.

Item	Horsepower Required and Available		
	At 40 mph	At 60 mph	At 80 mph
Wind resistance hp required	1.68	5.57	13.20
Rolling resistance hp required (Fig. 9)	4.25	7.50	12.00
Power required at wheel hubs	5.93	13.07	25.20
Power available at wheel hubs	92.17	92.17	92.17
Acceleration Power Available	86.24	79.10	66.97
Lb/APA	29.00/1	31.60/1	37.38/1

Frontal Area	=18 sq ft
C_d	=0.21
$FAC_d = F.A. x C_d$	=3.78
Gross Weight	=2500 lb (with 2 people and 1/2 tank fuel)
SAE Rated hp	=115.21
hp At Wheel Hubs	=92.17 (80% of Rated hp)
Weight/Power Ratio - 21.7/1 lb/hp	

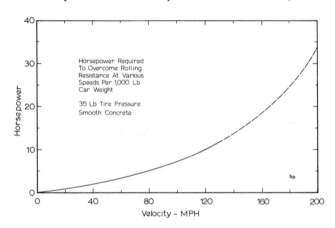

Figure 11. Horsepower Required to Overcome Rolling Resistance at Various Speeds.

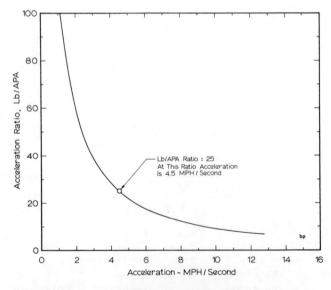

Figure 12. Variation of Weight-Acceleration Hosepower Available Ratio With Acceleration.

ment in acceleration, fuel economy, and/or reduced cost that may also be achieved by streamlining. It should also be emphasized these gains are within the present state-of-the-art--they only need application.

Table 2 lists hp requirements for both body types and speeds (V_s) up to 40 mph to show the effect of speed on power requirements in each case. Figure 11 shows the effect of speed on rolling resistance (weight). By the use of Table 2 and Figure 11 the hp required for either design with any weight and speed can quickly be calculated.

REFERENCES

(1) Korff, W. H., "The Body Engineer's Role in Automotive Aerodynamics," SAE Paper No. 649B, January 1963.

(2) Korff, W. H., "The Aerodynamic Design of the Goldenrod to Increase Stability, Traction, and Speed," SAE Paper No. 6600390, June 1966.

DISCUSSION

ALEX TREMULIS: I would like to concur with your emphasis on underpanning. I'd like to point out two classic examples. The first, the Jack Lufkin car that I have seen at the Bonneville Salt Flats for many years has been nurtured from a speed of the low 220's to a recent approach to 300 mph. This automobile has had absolute fantastic directional stability, and has shown little or no semblance of aerodynamic lift. I attribute its good behavior to the fact that it has the most beautiful underpan that I have ever seen on any car at Bonneville. The second example is a car called the Ford Mexico which we tested in 1955. It was a two-passenger T-Bird that had a C_D of 0.21 which confirms the rumor that automobiles can be beautiful and still have low C_D's. The University of Maryland said that we had developed a zero-lift automobile and here again, the main emphasis of the design is what we did to the underpan of the automobile. I am starting to resent these Can Am-type vehicles that are masterpieces of sheer brute force and are designed to dig a deep trench into the ground with their downforce. At the same time, I think it's a little inconsistent for the poor chassis designer to design a very low weight automobile and then subject it to tremendous downforces that just torture it.

BILL BETTES: In line with Alexe's remarks, some CalTech students have been developing some of their own designs in the wind tunnel and we think that we have come up with a vehicle basic body design that has zero lift. This is without wings and we get it by generating a vortex underneath. The vortex flow does two things; it lowers the pressure underneath and in addition it tends to entrain fluid from over the top of the car and on a fairly short car you get a smaller mean wake size and hence, lower drag. The drag reduction can be as great as 25 %.

JEFFREY KIRSCH: What about the economics of underpanning the car versus use of a simple spoiler at the front? If you have a small production car, you want to optimize its cost and performance for the best overall payoff.

KORFF: If the underside of a car is rough as a cob to begin with, it isn't going to get much air under it anyway. Ford showed this in their early work. So a spoiler doesn't add that much drag to the already rough surface and the download created by the negative pressure in the spoilers wake is far more important in such a case. However, if you start with a really clean automobile, you had better not hang a spoiler on it if you want to keep it aerodynamically clean.

BETTES: On rough underbody configurations, we have reduced the drag using a spoiler or as I prefer to call it, an underbody dam. We have obtained drag reductions of from 5% to as much as 10%. With regard to full underpanning of passenger cars, there are several problems. One is heat rejection from the engine and exhaust system. It is also a fire hazard. Seals that get old tend to leak and with the heat buildup you have the makings of a dangerous situation. Maintainance is another consideration. It costs money to remove those pans when you have to have a front end adjustment or the differential ripped out. In addition, mechanics tend to leave the covers off perhaps thinking that they are being nice guys for the next one who will work on the car.

DON VANDEGRIFF: On the Goldenrod, did you direct all the air around the sides and top?

KORFF: In tests we ran with Bill Bettes in the wind tunnel he runs at CalTech, we tried to split the air four ways, equally to each side and over the top and bottom. We also had a slight negative angle in the car which gave a little download. We were very concerned about lift and we had two nose configurations that we played with. But I think that the configuration we finally ended up with gave us equal flow over and under the car.

ROGER WICKS: On a speed record car where the ride height is nearly constant, you can get away with taking a lot of air in underneath it. But if you have a vehicle where the ride height and pitch attitude change quite a bit, I think you are playing with fire if you let a lot of air flow underneath.

KORFF: I couldn't agree more. However, I want to make this point. If you move the center of gravity forward, you get away from this problem. Aircraft have always had this same problem; an aft c.g. is pure dynamite. Height above the ground was not too critical on the Goldenrod (we went through three different changes there), but

pitch angle was. Now the sports cars that top the rise nose high and flip on their backs, that's what we're talking about here and in these cases, a further forward c.g. would help to hold the nose down.

AUD. QUESTION: What is the engine size of the Formula Delta car you referred to in your paper?

KORFF: We have a 750 cc two-cycle snowmobile engine with an automatic transmission.

DAVID WIER: With the present layout of your Delta car, that is, a single tire in the rear and the rear weight bias with the engine in the back, it looks like you might have some handling problems, oversteer and so forth. Have you thought about the reverse layout with the single tire in the front and the engine and two wheels in the rear? This layout might also have some aerodynamic advantages.

KORFF: We built one and it was so squirrelly I couldn't run it past 80 mph. I'm sure we had other problems with it too. I must say that the layout with the two wheels in front and one in back corners like it's on rails, but the center of gravity is at the one-third point of the wheelbase or further forward. We have had it back as far as 40%. The three-wheeler has been run on the freeways in the mid 80's and up into the 90's on one occasion. We shut it down pretty quickly, but it handled absolutely beautifully at those speeds.

AUD. QUESTION: Would you say that the application of your ideas on aerodynamic design to a compact sedan with marginal performance could bring the performance up to an acceptable level?

KORFF: I feel sure that it can. In many cases we have been talking here about apples and oranges. On the one hand, we talk about powerful racers which need spoilers and airfoils. On the other hand, I'm talking about freeway speeds and cars that our wives drive.

SOME ASPECTS OF THE DESIGN
OF LAND SPEED RECORD VEHICLES

Lynn Yakel
Rockwell International
Downey, California

Abstract

The vehicles that are utilized to obtain Land Speed Records take the form of
specialized, single-purpose, high performance devices. Many categories
exist which are little publicized, but contrary to popular belief, designing vehicles for them provides all of the challenges of building a 600 mile per hour
jet or rocket propelled car. Results obtained from the experience of acquiring
several National and World Records at the Bonneville Salt Flats are reviewed.
Data for a four-wheel streamliner and two streamlined motorcycles are presented.

1. INTRODUCTION

In many cases the development of land-borne,
record-setting vehicles in the small engine displacement categories requires much higher re-
finements in aerodynamic shape than those that
are designed for the unlimited categories. The
reasons are fairly obvious as there are really
only three determining factors for accomplishing
the task. The primary factor, of course, is the
power. Given enough, and applied in the proper
manner, the proverbial barn door can be made
to go fast. The barn door, of course, exhibits
copious amounts of drag and that is the second
consideration; aerodynamic drag. Assuming the
vehicle is driven by its wheels, the driving force
available is a function of the weight on the wheel
or wheels. Consequently, for any given vehicle
there is a point at which additional power applied
cannot be put to the ground without an increase
in the normal loading force (weight) on the driving wheels to prevent wheel slip.

In the early 1960's many of the new breed of re-

cord setting machines appeared; namely, those
that ignored the previously accepted standards for
this type of event. With the advent of the jet and
rocket propelled vehicles the traditional rules
went by the way-side. Horsepower was the name
of the game. From the standpoint of maximum
speed in the unlimited class, the system, of course,
has merit. By exchanging the driving force of the
wheels for engine thrust, the speed attainable is
then a function of the thrust required to overcome
the vehicle drag. In many cases little was done to
reduce the drag, as it was easier to simply increase the thrust.

In a sense it is easier to be a contender for the
unlimited Land Speed Record than it is for a "class"
record. Sponsors are available for subsidizing
such projects as the returns in the form of adver-
tising are much greater. The public, in general,
relates all land speed records to the ultimate and
therefore, does not fully comprehend the significance of a class record. It is difficult for the
layman to appreciate the difference between achiev-

ing 600 mph with 15,000 pounds of thrust and attaining 200 mph with 15 cubic inches of engine displacement. The latter kind of record is often a greater accomplishment.

2. THE LARSEN-CUMMINS CAR

The Larsen-Cummins streamliner shown in Figure 1 was conceived by Fred Larsen and Don Cummins in late 1965 following the annual Bonneville Nationals Speed Trials which are held in August. Their Modified A-Roadster, a supercharged Chrysler powered '27 T, had run for many years and reached its peak of development. It was the then current record holder in its class at 240.642 mph. In order to increase its speed by any appreciable amount would have required numerous and extensive changes to its non-aerodynamic shape and/or a phenomenal increase in horsepower. Neither of these alternatives held much promise, so consideration was given to the building of an all new car to attack the Bonneville Nationals class "D" Streamliner record, which then stood at 222.791 mph. The National Class D, as well as the International Class D, records were the ultimate goals.

Bonneville Nationals, Inc., sponsors of the annual Speed Trials, had classes oriented around the Federation Internationale de l'Automobile (FIA) at that time. Class D encompassed four-wheeled vehicles with an engine displacement of 2,000 to 3,000 cc. (122 to 183 cu. in.). Table I depicts the records that were in existence at the time the project got under way. It should be noted that the National 1-mile flying start record was amongst the oldest in the Record Book, which was a tribute to Frank Lockhart and Harry Miller, builders of the Stutz Blackhawk racing car.

Initial efforts in the project resulted in a rolling chassis being completed in early 1966. A considerable amount of work had been expended before any thought was given to aerodynamic design of the body, although most of the work had been directed toward the mechanical end of things. The configuration of the chassis is shown in Figure 2. Their body configuration work consisted of view-

Figure 1. Don Cummins and Fred Larsen Pose By Their Class D Record Holder.

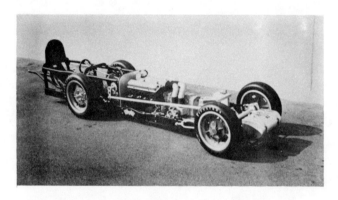

Figure 2. The Larsen-Cummins Record Car Chassis. The Cooling Water Tank Lies Just Forward of the Front-Mounted Roots Blower.

ing as many photographs of previous record setting vehicles as was available. Basically, all that was known was that the frontal area, as well as the overall length, had to be a minimum. The minimum frontal area was intuitive on their part. It just seemed logical that a small power plant demanded a small car. The length requirement was dictated by the size of the Larsen garage and the existing trailer which, with some modification, would be used to transport the new car. The logistics of Bonneville racing require either multitudes of money and equipment or in the case of Larsen and Cummins, a small compact rig capable of being transported to the Salt Flats with a minimum of expenditure and effort.

There was little hesitation on their part when help with the project was volunteered. They were able to concentrate on the other details of the pro-

Distance	Date	Place	Driver	Car	Time	Mph
International Class D (2,000-3,000 cc.), Flying Start						
1 kilo.	9-2-39	Reichsautobahn	R. Caracciola	Merc-Benz	9.04	247.4
1 mile	9-2-39	Reichsautobahn	R. Caracciola	Merc-Benz	14.50	248.3
5 kilo.	8-22-54	Bonneville	D. Healey	A-H 100S	1:01.36	182.3
5 miles	8-22-54	Bonneville	D. Healey	A-H 100S	1:37.97	183.7
National Class D (2,000-3,000 cc.), Flying Start						
1 kilo.	8-22-54	Bonneville	D. Healey	A-H 100S	11.61	192.74
1 mile	4-25-28	Daytona Beach	F. Lockhart	Stutz Spl.	18.15	198.29
5 kilo.	8-22-54	Bonneville	D. Healey	A-H 100S	1:01.36	182.26
5 miles	8-22-54	Bonneville	D. Healey	A-H 100S	1:37.97	183.73
International and National Class E (1,500-2,000 cc.), Flying Start						
1 kilo.	10-3-59	Bonneville	P. Hill	M-G Ex 181	8.7755	254,91
1 mile	10-3-59	Bonneville	P. Hill	M-G Ex 181	14.1415	254.57
5 kilo.	10-3-59	Bonneville	P. Hill	M-G Ex 181	48.0095	232.97
5 miles	10-3-59	Bonneville	P. Hill	M-G Ex 181	1:15.5175	238.36

ject still required for its completion. The con-figuration was determined, but the myriad refine-ments were yet to be worked out. It was suggest-ed that in order to build this small, lightweight, land borne missile as efficiently as possible, serious thought should be given to wind tunnel test-ing. In addition to the reduction of drag, perhaps more importantly, the stability of the vehicle could be determined. However, the budget was too meager, so no testing was planned.

As a concession to the desire for some kind of drag force measurements, Mr. Larsen did con-sent to a tow line test of the actual vehicle once it had arrived at the Salt Flats. With a 200 ft. tow line and a Dillon force gauge we attempted to determine the drag of the vehicle while towing it at approximately 80 miles per hour. This test was inconclusive as the drag (rolling plus aero) was so minimal that a steady state reading was

never achieved.

2.1 DESIGN AND FABRICATION

The chassis, as stated above, had been layed out for a minimum of frontal area. The front tread was fixed at 34 inches while the rear was an inch narrower. The wheelbase was also at a minimum at 90 inches. With the intended pow-er plant and gear box based on Chevrolet 283 series components, coupled to the early vintage Ford differential fitted with a Halibrand quick-change center section, it would have been diffi-cult to squeeze it any more. Tire/wheel sizes selected were also minimum, which helped to hold the frontal area down in size.

With sufficient dimensions to produce an outline drawing of the chassis and its components, pre-liminary sketches of the body shape were made. It appeared that there were two approaches that could be taken. The first, and most obvious, was the one that Larsen and Cummins had taken; i.e., minimum frontal area. The other was to achieve a minimum drag shape at the expense of the frontal area. The latter approach was ultimately chosen as it was felt that there was more to be gained through this approach.

The horsepower required to propel a vehicle at any given speed is essentially a function of the aerodynamic drag due to air resistance and is given by

$$HP = \frac{D \, V}{550} . \qquad (1)$$

The drag, D, is given by

$$D = C_D \frac{\rho}{2} \, S \, V^2 . \qquad (2)$$

As can be seen the power required is a function of the velocity, V, to the third power. Since one can not do much about reducing the air density, ρ, reductions in either the drag coefficient, C_D, or the projected frontal area , S, are the prime candidates for a reduction in the power required for a given speed.

There is, of course, some loss due to rolling resistance on the medium, whether it be on concrete, macadam or hard-packed salt. There are also mechanical losses in the gear boxes, bearings, etc. These losses can account for a major percentage of the power required up to about 60 miles per hour in a normal automobile.[1] At that point the aerodynamic drag equals the mechanical loss but rapidly surpasses it due to the V^2 term. The mechanical/rolling losses are real, but they are small in comparison to the aerodynamic drag. In general, these losses are always present, and probably are of the same order of magnitude regardless of the vehicle. A four-wheel drive vehicle should have slightly higher mechanical losses than a two-wheel drive vehicle due to the additional components involved. Besides the elimination of two of the wheels, a two-wheel vehicle should have a reduction in weight. However, it is felt that these losses are still in the same "ball park", and that the predominating speed limiting factor is the shape and

size of its envelope.

Figure 3 depicts the outline configuration of the vehicle as it was built, while Figure 4 shows it in cross section. The plan was to produce as near as possible a symmetrical shape both in planform and elevation thereby eliminating unwanted lift. A small negative angle of attack was built in to further ensure that there would be no adverse lifting characteristics.

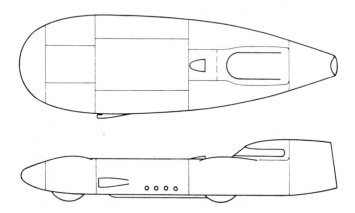

Figure 3. Plan and Profile of the Larsen-Cummins Car.

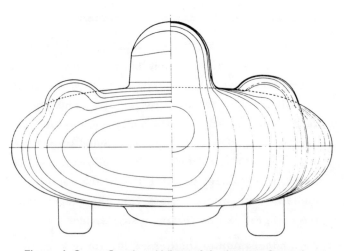

Figure 4. Cross-Sectional View of the Larsen-Cummins Car. The Left Side of the Drawing is Looking Aft; the Right Side is Looking Forward.

The driver's location was fortuitous from a design standpoint for several reasons. Fully streamlined vehicles that are compact as possible generally require the driver to be placed either ahead of the engine/driveline assembly or in the rear behind everything. From the driver's point of view, it is better to be at the rear with full view of everything rather than up in front not knowing what the tail is doing. A yaw string can help, but it is no substitute for a vast expanse of hood. The rear location of the driver has an additional benefit; the canopy and fairing provide a considerable increase in the vertical area aft of the rear wheels, thereby providing longitudinal stability.

In order to maintain a low silhouette, a front-mounted blower was chosen rather than the more conventional top-mounted configuration. A top-mounted blower generally provides a better fuel distribution to each cylinder of the engine, but several hundred square inches of frontal area are the penalty for this slight advantage.

There were several options available in supplying intake air for the engine. The most obvious was in the nose of the car where the dynamic pressure would be at a maximum. The problem with this location was that it required a long and tortuous inlet duct, which would also be limited in size due to the many obstacles in the way. The second alternative was to place a scoop on top of the hood. This would shorten the inlet tract considerably, but would require two 90° bends because of the side inlet to the blower. The configuration chosen required only one 90° bend in the duct and was considered the most efficient for this particular system. This side location can be seen in Figure 3. It is somewhat unusual by conventional standards and could have caused a blockage problem in a severe wind crossing from the right. However, this problem was discounted as it was considered unlikely that the car would be run under those conditions.

Due to its unusual shape the duct was fabricated in one piece from fiberglass. A male mold was used to ensure a smooth inner surface with no abrupt changes in the contour. These range from a vertical rectangle with rounded corners at the leading edge to a vertical ellipsoidal cross-section through the bend to a horizontal ellipse at the blower inlet. The part was removed from the mold with two longitudinal cuts. The two

halves were then bonded together. This was in turn bolted to an adapter plate with suitably radiused holes to match the two holes of the Hilborn injection system at the blower inlet. The unit was bonded to the body panel with fiberglass.

In order to clean up the flow externally, the duct was faired to the body and provided with a splitter since it was built to extend approximately one inch from the body surface. The duct was made serviceable by cutting it transversely midway between the body skin and the injector. The resulting small gap (approximately 1/8 in.) was sealed with a sheet of rubber wrapped circumferentially and held in place with two large hose clamps.

The only other planned protuberances from the otherwise smooth shape was a fairing on the underside to house the oil pan and the Halibrand quick-change center section, as well as the exhaust system. One other was added directly in front of the windshield as construction progressed. This was a small fairing to house the engine tachometer, or rather, a small portion of it. It was felt that this instrument should be within the driver's line of sight, thereby avoiding the necessity for a shift in vision. The time required to refocus from far to near to far again is relatively small, but one second at 300 miles per hour amounts to 440 feet travelled. Three seconds are probably required due to refocussing, light adaptation and reading the instrument, and in that time the car has gone a quarter of a mile. This is much too far to maintain a steady course.

The concept drawings for the vehicle were done in 1/10 th scale and provided the baseline for many discussions for all concerned with the project. Initially it was planned to bring the aft body to a point in planform, but with the overall length requirement of 15 feet on the part of the owners it soon became evident that this theoretical smooth shape would be full of bumps and protrusions. The width of the already constructed chassis was just too wide, particularly at the rear wheels. Even with the rear track narrower than the front, at 33 inches it meant adding several more feet to the overall length. Rather than add this addition-

Figure 5. Three-Quarter Rear View Showing the Parachute Container in the Cut-Off Tail. Just Visible Ahead of the Windscreen is the Fairing for the Tachometer.

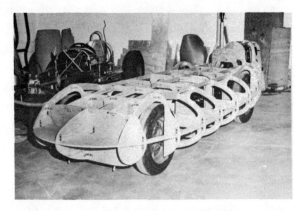

Figure 6. The Buck or Form to Which the Body Panels Were Shaped.

al length, the tail was cut off abruptly as shown in Figure 5.

While the drag probably would have been somewhat less with the full tail, the main advantage realized by the shortened tail was a location for the parachute container. If the tail had been brought to a point some sort of removable fairing would have been required to allow the parachute to be deployed. Additionally, several feet would have been added to the overall length, which would have required a new garage.

Referring again to Figures 3 and 4, it can be seen that there are no flat panels on the entire car. Figure 6 is a photograph of the buck which was built directly on the completed chassis. The buck is a form to which the body panels are shaped and is critical to the end product in several ways. It must faithfully represent all the contours desired of the finished shape and it must withstand considerable abuse during the body fabrication phase. The body panels are continuously fit-checked to the buck as shaping progresses and a lack of rigidity can cause severe deviations in the completed product. Using the actual chassis to which the body is to be mounted eliminates the potential deviation from the master reference lines which might result if a separate structure is used.

The body for the car was fabricated from 0.063 in. thick 3003 aluminum alloy. This thickness, together with the compound curves of the various

panels, provided an extremely rigid body shell. The dynamic pressure at 300 miles per hour amounts to about 200 pounds per square foot and dented sheet metal is not an unknown quantity in record attempt machines.

Symmetry was maintained about the horizontal reference line as much as possible, which served two purposes. The ellipsoidal cross-section provided a smaller frontal area than a rectangular section and with three inches of ground clearance there was little chance of trapping air below the car with the underside sloping up toward the sides.

Figure 5 also shows the individual exhaust headers protruding from the side of the car. These were provided with an additional bend at the body outlet to ensure that whatever small amount of thrust was produced would be directed in the right direction. More importantly, there were benefits to be gained by accelerating the boundary layer with the high velocity exhaust gas, thereby delaying flow separation.

2.2 PERFORMANCE

The vehicle was semi-complete in August of 1966 when it was trailered to the Bonneville Salt Flats in Utah for the first time. Since the Bonneville Nationals Speed Trials are held only one week a year, missing this event would mean waiting another full year. Time had not permitted the car to be painted and finished; however, mechanically the car was ready.

After filling the three gallon fuel tank with methanol and topping off the coolant tanks with water, the engine was warmed up and the car pushed to the starting line. The initial run was made to check out the handling of the chassis, the parachute deployment operation and the general over-all feeling of the car. This first run netted a speed of 225 miles per hour.

Two problems were encountered. First, a lack of oil pressure and subsequent engine noise indicated a malfunction in the 180 cu. in. power-plant. Second, the vehicle tended to wander slightly when power was removed. This was immediately arrested by deploying the parachute. The oil pressure problem resulted in a broken connecting rod, which prevented any further runs in 1966.

The next opportunity to run the car came in August of 1967. The engine was repaired and a different pickup installed in the pan to eliminate the oil starvation problem. The vehicle was weighed for the first time and was found to be considerably more biased toward the rear than anticipated. The distribution of the 1,950 pounds was 36% to the front and 64% to the rear. This included the driver. With the seat behind the rear axle the center of gravity was more adversely affected than with a between-the-wheels seating position. The nose of the car was 28.5 inches a-head of the front wheel centerline. This meant that the center of gravity (c.g.) was located 86 inches aft of the nose or approximately at the 48% line.

In order to provide more longitudinal stability it was necessary to move the c.g. forward to an assumed center of pressure at the 25% line, or 45 inches from the nose. Calculations indicated that 440 pounds was required 8 inches ahead of the front axle in order to accomplish this. Space was at a premium so a compromise was made at 250 pounds of ballast on a slightly longer moment arm than 8 inches.

The functioning of the entire vehicle was up to the design expectations at its second outing. During the week of the 1967 Speed Trials at the Salt

Flats the car averaged 255.870 miles per hour. Subsequent to the Speed Trials an invitation to participate with FIA Sanction was made by the Autolite Division of the Ford Motor Company for the last week in October.

This invitation was conditional on a non-interference basis with the Ford sponsored cars. Several days went by waiting for a lull in the Ford activities. Finally on October 30, 1967 Chief Steward Joe Petrali advised that the course was available if we were ready. The car was warmed up and pushed to the starting point, a distance of 2 miles from the start of the timed 5 mile course. The required two runs were made in 45 minutes and 24 seconds; well within the 60 minute maximum required by the FIA. The car performed fault-lessly, as exemplified by the fact that only two runs were required to establish a total of eight new records; four nation and four international.

Figure 7 shows the car at speed on the Bonneville Salt Flats. The attitude is essentially the same as at rest, indicating that the lifting forces are minimal.

The highest average speed to date with this car was attained in August of 1969 when it was timed at 289.508 miles per hour. Additional attempts have been made, but tuning problems and weather conditions have prevented any further increases in speed.

A new engine with a displacement of 2 liters was built by the owners for the 22nd Annual Speed

Figure 7. The Larsen-Commins Car Travelling in Excess of 250 Miles Per Hour.

Trials in August of 1970. This 122 cu. in. engine powered the car on its first run for a speed of 243.07 miles per hour. Due to insufficient warm-up, the Record average was only slightly over 227 miles per hour even though the return run was in excess of 245 miles per hour.

2.2.1 ACCOMPLISHMENTS

Table II is a summary of the Larsen-Cummins Streamliner accomplishments. A comparison of these figures with Table I shows that the International Class "D" Record (1 kilo.) was increased by almost 29 miles per hour. The Mercedes-Benz streamlined racing car which held this record for 28 years is shown in Figure 8.

Figure 8. The Mercedes-Benz 3-Liter Record Car Which Developed 485 BHP.

Table II
Larsen-Cummins Streamliner Run History

Date	Place	Speed (mph)	Remarks
August 1966	Bonneville Nationals	225.00	One way run - engine malfunction
August 1967	Bonneville Nationals	255.870	BNI Record
Oct. 1967	Bonneville (FIA)	275.994	1 kilometer - flying start average
Oct. 1967	Bonneville (FIA)	275.103	1 mile - flying start average
Oct. 1967	Bonneville (FIA)	248.400	5 kilometer - flying start average
Oct. 1967	Bonneville (FIA)	232.974	5 mile - flying start average
August 1969	Bonneville Nationals	289.508	BNI Record
August 1970	Bonneville Nationals	243.07	BNI one way run
August 1970	Bonneville Nationals	227.178	BNI Record (2 Liter)

2.3 PERFORMANCE ANALYSIS AND TECHNICAL DATA

Actual horsepower figures have never been available for either of the engines used in the Larsen-Cummins car. Both engines have a 6.0:1 compression ratio, a blower drive ratio of 1:1 and burn pure methanol for fuel. Two horsepower per cubic inch is probably a reasonable estimate for these powerplants at sea level. This would yield about 360 horsepower for the 3 liter engine and 240 horsepower for the 2 liter engine.

Because the altitude at the Bonneville Salt Flats is 4,300 feet, the power output there is considerably less. An approximate formula[2] for the horsepower at altitude is given as

$$hp_{alt} = hp_{s.l.} \left(\frac{\text{air density ratio} - 0.1}{0.9} \right). \quad (3)$$

Since air density is affected directly by pressure and inversely by temperature, the air density ratio at Bonneville on a hot summer day is about 0.84. In the case of the 3 liter engine then, the horsepower available at the clutch would be about 296.

If one assumes an efficiency of 95% for the transmission and 90% for the rear axle, the overall efficiency is approximately 86%. The power at the rear wheels is then about 253 hp. Based on the amount of heat generated during a run in the gear box, this is not an unreasonable estimate.

Using the expression for the rolling resistance

74

given in Reference 3, we have

$$R = \frac{K_R \, W \, V}{375} \qquad (4)$$

where $K_R = 0.005 + \dfrac{0.15}{P_{psi}} + \dfrac{0.000035 \, V^2}{P_{psi}}$.

The velocity, V, is in miles per hour, the weight of the car, W, is in pounds and P is the pressure of the tires. At V = 290 mph this expression says the rolling resistance is equal to 56.0 hp. The net aerodynamic horsepower is therefore 197 hp. Using equation (1) to find the aerodynamic drag, D, (the velocity is in feet per second in this equation) we obtain 254 pounds of drag force due to air resistance. The drag coefficient, C_D, is then obtained from equation (2) and is calculated to be 0.152.

Figure 9 is a graph of the horsepower required as a function of the velocity using this drag coefficient and a frontal area of 9.2 square feet, based on the rolling resistance derived from equation (4). It does not include the mechanical losses which, as stated above, amount to about 14%. Figure 9 was derived from data on the 3 liter powerplant; however, it agrees fairly well with the few data points available for the 2 liter engine. At V = 240 mph approximately 150 hp are required to compensate for both the rolling resistance and aerodynamic drag. Adding the mechanical loss of approximately 27 hp gives an estimated power output at the clutch of 177 hp. At sea level this would be equivalent to a power output of 215 hp, which is some 25 hp below the originally estimated 240 horsepower output of the 2 liter engine. Hopefully this indicates there is a potential for capturing the International Class "E" (1,500 to 2,000 cc.) Record of 254.57 mph set in 1959 by Phil Hill in the MG Ex 181.

Figure 10 shows the Larsen-Cummins car in phantom. Forward of the front wheels is the fuel tank. Also visible is the front-mounted Roots blower between the engine and the water coolant tank. The rear wheel brakes (there are none in the front) are Edco discs assisted by a 14 foot diameter ribbon 'chute. Use of the brakes only for stopping has been effective at speeds up

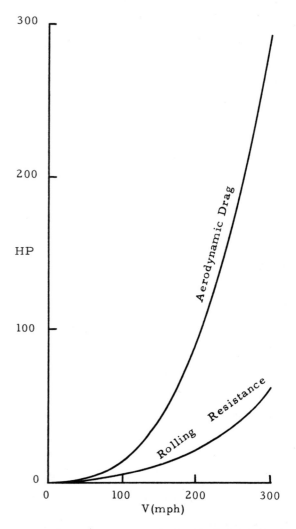

Figure 9. Horsepower Required at the Wheels for the Larsen-Cummins Streamliner as a Function of the Velocity at the Bonneville Salt Flats.

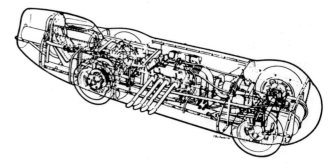

Figure 10. Cutaway Drawing by Clarence La Tourette of the Larsen-Cummins Streamliner.

to 270 miles per hour. However, the parachute is an effective "anchor" should the vehicle tend to wander. Except for a small drain hole below the engine in case of a fuel leak, the exhaust pipe penetrations and the drag chute container, there are no holes in the body. Breathing air is supplied to the driver via a medical-type oxygen bottle behind the seat. Table III summarizes the technical data pertaining to the car.

Table III
Larsen-Cummins Streamliner Technical Data

Dimensions

Length overall	180 in.
Width (maximum)	54 in.
Height (to cowl)	25 in.
Height (at tail)	36 in.
Wheelbase	90 in.
Track, front/rear	34/33 in.
Ground Clearance (minimum)	3 in.
Frontal Area S	$9.2 ft^2$
Weight, Total	1,950 lbs

Chassis

Frame, Rails	0.125 x 2 x 4, 1010 steel
Frame, Roll Cage, etc.	0.125 x 1.75 dia., 1015
Suspension, Front	transverse leaf, solid axle
Suspension, Rear	quarter elliptics

Brakes

Rear Wheels Only	Edco discs
Diameter, in.	12.5
Area, $in.^2$	273.2

Wheels/Tires

Wheels, Front	Halibrand, 4.5 x 15
Wheels, Rear	Halibrand, 5.0 x 16
Tires	Firestone Bonneville
Rear	6.00 x 16, dia. =25.5"
Front	5.50 x 15, dia. =24.0"
Inflation Pressure	90 psi

Engines

Block	1959 Chevrolet V-8
Bore, in.	3.48, 3.562
Stroke, in.	2.38, 3.000
No. Cylinders	8, 4
Displacement, $in.^3$	180.2, 120.0
Compression Ratio	6:1, 6:1
Blower, Roots	4-71, 3-71

Table III [Continued]

Engines (Cont.)

Manifold Pressure, psi	36, 36
Fuel	Methanol

Drive Train

Clutch	Schieffer
Gear Box	Chevrolet T-85
Ratio	1.31:1, 1.0:1
Differential	Ford/Halibrand
Ring & Pinion	3.27:1
Final Drive	1.96:1

3.0 THE MANNING-TRIUMPH STREAMLINED MOTORCYCLE

3.1 DESIGN PHASE

In 1970, prior to setting the World Land Speed Record at 265.492 miles per hour, preliminary consultations were held with Dennis Manning concerning his existing streamlined motorcycle. This was a modified aircraft wing tank with ample power, but lacking in controllability. This was due primarily to the poor vision afforded the driver since he had to peer to either side of the front wheel in order to see. In spite of this, the above record was attained, but afterward it was decided that a new shell was required if the land speed record for motorcycles was to be increased. It was also stressed that wind tunnel testing was most desirable.

The vehicle was layed out in 1/4 scale following essentially the same approach as used on the Larsen and Cummins Streamliner. However, there was less constraint on this vehicle since the chassis was not yet constructed. After laying out the plan and profile, the various cross-sections were determined as shown in Figure 11. The projected frontal area of this configuration amounted to 3.92 square feet. This was approximately 0.7 square feet larger than the original Manning-Harley Davidson record holder.

It was determined that in order to house the dri-

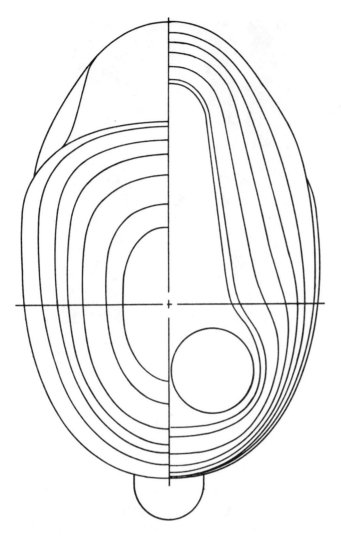

Figure 11. Cross-Sectional View of the Manning
Motorcycle. The Left Side of the Drawing is Looking Aft;
the Right Side is Looking Forward.

ver and the proposed Harley-Davidson V-Twin powerplant, a wheelbase of 120 inches was required. This placed the driver's head at the engine firewall and his feet some two inches behind the front wheel. The overall length was minimized at 181 inches. Mechanical details such as the suspension and drive train were to be similar to the existing record holder. Manning pursued the design and refinement of these components while the fabrication of the 1/4 scale wind-tunnel model was undertaken. Simplicity of the model had to be a key factor in its construction due to the limited funds available for testing.

Construction of the model was begun after consulting with Mr. W. E. Bettes, Director of the

GALCIT 10' Tunnel at the California Institute of Technology regarding model size and structural requirements. Figure 12 shows the solid block of wood selected for the body during the early stages of construction. Two of the twenty templates required for cross-section contour checking are visible also. In order to maintain accuracy an aluminum bar (0.50 x 2.00 inches) was inletted to the block of wood and then attached to a piece of 1/4" aluminum plate inscribed with the various station planes. These station planes, located at 5% intervals, provided the checking points for the templates. Figure 13 shows the model as it was nearing completion, while Figure 14 is a closeup of the rear wheel and the aluminum bar which rigidly connected the wheels together.

This bar was identical in cross-section to the one attached to the template fixture thereby assuring that the completed model was oriented accurately to the wheels. The bar was fitted with threaded inserts at each end, while the wheels were provided with slots to allow vertical adjustment both fore and aft of the entire model. The body was attached to the aluminum bar by two long Allen screws (#8-32 x 3") and each wheel was clamped by a single 1/4" Allen screw. Thus only two Allen keys were required to remove the body and make adjustments. Holes were provided in the body in alignment with the wheel height adjustment screws. This allowed ride height and angle

Figure 12. Wind Tunnel Model in the Early
Stages of Fabrication.

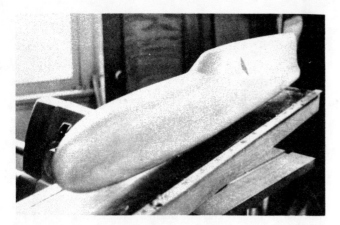

Figure 13. Model Nearing Completion.

Figure 14. Closeup of a Portion of the Model Rear Wheel and Bar Connecting the Wheels. Vertical Slot Provides Adjustment of Ride Height.

of attack changes in a matter of minutes. Figure 15 is a view of the bottom side of the model and shows the wheel cutouts, the aluminum bar connecting the wheels and the small hole at the front which provided access for adjustment. Gross configuration changes were not anticipated and consequently were not provided for.

Air inlet ducts for engine breathing and cooling were placed at either side of the cockpit canopy in order to take advantage of the ram air pressure. At V = 300 mph this amounts to about 1.3 psi, and at 320 mph it is over 1.5 psi. Since the model was built at as low a cost as possible and no pressure measurements were planned, there was no internal flow simulation. These ducts were therefore faired with clay for testing. The model was finished with a smooth coating of dull black paint. This provided good contrast for the

Figure 15. Details of the Bottom Side of the Model.

white interior of the wind tunnel and for the tuft studies.

3.2 TEST PROGRAM

Bill Bettes was relied upon heavily for the wind tunnel setup at GALCIT because of his great knowledge and past experience in the testing of vehicles in the proximity of a ground plane. Prior coordination ensured that installing the model in the tunnel was accomplished with the least amount of effort. Figure 16 shows the assembled "undercarriage" mounted to the yaw table in the test section of the tunnel. It was attached to the six component balance located under the table with two 7/16" diameter studs; one through each wheel. The wheel height above the ground plane was determined by the boundary layer thickness and was about 3/16 inch. The resulting gap between the wheels and the table was sealed with low density foam. Figure 17 shows the complete model in the tunnel in its initial test configuration, which was with four inches of ground clearance and zero angle of attack. Seventeen runs were made in all. With the exception of Run #2, in which the dynamic pressure, q, was varied, all of the test q's were at 56 lb/ft^2. This equates to a Reynold's number of approximately 3×10^6, based on the model wheelbase.

Figure 16. Yaw Table in the GALCIT Wind Tunnel With Model Undercarriage Installed.

Figure 17. Test Configuration Prior to Addition of Clay Inlet Fairings.

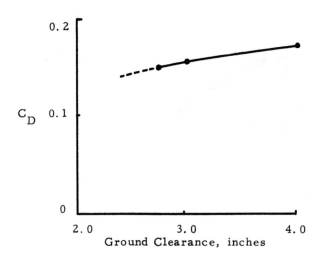

Figure 18. Variation of Drag Coefficient C_D Versus Ground Clearance.

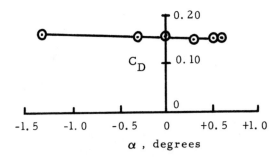

Figure 19. Variation of Drag Coefficient C_D Versus Angle of Attack.

All of the data obtained in the wind tunnel will not be presented here. However, some of the pertinent findings are shown in Figures 18 through 23. Following Runs #1 and #2, which established baseline data for the basic configuration, the inlet ducts were faired with clay. No significant changes in the coefficients were noted after addition of the fairings. Prior to this it was not known whether flow separation was occurring at the blanked off inlets or not. Initial results indicated a higher C_D than anticipated, coupled with positive pitching and yawing moments. The lift coefficient, C_L, was negative through a range of $\pm 6^o$ of yaw angle.

The next seven runs were made to determine the effects of ride height and angle of attack, α, on the baseline coefficients. Reducing the ground clearance to 3 inches lowered the C_D from 0.1725 to 0.1595 at zero angle of attack. This was further reduced at slight positive angles of attack with the lowest drag coefficient achieved with $\alpha = +0.30^o$. With this attitude lift was still negative and even with the positive pitching moment, there was still a slight download on the front wheel. As would be expected, the maximum neg-

ative lift was achieved with the largest negative angle of attack tested which was -1.32^o. This was accompanied by a drag increase of about 8% as compared to that obtained at the optimum angle of attack, $\alpha = +0.30^o$.

Subsequent tests were conducted with $\alpha = +0.50^o$ and included two different sized dams ahead of the front wheel, a very shallow inclination of the windshield (about 15° to the horizontal rather than 30°) and a small lip at the top of the trailing edge. The modifications were done with clay. No noticeable changes were evident due to the first three alterations. The 1/4" high lip or flair at the tail added substantially to the rear loading as the lift coefficient on the rear wheel increased in the negative direction approximately 2 times; i.e., from $C_{L_R} = -0.075$ to $C_{L_R} = -0.156$. With this high download at the tail, the C_{L_F} was slightly positive at 0.007, due primarily to an increase in the positive pitching moment. Additional runs were not

79

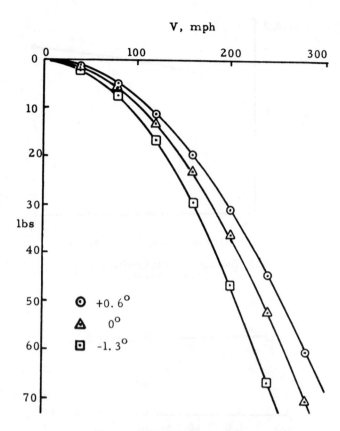

Figure 20. Variation of Total Aerodynamic Download Versus Velocity in MPH.

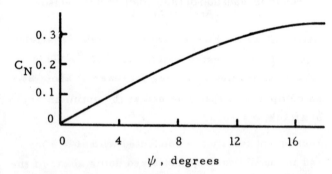

Figure 21. Yawing Moment C_N Versus Angle of Yaw.

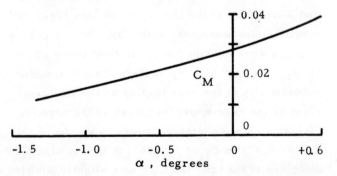

Figure 22. Pitching Moment C_M Versus Angle of Attack.

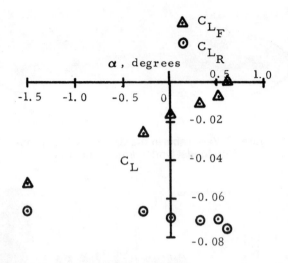

Figure 23. Lift Coefficients Transferred to Axles and Moment Center Location With $\psi = 0$.

made at other angles of attack. However, negative lift probably would have been restored with a small negative incidence.

The final run in which data were recorded was number 16. This was with the basic configuration plus the clay inlet fairings, a ground clearance of 2.7 inches and zero incidence. A minimum drag coefficient was obtained of 0.150.

Run #17 was a tuft study for flow visualization. Unfortunately there was a malfunction in the photographic equipment. Consequently, no photographs are available of this test. The tufts did show that the only area where flow separation occurred was immediately aft of the rear wheel.

3.3 FABRICATION AND TECHNICAL DETAILS

Due to the limited funds available, construction of this vehicle took place over a span of approximately two years. During this time there was a change in plans regarding the powerplant to be used. Rather than the Harley-Davidson of 90 cu. in. displacement being fitted, the chassis was built to accomodate two 650 cc Triumph engines. This necessitated lengthening the wheelbase for the additional engine and refairing all of the lines aft of the driver's compartment. This was an area of more or less constant tapering section so it was felt that the data obtained would still be representative.

Fiberglass was chosen for the body material in order to keep the costs down. A 16 foot long 4 X 4 was used as a backbone on which to mount the station bulkheads. Photo templates were made at each station and transferred to 3/4 inch marine plywood. These were made 3/8 inch undersize for the desired cross-section and provided with oversize square holes to fit over the 4 X 4. All station bulkheads had centerlines scribed on them and final alignment was made with the use of shims and a transit. Once these were in place the entire framework was covered with 3/8" X 1-1/8" oak stringers nailed in place. The entire body was thus faired from station to station. After three coats of epoxy resin, the ensuing shape was block sanded using alternately black and white primer. When the form was completed it was taken to the Wixon Brothers glass shop in Long Beach, California where the female molds and the complete body panels were made.

The tubular chassis was completed during the time the fiberglass body was being constructed. Several components were available from the previous Manning-Harley Davidson record holder. A freon fire extinguishing system was installed with a distribution of half to the driver's compartment and half to the engine compartment. Mercury switches were provided to shut off the fuel supply and deploy the parachutes in the event the motorcycle should get upside down. The two parachutes, one a 2-1/2 foot diameter on a 65 foot line, the other a 6 foot panel ribbon chute on a 50 foot line, were each housed in 6 inch diameter by 13 inch long tubes. These were located in a horizontal plane at the base of the tail. Unique for a motorcycle was the application of a Morse foot operated cable for the throttle. These were also used for the shifting and braking mechanisms. A nitrogen bottle charged to 450 psi actuated the parachute deployment and landing skids via appropriate solenoid valves. Power was supplied by two 6 AH, 12 volt Honda motorcycle batteries. Due to known problems with previous record attempt machines, all hardware was standardized as to size. This allowed a complete engine or

transmission replacement in approximately 15 minutes. Kim Tab 3.50 x 19 magnesium wheels, interchangeable fore and aft, were used. Final weight of the machine including the driver was approximately 900 pounds. Each of the two 650 cc Triumph engines reportedly produced 80 horsepower on a mixture of 92% nitromethane and 8% methanol.

3.4 PERFORMANCE

A preliminary test run was made during the 25th Annual Bonneville Nationals Speed Week in August of 1973. Because of the inclement weather conditions, very few days for running were available. And when they were, the course was quite rough. Initial checks were made with a tow line to familiarize the driver with the characteristics of a long wheelbase streamlined motorcycle, which are quite different than an ordinary two-wheeler. Following these familiarization tests, one timed run was made at 134 miles per hour.

Figures 24 and 25 show the completed vehicle on the Salt Flats in early October of 1973. Several problems were encountered during this record attempt session. The landing skid mechanism was not operating as expected and the single Triumph gearbox was inadequate for the power applied to it. Consequently, four gear boxes were disintegrated in all; they simply would not hold up under a hard acceleration. The fastest clocked time was 248 miles per hour and accomplished with only the use of high gear. (The first three gears had let go while getting under way.) Some minor crashes were incurred, which were attributed partially to the cause for the gearbox failures. The extremely rough salt course imposed high shock loadings on the drive line as well as the front steering mechanism. The front wheel steering bearings were replaced several times due to failure.

Following this attempt for a new record, the crew returned home to effect repairs. A Harley-Davidson 74 gearbox was modified and installed. Additional sealing was provided at the engine firewall due to fumes in the driver's compartment, and the exhaust system was rerouted. Upon re-

Figure 24. Profile of the Manning-Triumph Motorcycle
on the Salt Flats.

Figure 25. Another View.

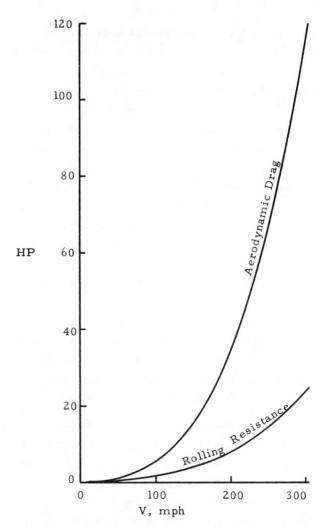

Figure 26. Horsepower Required at the Wheels on the
Bonneville Salt Flats for the Manning-Triumph Motorcycle.

turning to the Salt Flats, the motorcycle was
geared for a top speed of 270 miles per hour. A
standing start run was made at 225 miles per
hour in which all systems and handling were completely satisfactory. An attempt was then made
with a four mile approach. A front wheel steering bearing again failed as the vehicle was approaching the timed mile. At this point the engine tachometer indicated a velocity of 250 miles
per hour. Weather and course conditions pre-
cluded any further running in 1973. However,
the performance potential had been demonstrated.
Figure 26 is a plot of the horsepower required at
the wheels as a function of the speed in miles per
hour for the Manning-Triumph streamlined motorcycle at the Bonneville Salt Flats. The same
basic equations as those used to determine the
Larsen-Cummins power requirements were used.

4.   THE VESCO-YAMAHA STREAMLINED
MOTORCYCLE

4.1 DESIGN AND FABRICATION

The present Vesco streamlined motorcycle was
conceived in early 1971 and is a refinement of his

previous record holder. Don Vesco had broken
the land speed record in 1970 at 251.924 miles per
hour with the vehicle shown in Figure 27. This
was built primarily from a surplus aircraft fuel
tank. The frontal area was quite small at slightly
over three square feet and was the major contribution to its success. It had, however, reached its
potential. Consequently, Don held the record for
only one month before it was taken away.

It appeared that a reduction in drag was in order
if the Yamaha powerplants were to remain in con-
tention. The maximum horsepower available at
sea level for each of the two 350 cc two-stroke
engines was 55, or 110 hp total for the pair. Being
a Yamaha dealer somewhat limited Don's choice
as to powerplants. The 350 cc engine was the

82

Figure 27. The Vesco-Yamaha 1970 Record Holder Prior to Modification.

Figure 28. Plywood Buck for Shaping Panels.

Figures 29, 30, and 31. The Aluminum Body as Fabrication Progressed.

highest horsepower unit available at the time.

Working with drawings and the actual chassis, much the same as with the Larsen-Cummins car, a new shape was arrived at with a total projected frontal area of 3.4 square feet. It was planned to use aluminum for the body material so a form was required so that Pete Wilkins of Profab (the body builder) could shape the metal to it. Due to the complexity of attaching all of the station bulkheads to the existing chassis and the extreme body length (260 inches), a ten-inch square hollow beam was built of plywood for the backbone. Station bulkheads were then attached as shown in Figure 28. Figures 29, 30 and 31 show the body as shaping progressed, and Figure 32 shows the completed shape ready for paint and finish.

Because of the adverse yawing moment experienced in the Manning design, it was decided that a vertical stabilizer should be incorporated. The mounting base for the NACA 0006 airfoil section can be seen in Figure 29.

In order to maintain a low drag shape, NACA flush inlets were provided on either side of the body. Insufficient time prevented the proper

duct work to direct the flow internally and with the front engine very close to the firewall, overheating resulted. Since the access area through the bulkhead was limited for ductwork, it was later decided to incorporate external scoops for engine breathing and cooling.

The baseline design included an ejectable tail cone covering the parachute housing in order to gain a few more percent reduction in drag. Again, be-

Figure 32. The Completed Shape Ready for Paint.

Figure 34. Don Vesco Being Strapped into the Streamliner.

cause of limited time, this component was not fabricated and to date the vehicle has been run as shown in Figure 33.

4.2 PERFORMANCE AND ACCOMPLISHMENTS

Last minute details were completed and the new streamliner arrived at the Bonneville Salt Flats in time for the 1971 Nationals. As mentioned previously, the front engine overheated which prevented full power runs with both engines. However, by uncoupling the front engine, runs were made utilizing the rear engine only since it was receiving adequate air.

Figure 34 shows Don Vesco squeezed into the diminutive cockpit prior to his record breaking run of 182.278 miles per hour using a single 250 cc engine burning gasoline. This was some 6 miles per hour over the previous AMA Record of 176.82 miles per hour held by Harley-Davidson.

Additional records were set in 1973 in small displacement categories with this motorcycle as

given in Table IV. These were conducted under both AMA and FIM supervision and sanction.

Table IV
Vesco 1973 Records

Category	Record (mph)
250 cc	189.529
350 cc	202.445
750 cc	222.903

It is interesting to note that the tail fin was removed for the 250 cc and 350 cc Records. The increased area due to the fin caused the vehicle to be more susceptible to cross wind forces. At one point, prior to removing the fin, the vehicle was blown off the course at an estimated 45° angle due to a crosswind. From this, and other peculiar handling characteristics, it is evident that 2-wheel vehicles are more critical as to stability than their 4-wheel counterparts.

REFERENCES

(1) P. R. Kyropolous, K. B. Kelly and W. Tanner, "Automotive Aerodynamics", SAE Paper No. SP-180, March 1960.

(2) "Aeronautical Vest-Pocket Handbook", Pratt & Whitney Aircraft, East Hartford, Conn. 1952.

(3) S. F. Hoerner, "Fluid-Dynamic Drag", 148 Busteed Drive, Midland Park, New Jersey, 1965.

Figure 33. Profile of the Vesco-Yamaha Motorcycle on the Salt Flats.

KEVIN COOPER: Two questions. First, what was the Reynolds number of the wind tunnel tests you ran? Second, why did you cut the tail of the motorcycle off as you did? I've seen data that suggests shortening a long slender body by 14 % increases the drag coefficient perhaps 30 %. That's a very big price to pay for a small reduction in length.

YAKEL: The Reynolds number of the wind tunnel tests was 1.3 million per foot. Regarding the chopped off tail, Larson told me that no way was that thing not going to fit into his garage, so I had to come up with this compromise on length. I agree with you. I would rather have the tail on it. I had the same problem with the Manning motorcycle and on Vesco's I had planned to use a conical tail section to cover the parachute housing. It would have added another three feet and you can see in Figure 33 that Vesco's bike is already six feet longer than the other two.

AUD. QUESTION: How did you reference the angle of attack on the motorcycle wind tunnel model?

YAKEL: The aluminum bar that tied the two wheels together (Figure 14) was referenced to the centerline of the wooden body. By using a height gauge fore and aft, I could measure the distance of the bar above the yaw table to within thousandths of an inch. With this information it was just a matter of computing the tangent of the angle.

JON McKIBBEN: I notice that on the latest Manning machine you did away with the high tail fin but you still have a pretty good sized fin on the Vesco machine. With regard to yaw and roll problems in sidewinds, what are your feelings about the use of a large tail fin?

YAKEL: I can see some advantages in both approaches. A large fin generates a lot of crosswind force and on a two-wheel machine that's not a good idea. Don Vesco was blown off the course several times just due to the fin but he didn't get it upside down or sideways. It just laid him over so he went that way. To avoid this problem on the small class record machine, he ran without the fin.

CHUCK CONTRATA: What is the effect of surface texture on drag? For example, the dimpled surface on a golf ball adds 150 yards to its range and there is a big difference between a rough and a polished cylinder head.

YAKEL: There is a lot of literature on this, Hoerner's book Fluid-Dynamic Drag, for example. It's basically a function of the Reynolds number. The surface roughness doesn't become important until you reach Reynolds numbers of 10^5 and 10^6 where transition from laminar to turbulent flow would be expected.

THE CAN-AM CAR AND GROUND EFFECT

Peter Bryant
Majestic Motorhomes, Inc.
San Jacinto, California

Abstract

The concept of "aerodynamic ground effect" as it applies to high performance automobiles is defined and its historic development reviewed. Based on experience in the design and development of a series of Can-Am cars, methods are presented for achieving aerodynamic ground effect and for measuring its effects on vehicle performance and handling.

1. INTRODUCTION

The advent in 1966 of the Canadian-American Challenge Cup series for sports racing cars is probably responsible for more aerodynamic innovation in road racing car design than any other series in racing history. Unlimited engine capacity allowed more horsepower to be used than anyone had seen since the pre-war days of the powerful Mercedes and Auto-Union cars and perhaps it was this factor that urged car designers to look for new ways to improve tire traction and thus increase cornering power. The changes which resulted can best be described as a more intensive application of the general principles of "aerodynamic ground effect" to vehicle design.

What these new concepts in aerodynamic ground effect have meant in terms of increased performance is quite significant, so much so that the practice of using ground effect devices is now universal and is not limited to Can-Am cars although that is the area where it first became predominant. Many forms of racing now are using such devices to increase traction and lateral cornering power. Among them are Indianapolis cars, Formula 5000 cars, Grand Prix cars and dragsters.

In this paper, the concept of aerodynamic ground effect as applied to high performance automobiles is defined and its historical development is reviewed. Then, based on the experience of the design and development of a series of Can-Am cars, methods are presented for achieving aerodynamic ground effect and measuring its effects on vehicle performance and handling.

2. BACKGROUND

2.1 DEFINITION OF GROUND EFFECT

The concept of aerodynamic ground effect is used here in a broader sense than is conventionally used in the field of aircraft. A vehicle moving in close proximity to the ground experiences an aerodynamic force system differing from that which it experiences in free air. This difference traditionally is referred to as ground effect. With regard to high speed race cars, the term "ground effect" is broadened here to also include the effect of any aerodynamic device which, through its direct action, modifies the normal load on the vehicle tires. It is necessary to take this viewpoint with regard to high performance automobiles since the tire force system is the major one affecting vehicle performance and handling. However, aerodynamic download has a strong effect on the tire force system through its direct effect on the tire patch normal load and its indirect effect on vehicle suspension which in turn modifies the tire characteristics and the aerodynamic loads carried by the body. It is the strong interaction between the tire and aerodynamic force system which necessitates their simultaneous consideration in any meaningful definition of aerodynamic ground effect.

A unique example of a "ground effect" machine is the Chapparal 2J shown in Figure 1. The 2J was a Can-Am Group 7 car made in Texas by Chapparal Cars, Inc. It was propelled by a 465 cu.

inch aluminum Chevrolet engine but it also had an auxiliary engine which drove two fans mounted in the rear underbody as shown in Figure 2. These fans evacuated the air from the underside of the car as in a vacuum cleaner and literally sucked the car to the ground to increase tire traction. It is rumored that the force of this suction was equivalent to 1 "g"; that is, the car theoretically could have clung upside down to the ceiling by virtue of this unique form of ground effect.

More conventional examples of ground effect devices used in racing are wings and flaps attached to the vehicle as shown in Figure 3. These devices are installed so that when the vehicle is at speed, a large aerodynamic download is developed and the tractive force of the tires is greatly enhanced. Other frequently used devices shown in Figure 3 are body mounted fins and side fences and rear spoilers.

Figure 1. The Chaparral 2J Can-Am Ground Effect Car.

Figure 2. Installation of Rear-Mounted Fans in Chaparral 2J.

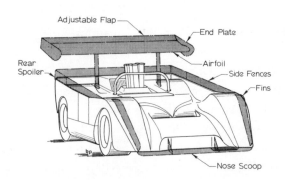

Figure 3. Aerodynamic Devices for Increasing Downforce on the Car.

Land speed cars still vie for low drag and generally clean lines but some use of ground effects is generally necessary for stability at high speed. This is not to say that in order to obtain the best ground effects, Can-Am cars have to have high drag, but usually when an attempt is made to increase the downforce on a car and thus its traction, the drag of the car does increase. This factor then becomes an important part of the design problem, which is essentially the development of aerodynamic configurations which will generate large amounts of download without an excess penalty in drag.

2.2 HISTORICAL BACKGROUND - THE INFLUENCE OF RULES MAKERS

There are complicated rules governing auto racing in general and vehicle design in particular. An important segment of these rules legislate the use of aerodynamic devices, their size, location and method of installation and operation. Apart from general configuration, there were not many regulations prior to 1968 which specifically mentioned aerodynamics. In 1969, following a series of spectacular accidents which the racing authorities put down to the use of aerodynamic devices, new legislation was written for racing which attempted to limit the use of these devices. These rules are mainly responsible for the changes which were made to chassis and suspension to accommodate ground effects.

The reason why the rule changes caused an upheaval in chassis design is quite easy to explain. Pre-1969 cars had very few restrictions regarding the size, shape, and method of installation of flaps, wings, and other aerodynamic devices. Thus, designers found that the best way to increase traction without affecting drag too badly was to place the airfoils, devices, etc., in clean air away from the bodywork and transfer the negative lift through the struts and mountings directly to the hub components of the wheels themselves. A typical installation of this type is shown in Figure 4. This layout achieved two main

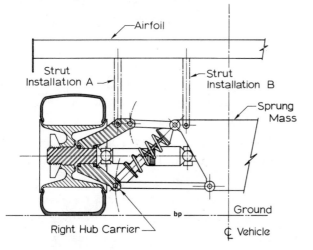

Figure 4. Sketch of Right Rear Suspension Assembly With Airfoil Mounted [A] On the Unright, [B] On the Sprung Chasis.

objectives. First, by taking the downforce directly through the hub components, the tire normal force was increased without excessive deflection of the suspension system. This extra traction meant higher cornering power for the vehicle and as road race cars spend proportionately more time going around corners than along straights, lap times were lowered considerably. Secondly, because the airfoils used were up and away from the bodywork of the car, the car itself could be designed for low drag and minimum interference with the airfoil, thereby having the best of both worlds from an aerodynamic standpoint.

Unfortunately, some of the devices used had problems regarding strength. Sometimes an airfoil would break or get loose due to weak mountings or overloading, etc. These failures caused a couple of incidents which unfortunately ended in near tragedy. Everyone involved was nervous regarding the consequence of such accidents and before things reached a disaster of major proportions the racing legislators changed the rules. It was a shame that this had to come about because of apparent ignorance on the part of some constructors or lack of quantitative data on aerodynamic devices.

Regardless of all the opposition by constructors, the rules were changed nevertheless and 'all aerodynamic devices' had to be fixed firmly to the sprung mass of the vehicle, as shown in Installation (b) of Figure 4. A limit was also placed on the height from the ground that the device could be located on the respective vehicles.

The operative words in this rule changing were sprung-mass and height. Suddenly all the loads and forces acting on the tires had to be transmitted via the springs and suspension components and the airfoils were now down lower relative to the car body. Their aerodynamic efficiency could be a problem if the aerodynamics of the car as a whole were not to be changed. Unfortunately, this could not be, because now the car and devices had just about become a single entity.

3. MEASUREMENT OF AERODYNAMIC FORCES

3.1 AERODYNAMIC DOWNFORCE

The various combinations of downforce at the front and rear of the car must be correlated to the best obtainable performance on the track. It is not really necessary to know to the mil what the downforce is in pounds, but rather, how to obtain the best results in varying configurations. To do this, a fairly simple method can be used. It is possible to measure the aerodynamic download with reasonable accuracy by measuring the vertical movement of the suspension system, resulting from these downloads. Relating the deflection of the suspension system in inches to download in pounds and then taking readings on the front and rear suspension over a range of speeds will allow one to get a good reading on the aerodynamic loading acting on the car. In particular, the small changes in aerodynamic loading which are produced by modifications in aerodynamic devices can be measured with very good accuracy.

A height recorder is one instrument which is frequently used for measuring suspension system deflection. A schematic of a typical height recorder is shown in Figure 5. The recorder is mounted in a suitable free space in the car and the cable is routed and anchored to the rear suspension so that it is pulled when the wheel goes from jounce to rebound. The return spring pulls the slide and

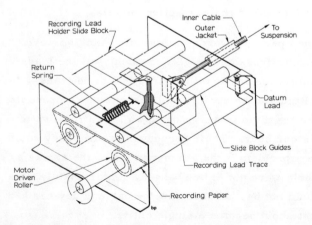

Figure 5. Schematic of Height Recorder.

cable back. A motor driven roller operated by a switch in the driver compartment moves the recording paper under the lead mounted on the slider block when data is being taken. A similar cable-block system, not shown in Figure 5 for clarity, is provided in this unit for the front suspension system so that data may be obtained fore-and-aft simultaneously.

In using the height recorder the following procedure is followed. First, the normal suspension system springs are replaced, with the softest ones available, softest referring here to the lowest practical spring rate for the vehicle. This is done so that the changes in ride height will be more significant and more easily measured. The system is next calibrated. The first reading is taken with the vehicle in the basic test configuration and with zero downforce. This is the baseline reading and it should be taken before and after each test run. This reading is taken with the car prepared for normal testing on the track, that is, with tanks half full of gasoline and with the driver at the wheel. The baseline reading is taken at 5 mph on a LEVEL surface at constant speed. In order to relate the change in suspension system height to download, the system is calibrated by adding weight in known increments and taking readings. This can be done, for example, by adding 50-lb bags of sand at the front and rear, alternately followed by 100 lb, etc., to 500 lb if so desired. After each calibration is made the zero height readings are rechecked to maintain control. All of these readings are taken at 5 mph constant speed on a level surface.

With the baseline readings taken, tests are then made to determine the forces caused by aerodynamics. By making test runs at various constant speeds the readings obtained will determine with reasonable accuracy as to how much the suspension has moved. Then by comparing these data with the calibration runs taken at 5 mph it can be determined how many pounds force it took to cause the measured deflections. Thus, we can determine what forces are caused by the various aerodynamic configurations tested. Note that the speed readings are taken only after the vehicle has sufficiently stabilized at the desired speed. Once the tests have been completed and evaluations made of the various aerodynamic devices and configurations, the vehicle is then returned to its standard trim and springs, etc.

It is suggested that any new aerodynamic devices that may be considered for use be tried under these conditions. However, one note of caution is required. Tests run at high speed, say 100 mph and greater, should not be attempted until it is established that the vehicle has sufficient aerodynamic stability to be safe at the higher speeds in whatever trim the particular run may be made.

3.2 AERODYNAMIC DRAG

By checking the time with a stepwatch while coasting from a constant test speed between reference points a known distance apart, a comparable coefficient of drag can be deduced. This procedure must be practiced with great care since the results are affected by the slope of the ground and by the prevailing winds, even crosswinds. Furthermore, since an undetermined part of the decelerating force is made up of tire rolling resistance and other mechanical losses, a precise coefficient of drag cannot be easily determined. The important point here is that if done carefully, these tests will provide a measure of the difference in aerodynamic drag between configuration changes.

3.3 TYPICAL TEST RESULTS

Results of one day's testing of the Shadow MK. 3 Can-Am car are presented and discussed here in order to show the usefulness of the testing techniques described above. These tests were performed in February 1972, at the Orange County Raceway, California. The objective this day was to determine the effects of a set of aerodynamic changes to the Shadow at a speed of 120 mph. The basic configuration of the car was:

- The as-designed body; no appendages
- Static design ride height
- A rear mounted wing set at 6-deg angle of attack. End plates but no flap
- No front wing, side fences, spoilers, or add-on devices

The test results are summarized in Table I.

The downforce characteristics of the basic configuration were determined in Run 1. A total downforce of 670 lb was obtained and the car appeared to handle well indicating that for this particular setup there was a good balance of aerodynamic downforce, fore-and-aft. Examining the results of Run 2, it is seen that increasing the rear wing angle of attack from 6 deg to 8 deg decreases the rear downforce by 70 lb. This loss means that the extra 2 deg has caused the wing to stall and this also means an increase in drag. However, if we examine Run 8, we find that by leaving the rear wing at 6 deg and adding a flap to the trailing edge set at 30 deg, stall has been eliminated and an extra 80 lb download is obtained at the rear.

Further analysis of these runs reveals another important characteristic. Changes made to the rear of the car affect the front and vice-versa. This is because when the downforce at one end of the car changes, so does the ride attitude. This attitude change affects the general aerodynamic configuration of the car as a whole. This means that if we want to find out the true effect of each device or configuration change, we should readjust the STATIC ride height in another series of tests before each ride to try and neutralize the attitude change and thus, at speed, get even more accurate readings. The problem of changing ride height can complicate the issue and is perhaps better left alone but not ignored.

No data on drag is presented in Table I. The drag characteristics of the car were checked in another test which was conducted at Riverside Raceway. Due to the comparisons made of each test run configuration in terms of cornering power and the amount of horsepower available, it was decided to ignore the drag figures as being insignificant in terms of overall performance. Coincidentally the configurations that exhibited excessive drag gains were not usually the best regarding all round performance anyhow.

The effect of configuration change on cornering power can only be assessed by trying each one

91

Table I
Summary Of Test Runs at 120 MPH Shadow Mk 3 Can-Am Car

Run No.	Configuration and Changes	Measured Downforce, lb			Remarks
		Front	Rear	Total	
1	Basic[*]	150	520	670	Car is stable. Ride attitude good.
2	Increase rear wing angle of attack from 6 to 8 deg	150	450	600	Car shows increase in drag as well as loss in downforce at rear. Rear wing stalled.
3	Rear wing returned to 6 deg. Front dams added. 4-in. high fitted full length front fender downslope. 2-in. from edge and parallel to vehicle centerline.	230	500	730	Car shows no noticeable change in stability from Run 1. Drag same as Run 1.
4	Same as Run 3. Side fences added to body from apex of front fender to apex of rear.	240	480	720	Side fences seem to change lift characteristics of rear wing. Possible mild stall or change in inflow angle.
5	Same as Run 4. Rear wing angle of attack lowered to 4 deg.	260	460	720	Rear lost 20 lb; front gained 20 lb. Caused by change in car attitude at 120 mph.
6	Rear wing back to 6 deg. Front wing mounted between front fenders and ahead of wheel. Set at 6 deg.	275	470	745	The front wing is increasing the front downforce but also affecting the rear adversely.
7	Increase front wing angle to 10 deg.	300	470	770	Drag increase noted. Steering seems to be heavy.
8	Front wing removed. 3-1/2 in. flap added to rear wing trailing edge. Set at 30 deg to wing chord.	180	600	780	Drag slightly greater than Run 3. Steering easier. Stability good. If anything, front seems light to driver.

[*]Basic Configuration:

- As-designed body; no appendages
- Static design ride height
- Rear-mounted wing set at 6 deg angle of attack. End plates but no flap.
- No front wing, side fences, spoilers, or add-on devices.

around a suitable corner, i.e., turn 9 at Riverside Raceway. Turn 9 can be taken at approximately 120 mph and it is easy to get comparative times between its entry point and exit point. Good analysis of all test results is important and one must be very careful and thorough to ensure that maximum benefit is obtained. Driver comments and "feel" regarding stability must also be analyzed carefully. These comments can be very useful regarding new directions to be taken.

Various other combinations of the 8 test runs made can be tried and it can be easily deduced that almost any desired effect front or rear or both can be obtained but it is still the downforce-to-cornering power ratio that will be the deciding factor for all. Incidentally, the configuration used at the first race at Mosport, Canada in 1972 was that used in Run 8 but with the front wing on at 10 deg. Total downforce at 120 mph was in excess of 900 lb. The car equalled the lap record in testing and qualifying and retired in the race with a broken transmission.

4. TUNING THE DOWNFORCE TO THE TRACK

By comparing the various downforce readings with the corresponding drag readings, a fair idea of the most efficient direction to take is found with the various devices. However, this does not necessarily mean that one should discard an otherwise promising configuration because it has high drag. To establish the true value of a particular configuration, it is necessary to evaluate it in the context of the race course on which it will be running.

A simple and effective method of evaluating the various courses is to rank them from fast to slow. This can be done by comparing average speeds per lap for our class of car. For example, Laguna Seca Raceway in California is 1.9 miles around and Can-Am cars can negotiate it in around 60 seconds. Thus, the average speed for one lap is approximately 114 mph. The top speed attained is about 165 mph and the lowest around Turn 9 is about 35 mph. Conversely, the Can-Am track at Riverside, California is 3 miles around. The top speed on the long straight is close to 195 to 200 mph and the slowest corner is about 65 mph. The average speed for a Can-Am car is around 125 to 135 mph so Laguna Seca can be put on file as a "slow circuit" and Riverside as "fast."

It can be deduced that as the cars are geared to utilize the available horsepower at each track, our car may not reach its 'terminal velocity' for the horsepower available at Laguna Seca. This is simply because there is not enough straight road. Here is a chance to use some of that total horsepower to overcome the extra drag we have if we change our aerodynamics to increase the downforce, and thus the lateral cornering force. Of course, we can only do this properly, if we know what we have and what is available. That is where we reap the benefits of the previous tests.

The next phase in development is simply the process of checking out the lateral cornering forces generated by various aerodynamic configurations, the relative merits of which have already been assessed. This can be done by recording the times through a given corner, and comparing one with another, thus deducing which combination best increases the cornering force generated. During these tests, attempts should be made to keep the prepared state of the vehicle constant, so as not to confuse the data by introducing other variables. For example, variables such as full tanks of gas at the start and empty at the end should be avoided.

5. SUSPENSION SYSTEM AND HANDLING CHANGES

It is apparent that, at speed, what is happening to the car with wings mounted on the sprung mass is a different proposition from the early designs which had their wings mounted to the hub components of the wheels. Direct readings from track tests show increases in the vertical axis of the front and rear suspensions of as much as 0.75 "g" or better. Downforce in excess of 600 lb at the rear and 250 lb at the front is easily attained. Such loads have actually been measured in tests of the Ti 22 car. For a vehicle weighing 1700 lb gross, aerodynamic downforce of this magnitude is a substantial increase and means, of course, that if the car is to maintain a fairly constant ride height through all ranges of speeds, then changes to the ride system must be made.

In order to meet this problem, the use of progressive rate springs is now fairly common and in some instances progressive rate geometry is used for the suspension spring mountings. On the subject of springs, it would seem that a new factor has also crept in to confuse the issue. The downforce is now using up the available spring travel. In cornering, the suspension is bottoming out and as the spring rate goes to infinity the car now rolls about the tire contact patch, and therefore rolls more. Because of this, the roll stiffness has almost doubled on contemporary cars, this being another good reason to use stiffer springing.

Along with lower roll angles, it is necessary to revise the geometry to produce less camber-change at the wheels. A bi-product of this geometry change is a change in the static roll center height. To explain: in most racing cars using independent suspension, unequal length 'A' arms are often used. In this practice, it is usually found that when the camber change of the wheel is quantitatively lessened, then the roll center also is lowered relative to the center of gravity. This causes a higher rolling moment to be generated during cornering, but because we have already increased the roll stiffness this does not seem to affect the cornering performance, and, in fact, may help on slow corners where the extra weight transfer caused by this moment is needed to increase the traction on the outside cornering wheels.

In summing up, the most significant changes made to the chassis because of aerodynamic developments are seen to be in three main areas. First, it has become necessary to increase the capacity of the suspension to accept the extra loads. Second, the roll stiffness has been increased and the total amount of camber change to the wheel reduced. Third, the philosophy regarding suspension geometry and vehicle dynamics has been totally revised.

6. GENERAL COMMENTS ON CHASSIS TUNING

There are various philosophies regarding the best approach to testing and chassis tuning. Most agree that instrumentation of the vehicle, wind tunnel testing, etc., are all valid methods to arrive at a good compromise for performance at any track. The word compromise is used because of the difficulty in getting all the desired features of handling and aerodynamics to work as one. For instance, if the car goes around a certain fast corner well, it may lose something in a slow corner and vice-versa.

The hardest problem facing a racing team at any track is in analyzing the performance of the car and driver to decide how it can best be improved. The key to this is usually in the ability (or lack of it) of the driver to communicate symptoms of handling and performance to his crew chief or engineer. If the engineer has doubts in his mind regarding the drivers' comments, he can take steps to find out what is happening by various methods: (a) He can go out on the track and observe what is happening to the car; (b) he can make a change to the car to see if the driver can detect and analyze correctly; or (c) he can try and remedy the situation by trial and error.

All these actions and more can be taken without danger if the problem area does not concern aerodynamics or radical changes to the basic chassis configuration. The biggest problem seems to be when to start making aerodynamic changes to a chassis that perhaps performs well at a different track in different conditions than those present. To make this decision easier, a few basic steps can be taken beforehand. For instance, the engineer and the driver should go around the track together and examine its peculiarities. Does it have any sharp inclines? How bumpy is it, and is it in good condition? Are there any areas where strong side drafts could affect the handling, etc.? Simple problems such as these should be taken into consideration before testing begins. By coupling the answers to these questions with the fast track-slow track evaluation made earlier, it should not be difficult to arrive at the best basic aerodynamic configuration for any track and the engineer should strive to stay within his acquired test data to insure a successful test and race.

7. REFLECTIONS ON SEVERAL CAN-AM PROJECTS

I have tried two basic configurations in cars of my own design, and would like at this juncture to make brief comment on them. The first car called the Autocoast Ti 22, shown in Figure 6, was designed in 1969, just as the rules were

Figure 6. The Autocoast Ti 22 Can-Am Car
With Rear Deck Mounted Spoiler

Figure 7. The Low Profile MK II Shadow Can-Am Car.

being changed regarding wings, etc. The car
raced in four Can-Am races in 1970, and finished
second in three of them, so I think in all modesty
that it was fairly successful. As can be seen from
Figure 6, I tried a new approach with the body
shape. I maintained a wedge type profile from
front to back, and then put "air fences" running the
entire sides of the car, the idea being to prevent
the air from spilling over the sides, and thus increasing the downforce. Incidentally, had I not
put these fences on the car, it would have been
illegal in terms of door requirements.

The car was raced first without a wing, but with a
rear spoiler added (see Figure 3). In its second
race in 1969, I added a wing to the rear which was
mounted directly to the hub component, as in
Installation (a) of Figure 4. This was the configuration that worked best for both handling and
speed. When the new rules came into effect in
1970, before going to the first race we tested all
the devices shown in Figure 3. The airfoil, under
the new rules, had to be lowered until it was
31-1/2 inches from the underpan. In this position,
it was so close to the rear body covering that it
would not work. The air flowing over the body itself would not pass around the airfoil in the prescribed manner. We concluded that the height
between the airfoil and the body (11 inches to be
specific) was insufficient to allow the airfoil to
work as it had done higher up in clean air. Also,

we had to mount it on the sprung mass. The wing
was removed and a rear spoiler replaced it.
Later, we added the side fences, fins, and nose
scoop. All these devices gave more downforce
and brought the car to peak handling performance.
But they did seem to affect the terminal velocity
more than the high mounted airfoil, so I concluded that perhaps a better approach would be to
design a car with a very low profile. This would
then allow a relatively better position for the rear
airfoil to perform in. The Ti 22 Mk I was destroyed after it flipped over backward while peak-
ing a hill in St. Jovite, Canada, in 1970.

In 1971, working for Advanced Vehicles Systems,
I designed a low profile car called the Mark II
Shadow (Figure 7). The Shadow had 12-inch diameter front and 15-inch diameter rear wheels.
Consequently, it presented a fairly low wedge-
shaped profile to the air. The rear airfoil was
mounted behind the centerline of the rear wheels
on the back of the transmission. By giving the
body a down-slope from the apex of the rear
wheel arch to the back tip, I managed to make the
rear airfoil work quite well. The car was fast on
the straights, but due to problems of trying to
develop the experimental tires for this configuration, no conclusions could really be made regarding its handling. Since then, this size of tire has
been developed more, and I feel that this concept
could be made to work best of all.

8. SUMMARY AND CONCLUDING REMARKS

The use of "ground effect" to increase cornering power of racing cars is still largely a factor of the available horsepower. A car that is limited in engine size or by formula or rules to a certain range of power cannot obviously ignore the drag factor and use all its power to go around corners. A line has to be drawn somewhere; where to draw the downforce line is a question that will now have to be answered by Can-Am car designers as well as the others. The reason? The rules. For 1975 and on, all Can-Am cars are limited to two basic sizes: 5-litre stock-block or 3-litre racing. The available horsepower will no longer be un-limited and it will take some time and perhaps too much money to build engines with more than 600 hp. Compare this figure to the 900-1200 hp of the turbocharged cars of 1973, and it is immediately apparent that the '73 cars had horsepower to "play with." A similar picture is drawn for Fomula 5000 and Indianapolis.

The answer to this problem may still be found in ground effects. How? A hard question to answer at this time, but if a re-examination of the defini-tion of "ground effefts" is made along with a close scrutiny of the rules, a loophole can no doubt be found. Perhaps the aircraft industry will point the way and obviously every angle has not been explored. Regarding the use of aerodynamic de-vices to increase negative lift, regardless of the solution, the aerodynamic qualities relative to the cornering power of the car will still be worth evaluating and the methods outlined in this paper will still be valid.

By examining the test results contained in this paper, it is obvious that it is impossible to just add devices, wings, etc., to any car and run it without proper testing. The very fact that an in-crease of only 2 deg on a wing will cause it to stall and lose its effect is easily apparent, but every competitor and car owner is not always able to secure testing facilities easily. Neither are they all able to afford the expense. The only ap-proach open to many is to make whatever changes are possible and run them against the stop watch at an actual race practice. Although this proce-dure can be time consuming at a race and even dangerous, it also is valid if it works. If most competitors would use the services of a qualified consultant before they use their not quite adequate funds to develop new ideas, they could save money in the long run and in most instances come out ahead both in terms of performance and economy. Many knowledgeable people are available at a reasonable fee and despite rumors to the contrary some people can even keep secrets.

DEDICATION

I respectfully dedicate this article to the memory of the late Peter Revson, whose car I prepared for the 1967 Can-Am series, and whose inspired driving made him Can-Am champion of 1971.

DISCUSSION

PAUL LAMAR: How much total downforce did you get on the Shadow?

BRYANT: The height recorder was unavailable to us until rather late in the game by which time we had made a number of changes and moved the wing around. I do know that the wing was gener-ating much more downforce than the one mounted low on the TI 22. It may have worked better be-cause the body was lower, but I think, more im-portant, it was in clean air. In the later Shadow, I vented the rear fenders at the top of the hump and the air coming out was helping the flow under-neath the wing making it work better. It's quite possible that had I vented the fenders on the TI 22 its low wing may have worked much better.

HENRY JEX: Have you measured the drag of these cars with all their download-generating devices?

BRYANT: We did not get a good measure of the all-up vehicle coefficient of drag. We were mainly interested in a comparative measure of the drag coefficient of each of the devices we were testing. It's not necessary to know to the nearest pound what the download or the drag of a given device is, but rather how much a given aerodynamic change improves or degrades the downforce and drag. In our testing procedures, we got a comparative reading of the drag of each aerodynamic change by timing a coast-down with a stop watch. But even then, the drag didn't really mean that much to us since we were ultimately interested in going around a corner faster than we could before. Since there are more corners on road racing circuits than there are straights, we could lower lap times by improving the cornering even though it meant more drag. The Chaparral proved that. A Lotus 23 could go down the straights faster than the Chaparral 2J, but there was no way it could stay with the 2J in the corners.

LAMAR: Can-Am cars still have a lot of acceleration capability at the end of the straightaway. Drag is near the bottom of the priority list. If you have to increase the weight of the body by 50 pounds to reduce the drag, it's a bad trade-off.

WAKE PROPERTIES OF TYPICAL ROAD VEHICLES

J. P. Howell
Department of Aeronautics,*
The City University
London.

Abstract

A considerable degree of driving discomfort can be experienced when driving a vehicle in the wake of others. This is especially true in either wet or dusty conditions when both forward and rearward vision becomes obscured. This report investigates the wake properties of various vehicle types, principally a saloon car, from a series of wind tunnel tests. Longitudinal and transverse velocity distributions derived from pressure measurements are shown for various downstream positions in the wake. Hot-wire anemometer measurements are used to map the shape of the base flow recirculation bubble for a variety of typical rear end designs; to show the distribution of mean velocity and turbulence intensity in the wake, and the deformation and decay of the trailing vortex sheet. Periodic effects arising from instabilities of the separated shear layer are investigated and a yawed flow is shown to have an influence on the wake.

NOMENCLATURE

B	= vehicle width		$P_1 P_2$	= pressures in two hole probe
C_L	= lift coefficient (based on frontal area)		P	= total head pressure
e	= r.m.s. voltage		R_e	= reynolds number
e_w	= turbulent energy within bandwidth		S	= static pressure
w	= bandwidth/tuned frequency		u, v, w	= r.m.s. velocity in X, Y, Z direction
E	= d.c. voltage		U, V, W	= mean velocity in X, Y, Z direction
f	= frequency		x	= distance from ground board leading edge
H	= vehicle height		β	= yaw angle
k	= constant		δ^*	= boundary later displacement thickness
$n\Phi(n) = \left(\dfrac{e_w}{\frac{e}{w}}\right)^2$			ρ	= density
			ψ	= flow angularity
			∞	= free stream

* Now Research Fellow, Magnetic Levitation Project, Department of Engineering, University of Warwick, Coventry, England.

1. INTRODUCTION

A wake flow is generated because in a real fluid shear stresses arise. This gives rise to drag forces which do not occur in an inviscid flow, while a number of the unpleasant features of modern driving are also directly attributable to the effects of the wake. A fastback car with a poorly designed rear window slope will suffer fluctuations in rear wheel lift caused by a shifting of the flow separation point under varying external flow conditions. Rearward visibility on estate cars becomes restricted[1] when dust or water particles thrown up from the road by the tyres enter the recirculation bubble flow and settle on the rear screen. For similar reasons rear lights on any vehicle become obscured by mud[2], and exhaust gases can enter the vehicle if the exhaust pipe is incorrectly sited[3]. The process of turbulent mixing ensures that the wake region is rapidly filled by any particles of dust, water or smoke entering it. This means that where vehicles are travelling fairly close together on very dry or wet surfaces the forward visibility of the downstream car is impaired. This can be serious when the upstream vehicle is large and travelling at high speed as occurs with lorries or coaches on motorways. Water droplets thrown up by the front tyres cause the most disturbance by breaking down on hitting the bodywork immediately aft of the wheels, the atomised droplets then filling the separated region that usually exists around the front end of these vehicles, restricting forward visibility well into the adjacent lane. Efforts to reduce this particular problem have achieved little success[4].

Racing cars with their large exposed tyres suffer accutely from this problem, among others, when wet track conditions prevail. Even when normal conditions occur, however, the closeness of the cars combined with high speed, and a large vertical flow component in the wake can cause severe handling difficulties. In Can-Am racing three experienced drivers have had their cars turn completely over when travelling close behind another. Interference effects occurring between road vehicles are generally less noticeable because speeds are lower and separation distances greater but certain types of lorry can produce discomforting handling effects on a car travelling just downstream of the recirculation bubble where high turbulence levels would be expected. Lateral force and moment interference between a large and small vehicle in general constitutes a more noticeable effect[5]. A reduction in drag force when travelling within the wake is probably the only gain experienced[6,5,2]. Racing drivers perform the slipstreaming manoeuver when overtaking by utilising the low drag region behind the car to be overtaken for accelerating alongside where the greater momentum carries the car through the high drag region experienced when two vehicles are side by side to complete the procedure. Alternatively the following car can conserve fuel by maintaining station in the low drag region where less power is required to travel at a given speed, effectively reducing the strain on the engine. Some long distance lorry drivers are believed to travel dangerously close together on motorways in order to realise a similar gain in fuel consumption.

As all the problems cited above arise directly from the effects of the wake it was felt that further information on wake properties would be desirable. A series of wind tunnel tests was therefore devised. Measurements were taken within the wakes of various typical road vehicles. Previous work on road vehicle wakes has included flow visualisation studies of exhaust smoke patterns[3] and by tuft grid[7], while different rotating vane devices have been used for quantitative wake surveys at both full scale[8,9] and in the wind tunnel[7].

2. EXPERIMENTS

2.1 MODELS

The models tested are shown in Fig. 1. The results given in this paper predominantly refer to the saloon car model but investigations were also

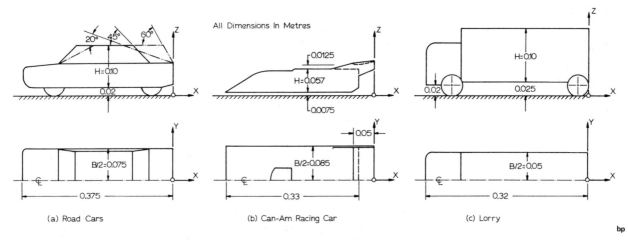

All Dimensions In Metres

(a) Road Cars (b) Can-Am Racing Car (c) Lorry

bp

Figure 1. General Arrangement of Models Utilized in the Wind Tunnel Test Program.

made of estate and fastback types while variations in boot length were possible on the saloon. A removable upperbody section facilitated these changes in the side profile. Roughness elements were attached to the underside to simulate various underbody component. Transition strips were fitted to the vehicle nose. The Can-Am type racing car was used to represent the extreme negative lift machine while the lorry represents a virtually zero lift case. All the models are approximately 1/10th scale for typical European vehicles except for the lorry which is approximately 1/20th scale. The origin of the axis system is located as shown where the ground plane intersects both the vehicle plane of symmetry and the vertical plane through the trailing edge. The X-axis is positive in the free stream direction. This axis system has been applied for all conditions of yaw.

2.2 WIND TUNNEL

The wind tunnel used for these experiments was The City University T.3. low speed tunnel which has an octagonal working section 1.14 m wide by 0.93 m high and 1.53 m long. Ground simulation was provided by a full span full length fixed ground board mounted 0.2 m above the tunnel floor which gave a working section above the board of 0.75 m^2. Circulation control was provided by a short span flap mounted centrally on the undersurface of the ground board at model

position, as shown in Fig. 2. Zero circulation was obtained by rotating the flap until the pressures from tappings situated in the upper and lower ground board surface just aft of the leading edge were balanced. Over the region occupied by the model and its wake, measurements in the empty tunnel with ground plane only fitted showed that the mean velocity variation was better than 1% with flow angularity less than ± 05°. Turbulence intensity at the model position was 0.6%. Boundary layer measurements along the ground plane centre line showed that the displacement thickness, δ* was given by the expression

$$\delta^* = 0.048 \text{ x } Re_x^{-1/5} \qquad (1)$$

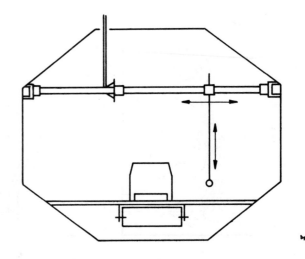

Figure 2. Front View of the Wind Tunnel Working Section.

101

where x is the distance downstream of the ground board leading edge and Re_x is the Reynolds number based on the distance x. At mid length the displacement thickness was 0.002 m. The only situation where the use of a fixed ground plane would cause serious error in the results is the Can-Am model case where the very small ground clearance produces an unrepresentative separation on the ground plane immediately aft of the model. The influence of this on the vortex flow here considered would however be limited.

2.3 TEST EQUIPMENT

A traverse gear was built to carry either a pitot rake, a two hole yaw probe, or a hot wire anemometer. Other instruments were used[10] but they are not relevant to this paper. Traverses were possible in the vertical and lateral directions while the longitudinal station was set by clamping the traverse gear to slide rails running the length of the working section. The pitot rake was used to measure total head pressure values through the wake while yaw angles were obtained by comparing the readings from a two hole yaw probe with the total head values. Mean and turbulence velocity measurements were taken using a DISA constant temperature hot wire anemometer, which

was temperature compensated, and linearised. The probe wire for all these experiments was mounted normal to the free stream direction and parallel to the ground. For measurements of periodic phenomena the hot wire signal was fed to a frequency analyser with a one third octave and narrow band facility.

2.4 TEST PROCEDURE

The models were mounted with 0.001 m clearance between wheels and ground surface as used for force measurements. All runs were performed at a nominal 30 m/s which gave a Reynolds number based on model length of approximately 0.85×10^6 for all models. The pitot rake which included a static tube, was traversed vertically across the wake in a number of downstream locations. This established the principal features of the wake. Horizontal and vertical traverses were then made through the positions of minimum total head, using the yaw probe and the hot wire anemometer. Vertical traverses were made through the wake centre line at all these downstream stations and also immediately aft of the model base to determine the extent of the recirculation bubble. A sample of the results taken are reproduced here.

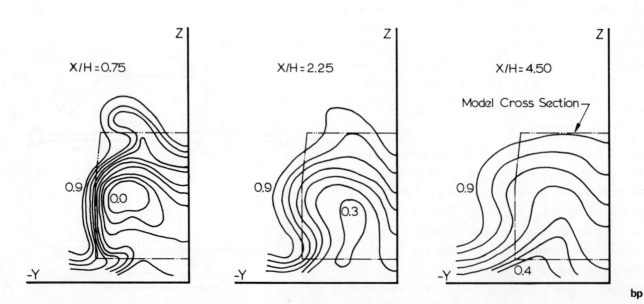

Figure 3. Contours of $[P-S]/[P_0-S]$ for the Saloon Car Model.

3. EXPERIMENTAL RESULTS

3.1 SALOON CAR WAKE

Contours of total head at several downstream stations were derived from a series of pitot pressure traverses. A typical result is shown in Fig. 3. The contours plotted are for equal values of $(P-S)/(P_O-S)$ where P is the local pitot pressure, S the static pressure outside of the wake, and P_O is the reference total head. In a turbulent flow the reading of a pitot probe is given by[11]

$$P = S + \tfrac{1}{2}\rho\left[(U^2 + V^2 + W^2)f(V, W) + (u^2 + v^2 + w^2)\right] \quad (2)$$

where U, V, W are the mean velocities in the X, Y, Z directions and u, v, w are the corresponding turbulence velocities. Where the transverse velocities are less than 0.3 U, f(V, W) can be taken as unity. The contour values are therefore approximations to $(U/U_\infty)^2$. For all the contour plots in this paper only the inner and the outer contour are given values to avoid confusion. The intermediate contours represent equal valued steps. Comparison of the three contours shows that there is a noticeable decay of the maximum total head deficit while the vortex flow rapidly loses its identity. Most saloon cars do not have a very high lift coefficient; for this model $C_L = 0.17$. At the station nearest the vehicle base a second pair of longitudinal vortices is noticeable above the main pair. This weaker vortex results from the rolling up of the vortex sheet separating at the roof.

The yaw probe was traversed vertically and horizontally through the total head minimum position to record both pitch and yaw. Provided that flow angles are less than about 15° flow angularity, ψ, is given by[11]

$$\psi = k(p_1 - p_2)/(P - S) \quad (3)$$

where p_1, p_2 are the pressures at each of the yaw probe holes, and k is a constant of calibra-

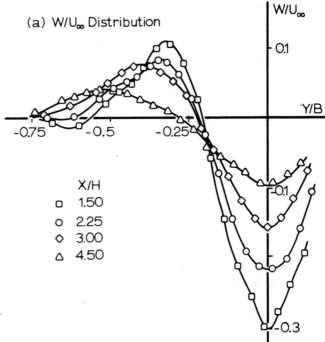

(a) W/U_∞ Distribution

X/H	
□	1.50
○	2.25
◇	3.00
△	4.50

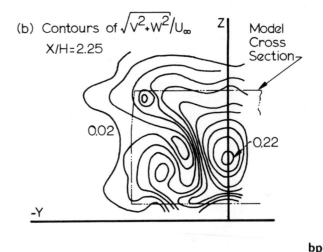

(b) Contours of $\sqrt{V^2 + W^2}/U_\infty$
X/H = 2.25

Model Cross Section

bp

Figure 4. Velocity Distributions - Saloon Car Model.

tion. The effects of turbulence are negligible but a shear flow can introduce problems. For this reason a two hole probe was used as it was the smallest practical instrument available. Fig. 4(a) shows the results of horizontally traversing the probe, on this occasion to measure pitch at a number of downstream positions. It is evident that a strong downwash exists at the wake centre typical of a vortex pair. If the zero downwash position is taken as the centre of the vortex, ignoring the fact that one vortex system superimposes a flow on the other, the vortex centre moves outward and downward as it travels downstream, which is the expected motion of a vortex pair near to ground. At X/H = 2.25 a contour plot was made of $\sqrt{V^2 + W^2}/U_\infty$. From this contour it is evident that the vortex centre is given by the total head contour. The flow field tends to be symmetrical about a line through the origin and the vortex centre. The drastic changes in circumferential velocity around any given circular contour implies that a rotating vane device for measuring vorticity must have a diameter at least an order of magnitude less than the distance between any pair of vortex centres.

Traverses with the hot wire anemometer were similarly performed and Fig. 5 shows variation in turbulence intensity from vertical and horizontal traverses through the vortex core. A hot wire anemometer essentially measures the flow components normal to the wire so for this experiment the value e/E_∞ plotted, where e is the r.m.s. signal voltage and E_∞ is the D.C. signal outside the wake represents $\sqrt{u^2 + w^2}/U_\infty$. The presence of the vortex sheet is clearly shown by the turbulence intensity peak. The vortex sheet disappears into a virtually uniform turbulent flow by the time it reaches the furthest downstream position measured. The sheet initially moves downstream with a velocity of 0.6 U_∞.

Comparison between vertical and horizontal traverses also shows that the separated shear layer barely rolls up at all and merely becomes distorted downwards at the centre line as shown by a contour plot of e/E_∞ at X/H = 2.25, Fig. 6. The comparatively low energy flow arising from the vehicle underside produces a weak vortex sheet. It is interesting to note that the vortex

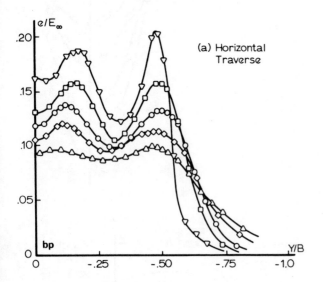

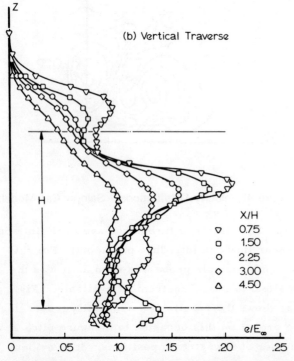

Figure 5. Turbulence Profiles - Saloon Car Model.

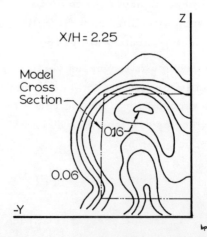

Figure 6. Contours of e/E_∞ - Saloon Car Model.

104

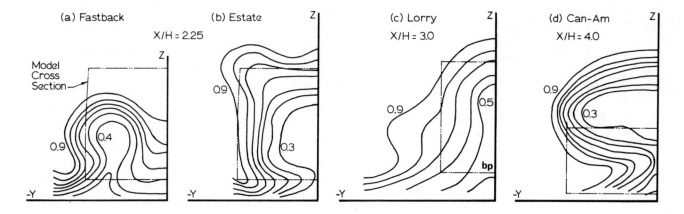

Figure 7. Contours of [P-S]/[P$_0$-S] for the Fastback, Estate, Lorry, and Can-Am Models.

lattice method, due to Stafford[12] for calculating the flow around motor vehicles assumes, for simplicity, that the wake consists of a semi-infinite cylinder of streamwise trailing vortex filaments emanating from the edges of a well defined base. This assumption is seen to be valid.

3.2 WAKES OF OTHER VEHICLES

Wake studies were similarly performed for a number of other vehicles. For brevity only a single total head contour at a stated downstream distance is given for each model, Fig. 7. The trailing vortex sheet of the fastback ($C_L = 0.31$) distorts considerably more than the saloon shape to give a flow containing a more distinct vortex pair. The estate car ($C_L = -0.1$) displays very little distortion from the rectangular shape which is expected for a vehicle with nearly zero lift. The lorry shape ($C_L = 0$) similarly has very little distortion but in this case the sharp longitudinal edges give rise to distortions in the vortex sheet which induce longitudinal vortices in the wake that produce the result shown. The effect of the lower energy underbody flow is apparent for this case, the sharp lower leading edge being partly responsible.

The Can-Am shape ($C_L = -0.7$) typifies the extreme negative lift racing vehicle. Open wheeled racing cars would probably have a fairly similar wake configuration for the same lift because they are similarly bluff vehicles. High vertical velocities occur in the wake and the whole vortex system moves fairly rapidly upwards. Results have shown that an upwash angle in excess of 20° persists even at a vehicle length downstream.

3.3 RECIRCULATION BUBBLE

A series of vertical traverses was made with the hot wire anemometer on the wake centre line immediately downstream of the base to measure e/E_∞, Fig. 8(a). The mean flow variation E/E_∞, Fig. 8(b) by a similar argument to that given in 3.1, will measure in this case $\sqrt{U^2 + W^2}/U_\infty$. Fig. 8(a) shows that initially the vortex sheet arising from the roof is more pronounced than that from the boot, because the latter is immersed in the turbulent field of the former, but as the flow moves downstream this situation is reversed, while the underbody vortex sheet is the weakest of the three. It is also noticeable that the lower sheet moves parallel to the ground while the upper sheet curves downwards.

A hot wire is unfortunately unable to provide information regarding the direction of a flow so the contours of the recirculation bubble rely on interpretation of the data obtained. At the boundary of the recirculation region the flow velocity becomes zero so theoretically the ratio e/E becomes infinitely large. In practice the D/C values are always finite while the local turbulence levels reduce so a local e/E maximum is taken as the limit

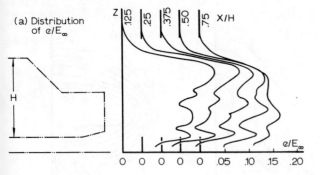

(a) Distribution of e/E_∞

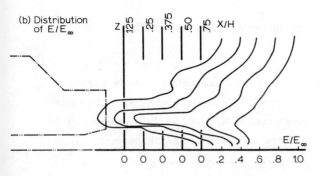

(b) Distribution of E/E_∞

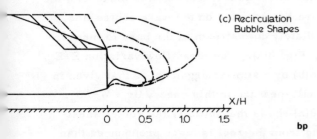

(c) Recirculation Bubble Shapes

bp

Figure 8. Wake Turbulence Characteristics and Recirculation Bubble Shapes.

boot dominates the flow. The process whereby mud gets onto rear surfaces can be readily seen. Particles thrown up by the tyres are entrained by the lower shear layer. On separating from the rear of the body some of those particles will travel downstream in the wake while others will cross the shear layer to the reverse flow region where they will be transported to any part of the surface enclosed by the separated shear layer, and deposited. When the length of the boot is reduced sufficiently the flow separating from the roof cannot reattach to the upper surface of the boot so that the flow over the entire rearward facing surfaces is enclosed by the same recirculation bubble. From Fig. 8(c) it would seem that for the particular rear window slopes and height of roof above the boot adopted, the limiting case, where flow reattachment fails to take place on the boot, is given by a boot length approximately equal to the height of the roof above the boot. Any design which has a boot length less than the limiting case would therefore tend to suffer from an obscured rearward vision in wet or dusty driving conditions. The estate car has a symmetrical bubble which extends rearwards a distance 20% greater than the vehicle height. The fastback shape has a bubble which is virtually identical in shape to the saloon shape although the upper vortex sheet tends to leave the base tangential to the rear body slope.

For all models a forward velocity as high as 35% of the free stream velocity was recorded just forward of the bubble closure. Immediately aft of the bubble closure the turbulence intensity based on local velocity reaches a peak of 55%, while based on free stream velocity a peak of 35% is reached. At these intensities the hot wire results are subject to errors as analysed but the length of the bubble may be taken as accurate, as can the width where the flow is nearly parallel. A feature of separated flow is that they are independent of Reynolds number and this was verified with the saloon car model for an increase in Reynolds number of 50%.

of the reverse flow bubble. In addition inspection of the turbulence intensity distribution for the case $X/H = 0.125$ reveals that in the lower half two distinct turbulence intensity minima appear which typically occur at the bubble boundary[13]. The bubble is drawn in Fig. 8(c) for the saloon car previously considered and a selection of other typical rear end designs. Considering this saloon case first it is obvious that the bubble shape arises from an asymmetric separation of the shear layers. As the bias is towards the lower side of the vehicle it can be assumed that the recirculating flow arising from the upper edge of the

3.4 PERIODIC PHENOMENA

Periodic effects arise from distortions of the vortex sheet. In the case of two dimensional flows the resulting Karman vortex sheet dominates the wake and is of primary importance. It can for instance cause severe oscillations in chimney stacks or bridge structures. With three dimensional bodies, however, the periodicity is less marked but it can still be detected[13]. Fig. 9 shows a typical spectrum from the signal of a hot wire placed just outside the vortex sheet of the saloon car model. The function $n\phi(n)$ is a measure of the turbulent energy contained with a given frequency bandwidth. Similar spectra can be obtained throughout the wake downstream of the recirculation bubble but the peak frequency and number of peaks will vary according to local dimensions of the vortex sheet. The estate car produces a sharper peak indicating that a more highly periodic wake exists. This is because its lift is more nearly zero. A vehicle wake at normal road speeds would exhibit frequencies of between 1 - 2 Hz. It is not likely that any oscillatory forces will arise either on the generating vehicle or on a vehicle submerged in its wake, but the author feels that an acoustic effect could result.

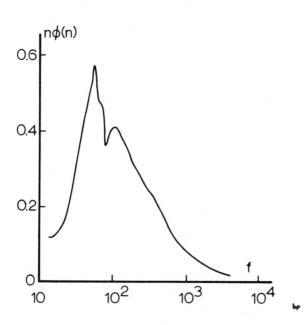

Figure 9. Frequency Spectrum - Saloon Car Model.

In the case of a large bluff body such as a lorry it is quite possible that these periodic effects could have an upsetting influence on a small car's handling. The author has noted that behind some lorries particularly the unloaded, open top type, there is a point in the wake where a following small car suffers a disturbance which is in no way dangerous but is sufficient to cause momentary discomfort.

3.5 THE INFLUENCE OF YAW

A typical feature of a motor vehicle at yaw is the very sharp rise in lift force. Total head contours have been plotted at various downstream positions in the wake at 5°, 10°, 15° of yaw. Fig. 10 shows the result for the saloon car at $X/H = 3.0$. It is apparent that the flow becomes increasingly defined by two distinct vortices of equal rotation. The windward vortex results as before but the leeward vortex arises from the cross flow over the roof of the car. The vortex which at zero yaw arises from the leeward side of the yawed vehicle rapidly loses its identity with increasing yaw.

4. DISCUSSION

A number of solutions to the problems posed in the introduction have been tried with varying degrees of success. It is hoped that an understanding of the wake structure may enable further solutions to be made or help to explain why some of the existing ones work. In the case of the fastback car the addition of a spoiler[14] at the rear fixes the separation point forward of the spoiler. This increases the pressure immediately in front of the spoiler, allows predictability with respect to steering, and may reduce the drag. Deposits on rear windows are supposed to be prevented by using a slot arrangement similar to a Townend ring, which adorned many radial engined fighters, in reverse[1,2]. High energy is directed into the base region but care must be taken to avoid flow separation on the flap itself otherwise the advantages will be negligible. Daimler-Benz claim to have solved the problem of dirt deposits on rear lights by a ridged surface[2] which again induces high energy

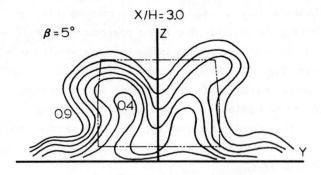

X/H = 3.0

$\beta = 5°$

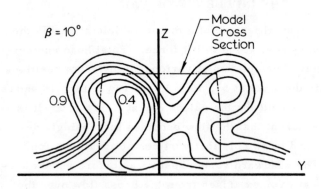

$\beta = 10°$

Model Cross Section

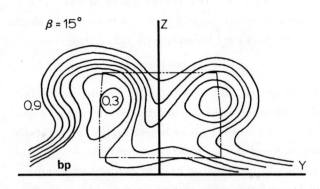

$\beta = 15°$

Figure 10. Effects of Yaw. Contours of [P-S]/[P₀-S] - Saloon Car Model.

air into the edges of the base region. Attempts to solve the spray problem from lorries has achieved little success[4], although a number of ingenious attempts have been made. To improve the handling of racing saloon cars; and to a limited extent road going sports cars, lower leading edge mounted spoiler have recently appeared. When originally fitted these had the effect of lowering the front stagnation point so that the effective incidence of the car was lowered, (increasing the camber however) reducing lift at the front wheels. More recently still the spoilers have grown so that they nearly touch

the ground. The car becomes virtually insensitive to small pitch changes so that when the car is travelling in anothers' wake the handling remains consistent.

5. CONCLUSIONS

Wake measurements of which a sample have been presented here show that the wake does not consist of an isolated vortex pair as for an aircraft but merely a distorted vortex sheet which rapidly becomes a nearly uniform turbulent flow with small swirl. Fairly large transverse velocities can appear close to the vehicle.

The recirculation bubble must always exist but thoughtful design of the vehicle rear end should prevent deposits from forming on rear windows. Partial cures for deposits on rear lights, etc. exist. Periodic effects are of secondary importance. The effect of yaw is to alter the shape of the wake so that it becomes dominated by a pair of vortices rotating in the same direction.

REFERENCES

(1) Dawley, M.W., "Aerodynamic Effects on Automotive Components," SAE Paper, Int. Automotive Engn. Cong., Jan. 11-15, 1965

(2) Goetz, H., "The Influence of Wind Tunnel Tests on Body Design, Ventilation, and Surface Deposits of Sedans & Sports Cars," SAE 710212, 1971

(3) Prinham, H.E., & Bowman, W.D., "Exhaust Flow Pattern Study in a Wind Tunnel," SAE 730236, 1973

(4) Sherard, T.D., "Suppression of Vehicle Splash and Spray," SAE 730718, 1973

(5) Howell, J.P., "The Influence of the Proximity of a Large Vehicle on the Aerodynamic Characteristics of a Typical Car," Advances in Road Vehicle Aerodynamics, Published by B.H.R.A. Fluid Engineering, Bedford, England, 1973

(6) Romberg, G. F., Chianese, Jr. F., & Lajoie, R. G., "Aerodynamics of Race Cars in Drafting and Passing Situations," SAE 710213, 1971

(7) Pothoff, J., "Luftwiderstand und Auftrieb Moderner Kraftfahrzeuge," Road Vehicle Aerodynamics, Published by The City University, London, 1969

(8) White, R. G. S., Paish, M. G., "A Study of Aerodynamic Lift," MIRA Report 1966/16

(9) Lind-Walker, G. E., "Car Aerodynamics - Pt. II," Automobile Engineer, July 1958

(10) Howell, J. P., "Wake Characteristics of Simple Bluff Bodies Near to Ground with Application to Road Vehicles," Thesis - in preparation

(11) Bryer, D. W., & Pankhurst, R. C., "Pressure Probe Methods for Determining Wind Speed and Flow Direction," Published by H. M. S. O., London, 1971

(12) Stafford, L. G., "A Numerical Method for the Calculation of the Flow Field Around a Motor Vehicle," Advances in Road Vehicle Aerodynamics, Published by B. H. R. A. Fluid Engineering, Bedford, England, 1973

(13) Calvert, J. R., "Experiments on the Low-Speed Flow Past Cones," Jnl. Fl. Mech. Vol. 27, p. 273

(14) Scibor-Rylski, A. J., "Negative Lift Devices on Racing Cars," Road Vehicle Aerodynamics, Published by The City University, London, 1969

TRAPPED VORTEX FLOW CONTROL FOR AUTOMOBILES

J. J. Cornish III
Chief Engineer, Lockheed-Georgia Company
Marietta, Georgia

Abstract

Recent aerodynamic research has produced a unique method for controlling the air flow over aircraft wings and fuselages. The use of suction or blowing air at discrete locations results in "trapped" vortices which redirect the flow and thus affect the aerodynamic forces on the body. Recent applications of this technique to automobiles are displayed by smoke-flow visualization studies.

1. INTRODUCTION

The fundamental and normal concern of the aircraft industry for minimizing fuel usage has been greatly intensified by the problems imposed on all of us in every aspect of the current energy crisis. Since Lockheed is seeking to inject into the national economy any products of aerospace research that may help to relieve that crisis, we are taking a new and special interest in the field of automotive aerodynamics. In particular, we are carefully sorting out the many things being accomplished in the aircraft business which might be applied to reduce the drag, and therefore the fuel consumption of many ground vehicles.

2. AERODYNAMICS AND THE AUTOMOBILE

2.1 STABILITY AND LIFT EFFECTS

The automobile makers have long been interested in aerodynamics for a number of reasons. The past emphasis has primarily been placed on providing stability and control in side gusts. As the speed of touring and racing cars increased, however, designers became more concerned with lift effects on the automobile. Indeed, the lift problem has been made only too evident in recent years by the distressing tendency for automobiles to do loops during some road races. Certain automobiles, such as the broad and low CAN-AM cars, have topped hills in the face of gusts, kept on sailing, and then half-looped and landed on their backs. The personal risks, not to mention the damage to the professional pride of drivers and owners, are enormous.

Thus, it is obvious that designers want to learn how to counteract the lift on these vehicles, to keep the wheels firmly and continuously on the ground so that all those thousands of horsepower can be applied productively. We have seen all sorts of attempts to hold cars down, including the use of auxiliary power units and powerful fans designed to suck the automobile down snugly to the road.

2.2 ACOUSTICS

The acoustics problem also has been drawing the interest of automotive designers. The interior volume and nature of the air flow in some cars, in cases where a window may be open to a certain degree, forms a powerful Helmholz resonator which creates a low-frequency beating effect that is intolerably uncomfortable to the driver. Exterior airflow can also cause extremely loud hissing and swishing noises, which create interior sound problems similar to those of a light aircraft. So, the automotive industry is very seriously seeking to learn more about the aerodynamic noises which are affecting their products.

2.3 DRAG

Above all, however, aircraft and automotive designers have a special area of mutual interest in the problems created by aerodynamic drag. The Department of Transportation and other agencies have offered great inducements in the forms of honors, prizes, and contracts to get the most capable people working to reduce the drag of highway vehicles. As discussed in the following sections, an interesting type of Lockheed research holds much promise for application to this aspect of automobile aerodynamics.

3. THE MECHANISM OF VORTEX SHEDDING

3.1 BASIC PROBLEM AND SOLUTION

As air passes over the surface of a moving body, it loses energy because of friction, and the extracted energy results in drag. More generally this is in the form of pressure drag, which is caused when the flow separates from the rear of the vehicle. We want the flow to close cleanly behind the vehicle and to recover the lost pressure. Through many research studies we have developed some means to prevent the vortex flow from being shed. Instead of separating, the flow is held on to the surface by the creation of a "trapped" or "locked" vortex. The development of this technique can be applied to reduce automotive drag.

3.2 SEEING THE FLOW

3.2.1 The Vortex Street

Figure 1 presents a view inside a smoke tunnel which is used in experiments to visualize flow. The flow is moving from left to right, and the white lines are smoke filaments which have been injected upstream to trace out the patterns of the

flow as it moves past the 1/2-inch cylindrical rod. Vortices are shed more or less regularly from blunt bodies as shown here. The series of smoke whorls trailing off downstream is known as a "vortex street."

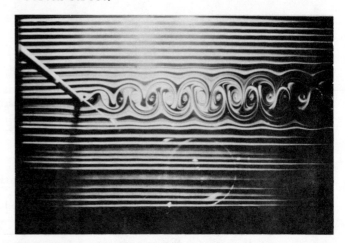

Figure 1. Non-Stagnant Vortex Street.

3.2.2 Strouhal Number

The frequency of shedding, relative to some dimension of the body in the freestream flow, is described by a measurement called the Strouhal number, as indicated in Figure 2. It is evident that, over a very wide range of Reynolds numbers (roughly a hundred to a million), the Strouhal number is virtually constant for almost all kinds of bodies of any size. This means that the kind of vortex shedding that will occur with low Reynolds numbers is the same as that expected to occur in

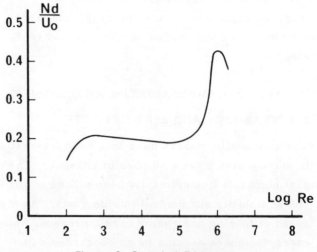

Figure 2. Strouhal Frequency.

the higher full-scale numbers. This principle of constancy is thus valid for studying vortices being shed in the wake of a large island, down to the very low Reynolds numbers which created the effects shown in Figure 1. Our initial goal is to make the Strouhal frequency go to zero by locking the vortices on the moving body and preventing their being shed at all.

3.2.3 Vortex Shedding and Flow Patterns

It should be made clear at this point that, although we visualize vortex streets in two dimensions, the phenomenon is actually three-dimensional. This is portrayed in Figure 3. At one point the vortices will be shed off the top of the body, and at some distance further over they will be shed off the bottom, alternating back and forth. Between these shedding points or nodes there is an oscillating flow that moves in a span-wise direction.

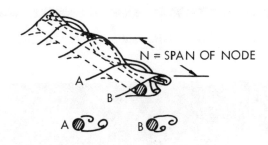

Figure 3. Span of Nodes.

Vortices are formed ahead of bodies as well as behind. The surface upstream of such a disturbance is shown in Figure 4, which involves another cylindrical shape. Friction causes energy to be lost in the boundary layer as the flow approaches the high pressure in front of the cylinder, reverse flow occurs and, again, a vortex is formed. In constrast with the previously illustrated cases, however, the vortex here is not shed. It is stationary and locked in place because the flow is moving along through the core and then around the sides of the cylinder.

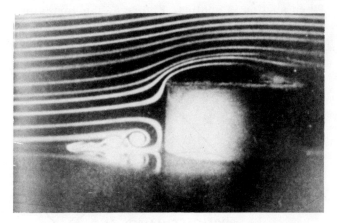

Figure 4. Vortex in Front of a Cylindrical Body.

Figure 5 shows the flow gathering in the front and then moving span-wise. Since the flow is being sucked out of the vortex as fast as it is collected from upstream, the vortex is "trapped" or locked in place. It seems clear that, if we could suck the flow out of vortices behind such a body, they would remain locked there just as this vortex is trapped in front. That approach was the basis of our following studies.

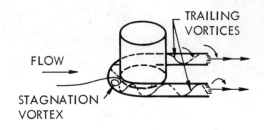

Figure 5. Stagnation and Trailing Vortices.

4. BASIC EXPERIMENTS IN FLOW CONTROL

On the airfoil section shown in Figure 6, we built a place for the vortex to remain if we succeeded in locking it in place. At the nodes near the flap, we placed suction ports to draw the flow out of the vortex cores as fast as it collected.

Figure 7 shows a model of our device in a tunnel; with no suction at the little ports, the flow moves along the top and separates.

When suction is applied, Figure 8, the vortex is locked in position, which is the basic control result we wanted.

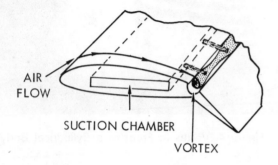

Figure 6. Lift Generated by Locked Vortex.

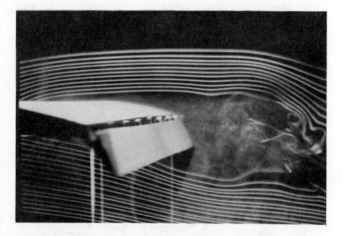

Figure 7. Lift Generated by Locked Vortex
- Without Suction.

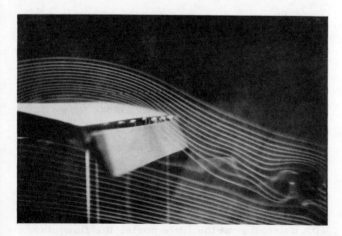

Figure 8. Lift Generated by Locked Vortex
- With Suction.

We then applied this technique to several other types of bodies. Around a quite randomly conceived aerodynamic shape we placed a number of suction nodes, which disturbed the flow and created much turbulence when there was no suction, as in Figure 9.

When suction was applied, Figure 10, a ring vortex was locked between each pair of plates. The flow recovers very rapidly and goes smoothly downstream because of the trapped vortices.

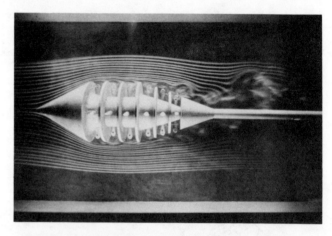

Figure 9. Body of Revolution - Without Suction.

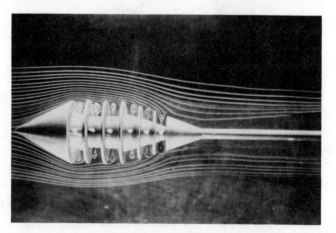

Figure 10. Body of Revolution - With Suction.

To continue our basic investigations, we created the body shown in Figure 11 to provide a friction layer at the front and a large bluff shape at the back. We then inserted two suction ports to determine whether it would be possible to lock a vortex behind that extremely blunt afterbody.

Without suction, Figure 12, the slow-moving flow 'sheds vorticity downstream, producing high drag.

When we suck the flow through the two holes as shown in Figure 13, the low-energy flow moves in, gets caught in the middle of the vortex, and then is sucked down. The core of the vortex acts like a little pipe through which the low-energy can be extracted.

When the suction is gradually reduced, as in Figures 15, 16, and 17, more flow accumulates in the core than is being pulled away, and the vortex is finally shed off downstream.

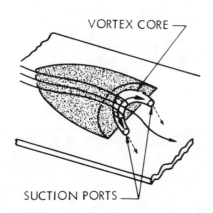

Figure 11. Half Body.

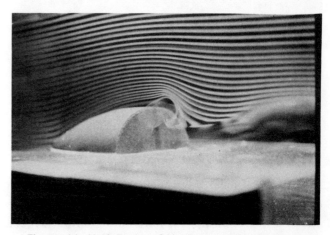

Figure 14. Half Body - 3/4 View - With Suction.

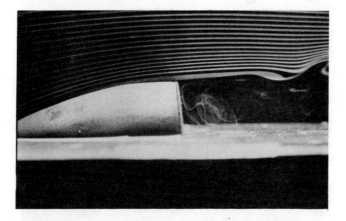

Figure 12. Half Body - Without Suction.

Figure 15. Half Body - 3/4 View - With Suction - Locked Vortex Starting to Shed.

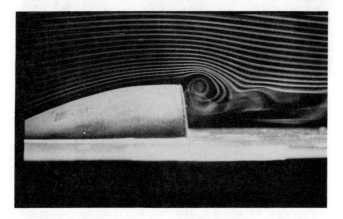

Figure 13. Half Body - Side - With Suction.

Figure 16. Half Body - 3/4 View - With Suction - Locked Vortex Shedding.

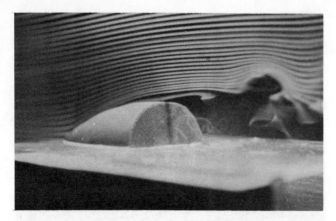

Figure 17. Half Body - 3/4 View - With Suction - Locked Vortex Further Downstream.

Figure 19. Vortex Aft Separation.

5. APPLICATION TO AN AUTOMOTIVE SHAPE

As a vehicle upon which to apply the knowledge derived from the vortex-locking experiments, we chose a model of the Corvette automobile. Figure 18 shows that a very undesirable flow condition is created when the flow separates off the extremely blunt rear window.

Figure 18. Vortex Aft Separation.

Figure 20. Locked Vortex on Rear Window.

Figure 21. Locked Vortex on Rear Window.

We were able to lock on a vortex by inserting a hole on each side of the vertical body aft of the rear window, Figure 19, and two holes in the area of the tail lights for suction.

When suction is turned on, there is a slow recovery and then smoothly moving flow down the back, Figure 20.

The close-up view of this locked vortex in Figure 21 indicates the points of sucking at the tail lights, and the motion of the vortex toward the holes.

Since the locked vortex created a good downward flow, aerodynamic forces are generated which help hold the tail of the car down. Now, as shown in Figures 22 and 23, the two vortices move the flow around the corners, and there is a stagnation region on the rear deck which produces a downward pressure. The flow has been made so clean that wake turbulence, associated aerodynamic noise, and drag are sharply reduced.

Figure 22. Locked Vortex on Rear Window and Rear of Car

Figure 23. Locked Vortex on Rear Window and Rear of Car.

6. SOME TECHNICAL OBSERVATIONS

A question that immediately comes forward relates to how much suction is required to accomplish effective vortex locking and substantial drag reduction. Although full-scale measurements have not yet been made on automobiles, our experiments with various other kinds of bodies and aerodynamic shapes allow some estimates to be made of the amount of suction needed to "lock" the vortices in position. For the size and speed of automobiles, the required quantity of suction is approximately proportional to the speed of the

vehicle and its length. Thus

$$Q/f = k U \ell$$

where Q/f is the suction flow quantity per unit width, cubic feet per second per foot.

U is the velocity of the automobile, feet per second

ℓ is the length of automobile upstream of the vortex, feet

k is an empirical constant (about $1/100$)

Thus, a car 15 feet long moving at a speed of 100 feet per second would require a suction quantity per foot of width of

$$Q/f = \frac{100 \times 15}{100}$$

or 15 cubic feet per second for each foot of width of the trapped vortex. If the vortex is, say, 4 feet long, then there will be a requirement for a suction quantity of about 60 cubic feet per second.

For a body of any shape moving through the air, there is a normal frequency of shed vorticity. If this series of vortices is exactly measured and related to the length and diameter of the body and the velocity of the flow, a precise Strouhal number is determined. By sucking up the flow we are changing this Strouhal number, actually making it go to zero and trapping the vortices. When the quantity of suction is reduced, it is not surprising that the vortex shedding begins again and finally returns to the original Strouhal frequency which existed before suction began.

7. CONCLUSIONS

The various phenomena associated with trapping vortices are now more clearly understood, and these phenomena can be isolated, defined, and developed into a technique for successful application to vehicles now in existence.

For the automotive designer, this interesting method for controlling air flow offers a promising approach to greatly reduced drag, noise, and fuel consumption.

Much remains to be done, of course, particularly in the determination of power requirements and in geometric optimization. We feel that our preliminary results are encouraging enough to draw the resources of the automotive industry toward a development area that is likely to bring large specific benefits.

DISCUSSION

PAUL LAMAR: You mentioned that there was no induced drag on a body in contact with a plane. Is that true in the case of automobiles? If you notice cars running in the rain you can see vortices coming up off the back of the car at an angle of about 45 degrees.

CORNISH: A car is not a body in contact with the ground. If you imagine a sphere moving through the air, it is well known that if you cut it down the middle, there would be forces to pull it apart. Now, if you don't allow any flow to move through the cut in the sphere and if you remove one of the hemispheres and replace it with a plane surface, there will be a strong force on the remaining hemisphere trying to lift it off the plane surface. That surface is a plane of symmetry and the remaining hemisphere doesn't know the other half has been removed so it feels no induced drag as a result of the lift acting on it. As long as you can absorb the lift through a plane of symmetry, there will be no induced drag. If you let flow go under the hemisphere, then you have a singular body upon which induced drag forces will act.

PETER BRYANT: On the Corvette model, did you try to increase the suction by some other aerodynamic means such as a venturi inside the car?

CORNISH: Yes. One of the things we did was to put a little fence or spoiler plate around the front. Instead of letting it go all the way around the car, we chopped it off at the front wheel well. The high velocity in that region created low pressures which sucked air out from the bottom of the car. We could then bleed the air from the base into this region. You can also pump the air with the exhaust or suck it up the carburetor; there are a number of things that can be done.

AUD. QUESTION: What sort of flow rates do you need for a standard type of car like a Corvette?

CORNISH: The momentum coefficient, $C\mu$, is about 0.5 and suction velocities required are of the order of the speed of the vehicle.

DEAN BATCHELOR: In the experiments you showed using the "quarter football" model, it was cut off almost at the widest point. How would the results of your experiment change if you extended the model and cut off, say, the last 30 %?

CORNISH: That type of change would reduce the amount of suction required. You could optimize the cut-off point of the body by going back to that point where you can't do anything more geometrically, that is, where the boundary layer has run out of energy and then at that point, apply suction.

BERNARD PERSHING: Some of the flow visualization pictures are reminiscent of work done by F.O. Ringleb on the control of separation using trapped vortices. His work is reported in the two volume set, "Boundary Layer and Flow Control", edited by G. V. Lachmann.

THE AERODYNAMICS OF AN ISOLATED ROAD WHEEL

J. E. Fackrell and J. K. Harvey
Imperial College
London, England

Presented by
Henry Jex
Systems Technology Incorporated
Hawthorne, California

Abstract

This paper reports a detailed study of the air flow around an isolated road wheel. The forces on the wheel were obtained by integrating pressure measurements thus permitting a full simulation of a rotating wheel in contact with the ground to be carried out. The effects of wheel width, shape and tread pattern were investigated and special features associated with the rotation are discussed.

1. INTRODUCTION

Despite the great interest in the aerodynamics of cars in recent years, the flow field associated with the wheels has received relatively little attention, mainly due to difficulties in obtaining an adequate simulation of the flow. Yet in many cases where aerodynamic design is important, the flow about the wheels can play a major role in the behaviour of the vehicle. The obvious example is the 'Grand Prix' racing car, which travels at high speeds with totally exposed wheels. A detailed understanding of the flow should also help in dealing with the hazard formed by entrainment and dispersal of spray from a wet road.

Another reason for examining the wheel aerodynamics is their relevance to the currently used wind tunnel simulation techniques for testing land vehicles. Car models are usually mounted in the wind tunnel with a clearance under the wheels because contact of the wheels with the floor would make balance measurements of the aerodynamic forces impossible. However, unless a full simulation, including the contact with the floor, is carried out, the error associated with this practice will remain unknown.

2. APPARATUS

2.1 TUNNEL CONFIGURATION

In performing our experiments, we have used a rotating wheel in contact with a moving floor (Fig. 1 and Fig. 2). The speed of the floor was matched to that of the wind to simulate the wheel moving forward through still air. The floor passes between the wheel and a supporting roller, so that movement of the floor causes the wheel to rotate.

Figure 1. Installation of Tyre in Wind Tunnel Test Section - View From Upstream.

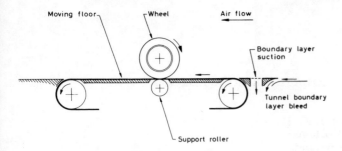

Figure 2. Wheel and Moving Floor.

The tunnel boundary layer was bled off ahead of the floor to prevent the low speed air in this layer from moving above the floor. By doing this, the speed in the layer above the floor was prevented from falling below 95% of the free stream value.

The choice of an essentially isolated wheel was made in order to provide results for a basic reference configuration. For the same reason the wheel is non-deformable and smooth-surfaced. Obviously, there are many factors which are going to influence the wheel aerodynamics, for example, body interference, fairings over or in front of the wheel, tread patterns, etc. We have so far only attempted to examine the effect of tread pattern, although it may prove interesting to look at the other factor at a later date.

Six wheel shapes were tested, a combination of three tread widths with two different edge profiles, their profiles being representative of the tyres used on 'Grand Prix' cars. The wheels were made of aluminium alloy and all had a diameter of 16-3/8 inches. This diameter in conjunction with the test speed of 61 ft/sec gives a Reynolds number of 5.3×10^5. A typical racing car wheel of 20 inches diameter has a Reynolds number of 5×10^5 at 30 mph and 2.5×10^6 at 150 mph, both of which are in the supercritical range for circular cylinders and spheres. Our Reynolds number is also in this range but at the lower end of the scale of racing car values. However, for reasons given later, we suspect that there will be no change at higher values.

2.2 PRESSURE MEASURING INSTRUMENTATION

As already mentioned, because of the difficulty of separating the aerodynamic forces from the ground reaction forces, the contact of the wheel with the ground precludes balance measurements. Instead, the forces have to be obtained by integrating the pressure over the wheel's surface. Skin friction effects will not then be included in the forces, but these are relatively small for bluff bodies with large separation regions.

As the wheel rotates, pressure sensing holes on its surface experience a cyclic variation corresponding to the pressure distribution around the perimeter. Superimposed on this are random fluctuations arising from the unsteady flow in the wake. The measuring system must respond sufficiently rapidly to follow the transient details of the pressure variation and then in the data handling some means must be employed to separate the mean cyclic variation from the random fluctuations.

The instrumentation system used to achieve this is shown in schematic form in Fig. 3. The rapid response was provided by a B & K 1/4-inch condenser microphone and its associated oscillator (DISA No. 51E32), both placed on the axis of rotation of the wheel to avoid centrifugal effects on them. The signal from these units is taken from the rotating assembly through slip rings to a DISA reactance converter and then via a filter to the 'data handling' part of the system, provided by a Hewlett-Packard correlator used in its 'signal

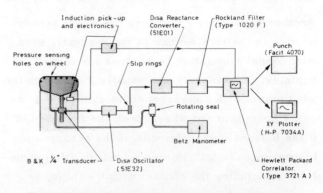

Figure 3. Schematic of Instrumentation System.

recovery' mode. A trigger pulse obtained each revolution of the wheel by an induction pick-up is also fed to the correlator and initiates one sampling cycle of the pressure signal. The correlator digitally averages several thousand such samples, thereby retaining the recurring mean variation but eliminating all fluctuations not correlated with the wheels rotation, including those due to turbulence and any electrical noise or hum on the signal. The correlator stores the mean distribution, ready for punching onto paper tape and for plotting on graphpaper, in the form of discrete points, each corresponding to a position around the wheel. The interval between points that was normally used corresponded to every 5°, but by introducing a time delay into the induction pick-up circuit and resetting the correlator interval any portion of the signal could be looked at in greater detail.

Two difficulties were encountered with the system. Firstly, because a length of tubing was used to connect the pressure hole on the wheel's surface to the microphone at the centre, resonance of the pressure signal was experienced at about 250 Hz. However, by a combination of electrical filtering and mechanical damping (in the form of a loose tuft of wire wool in the tubing), a frequency response of 0-450 Hz was achieved. For comparison, the frequency of rotation of the wheel was 14.25 Hz.

The other difficulty was the long term drifting of the transducer output signal. To overcome this, a branch was made in the connecting tubing and the pressure taken out, via rotating seals, to a Betz manometer. The slow response of this instrument meant that it measured only the mean signal level whilst the fluctuating part was supplied by the correlator with the drifting D.C. filtered off.

3. RESULTS

3.1 COMPARISON OF ROTATING AND STATIONARY WHEELS

Fig. 4 presents typical pressure distributions around a wheel centre-line, with the wheel rotating and stationary in order to highlight the specific effects of rotation. An obvious difference

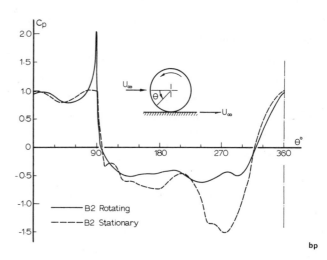

Figure 4. Pressure Distribution at Hole 10 - Wheel B2 Rotating and Stationary.

occurs at the floor ($\theta = 90$) where the rotating wheel has a sharp rise in pressure to a value of c_p much greater than one. This can only be due to viscous effects, associated with the moving boundaries of the wheel and floor, which we shall discuss later.

Over the rear, the pressure is not particularly constant in either case, but is lower for the stationary wheel. Then a major difference occurs over the top ($\theta \simeq 270$), where the stationary wheel has a region of large negative pressure which is absent on the rotating wheel. Smoke visualisation experiments (Fig. 5) show that the boundary layer remains attached over the stationary wheel, until about $\theta = 210^{\circ}$, but that separation occurs much further forward on the rotating wheel, at about $\theta = 280^{\circ}$.

This change in separation position appears similar to those observed on spheres and cylinders when the flow changes from subcritical, with

[a] Wheel Stationary.   [b] Wheel Rotating.

Figure 5. Smoke Visualization of Flow Past Wheel.

121

turbulent separation. However, measurements made of the turbulence in the boundary layer showed that the layer becomes turbulent far forward on the rotating wheel, within about 20° of the stagnation point. There is no sudden transition to turbulence, but its intensity gradually grows until separation is reached. By contrast, on the stationary wheel the layer is laminar up to 270°, when a short separation bubble forms, with turbulent reattachment and final turbulent separation at about $\theta = 210^{\circ}$. Another point worth noting is that one would normally expect a higher base pressure from the later separation of the stationary wheel, not the lower one found. Therefore, the observed changes are not simply transition phenomena but must be due to other special features associated with the rotation.

The cumulative effect of these changes in pressure distribution are important because they result in the rotating wheel having both a lower lift (a C_L of 0.44 against one of 0.76) and a lower drag (a C_D of 0.58 against 0.77).

3.2 SPECIAL FEATURES ASSOCIATED WITH THE ROTATING WHEEL

Fig. 6 shows our idea of what occurs at separation on the centre-line of the rotating wheel (Region A). Because the surface of the wheel is moving upstream and the air right next to the surface must move with it, the separation occurs at some point above the surface. At this point the mean tangential velocity, u, and its gradient in the normal direction, $\partial u/\partial y$, are both zero. We feel that it is this special form of separation which causes the separation position to move forward to a position where the boundary layer does not sustain any adverse pressure gradient. The reversed layer of air which moves with the wheel's surface will bring turbulent fluid from the wake region forward and probably accounts for the appearance of turbulence in the boundary layer so close to the stagnation point. (It is this early appearance which leads us to suspect that there will be no change in flow characteristics at Reynolds numbers higher than the 5.3×10^{5} used).

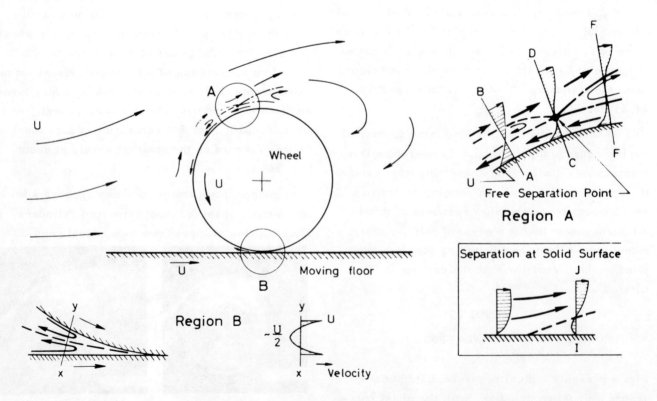

Figure 6. Details of the Separation Point and Jetting Flow.

The very high pressure encountered near to the floor on the rotating wheel are indicative of viscous effects associated with the coming together of the surfaces of the wheel and floor. A low Reynolds number solution for the two-dimensional flow induced by straight boundaries moving together at a corner, suggests the type of flow shown in Fig. 6, Region B, i.e., an upstream moving jet emerging between the two layers of air that move with the surfaces. A solution of this sort could only possibly be valid in a very small region under the wheel, but the effect of the jet should be noticeable over a much larger region. To examine this, some smoke visualisation was carried out on a simple two-dimensional analogue

[a] Cylinder Rotating as Wheel.

[b] Cylinder Stationary.

[c] Cylinder Rotating Opposite to Wheel.

Figure 7. Smoke Visualization of Two-Dimensional Flow.

of the wheel flow, consisting of an image system of two cylinders with their wakes separated by a long splitter plate. The results (Fig. 7) do show a large disturbed region in front of the cylinder when it is rotating in the same direction as a wheel, which is absent when the cylinder is stationary or rotating in the opposite direction. In three dimensions, this upstream flow is mostly lost around the side of the wheel and is not easily shown by smoke experiments, but it should still be important, not only for the small region of extreme pressure it produces, but also for its contribution to spray dispersal behind the tyre on wet roads.

3.3 LIFT AND DRAG COEFFICIENTS

The two different edge profiles tested gave different overall widths to wheels with the same width of tread in contact with the ground. Since we feel it is the latter width which is important for road-holding we have constructed two sets of coefficients; one being based on the conventional cross-sectional area normal to the flow and the other on an area constructed by multiplying the diameter by the tread width. These coefficients are shown in Fig. 8.

The conventional coefficients show a general increase with width in both drag and lift and both edge shapes give about the same values. On the other hand, the second set of coefficients have no clear trend with width, but do show that the sharper edge radiused (shape 2) wheels have a lower drag coefficient at all widths and are therefore a better choice from an aerodynamic point of view.

The coefficients shown do not include any contribution from the indented hub of the wheels. This would amount to an increase in the conventional drag coefficient of 0.07 for the narrowest wheels, 0.03 for the middle size and 0.01 for the widest, with little change in lift for all widths. Therefore, for the narrower wheels a flush hub cover would be worthwhile (brake cooling considerations aside), but on wider wheels the hub is contained in a separated region at the side of the wheel with no flow entering it and little would be gained.

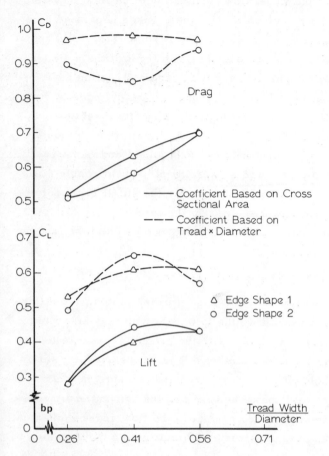

Figure 8. Variation of C_L and C_D With Width of Wheel.

It is important to note that the lift coefficients are always positive and fairly large, being about 2/3 the drag. This is in contrast to results presented by Morelli[1], who used a stationary ground plane and allowed a small clearance under the wheel (a gap/dia ratio of 0.016). This arrangement gave a C_D of 0.45 and a C_L of -0.1 for the isolated rotating wheel, i.e., negative lift. Other work by Stapleford and Carr[2] has also demonstrated that a small gap under the wheels can produce a complete reversal of the sign of the lift and that this change is greatly increased by having the wheels rotating and by using a moving floor.

The reasons for the change are not hard to deduce. The high pressure which we found under the wheel will be lost and, indeed, due to the venturi effect of air rushing through the gap, will be replaced by large negative pressures. This airflow under the wheel will only be increased by rotation and a moving floor.

3.4 EFFECT OF TREAD PATTERN

Our wheels are smooth surfaced as are the 'slick' tyres of current 'Grand Prix' cars and it might be supposed that having a grooved tread pattern on the surface might allow air under the wheel in the same manner as a small clearance. To simulate a tread pattern, we had three continuous grooves, each 1/4 inch wide and 1/8 inch deep, cut into one wheel. Fig. 9 shows the pressure around the centreline of this wheel before and after the grooves were cut, the hole being inside the groove in the latter case. The only difference occurs near the ground, where the high pressure has been converted into a large negative pressure, as suggested in the last section.

However, we found that for holes which were not in a groove, there was no noticeable change in pressure distribution. In particular the holes on the raised portions of the wheel still showed the high pressure at the ground, to some extent reflecting the localised nature of this phenomenon, nor was the base pressure altered by any flow through the grooves. The drag therefore was unaltered but the lift did decrease by about 10%. This is of the same order as the decrease in tread width in contact with the ground. Bearing in mind the large change in lift that was produced by a gap/dia ratio of only 0.016 this suggests that a very small clearance would be needed to reproduce the effect of tread pattern by using a small clearance.

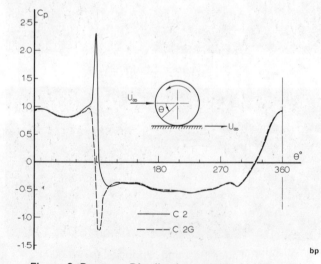

Figure 9. Pressure Distribution at Hole 11-Wheels C2 and C2G With Grooves.

4. CONCLUSIONS

We hope that we have demonstrated some of the unique properties of flow past a rotating wheel, including the movement of separation and the jetting at the floor. These features affect the forces on the wheel and can also have application to the study of spray generation by wheels on wet roads. In addition the lift and drag results may be of direct interest to those concerned with competition vehicles with exposed wheels.

In a more general context, the results throw doubt on the validity of testing car models with a clearance under the wheels. The greatest errors will occur for models where the wheel forces are an appreciable proportion of the overall forces but results from all such tests will incorporate some indeterminate error. For most car shapes this error will probably be accepted in order to take balance measurements, since the alternative, involving obtaining the forces from pressure distributions, is so much more time consuming and expensive. However, for the 'Grand Prix' type of car, the error will be large and if the clearance under the wheels is retained, it will only be made worse by rotating wheels and a moving floor. If to minimize the error due to the clearance, the wheels are not rotating, the change in separation position on top of the wheels will effectively alter the incidence of the flow onto the rear aerofoil and so greatly alter the overall force on the vehicle. For this case therefore the full simulation should be worthwhile and even necessary if accuracy is desired.

REFERENCES

(1)   Morelli, A., "Aerodynamic Actions on an Automobile Wheel," Fifth Paper at the First Symposium on Road Vehicle Aerodynamics, City University, London, 1969.

(2)   Stapleford, W.R. and G.W. Carr, "Aerodynamic Characteristics of Exposed Rotating Wheels," Motor Industry Research Association Report No. 1970/2, 1970.

DISCUSSION

BILL BETTES: That was an excellent piece of work. It considered the effects of rotation and wheel gap on lift and drag. However, the fact that a nondeformable tire was used suggests that another thing to look at is the effects of tread change. The tire would deform in the region where pressure coefficients greater than one were measured and this could change the lift characteristics measurably.

JEX: From theory, the less acute angle that a finite squash patch would produce should reduce the positive pressure slightly. On the other hand, the geometry becomes a little more two-dimensional and these factors tend to offset each other. Also, grooves which are undistorted in the solid tire would tend to close up in the deformable tire due to squirm in the contact patch. This effect would suppress the benefits obtained by flow of the air through the grooves.

MEL ROGERS: I am bothered a bit by the large positive pressure peak measured ahead of the tire contact point in the rotating case.

JEX: These values are plausible. Just at the tire contact point, there is a squeezing action of the air and very large positive pressures are developed; much as the large pressures developed in liquid film lubrication.

BOB WHITE: You are correct on your assumption of the tread behavior of a deformable tire. If you look at any film taken from underneath of a tire on a glass plate, you can see that the distorted tread has completely shut off the passage of the air.

JEX: Because of this behavior, I think the results presented in the paper may be a little more general than the solid tire implications might lead one to suspect.

125

LOW COST AERODYNAMIC TESTING
TECHNIQUES FOR AUTOMOTIVE DEVELOPMENT

Glen J. Brown
Developmental Sciences, Inc.
Industry, California 91744

Abstract

The requirements for effective testing leading to the development of competitive race car shapes are reviewed. Available methods are examined in light of these requirements. Included are the categories of road, wind tunnel, and moving model testing.

1. INTRODUCTION

The aerodynamic testing of race cars with the purpose of developing superior shapes has a unique set of requirements quite different from what one is accustomed to in aircraft wind tunnel testing. At this time, the range of possible automotive configurations has not converged appreciably to an optimum configuration. This fact is due, at least in part, to frequent rule changes. Thus, automotive development testing, to be effective, must span a wide range of allowable configurations, and indicate in an unambiguous manner the aerodynamic characteristics of each configuration relative to the others. Since, unlike aircraft, automobile performance depends on a complex combination of factors other than aerodynamics, absolute force coefficient values have little meaning except when related to other vehicles of known performance. *

It will be useful in this discussion to introduce the concepts of absolute and relative accuracy. We will say that test results with absolute accuracy

may be scaled in the usual manner to yield the total forces and moments on the full scale vehicle. It may be said that absolute accuracy is obtainable only by testing full scale instrumented automobiles actually traveling over the ground or in wind tunnel tests with scale models in which extreme care is taken to provide accurate ground and wheel simulation.

We will say that a series of tests has relative accuracy when changes to the model produce the same relative changes in aerodynamic forces in full scale vehicles traveling over the ground even though the actual value of the forces may not have absolute accuracy for a variety of reasons. That is, a change made to a model that produced a 10 percent increase in negative lift would produce nearly the same change if applied to an actual vehicle. One must be careful in deciding that a particular test setup has good relative accuracy. This is, in fact, a contradiction because the only way to know for sure is to have absolute accuracy. The types of inaccuracies described here will be limi-

---

* This applies primarily to closed circuit competition vehicles rather than speed record or drag vehicles that compete against the clock and are more readily analyzed.

ted to the use of non-metric wheels and some Reynolds' number disagreement.

Requirements for development testing are summarized as follows:

(1) Low enough cost to get started

(2) Relative accuracy

(3) Convenience in changing configurations

In the following sections we will examine the available test techniques in terms of accuracy, usefulness for the task of development and cost. This discussion is addressed primarily to the development of roadrace and speedway type race-cars.

2. FULL SCALE VEHICLE TESTING

2.1 UNINSTRUMENTED ROAD TESTS

Road tests in which the vehicle is uninstrumented except for the normal cockpit instruments are the most common form of testing for evaluating changes made to competition vehicles and even new designs. This type of testing has the advantage of reflecting the combined effect of aerodynamics, all other vehicle systems and the interaction of aerodynamic effects with the other systems. In this sense, road testing is the ultimate measure of success of any design or modification. In particular, the angular settings of wing are properly determined only through road testing.

For the purpose of development, road tests have very serious shortcomings. One must rely on limited data in the form of lap times, straightaway RPM, driver comments, and oil streak or tuft flow visualization. Such information cannot, in general, be interpreted with enough precision to see the effects of small changes that are often significant to the understanding of a complex aerodynamic problem. The situation is aggravated by the fact that driver comments may not correspond to the indications of lap times; is further confused by the interaction with suspension and changes thereto; and is made all but impossible if the testing is going on at the same time.

Despite its shortcomings, road testing remains the most universally used method today. The method results in evolutionary changes more often than large improvements leading to decisive competitive advantages.

2.2 INSTRUMENTED ROAD TESTS

Much information can be obtained through instrumented road tests. Lift force and pitch moment on the sprung structure can be obtained with good accuracy by measuring suspension deflection at speed while coasting. Drag on the wheels and sprung structure can be obtained and separated from rolling resistance through coast-down tests. As a minimum, the following quantities must be measured:

● Suspension deflection, 4 wheels

● Ground speed

● Air apeed

This type of testing can be quite accurate and highly useful, especially since handling and aerodynamics can be evaluated separately and together. Instrumented road testing is the logical extension of simple road tests and certainly within the means of any constructor. The only shortcoming of the instrumented road test for the purpose of development is that configuration changes are somewhat inconvenient and limited in scope.

3. WIND TUNNEL TESTING

Wind tunnel testing is traditional in aircraft development, but is generally too costly for widespread application to automotive development on a low budget. Certain considerations, particularly pertaining to scale, can have a strong impact on cost, and may serve to bring wind tunnel testing into more development budgets.

3.1 FULL SCALE

Full scale wind tunnel testing is extremely costly and is generally the province of auto manufacturers. As in the case of road tests, configuration changes are somewhat inconvenient on large models, thus limiting the scope of a development program.

3.2 MEDIUM SCALE (3/8)

Medium scale testing represents a good compromise in scale and cost. The scale is sufficient to obtain a degree of absolute accuracy if other conditions are satisfied. The cost, though not inexpensive, is typically a fraction of the cost of a racing engine. Models may be made of wood or clay with an aluminum or steel supporting structure. The convenience of working with these materials at medium scale allow configuration changes to be made quickly.

3.3 SMALL SCALE (1/10)

Small scale testing can be quite inexpensive while retaining enough relative accuracy to be useful. Most importantly, model changes can be made almost spontaneously with pieces of clay and strips of shim stock.

The availability of suitable tunnels may limit small scale testing. Some colleges have small tunnels, but they are not always available to private users. The cost of construction of a small wind tunnel need not exceed that of a good dynamometer setup. Thus, the future may see those with continuing needs for testing capability building their own tunnels.

Figure 1 shows a 1/10 scale USAC race car model installed in the Merrill wind tunnel at CalTech. Because of the small gap between the mod-

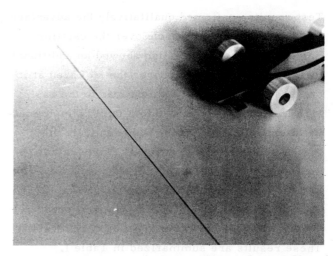

Figure 2. Boundary Layer Suction Slot in Ground Plane.

el and the ground plane, a suction slot was incorporated in the ground plane to insure a thin boundary layer at the model, Figure 2. The test setup was further simplified by mounting the wheels directly to the ground plane and not measuring forces on them.

Since the purpose of these tests was to develop an aerodynamically improved shape over the best competing car at the time, models were built of the competing car (McLaren M16), the client's current car (1971 Eagle), and the proposed new design, Figure 3. In addition, extensive modifications were made to the basic McLaren chassis to explore a broad range of aerodynamic possibilities.

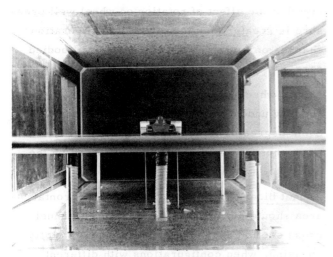

Figure 1. Model and Ground Plane in CalTech's Merrill Tunnel.

Figure 3. Eagle Model in Tunnel.

129

Test results confirmed qualitatively the advantage the McLaren had at the time over the existing Eagle. The proposed design showed an additional increment in negative lift over the McLaren at increased drag levels. Modifications to the basic McLaren chassis indicated that fairly simple modifications to the McLaren would duplicate the forces on the proposed design. Fairly extensive modifications to the basic McLaren chassis, Figure 4 showed clearly that wings in ground effect, even in the influence of the tires, could produce substantial negative lift at reduced drag levels. These results are summarized in Table I.

Table I
Summary of Results - 1/2 Scale USAC Cars

Configuration	Forces on Sprung Structure at 200 mph* Full Scale, Lbs.	
	Lift	Drag
1971 Eagle	+120	570
McLaren M16	-165	525
Modified McLaren (side radiators)	-570	660
Development Eagle	-510	660
Best Modified McLaren (front radiator)	-600	515

Figure 4. Modified McLaren Chassis With Wings in Ground effect.

The tests described above were accomplished in three days and spanned nearly 50 configurations.

3.4 GENERAL GUIDELINES

Care must be taken that, in an effort to reduce cost in a wind tunnel program, even relative accuracy is not sacrificed. The following are guidelines that will insure acceptable accuracy. The reader is referred to references 1 through 5 for the experimental basis for this information.

Ground simulation. A ground board, in general, must be used. As a rule of thumb, the boundary layer displacement thickness should be 25% or less of the ground plane to underbody distance.

Wheels. No practical way has yet been developed to measure forces on rotating wheels without flow under the wheels. All simulations will therefore evolve a compromise.

Non-metric wheels are justified when the effect of the body on the wheels is unimportant compared to the effect of the wheels on the body. This is difficult to verify in any case since the interaction appears to be strong. A sports car nose on an open wheeled car is an example for which non-metric wheels are not acceptable.

Non-metric wheels can rotate. One may speculate that the effect of rotation on wheel well pressure is greater than the effect of configuration changes on forces on the wheels for full bodied cars.

Metric wheels must not touch the ground plane, yet flow under the wheels must be minimized. Some degree of compromise is, therefore, always present when forces are measured on the wheels of a model.

Tunnel blockage. A model's projected frontal area should not exceed 7 percent of the tunnel cross section above the ground plane. Strictly speaking, when configurations with different frontal areas are compared, the results should be corrected for the difference in blockage.

130

However, if the 7 percent guideline has been followed, this can probably be ignored. For example, a 20 percent change in model frontal area from 5 percent to 6 percent of the tunnel area will produce a drag result that is too high by 1/2 percent[4].

Reynolds' Number* (scale effect). Reynolds' number based on wheelbase should be kept above 2×10^6. Lower Reynolds' numbers may preserve relative accuracy for bluff bodies down to $Re \simeq 5 \times 10^5$. Airfoil characteristics do not scale well at low Reynolds' numbers, so wing angle of attack settings should be reserved for track testing. However, for the low aspect ratios typical of current race cars ($15 < A < 4$) induced drag dominates and airfoil characteristics have a relatively small effect on the wing drag polar below stall. For example, a wing of aspect ratio 2 operating at a C_L of 1 will have an induced drag coefficient of:

$$C_{D_i} \approx \frac{C_L^2}{\pi A} \left[1 + \frac{2/A}{1 + 2/A} \right] = 0.23$$

regardless of Reynolds' numbers.

Whereas, the section (airfoil) drag is about

$$C_{D_o} \approx 0.008$$

for most airfoils at this lift coefficient.

4. MOVING MODELS

Moving models combine the ground simulation and rotating wheels of instrumented road tests with the convenience of wind tunnel models. Two examples are given below of how moving models can be supplied to automotive aerodynamics.

4.1 HIGHWAY AERODYNAMIC TEST FACILITY

The Highway Aerodynamic Test Facility was built under contract to the U. S. Department of Transportation, National Highway Traffic Safety Administration to study the aerodynamic effects of buses and trucks passing in close proximity to passenger cars**. The facility has two "lanes" which can be operated singly or together, in either direction and at differing speeds simultaneously. The models are pulled by cables running beneath the tracks connected through gearing to a 20 H.P. motor. Top speed is about 100 mph depending on the weight of the model.

A model is shown in Figure 5 with the top fairing removed. Both the top fairing and the detailed underbody are attached to a 6-component strain guage balance. Non-metric wheels roll on the track, rotating on axes that do not tough the underbody fairing. Signals from the balance are transmitted by a telemetry system traveling with the

Figure 5. High Speed Moving Model With Lightweight Body Fairing Removed.

model, under the track, to a data recorder. Unwanted vibrations due to irregularities in the track are eliminated electronically using accelerometers.

The facility is specialized in that the complexity of the models is justified over wind tunnel testing only when accurate ground simulation or transient events are of importance.

---

* Reynolds' number in air is given by Re = Wheelbase (ft.) x Airspeed (MPH) x 10^4.

** DOT/DSI Contract DOT-HS-102-1-147.

Figure 6. Automotive Development's Push Model.

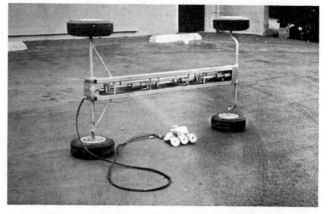

Figure 7. Model Chassis Showing Balance.

4.2 Push Models

A 1/2 scale push model of a Formula Ford car is shown in Figure 6*. The wheels are go-cart parts and appear to scale quite well. Bodies were made of foam and fiberglas to represent both an existing competitive vehicle, and the proposed development body. Configuration changes were reported to be reasonably convenient.

The test chassis is shown in Figure 7. Hydraulic cylinders were used to convert forces to pressure levels which were read on guages. Front lift, rear lift, and drag were resolved through a system of linkage to the cylinders.

Table II
Summary of Test Methods

	Method	Accuracy	Changes	Cost	Remarks
I.	Full Scale Road Test				
	Uninstrumented	Performance only	Limited	Low	No direct aero drag.
	Instrumented	Absolute	Limited	Low	Lift on sprung mass total drag.
II.	Wind Tunnel				
	Full Scale	Absolute	Limited	High	Primarily for mfg.
	3/8	Absolute/ Relative	Easy	Moderate	Good development method.
	1/10	Relative	Very Easy	Low	Best results/$ unless configuration range is narrow.
III.	Moving Models				
	Highway Aero Facility	Absolute/ Relative	Easy	High	Non-metric wheels. Cost may be reduced with experience.
	Push Models	Absolute	Easy	Low	Non-metric wheels. Low cost. Very effective.

* Photo courtesy Dave Bruns, Automotive Development, Inc.

The effectiveness of this approach has been well demonstrated by racing success. The necessary apparatus is certainly within the construction capabilities of any race car shop.

5. CONCLUSIONS

The methods available for testing automotive shapes with sufficient accuracy for development purposes span a wide range of both cost and effectiveness. Some pertinent facts on some methods are summarized in Table II.

Results are not proportional to cost, but are more nearly related to the range of configurations considered and the number tested. No single method is clearly best suited for race car aerodynamic development. Rather, the choice in each case must be based on the available resources and the technical requirements of the development program.

REFERENCES

(1)   Bettes, W.H. and Kelly, F.B., "The Influence of Wind Tunnel Solid Boundaries on Automotive Test Data", _Advances in Road Vehicle Aerodynamics 1973_, BHRA, Cranfield Bedford, England.

(2)   Beauvais, F.N. et.al., "Problems of Ground Simulation in Automotive Aerodynamics", SAE 680121.

(3)   Mason, W.T. Jr., and Souran, G., "Ground Plane Effects on the Aerodynamic Characteristics of Automobile Models - An Examination of Wind Tunnel Test Techniques", _Advances in Road Vehicle Aerodynamics 1973_, BHRA, Cranfield Bedford, England.

(4)   Pope and Harper, Low-Speed Wind Tunnel Testing, Wiley, New York, 1966.

(5)   Lissaman, P.B.S., V/STOL Notes, Cal Tech 1969.

DISCUSSION

BOB LIEBECK: Do you think you can get any meaningful data regarding download at the low Reynolds numbers of your tests?

BROWN: The test Reynolds numbers are on the order of 10^5. Ordinarily, this would be considered low but we are not looking for airfoil data; we're looking for relative data between one configuration and another. Even if the profile characteristics of the wing are quite far off (and that's usually a trend on the track anyway), as long as the lift-to-drag characteristics of that system are maintained, then the relative accuracy of that system can be measured. And the lift-to-drag characteristics are mainly a function of the effective span of the wing rather than the airfoil characteristics.

AUD. QUESTION: Do the canards help streamline the front wheels?

BROWN: We had no way of knowing that because the wheels weren't metric. Very specifically, this type of testing should never be used if you are thinking about a sports car type nose because there, the payoff is probably in reduced front wheel drag.

AN HISTORICAL SURVEY OF BONNEVILLE RECORD CARS

Dean Batchelor

Few enthusiast realize just how many "streamliners" have been built to run on the salt flats - either by hot rodders for the annual Bonneville National Speed Trials (now called Bonneville Nationals), or by some of the major automobile manufacturers seeking class records.

This is due in part to the vast amount of press coverage heaped on the all-out Land Speed Record cars, and in part to the general lack of knowledge (and, possibly, lack of caring) of the press relations people and the press itself. It has always been a pain in the backside to me as an editor, and as an ex-Bonneville competitor, to see news reports and press releases claiming WORLD RECORD when they actually meant International record, or National record.

So before getting into my discussion of Bonneville record cars, I'd like to clarify the record "system" a bit. Until the advent of the turbine, jet and rocket-powered cars, there were 10 International Classes, as follows:

Class A	IC engines over 8000cc
B	" 5000-8000cc
C	" 3000-5000cc
D	" 2000-3000cc
E	" 1500-2000cc
F	" 1100-1500cc
G	" 750-1100cc
H	" 500-750 cc
I	" 350-500 cc
J	" 0-350 cc

These classes still exist, of course, but due to human nature people tend to look at the biggest, best, most, or fastest, ignoring other efforts that may have been as great (or greater). The built-in "newsworthyness" of the big boys tends to overshadow the "lesser" achievements of the relatively slower cars in smaller classes.

Now, a World Record holder is the car/driver combination that covers the established distance in the shortest time, or covers the most distance in the established time. There is only one World Record holder for each distance or time reference, and the record holder can be from any class. There may be an International Record, however, for every distance and every time so there can be a large, and confusing number of records.

Regardless of which class the car fits, it is possible to establish a World Record, an International Record, and a National Record (for the country in which the actual record run is made) all at the same time. To become a National or International Record, it has only to be the fastest in the appropriate class, but to be a World Record, it has to be the fastest for the distance, period.

A good example of this is the 1937 Auto Union, which established new International Class B records for the standing start kilometer and mile, but because they were also the fastest times ever recorded for the distance, regardless of class, they became new World Records as well. In addition, they were new German National records both for class and absolute. In 1952, George Hill, in the Hill-Davis Bob Estes Mercury Special set new International Class C records for the flying start kilometer and mile (taken from Auto Union) and

Jack Harvey Streamliner - Muroc Dry Lake in the late Thirties. Car was big and relatively heavy, and its performance was not good enough to excite other competitors to build aerodynamic bodies.

The Spalding Brothers, Tom and Bill, brought a Ford V-8 powered streamliner to the dry lakes in the late Thirties. It, also, was too big and relatively heavy for the modest horsepower available in those days.

George tried for the standing start records as well. He was successful in setting new American records for the SS kilometer and mile but was not successful in gaining the International records for the distance.

The Bonneville Salt Flats had been the venue for many World Record attempts, both successful and unsuccessful, before the Southern California Timing Association ran the first Bonneville Nationals meet in 1949. Names like Ab Jenkins, Sir Malcolm Campbell, George Eyston, John Cobb and others are well known to anybody who follows this sort of thing and, because of the "news value" of their exploits, their names are fairly well known to most men - auto enthusiasts or not.

Hot rodders had done little with designed-from-the-ground-up streamliners before WW II and the only ones I know of were built by Jack Harvey, and the Spalding Brothers. Both were big, and

heavy, and probably didn't have an overabundance of horsepower. And they ran on the dry lakes of Southern California, which don't offer either superior traction or the available length of Bonneville. Neither car sparked the interest of the other competitors enough to cause a boom in aerodynamic body design.

After WW II, however, the hot rod movement was expanding so fast, particularly in Southern California, that somebody just had to go all out to build a "streamlined" hot rod and to the surprise of many, three appeared in 1949. The So-Cal Special, built by Dean Batchelor and Alex Xydias on an ex-Bill Burke belly-tank lakester chassis; Lee Chapel's "Tornado" Special, designed and built from the ground up by Bob Allington, and Howard Johansen's twin tank - a cattamaran type vehicle in the style of Piero Taruffi's successful "Tarf" and "Italcorse."

Howard Johansen's twin tank was entered in the 1949 Nationals. Driver sat in the left body, flathead Merc in right. Top speed was a disappointing 147.54 mph as the car, built at last minute, handled poorly.

Xydias-Batchelor So-Cal Special achieved top time at the 1949 Bonneville Nationals with a one-way run of 193.54 mph and a two-way record average of 189.745 mph. Engine was Edelbrock-equipped 274 cid flathead Merc.

Both the Chapel car and the So-Cal ran at El Mirage dry lake in the summer of 1949, but only the So-Cal and Johansen's twin tank appeared at Bonneville that year. Johansen had problems with his car and his best speed at Bonneville was 147 mph, but the So-Cal came away with a top speed of 193.54 and a two-way average of 189.745 mph.

Activity picked up in 1950 and there were four streamliners on the salt. The So-Cal Special was back with a new nose design as a result of throwing the tread off both front tires on the record run in 1949 and the subsequent installation of slightly larger front tires; Lee Chapel brought his Tornado to the salt for the first time, and two new cars appeared - the Kenz-Leslie twin Merc engined car from Denver, and the Marvin Lee-Wayne Horning GMC six "City of Pasadena."

So-Cal Special in 1950, driven by Ray Charbonneau, standing and Bill Dailey in cockpit. Top speed was 210.896 mph, two way average, 208.927 mph. Engine was still flathead with 210 bhp on straight methanol.

So-Cal Special completely rebuilt for 1951 season had clear canopy over driver and was to get independent rear suspension before Bonneville. Crash at Daytona Beach in February, 1951 totally destroyed car.

Lee Chapel's "Tornado", left, as it appeared in 1950 and 51. New Tornado ohv heads for flathead engine proved troublesome and the best run was 175.09 mph in 1950. The car was beautifully built, but hadn't reached potential.

Chapel's Tornado, below, with new smaller wheels and tires which allowed lower body line over wheels. Car set Class C Bonneville Nationals record of 224.144 mph in 1952, crashed in 1953 with minor injuries to driver.

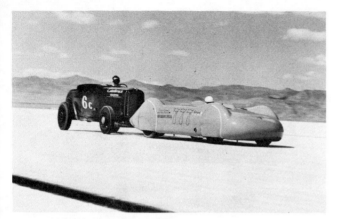

Kenz-Leslie twin Merc flathead from Denver, Colo. ran with this configuration in 1950, 51 and 52, then a covered canopy over driver was added for 53 and 54. Top record was 255.411 mph two-way average set in 1953.

In 1955 Kenz-Leslie car appeared on the salt with three Merc flatheads, four wheel drive, and the driver moved to the rear. Best run for car with this setup was 270.47 mph in 1957. Car has since been retired.

Chapel's car still wasn't running right, and the best time recorded was 175.09. The City of Pasadena crashed at speed, after a run of 195.652, but the driver Puffy Puffer walked away from the accident with minor scratches. It was a close duel between the So-Cal and the Kenz-Leslie cars for top speed - the So-Cal recording 210.8962, and Kenz-Leslie 210.6489. Each car set class records - the So-Cal at 208.927 average, and Kenz-Leslie at 206.5048 mph. This year the So-Cal was driven alternately by Bill Dailey and Ray Charbonneau, and the Kenz car was driven by Willie Young.

Early in 1951 the So-Cal Special was destroyed at Daytona Beach, with its driver, Bill Dailey, barely escaping with his life. Two cars appeared at Bonneville; Chapel's and the Kenz-Leslie, both for the second time. Chapel's car still didn't realize its potential and timed only 174.418 but the Kenz-Leslie car, still driven by Young, managed a time of 230.7692 one way and a two way average of 221.4795.

Things really began to happen in 1952 with six streamliners on the salt - four of them new cars. Kenz and Leslie were back with their twin-engined car, now called the Floyd Clymer Motor-book Special, and gained the top time of the meet at 250 mph. Willie Young was still the driver and his two way average was 244.66 mph. Lee Chapel came back also with his Tornado and this time it was running! Driver Sonny Rogers set a new class C record at 224.144 mph.

Marvin Lee-Wayne Horning "City of Pasadena" was powered by GMC six. First and only appearance at Bonneville was at the Nationals in 1950. After run of 195.652 mph, the car was destroyed in a crash.

City of Pasadena at speed shows extreme body rake to increase down pressure on nose, but flattened Clark Y type airfoil is one of the best lifting shapes known and could have caused traction loss and subsequent crash.

Bill Burke's first streamliner was the Hot Rod Magazine Special. It was Harley-Davidson powered and ran 138.14 mph one way and set a class record at 136.90 mph, both in 1952. Car was extremely small and light.

George Hill and Bill Davis brought Dean Batchelor-designed "City of Burbank-Bob Estes Mercury Special" to the salt in 1952. It set new Nationals records, and two weeks later set FIA/AAA International C record of 229.77 mph.

Bill Burke had a new car, powered by a Harley-Davidson motorcycle engine and Bill took it through at 138.14 one way and set a class record at 136.90 mph. George Hill and Bill Davis brought their new Dean Batchelor-designed car, called the City of Burbank, powered by an Adams-Mohler ohv on a Merc block and set a new SCTA class B record of 230.16 mph.

Harold Post's Chrysler special, driven by Otto Ryssman, achieved 217.65 one way in class C but couldn't beat out Chapel's car for the record, and Chet Herbert ran his "Beast III" Chrysler-powered car at 232.35 mph.

Chet Herbert brought his Rod Schapel-designed "Beast III" to Bonnevile in 1952. Chrysler V-8 powered, it attained a speed of 232.35 mph. Design was clean, but far too large for the power it got from Chrysler.

Two weeks after the Nationals, Hill and Davis came back with sponsorship by Bob Estes, Mobil, Thalco and Iskenderian to set new International Class C records for the flying start kilometer and mile under AAA sanction. With Hill driving, the car averaged 229.77 mph. He later tried for the standing start kilo and mile and was successful at setting new American records, but fell far short of the International marks. This car simply wasn't set up for acceleration and the combination of weight, gearing and traction were against it. But it was a break-through for "hot rodders" because nobody in AAA or most other professional racing organizations believed it possible.

Dana Fuller's 671 GMC Diesel "Big Mamoo" is the ex-Herbert "Beast III". In this form, Fuller set a new World Diesel mark, at the 1953 AAA record runs, of 169.32 mph two-way average over the measured mile.

Harold Post's car started with flathead Merc, but ran Chrysler V-8 at Bonneville in 1952, 53, and 54. Top speed attained was 222 mph before it crashed at 1954 Bonneville Nationals destroying the car.

Chet Herbert's "Beast IV" ran in 1953 powered by a single Chrysler V-8, re-appeared in 1954, top, as "Beast V" with two Dodge V-8s, four wheel drive and driver in the middle. Best run was 246 mph. Herbert-Hermann-Walker-Sorrell Engineering Special, above, is the ex-Herbert "Beast IV" with three Chevrolet V-8s and four wheel drive. The drivers cockpit has been moved to the rear to accommodate all the machinery.

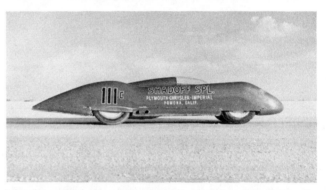

Mal Hooper's Shadoff Special, another Batchelor-designed car, held at various times 15 International and 16 National records in Classes B and C. Top average speed for Chrysler-owered car was 272 mph.

If things were good for the record enthusiast in 1952, they were even better in 1953, with nine streamliners actually on the salt (10 had been entered); five of them new cars. Chet Herbert had built "Beast IV" and the Hill-Davis, Kenz-Leslie and Chapel Tornado cars were back. Top time of the Nationals was gained by the Kenz-Leslie car at 255.411 (two way average).

New this year were the Le Blanc twin Chrysler powered car, which was rejected by the technical committee and didn't make a run, the Mal Hooper-Ray Brown Shadoff Chrysler Special, Tommy Thompson's Olds V-8 powered car, and Fred Carillo's unique Chrysler powered vehicle.

Chapel's car crashed during the Bonneville Nationals after a run of 230.62 mph, but its driver, Sonny Rogers, escaped with minor scratches. Carillo's car crashed the following

week during the AAA sanctioned runs costing Fred his left foot and causing other minor injuries. Both cars were totalled.

The Shadoff car, Chet Herbert's car, and Hill-Davis' car stayed over after the Nationals to run AAA and the Carillo car and Dana Fuller's GMC 671 Diesel (the ex-Herbert Beast III) appeared only for the AAA runs. At the end of the FIA-AAA week the Shadoff Special had set six International and six American records - 1 kilometer to 10 miles - in Class C - the best time being 236.36 mph average; the Chet Herbert Chrysler had set two International and two National Class B records - 1 kilometer and 1 mile - the best at 233.31 average; and the Dana Fuller Diesel had set two World Diesel records, two International class records and two American records - 1 kilo and 1 mile - recording 169.32 for the measured mile.

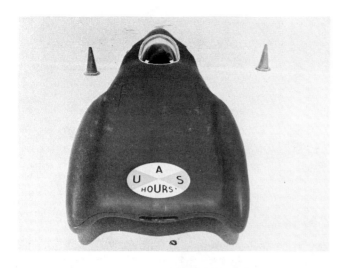

Fred Carillo's Chrysler-powered car, left and above, was to have been a 3-wheeler, but finally was built with rear wheels only 24 inches apart. Super-slick design never proved itself because of a crash at the AAA record trials in 1953.

Le Blanc Special, left and below, was designed to duplicate shape of John Cobb's Napier Railton record car. Two Chrysler V-8s and four wheel drive were used; driver was completely enclosed and looked out through plexiglas panel.

For the 1954 meet, 12 streamliners - from John Fox's tiny 500cc Norton-powered Cooper to Dana Fuller's big 671 GMC Diesel (including four two-engined cars) were entered.

Part of the Bonneville Nationals week was lost to rain and speeds were not high. The Kenz-Leslie twin Ford was the top car of the meet at 251.92 mph. The Potvin-Hartelt entry (Harold Post's car) crashed at over 200 mph when a rear tire went flat because it rubbed on the chassis, slightly injuring its driver, Otto Ryssman.

The combination of weather, poor salt conditions and problems caused by the Great Salt Bear (the Bonneville equivalent of Leprechauns, Poltergeists and Gremlins) kept the meet from becoming one of the great ones. With all but one of the streamliners entered actually appearing on the salt, records should have been broken right and left, but it was not to be.

The 1955 meet was also disappointing from a top speed standpoint. The Hill-Davis-Duncan-Losinski-Capanna car got top time of the meet at 238.56 mph. And another car was destroyed. The Le Blanc twin Chrysler spun and turned over several times, flinging pieces over a quarter of a mile, severely injuring its driver Glen Pengry.

When this car first appeared on the salt in 1953, it had been rejected by the technical committee for a long list of things - mostly construction. It had clearance problems for some moving parts, aircraft control cable for steering (with no consideration by the builder for prestretching the cable), butt welded steering arms and when a jack was put under the jackpad built into the tail to elevate the car to change rear wheels, the center of the chassis sagged several inches. The owner-builder completely revamped the car and it was successfully passed in tech inspection in 1954 and 1955.

Howard Johansen's second twin tank ran in 1954 with Dodge V-8 in left body, driver in right. Car was much smaller than first design in 1949 but still never realized speed potential it should have.

The 1956 meet had to be one of the dullest ever for aerodynamics enthusiasts. Three cars appeared on the salt; Kenz-Leslie - which also had fast time of the meet at 261.81 - Tommy Thompson, and the Bob Herda Attempt I. Chet Herbert's "Beast V" got as far as Wendover but never got to the salt.

Again in 1957 streamliner activity was down - the Kenz-Leslie car taking fast time of the meet again, with Roy Leslie driving, at 270 mph - as speeds in other Bonneville classes were far more impressive for their class than were the streamliners.

A. R. "Tommy" Thompson ran his Olds V-8 powered "Golden Rod" in 1953, 54, 55, 56, 57, 58 and 59, with a best run of 205 mph in 1959. Shape was good, but full-width chassis made frontal area too large.

The cars that were being built to run in the streamliner classes exhibited a tremendous difference in design philosophy and quality of construction. There had been two wheel drive - front and rear - and four wheel drive; cars with full suspension - from the simple and unsophisticated solid axle and transverse leaf springs to full independent (usually swing axle because of fabrication simplicity); De Dion rear, and cars with no suspension at all.

Some were beautifully built in all respects, and some were barely acceptable by the technical committee, but most had one quality in common - enough horsepower to make them go like hell.

John Vesco's Offenhauser-powered streamliner was one of first to appear at Bonneville Nationals with extra narrow track to achieve smaller frontal area. John's son, Don, drove it 222.791 mph with no apparent trouble.

Bob Herda's "Attempt I" also had good shape that was hurt by a wider than stock car track and its resultant enormous frontal area. Car never really ran right and best run was 149 mph in 1956.

Some of the subsequent crashes were explainable; the Potvin-Hartelt-Post car blew a tire. The Hill-Davis-Duncan-Losinski-Capanna car broke a rear axle. It appears that the Lee-Horning, Athol Graham and Chapel cars simply lost traction and subsequent directional control. Fred Carillo probably over corrected to bring his car back on course after drifting outside the markers. The others are unknown quantities because the SCTA and Bonneville Nationals Boards have been paranoid about allowing photographs to be taken of wrecks or allowing time for thorough examinations a la FAA.

The more recent exploits of Bonneville competitors have been covered well enough in magazines, newspapers and books that further detailed examination and description here is unnecessary. It does appear though that many of the car builders could have used some competent professional help.

There's an engineering axiom to the effect that "what looks right, is right" but there's an enormous fallacy involved. What looks right to a trained engineer isn't necessarily what looks right to the untrained but ambitious amateur car designer, and there have been some wierd and downright dangerous cars appear on the salt - ones that passed all the technical rules of the organizers but would have made an engineer cringe.

Hammon-Whipp-McGrath "Redhead" was one of the most bizarre shapes to run at Bonneville, but it must have worked. Single Chrysler V-8 pushed car to 331 mph one way and a two-way record average of 306.35 mph.

Athol Graham' Allison aircraft engine-powered "City of Salt Lake" had run 344 mph in 1959, but in 1960 attempt on Land Seed Record, the car crashed killing Graham. Enormous power, two-wheel drive, and over-eager acceleration were probable causes of car getting sideways in course before flipping.

Bill Burke and Bob Laster set new Bonneville Nationals Class D record in 1960 with Falcon six-owered "pumkin seed" at 205.95 mph. In 1961 it went 235.22 mph with a Mickey Thompson 4-cylinder Tempest.

Bud Hare's 40 cid Triumph motorcycle-engined car set two-way average record of 144.436 mph in 1960. Hare ran motorcycles at Bonneville for years, finally decided to put his efforts into a car.

143

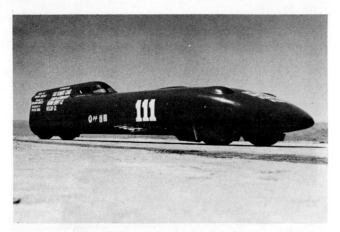

Summer Bros. approach in 1961 was supercharged Chrysler V-8 driving paired front wheels, and the rear "idle" wheels mounted in tandem. Top speed was 302.317 mph, 262.232 mph average from 302 cid engine.

Bob Herda really got his act together in 1965, setting a two-way average of 325.85 mph for new Bonneville record. Car was one of the most beautifully built cars ever to run on the salt flats.

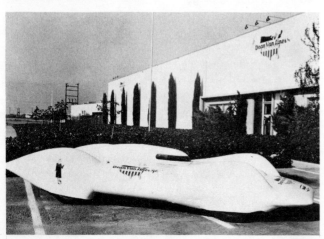

Ermie Immerso's first streamliner, the Dean Van Lines Special, built in 1960 for the 1961 season had two supercharged Lincoln V-8s. His goal was 400 mph but the car never achieved the target speed.

Chassis and aerodynamic requirements are not always compatible, and it takes a combination of knowledge, common sense and luck to reach the right combination. And some of the amateur car builders haven't reached that combination even with help from supposedly competent aerodynamicists. The problem being that what works in "free" air at, say 10,000 feet altitude doesn't necessarily work at ground level.

I designed the bodies for three Bonneville streamliners - the So-Cal Special, the Hill-Davis-Bob Estes car and the Mal Hooper-Shadoff Special. Then I quit because speeds were getting higher at a rapid rate, and I didn't feel qualified to design what I would consider to be a completely safe car. If I designed it, I would want to be willing to drive it and feel safe in it.

Thinking about how I would design a car - if I were to design another streamliner - I would make it as small as possible, compatible with engine, driver and tires which are the three significant components. I would aim for a high polar moment for directional stability. It might have the engine in front, with front wheel drive, or it might be midship with rear wheel drive, but I'd want the CG ahead of the CP as far as reasonably possible. The car would not have a fin - I don't believe in them as either necessary or desirable.

And the car would have full suspension. Many car builders (and some of the very successful

Ermie Immerso re-built his 1961 car using four Ford V-8s recording 283 mph in 1962, and 302 in 1963. Few multi-engined cars have worked well and fewer yet have done it without long debugging periods.

ones) argue that suspension is unnecessary at Bonneville because of the super-smooth surface. This is fanciful fiction in light of known history of the salt conditions and it is a long wait 'til next year if the surface is too poor for maximum performance.

Our So-Cal Special was indicating over 200 mph (engine rpm, gear ratio and tire size) in 1949 when I clocked 193 mph. A year later, at the same rpm with the same gears and the same tires Bill Dailey clocked 210 in the car. It had no rear suspension and in 1949 it had simply been getting wheelspin from a less than perfect surface.

My "new" car would, I think, have Watt link suspension. The reason for this is to have all wheels independent, yet have a suspension that won't change wheelbase, track or camber. All commonly used independent systems affect one or more of these conditions. With fore-and-aft Watt links, the only change would be the caster angle of the front wheels and it would be minimal because wheel movement would be restricted to less than an inch up or down (if the salt is too rough for these limits, it is too rough for a record attempt).

It is my opinion that a well-controlled independent suspension system such as the Watt link would give the maximum stability and control obtainable. I don't believe in, and wouldn't build, a car that has no suspension because even with tire flexibility

Fastest internal combustion reciprocating engine-powered car in the world was Mickey Thompson's four Pontiac V-8 engined car at 406 mph. Two-way record run was not completed so car didn't get official record.

Summer Bros. second streamliner was this four wheel drive, four engine (in line) Chrysler V-8 "Goldenrod". It is currently the World's Fastest Wheel-driven car, with a two-way average of 409.277 mph set in 1965.

Els Lohn tried various engines in several small streamliners and finall in 1967 coaxed 193.167 mph out of this sohc Coventry Climax-powered car.

One of the most successful cars to run at Bonneville was the Lynn Yakel-designed Larsen-Cummins car. With a 3-liter Chevy V-8 it set record of 289.51, then with 2-liter half-a-Chevy it did 240 mph one-way, 228 mph average.

The "Orangecrate", above, started out as a Honda powered car, ended up with a Triumph motorcycle engine and records in 1966 at 129.507 mph and in 1967 the two-way average was raised to 142.693 mph.

Top left. A Mercury outboard engine propelled this little streamliner to 153 mph. The popularity of smaller cars to try for the smaller engine class records has grown in recent years and will no doubt continue.

Matt Guzzetta's unique approach to a streamlined car, left, ran 137 mph with a 500 cc motorcycle engine but in a subsequent run with a 350 cc Yamaha, the car overturned on some rough salt - no damage to driver.

to absorb surface irregularities the inertial forces acting on the total weight of the vehicle running over a rough surface (and make no mistake, the Bonneville course gets rough!) are just too high for maximum directional control. An an independent suspension that allows wheelbase, track or camber changes has its effect on directional stability that may be even worse than no suspension at all. Obviously, we are talking about straight line running, the Watt link offers no advantage for a road car that I can see and would, in fact, probably be detrimental to its ride and control.

And, in my mythical car, I would do everything possible for fire prevention and fire control. Sitting in the usually cramped cockpit of a streamliner there is a surprising amount of time to think about all the things that can fail - tires, wheel bearings, engine, clutch, or ??? But the thing most feared is fire. At two or three hundred

miles an hour, it takes an eternity to get stopped if something is wrong, and the driver is completely alone and on his own until he can come to a stop, and even then he may be at the far end of the salt bed, five or more miles from help.

This design exercise is strictly academic as I have no intention of designing or building another streamliner, but it does satisfy some mysterious creative urge that comes over me when I think about Bonneville.

This historical survey started out to be the complete, all knowing, all inclusive, fully documented and illustrated presentation, but writers, like racers, often find time is against them. Not every streamlined car that has run at Bonneville is included here - for which I apologize - but an historical comparison is possible and illustrates the variety of design philosophy in these cars.

World Diesel mark is held by Bill Snyder in Corsair II at 236.034 mph. Power was supplied by six cylinder Detroit diesel. Car also holds Class C record, with four cylinder engine, at 197.876 mph.

Bonneville Nationals rules allow this to run as a sports car, but Bonneville regulars calls Knot Farrington's T-Bird a "streatliner". It ran 228.571 mph one way, set class record of 216.56 with superchared chrysler.

Another "sports car" is Jack Lufkin's turbocharged Chevy V-8 [in photo it is Ford powered] which ran 294.11 mph in 1973 and set new record at 291.736 mph. Both Lufkin and Garrington are within National rules.

It is, in most cases, a pastime that is rewarding only in the satisfaction that one gets from a personal achievement. The popular press and most of the automotive press will devote space to the likes of Campbell, Breedlove, Arfons, Gabelich, etc., but virtually ignores the cars built to run in smaller classes or cars that run the Bonneville Nationals but never attempt an international record. And nothing should be taken away from the super-heros, they risk their lives and very often their life savings (along with considerable money from sponsors) in their record attempts. These efforts should be recognized. But the 290 mph, 3-liter, supercharged Chevy of Larsen-Cummins has accomplished a feat just as remarkable, and just as worthy as the 600 mph jet or rocket cars, with little or no world recognition.

All these "little guys" are my heros, not the ones who build the super-bucks "grounded aircraft" type of record car.

IMPROVEMENT OF HANDLING CHARACTERISTICS OF
AUTOMOBILES BY REDUCING THE AERODYNAMIC LIFT

H.-H. Braess, H. Burst, L. Hamm, R. Hannes
PORSCHE Aktiengesellschaft
Stuttgart, Germany

Presented by
David H. Weir
Systems Technology Incorporated
Hawthorne, California

Abstract

The aerodynamic development of the PORSCHE 911 model is traced through a review of extensive wind tunnel experiments and empirical data on racing cars. The effect of aerodynamics on handling, both steady state and transient, is discussed.

1. INTRODUCTION

During recent years the field of automotive aerodynamics, among other problem areas, has also been examined with increasing concern.

Through the original attempts to reduce the flow resistance in order to achieve a higher top speed and a lower fuel consumption, one recognized in the 1930's the important influence of aerodynamics on the directional stability of the automobile.[1] Detailed experiments showed that so-called "streamlined" automobiles very often were not only too sensitive to side winds but also produced even stronger lift forces than nonstreamlined automobiles[2]. Because the primary safety of automobiles and in addition the competitiveness of sports and racing cars are generally reduced by these effects, intensive work has been undertaken during the last two decades to improve aerodynamic characteristics. As in many other areas racing has proved to be the pace maker. It was possible to examine a series of solutions obtained not only in the wind tunnel but also under actual driving conditions[3,4,5,6,7]. Additionally theory has shown how fundamentally aerodynamics effect the handling and side wind sensitivity of the automobile[8,9,10].

The present work, based on the previous systematic examination by the Porsche Company of the aerodynamics in the wind tunnel and on the test track, shows the effects of wind tunnel developed solutions on handling characteristics for the 911 production model. In addition to the practical applications of these results, which are seldomly encountered in the literature, there are two worthwhile reasons for bringing these results to light. Firstly, the basic value of the wind tunnel as an important developmental tool for improving the automobile is verified. Secondly, the results suggest ways to improve the theoretical models for determining the effects of aerodynamics on handling and stability at high speed.

2. WIND TUNNEL RESULTS OF FRONT AND REAR SPOILERS

As a result of the experience gained with racing cars, especially the type 917, work was begun in 1970 to modify the external form of the type 911 with the purpose of improving the flow around the car without appreciably changing the basic shape of the automobile. The firt results of these efforts may be seen in Figures 1 and 2.

Figure 1. Front Spoiler of PORSCHE 911 Carrera.

Figure 2. Rear Spoiler of PORSCHE 911 Carrera.

Figure 3. PORSCHE 911 in the Wind Tunnel.

The aerodynamic characteristics with these two spoilers were so improved, especially with regard to the reduced lift and the distance between the center of gravity and the center of pressure, (side wind moment arm) that these spoilers found application in the normal production automobiles.

Further development efforts were continued in the wind tunnel, Figure 3, resulting in the configurations shown in Figures 4 and 5.

As may be seen from the figures, the front spoiler is nearly fully integrated with the front section of the car, whereas the fiber glass reinforced polyester rear spoiler was executed as an addition to the engine cover. Two important design criteria were form stiffness in order to withstand high speed aerodynamic forces as well as vibration

Figure 4. Front Spoiler of the Modified
PORSCHE 911 Carrera.

Figure 5. Rear Spoiler of the Modified
PORSCHE 911 Carrera.

and also light weight. To improve the external aspects of the secondary safety of the automobile, the ends of the rear spoiler are protected with rubber.

While it is possible to design a form for racing cars which is relatively free of compromise, the normal street version requires that special attention be paid to such details as adequate ground clearance as well as details which are relevant to traffic conditions such as external safety features for the protection of pedestrians and cyclists.

Considering these restrictions, it is remarkable that the front spoiler reduces the lift of the front axle at zero angle of yaw by 90%, as shown in Figure 6.

The gradient of the frontal lift coefficient as a function of the angle of yaw could not be improved, as expected[11]; but the absolute values are lower throughout the whole range, Figure 7.

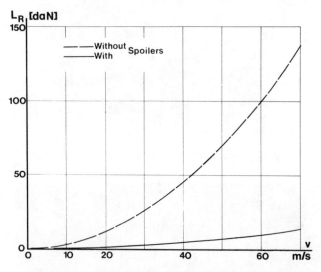

Figure 8. Rear Lift at Zero Yaw Angle.

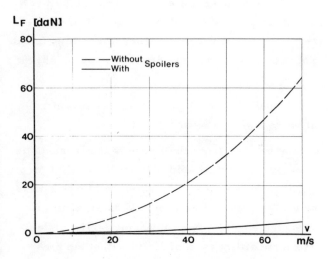

Figure 6. Frontal Lift at Zero Yaw Angle.

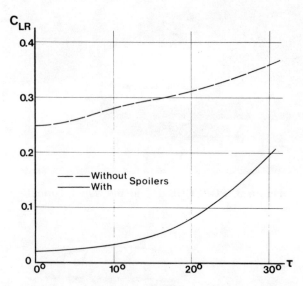

Figure 9. Rear Lift Coefficient as a Function of Yaw Angle.

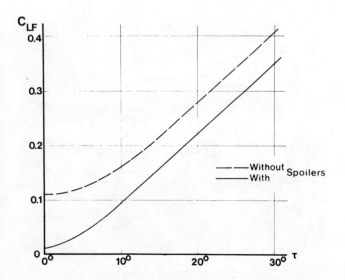

Figure 7. Front Lift Coefficient as a Function of Yaw Angle.

Because a higher down force on the rear axle improves the directional stability[12, 13], special attention was given to the rear spoiler. As may be seen from Figures 8 and 9, the results of this effort can be described quite satisfactorily.

With this rear spoiler it was possible to achieve a nearly zero rear lift at small angles of yaw. The relative down force at a speed of 40 m/s is

150

about 45 kp, which represents a gain in rear axle weight of about 6 to 7%. As it will be shown, this increase in rear axle loading results in an improvement of the directional stability and therefore in overall handling. As is the case with the front spoiler, we see from Figure 9 that the rear lift coefficient increases with the angle of yaw[11].

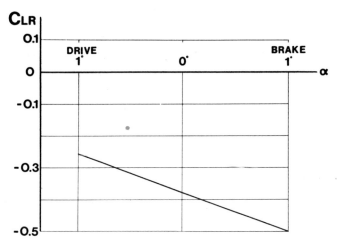

Figure 10. Rear Lift Coefficient as a Function of Pitch Angle (917-20 Racing car).

Braking manoeuvers are often of even greater importance than constant velocity driving conditions. This is true because during heavy braking manoeuvers, the directional stability of the automobile is reduced primarily as a result of the lower cornering power of the rear axle[14]. Whereas the rear down force increases markedly with the braking dive angle on the 917-20 racing

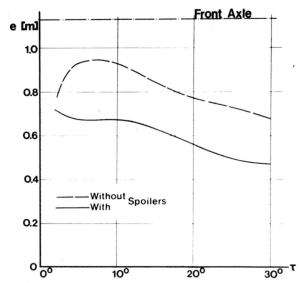

Figure 13. Distance Between Center of Gravity and Center of Pressure as a Function of Yaw Angle.

car, Figure 10, it was possible to realize only a small portion of this effect on the 911 car. But the experience tells us that progress will be possible.

As a result of the improved air flow around the automobile due to the spoilers, as shown by the tuft studies of Figures 11 and 12, the important parameter characterizing the side wind sensitivity also shows an improvement. Figure 13 shows that the characteristic quantity of the distance between the center of gravity and the center of pressure as a function of the yaw angle is appreciably reduced for the Carrera with its spoilers.

Figure 11. Airflow at the Rear End Without Spoiler.

Figure 12. Airflow at the Rear End With Spoiler.

151

This quantity, which represents a moment arm for the resultant side wind force about the vertical axis through the center of gravity is known to be an important factor in the sensitivity of the car to sidewinds[10, 15].

Lastly, it would be of interest to note that all presented improvements did not induce an increase of the total drag. Even this value is reduced by 2%. At higher angles of yaw the reduction is even more pronounced.

3. RESULTS OF ROAD TESTING

As previously mentioned, road testing of the automobiles with spoilers was employed to determine how the modified aerodynamic forces influence the handling and stability.

3.1 STEADY-STATE CORNERING BEHAVIOUR

Because steady-state cornering behaviour is the basis for evaluating handling characteristics, and also because it is especially suitable for determining the primary influence of the spoiler, namely the increased front and rear axle cornering force capability, numerous circular skid pad tests were carried out. The results, obtained on two different skid pads with various radii, are shown in Figure 14.

In order to be able to compare the test results with those of other cars, the usual presentation of

the actual steering wheel angle as a function of vehicle velocity or lateral acceleration was not chosen, rather the steering wheel angle was divided by the product of the wheelbase and the overall steering ratio. This value can be considered as the static steering sensitivity[16, 17].

It is surprising that the effect of the spoiler is felt at speeds as low as 17 m/s. Because the increase in wheel load due to the spoiler is greater on the rear axle than the front axle, the test car, which in unmodified form oversteers at the friction limit, exhibits with spoilers a continuously but slightly increasing steering wheel angle.

The curves of Figure 14 show that the spoiler is a good means for achieving an increased cornering limit. Additional benefits obtained with spoilers are a slightly understeering effect at high speeds as well as a more neutral tendency at slow speeds in tight corners. This behaviour is considered to be worthwhile based on the years of experience gathered by the Porsche Company.

Experience has shown that at the limit of adhesion where the automobile behaves in a nonlinear fashion, sometimes small changes in the dynamic parameters can have a strong influence on the behaviour in this region, as indeed these tests also indicate. Theoretical considerations verify that these empirical results are well founded[18, 19]. For this reason, no attempt was made to determine stability coefficients, or understeer parameters, which derive from linear theory of vehicle dynamics.

3.2 TRANSIENT BEHAVIOUR

Because the control of the vehicle in actual driving situations, especially during difficult manoeuvers, is only possible by means of a closed loop man-machine-system, all aspects of transient response must be taken into consideration.

The first example deals with the so-called power-off effect, in which a vehicle cornering at the limit normally exhibits oversteer when the power is removed[20].

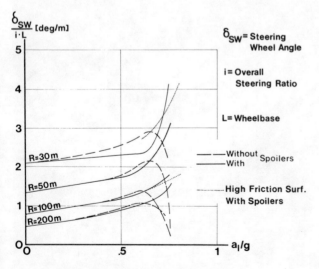

Figure 14. Steady-state Corner Behavior.

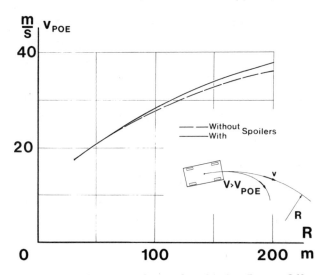

Figure 15. Cornering Speed Considering Power-Off Effects.

As Figure 15 shows, the velocity at which the car oversteers into the corner increases due to the improved cornering capability as a function of the turn radius. The improvements, which are naturally small in tight corners, can however be reproduced by a highly qualified test driver.

In a critical situation, for example in a suddenly necessary avoidance manoeuver, the vehicle must be able to respond quickly to a drastic steering input, however following such a manoeuver, the vehicle movements must be rapidly damped[21].

Figure 16 shows a comparison of two tests with and without spoilers. The two cases were selected from records containing a large number of tests. The two selected cases are practically identical with regard to the steering wheel time histories.

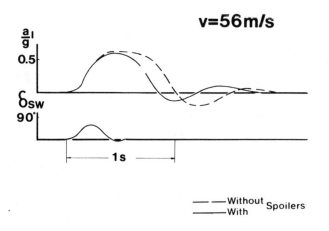

Figure 16. Transient Behavior at High Speed.

The time function depicts a reduction in the phase lag between the lateral acceleration and the steering wheel movement as well as a reduction in the damping time for the vehicle with spoilers. Because Porsche experience indicates that both of these quantities greatly enhance the driver's feeling during this manoeuver, especially at higher speeds[22,23,24], this improvement, which is based on the increase in lateral force capability, is considered significant[25].

Because braking in a turn presents problems owing to high demands placed on the available adhesion between tires and road and also as a result of the dynamic effects (especially load transfers), this situation must be examined[19].

Figure 17 shows the stopping times of a vehicle, which enters a narrow, pylon-defined turn with a speed of 40 m/s. Due to increased directional stability of the car with spoilers, a markedly improved deceleration was made possible. In addition there was a tendency for less scatter in the data, which speaks well for improved handling.

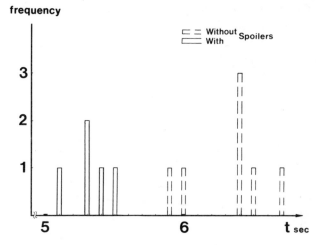

Figure 17. Braking in a turn.

This effect, which shows the consistency of handling, is well known also from other driving tasks. Note that the degree of difficulty experienced by the driver is reduced significantly. As Figure 18 shows, only small steering wheel corrections are necessary with spoilers at equal initial velocity and even increased deceleration, whereas the driver was able to control the artificially hard

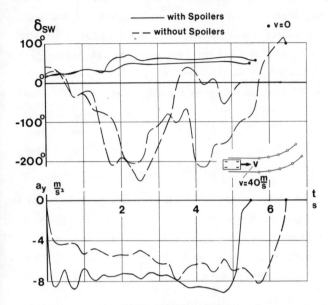

Figure 18. Braking in a Turn.

situation without spoilers only with considerable steering wheel movements.

3.3   SIDE WIND SENSITIVITY

Even though the lateral path deviation of the automobile with constant steering wheel position under the influence of side winds is not an absolute criterion for evaluating the side wind sensitivity[10], the results of the current work are presented so that the influence of the down force and the position of center of pressure can be recognized.

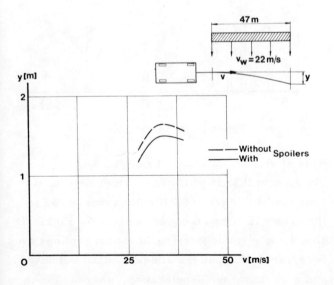

Figure 19. Side Wind Sensitivity.

Figure 19 depicts a reduction in lane deviation due to wide winds. From these data it may be seen that a maximum deviation occurs at 33 m/s, however it must be remembered that at higher velocities the shorter time of side wind exposure has a great influence on the results.

The reduction in lane deviation is smaller than one would expect from wind tunnel measured side wind moment arm. Even though this quantity has an important influence, other phenomena such as the magnitude of the resultant wind force (which is slightly increased as a result of the spoilers), the rolling moment, the transient behaviour of all forces and the interaction between the chassis dynamics and the aerodynamic forces are also important[10,26].

4.   CONCLUSIONS

The present work has shown that all important aerodynamic forces acting on a car body can be improved by properly designed front and rear spoilers.

The result of the spoiler-induced downthrusts is an increased lateral force capability which improves the steady-state as well as the transient lateral behaviour of a car.

ACKNOWLEDGEMENT

The authors wish to thank Mr. Stokley for his help with the translation.

REFERENCES

(1)   Sawatzki, E., "Einfluss der Luftkräfte auf die Stabilität des Kraftfahrezeuges," DKF Nr. 70, 1941.

(2)   Barth, R., "Einfluss der Form und der Umströmung von Kraftfahrzeugen auf Widerstand, Bodenhaftung und Fahrtrichtungshaltung," VDI-Z, 1956, pp. 1265-1275.

(3)   Walker, G.E. Lind, "Car Aerodynamics," Automobile Engineer, 1958, pp. 262-270.

(4) Mezger, H., "Der Porsche 4,5 1 - Rennsportwagen Typ 917," <u>ATZ</u>, 1969, pp. 417-423.

(5) Boyce, T.R. and P.J. Lobb, "An Investigation of the Aerodynamics of Current Group 6 Sports Car Design," <u>Advances in Road Vehicle Aerodynamics</u>, 1973; Published by BHRA Fluid Engineering.

(6) Scibor-Rylski, A., "Experimental Investigation of the Negative Aerodynamic Lift Wings Used on Racing Cars," <u>Advances in Road Vehicle Aerodynamics</u>, 1973; Published by FHRA Fluid Engineering.

(7) Mezger, H., "Der Porsche Turbo-Rennwagen 917," <u>ATZ</u>, 1973, pp. 362-367.

(8) Mitschke, M., "Fahrtrichtungshaltung und Fahrstabilität von vierrädrigen Kraftfahrzeugen," Deutsche Kraftfahrtforschung Heft 135, 1960.

(9) Pershing, B., "The Influence of External Aerodynamics on Automotive System Design Requirements," <u>Advances in Road Vehicle Aerodynamics</u>, 1973; Published by BHRA Fluid Engineering.

(10) Gnadler, R., "Beitrag zum Problem Fahrer-Fahrzeug-Seitenwind," A.I. Nr. 3, 1973, pp. 109-138.

(11) Potthoff, J., "Luftwiderstand und Auftrieb moderner Kraftfahrzeuge," <u>Proc. First Symp. Road Vehicle Aerodynamics</u>, 1969, London.

(12) Toti, G., "Aerodynamic Effects on Vehicle Moving in Stationary Air and Their Influence on Stability and Steering Control," SAE Paper 948 D , 1965.

(13) Hales, F.D., "External Aerodynamics and the Stability of Road Vehicles," von Karman Institute, Brussels, April 1972.

(14) Lugner, P., "Untersuchungen über die Kurvenfahrt eines Kraftfahrzeuges," Diss. T.H., Wien, 1969.

(15) Mitschke, M., "Dynamik der Kraftfahrzeuge," Springer Verlag, 1972.

(16) Hoffmann, E.R. and P.N. Joubert, "The Effect of Changes in Some Vehicle Handling Variables on Driver Steering Performance," <u>Human Factors</u>, 1966, pp. 245-263.

(17) Braess, H.-H., "Theoretische Untersuchung des Lenkverhaltens von Kraftfahrzeugen," Diss. T.U., Munchen, 1971.

(18) Rompe, K., "Zum Lenkverhalten von Kraftfahrzeugen bei stationärer und instationärer Kreisfahrt im Grenzbereich," Diss. T.U., Hanover, 1972.

(19) Sorgatz, U., and F. Ammesdörfer, "Einfluss von Traktion und Rollwiderstand auf das Fahrverhalten bei höheren Querbeschleunigungen," <u>ATZ</u>, 1974, pp. 8-11.

(20) Sorgatz, U., and F. Ammesdörfer, "Die Lastwechselreaktionen von Personenkraftwagen bei Kurvenfahrt mit höheren Querbeschleunigungen," VDI-Z, 1974.

(21) Ervin, R.D., et al, "Refinement and Application of Open-Loop Limit-Manoeuver Response Methods," SAE Paper 730491.

(22) Seznec, M., "Vehicle Dyanmics in Safety Research," Report 1, Int. ESV Conference, Paris, 1971, pp. 75-79.

(23) Chatelet, A., and P. Auhtuan, "Dynamique du Système Conducteur-Vehicule," <u>Ingenieurs de L'Automobile</u>, 1973, pp. 757-810.

(24) Jones, G., "Vehicle Handling," Report 3, ESV Conference, Washington, 1972, pp. 2-75 - 2-78.

(25) Strackerjan, B., "Fahrversuche und Berechnungen zur Kurshaltung von Personenkraftwagen," Diss. T.U., Braunschweig, 1973.

(26) Hawks, R.J. and E.E. Larrabee, "The Effectiveness of Automatic Guidance in Reducing Automobile Cross-Wind Response," <u>Advances in Road Vehicle Aerodynamics</u>, 1973; Published by FHRA Fluid Engineering.

AUD. QUESTION: Was the data on front end and back end lift of the Porsche obtained from wind tunnel tests or from actual road tests?

WIER: It is my understanding that all the data in the presentation are wind tunnel other than the handling data, of course, which were full scale skid pad results.

AUD. QUESTION: Do you have any comment on the change in steering characteristics from understeer to oversteer for only a 30 meter radius (Figure 15). That would correspond to a speed of 30 to 35 mph.

PETER BRYANT: The normal response of a sports car when you back off the throttle is to oversteer.

WIER: That's right. Figure 15 shows the velocity at which oversteer transition occurs. They must have made a number of repeat runs observing how fast they could go and get an oversteering situation when they did go on tread and throttle. Figure 15 shows a minor effect with spoilers on; it's not really very much.

BOB WHITE: I've been at the test track and watched them run some of those tests and I can attest to the fact that the car does that. I drove a Carrera prototype a year or so ago and found that when you take the power off on these rear engine cars, you go into an oversteer condition.

WIER: Figure 14, which plots the steady state cornering behavior, shows that at the higher lateral accelerations there is a dramatic effect from the spoilers. The car is oversteer without the spoiler and understeer with it, even at the very small turn radius of 30 meters (about 100 feet) which

would correspond to a velocity of about 35 mph. It is surprising that there would be so strong a spoiler effect at that low speed.

PAUL LAMAR: If they had changed the swaybar of the car to compensate for the addition of the spoiler, they can get the characteristics with and without spoilers shown in Figure 14.

WIER: That's a very good point. It's not clear in the paper but they may be comparing the '74 Carrera with the basic 911 in which case there would be a significant difference in suspension as well as in rear tires.

WHITE: This may also have been an experimental model because the values of lateral acceleration are low for a Carrera. They typically get 0.9 on that same skid pad.

WIER: They may not have pushed it to that point in this series of tests.

RAY KILLS: To what would you attribute this abrupt transition shown in Figure 14 from understeer to oversteer without spoilers, and how would the spoiler so strongly affect that transition?

WIER: The understeer-oversteer transition without the spoiler is a typical behavior pattern and is due to tire and suspension characteristics; just a basic dynamic effect. The continued understeer at the high lateral accelerations spoiler-on is probably due to the difference in suspension between the Carrera and 911. It is more reasonable to attribute the difference to that since at those low speeds the spoiler is not generating very much download as shown in Figures 6 and 8.

The Effect of Aerodynamic Download on Automobile Handling

Roger J. Hawks
Assistant Professor of Mechanical Engineering
Clarkson College of Technology
Potsdam, New York 13676

Abstract

A series of calculations have been performed which investigate the effect of various forms of aerodynamic download on stability, steady-state steering response, and path response using both small
disturbance equations of motion and a ten-degree-of-freedom computer simulation of automobile
dynamics. It was found that aerodynamic download will improve cornering performance but that
the cornering performance in a vacuum may be a practical upper limit.

NOMENCLATURE

AT = Tire aligning torque (lb-ft/rad)

A_0 = Empirical constant (lb/rad)

A_1 = Empirical constant (rad^{-1})

A_2 = Empirical constant (lb)

A_3 = Empirical constant (rad^{-1})

A_4 = Empirical constant (lb)

C = Tire cornering stiffness (lb/rad)

CT = Tire camber thrust (lb/rad)

N = Yawing moment (lb-ft)

W = Vehicle weight (lb)

Y = Side Force (lb)

Z = Tire load (lb)

ℓ = Vehicle Wheelbase (ft)

n = Dimensionless yawing moment

r = Turn rate

t = Tire pneumatic trail (ft)

α = Tire slip angle

β = Vehicle side-slip angle

γ = Tire inclination angle

δ = Steer angle

1. INTRODUCTION

The effect of aerodynamic download on an automobile during cornering involves a very complex
process which is not yet fully understood. The
multiplicity of parameters involved in cornering makes
any rational analysis very difficult so that the
empirical approach must be utilized. However, a
carefully planned set of experiments aimed at a
complete understanding of the aerodynamic influences
on cornering, while of great academic interest, would
be of little practical use to the race car designer.
Thus, the more common approach has been to make
various changes, such as wing size and location, all
at once and then test to see if an improvement in
cornering speed was achieved. This process continues
until the optimum (from the viewpoint of the driver)
cornering performance is obtained. By this process
the optimum aerodynamic configuration has evolved.
This configuration consists of a large aerodynamic
download located as far to the rear of the vehicle as
possible along with a somewhat smaller download
located very far forward.

In an effort to better understand these results, a series of analyses have been performed attempting to describe the aerodynamic effects on cornering. In the first of these[1], it was shown that aerodynamic download could increase the maximum cornering speed of the vehicle. Brunelli[2] and Pershing[3] both showed that the simple static stability of the vehicle could be enhanced by adding download at the rear. Pershing[3] also investigated the effect of download on the steady-state steering response of a rigid automobile.

Even though static stability is a sufficient condition for stability in a rigid automobile, it is not necessary since a statically unstable vehicle could still be dynamically stable. When the suspension system is included, the vehicle must have both static and dynamic stability. The suspension system also greatly affects the handling qualities. Thus a more careful analysis must consider both dynamic stability and handling for an automobile with a suspension system. Furthermore, the actual path response of the vehicle will also depend on the response time, the lateral velocity, and the turn rate so that simply classifying the steering characteristics will not be sufficient to determine the maximum cornering performance of the vehicle.

This paper describes a series of calculations which investigate the effect of various forms of aerodynamic download on stability, steering response, and path response using both small disturbance equations of motion and a ten-degree-of-freedom computer simulation.

2. SAMPLE VEHICLE

All of the calculations described in this paper were based on the Lola T-140 Formula A car. This car was selected since its inertia and geometric properties are well known. The basic vehicle (with driver) weighs 1740 lbs and has a wheelbase of 8 ft. The center of gravity is located 5.13 ft behind the front wheels. Both front and rear suspensions are of the double link independent type. The roll centers are consequently very low, and the suspension has very high roll stiffness.

The force and moment characteristics of a pneumatic tire are determined primarily by the normal load on the tire and by the slip and inclination angles. Except for a few extremely violent maneuvers (such as skids and spins) most automobile motions involve relatively small values of slip angle and inclination angle. The tire side force can then be represented by

$$Y = C\alpha + CT\gamma \tag{1}$$

where C is the cornering stiffness and CT the camber thrust of the tire. Both C and CT are functions of normal load on the tire and inflation pressure. The relationship between C, CT, and the normal load Z can be described by equations of the form[4]

$$C = - [A_0 + A_1 Z (1 - \frac{Z}{A_2})] \tag{2}$$

$$CT = A_3 Z (1 - \frac{Z}{A_4}) \tag{3}$$

Both of these equations apply for normal forces such that

$$Z \leq \Omega A_2 \tag{4}$$

Above this load, the tire is operating in an extreme overload condition and C and CT are assumed to have the values obtained for a load of ΩA_2.

The aligning torque produced by a tire is given by

$$N = AT\alpha \tag{5}$$

where AT is related to the cornering stiffness by

$$AT = - tC \tag{6}$$

t is the pneumatic trail and is assumed to be a constant in this analysis. The values of the tire constants used are given in Table 1.

Table I
Tire Properties For Lola-T-140

Constant	Front Tires	Rear Tires
A_0 (lb/rad)	4400	6600
A_1 (rad^{-1})	12.7	9.16
A_2 (lb)	2900	3500
A_3 (rad^{-1})	1.78	1.78
A_4 (lb)	3900	3550
Ω	1	1
t (ft)	0.389	0.32

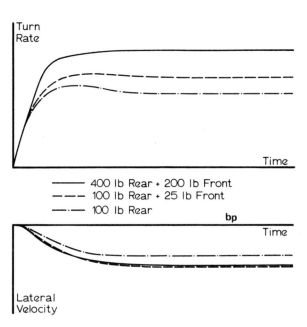

Figure 1. Effect of Download Distribution on Rigid Car.

3. RIGID BODY ANALYSIS

If the suspension system is ignored, the vehicle becomes a rigid body. The requirement for static stability of the rigid automobile is that

$$n_\beta = \frac{1}{W\ell} \; \frac{\partial N}{\partial \beta} > 0 \qquad (7)$$

n_β is a function of the cg location of the vehicle and the values of C and AT for the tires. Ignoring aerodynamic effects for the Lola produces a negative value for n_β ($n_\beta = -0.41$). Thus, the vehicle is statically unstable at all speeds. However, if the dynamic stability is considered,[5] it is found that the vehicle is dynamically stable for all speeds up to the critical speed of 182.5 mph. The vehicle is stable below 182.5 mph but has a static instability (divergence) above that speed. By considering the steady-state turn rate (r_{ss}/δ), it is found that the Lola is oversteering at all speeds.

To determine the effect of aerodynamic download on the handling, the rigid body equations of motion were first programmed on an analog computer. A series of runs were then made to assess the effect of various aerodynamic configurations on the turn rate and lateral velocity at a speed of 140 mph. It was found that the response, in terms of both steady-state values and response time, was best when additional download was added to both the rear and the front of the vehicle (Fig. 1).

On the basis of these results, a particular aerodynamic configuration was selected for further study. This configuration consisted of a rear mounted wing with an area of 6 ft^2 and a lift coefficient of 1.6 and a wing mounted on the front of the vehicle with an area of 5 ft^2 and a lift coefficient of 0.8. The aerodynamic download on the front of the vehicle is then about 40% of that on the rear and the center of pressure is located 56.5% of the wheelbase behind the front wheels (or 7.3 in ahead of the cg).

The effect of download on the rigid body static stability of this vehicle is shown in Fig. 2. The aerodynamic download produces static stability in the vehicle at a speed of 143 mph. Thus, with the wings attached, the vehicle is stable at all speeds, having dynamic stability below 143 mph and static stability above that speed. Fig. 3 shows the steady-state turn rate of the vehicle. The vehicle is now oversteering below 143 mph but is understeering for higher speeds.

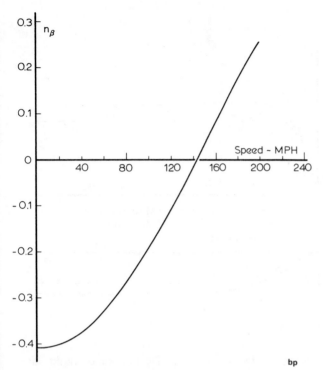

Figure 2. Static Stability of Rigid Car With Download.

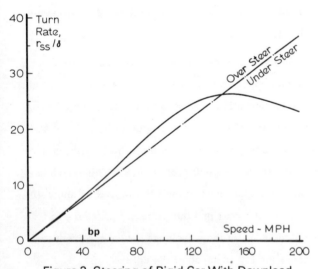

Figure 3. Steering of Rigid Car With Download.

4. EFFECT OF SUSPENSION SYSTEM

The next step is to consider the effect of the suspension system. The basic equations of motion for an automobile with suspension system are available in the literature[5,6]. These equations are linearized by assuming that the vehicle motions are small. In general, there are no simple stability relationships

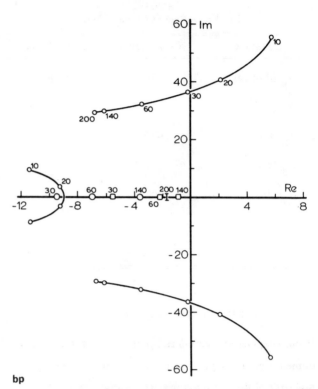

Figure 4. Stability of Car With Suspension-No Download.

for the automobile with a suspension system. A critical speed can be found which is the maximum speed at which the vehicle is statically stable. However, the vehicle need not be dynamically stable below the critical speed. Therefore a more general stability criterion is needed. In order to find the effect of a given parameter on stability, the usual approach is to construct a locus of roots diagram for the characteristic equation of the system. Since the characteristic equation for an automobile with a suspension system is a quartic, the digital computer is often used to obtain these plots.

For the Lola T-140 without wings but with a suspension system, the critical speed is found to be 171 mph. Above this speed, the car is statically unstable. From the root locus plot (Fig. 4), it is found that the vehicle has both static and dynamic stability for speeds less than the critical speed. (There is a slight roll instability for speeds less than 30 mph but this

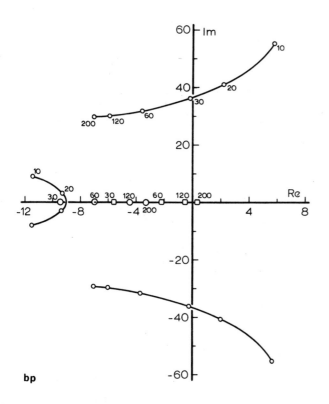

bp

Figure 5. Stability of Car With Suspension and Download.

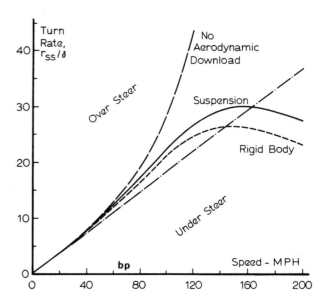

Figure 6. Steering of Car With Dowload.

has little effect on controlability.) From a consideration of steady-state turn rate, it is found that the vehicle is oversteering at all speeds.

When the wings are added to the vehicle with the suspension system, the vehicle is stabilized for all operating speeds. The root locus plot (Fig. 5) shows that the stability decreases to 140 mph but then increases as the aerodynamic loads build up. The steady-state steering response is shown in Fig. 6. With the suspension system acting the vehicle oversteers for speeds less than 163 mph. This is a higher transition speed than was obtained for the rigid car. Basing download requirements on the rigid car model thus will not provide sufficient download when the suspension system is acting. Larger downloads will be required with the suspension system in order to produce high speed understeer.

5. DIGITAL COMPUTER SIMULATION

Even when the stability and handling characteristics of a vehicle are well known, a prediction of the max-

imum cornering speed attainable by the automobile is difficult. Since high speed cornering involves high lateral accelerations and large tire slip angles, small-disturbance equations of motion cannot be used to study the effect of aerodynamics on cornering ability. Therefore, in order to analyze the effect of aerodynamics on cornering one of the more sophisticated computer models must be used. The most successful of these is the HVOSM (Highway-Vehicle-Object Simulation)[4] which has been modified to include a full compliment of aerodynamic forces and moments and a general wind gust input.[7,8] This digital computer simulation was used to study the effect of aerodynamics on cornering ability. As a measure of cornering ability, the maximum speed at which the vehicle could negotiate a 90° turn of constant radius was determined. The test conditions used were a turn of radius 350 ft with a vehicle throttle setting which would produce an acceleration of 0.1 g if the vehicle were traveling in a straight line. The vehicle speed entering the corner was increased until the vehicle could no longer negotiate the turn within the limits of a 15 ft highway. The maximum entrance speed at which the turn could be negotiated was thus found.

In order for the vehicle to properly execute the turn, it was necessary to use some form of closed-loop steering control. The method used was the wagon-tongue path-follower system.[4,7] This system is very stable and has a high level of damping.

Aerodynamic data for the vehicle was obtained from wind tunnel testing on similar vehicles.[9] Several different aerodynamic configurations were studied. In addition to the basic vehicle (clean configuration), the effect of wings mounted on the rear suspension and front body work as well as nose canards (dive planes) were considered. Calculations were also made with all the aerodynamic forces set to zero (operation in a vacuum) for comparison.

Results of these calculations are shown in Table 2. The speeds shown are the maximum speeds at which the vehicle can enter the corner and still complete the 90° turn. These speeds represent the absolute maximums, since, at the entrance speeds given, the vehicle is actually sliding through the corner with the steering at full-lock.

Table II
Maximum Cornering Speed of Lola

Vehicle Configuration	Maximum Speed mi/hr
No Aerodynamics	62
Clean	60
Wing on Rear Axle	59
Wing on Rear Axle and Front Wing on Body	62
Wing on Rear Axle and Nose Canards	60
Wing on Rear Axle, Front Wing on Body, and Nose Canards	62

The most obvious feature of these results is that the best that can be achieved through the use of these aerodynamic download producing devices is no better than that which can be achieved in a vacuum. Cornering performance with the rear wing mounted directly to the rear axle was most surprising.

Popular opinion indicates that this is the most advantageous use of aerodynamics, and previous analyses have been directed toward this situation. The present results, however, indicate that this use of aerodynamic forces not only gives the worst cornering performance but actually reduces the cornering speed below that achieved with no auxiliary devices.

From the results obtained here, it can be concluded that aerodynamic download on the rear wheels alone will not improve cornering speed but will actually degrade it. In order to improve cornering speed, the lift on the body of the vehicle must be reduced and, preferably, aerodynamic download should be produced by the body. A nose-down pitching moment also helps to improve cornering speed, but is not as important as download on the body.

These results seem to contradict the experience of several racing organizations. The performance improvements which have resulted by adding wings to racing cars, while real, probably were not produced entirely by the rear wing. Improvements in tire and suspension design were made concurrently with the addition of wings. Furthermore, aerodynamic improvements were not limited to the addition of a single rear wing. In almost all cases, extensive redesign of the body shape of the vehicle was done at the same time. Front mounted wings and canards were usually also installed in order to provide more suitable handling. Thus the body lift was greatly reduced at the same time the rear wing was added, and the present results show that cornering performance is improved by reducing body lift.

REFERENCES

(1) Lamar, P., "Aerodynamics and the Group Seven Racing Car," Proc. Symposium on the Aerodynamics of Sports and Competition Automobiles (B. Pershing, Ed.), American Institute of Aeronautics and Astronautics, New York, 1969, p. 23.

(2) Brunelli, G., Style Auto, Feb. 1968, p. 41.

(3) Pershing, B., "The Influence of External Aero-Dynamics on Automotive System Design Requirements," Advances in Road Vehicle Aerodynamics (H. Stephens, Ed.), British Hydromechanics Research Association, Cranfield, England, 1973, p. 25.

(4) McHenry, R. and N. DeLeys, Vehicle Dynamics in Single Vehicle Accidents - Validation and Extensions of a Computer Simulation, Rept. VJ-2251-V-3, Cornell Aeronautical Laboratory, Inc., Buffalo, NY, Dec. 1968.

(5) Ellis, J., Vehicle Dynamics, Business Books Ltd., London, 1969, p. 79, 137-171.

(6) Steeds, W., Mechanics of Road Vehicles, Iliff and Sons Ltd., London, 1960, p. 236-261.

(7) Hawks, R., The Effect of Aerodynamic Forces on the Performance and Handling Qualities of High Speed Automobiles, Ph.D. Dissertation, Univ. of Maryland, Jan. 1972.

(8) Hawks, R. and E. Larrabee, "The Effectiveness of Automatic Guidance in Reducing Automobile Cross-Wind Response," Advances in Road Vehicle Aerodynamics (H. Stephens, Ed.), British Hydromechanics Research Association, Cranfield, England, 1973, p. 67.

(9) The Aerodynamic Characteristics of Racing Cars Fitted with Aerofoils, Research Rept., Jim Clark Foundation, London, 1969.

DISCUSSION

PAUL LAMAR: You say that in the Calspan computer simulation used in the analysis you set the throttle to maintain 0.1 "g" straight-line acceleration. Was the 0.1 "g" acceleration held in the corner as well?

HAWKS: In the simulation, the throttle setting was fixed. This is equivalent to applying a constant torque to the rear wheels.

LAMAR: But that isn't a real life situation.

HAWKS: The Calspan program has damn near everything needed to describe the vehicle chassis, tire, and suspension characteristics. Still, there is a lot of controversy about what those computer simulations mean. I don't claim that the results I obtain are real life situations, but they are the same for each case I examined. This is the important point since my objective was to show the effect of various aerodynamic configurations under the same operating conditions.

LAMAR: The issue I take with the computer simulation is the use of the constant throttle setting. At high lateral acceleration the front tire drag becomes very large, on the order of 30% of the front end weight and use of a fixed throttle setting is unrealistic. It will give erroneous results. At a fixed throttle setting, aerodynamic download is a detriment to speed. You also concluded from your work that download should be distributed fore-and-aft in proportion to the weight distribution and this is also based on your use of a constant throttle setting.

AUD. QUESTION: With a fixed throttle setting, the speed is fixed not by the aerodynamic characteristics but by the scrubbing of the speed due to front tire drag as pointed out. If you apply throttle to compensate for the front tire drag, aerodynamic download will greatly increase the speed through the turn.

The initial critical speed you computed, 184 mph, is terribly low. I have my doubts that the Calspan equations for tire characteristics are applicable for racing tires. There is a drastic difference between street tires which develop their maximum side force at slip angles of about 15 degrees and racing tires which reach their peak at about 5 degrees.

DAVE WIER: To clarify the Calspan tire model, it doesn't have any numbers in it; it's just a set of functional relationships which include the effects of normal load, camber change, and many other details. The key question is, did you use racing tire data and if so, where did you get it? I would be surprised if you were able to quantify all these characteristics because racing tires haven't been tested enough.

HAWKS: Racing tire test data was unavailable. I selected numbers to use in the Calspan tire model which produced cornering stiffness values that agreed with values that appear to be obtained on the track.

THE EFFECT OF AERODYNAMICS ON THE PERFORMANCE AND STABILITY
OF HIGH SPEED MOTORCYCLES

K.R. Cooper

National Aeronautical Establishment

National Research Council of Canada

Ottawa, Canada

ABSTRACT

The effects of aerodynamics on the terminal velocity, acceleration and fuel consumption of a motorcycle were investigated analytically using measured mean aerodynamic force data. These data were obtained for a variety of full-sized motorcycles with riders mounted in the National Aeronautical Establishment's (NAE) 6 ft. × 9 ft. working section wind tunnel. A four-degree-of-freedom model of the motorcycle dynamics, incorporating the measured mean aerodynamic forces and estimated unsteady lateral derivatives, were used to examine the role of aerodynamics in motorcycle stability.

It was found that significant gains in performance could be realized for road, road racing and record motorcycles by careful attention to drag reduction. It was further found that the steady aerodynamic forces and moments exerted a stabilizing influence on the motorcycle dynamics. However, for extensively streamlined record motorcycles the aerodynamic side force, yawing moment and rolling moment due to yaw rate may lead to an oscillatory instability at high speeds. This aerodynamic mechanism may, in part, explain the handling problems encountered by so many of these motorcycles.

NOMENCLATURE

A	frontal area, ft.^{2}; origin of vertical body fixed coordinate system
a_b	acceleration due to brake application, ft./sec.^{2}
a_c	lateral cornering acceleration, ft./sec.^{2}
a_1, a_2	coefficients related to rolling resistance
B	motorcycle wheelbase, ft.
a, b, e, f h, j, k, l	motorcycle dimensions, Figure 19
c	camber as a fraction of the chord
C	chord, ft.; total streamlined motorcycle length, ft.
C_D	drag coefficient, $D_a/\frac{1}{2}\rho V^2 A$
C_L	lift coefficient, $L/\frac{1}{2}\rho V^2 A$
C_Y	side force coefficient, $Y/\frac{1}{2}\rho V^2 A$
C_M	pitching moment coefficient, $M/\frac{1}{2}\rho V^2 AB$
C_N	yawing moment coefficient, $N/\frac{1}{2}\rho V^2 AB$
C_R	rolling moment coefficient, $R/\frac{1}{2}\rho V^2 AB$
C_{f1}, C_{r1}	front and rear tire cornering stiffness coefficients
C_{f2}, C_{r2}	front and rear tire camber stiffness coefficients
C_{rxz}	rear frame product of inertia about axes parallel to AXYZ through the rear frame mass centre, slug ft.^{2}
D_a	aerodynamic drag force, lb.
D_r	rolling resistance, lb.
d	stopping distance, ft.; wheel diameter, ft.
F	force, lb.
f	fuel consumption, gal./sec.
g	acceleration due to gravity, 32.16 ft./sec.^{2}
I_{rx}, I_{ry}, I_{rz}	rear frame moments of inertia about axes parallel to AXYZ through the rear frame mass centre, slug ft.^{2}
I_{fx}, I_{fy}, I_{fz}	front frame moments of inertia about axes parallel to $AX_1 Y_1 Z_1$ through the front frame mass centre, slug ft.^{2}
i_{fy}, i_{ry}	front and rear wheel polar moments of inertia, slug ft.^{2}
i	polar moment of inertia of engine crankshaft and flywheel, slug ft.^{2}
K	steering damping constant, ft. lb./(rad./sec.)

L	aerodynamic lift force, lb.
l	longitudinal distance from rear frame CG to the front wheel contact point, ft.
l_1	longitudinal distance from the rear frame CG to the lateral centre of pressure of the front frame, ft.
l_2	height of the front frame lateral centre of pressure above the ground, ft.
l_3	perpendicular distance from the front frame lateral centre of pressure to the steering axis, ft.
l_4	longitudinal distance from the centre of pressure of the unsteady side force to the rear frame CG, ft.
M	aerodynamic pitching moment, lb. ft.
m	mass, slugs
N	aerodynamic yawing moment, lb. ft.
P	engine power, hp (550 lb. ft./sec.)
p_t	tire pressure, lb./in.^{2}
Q	generalized force, lb.
q	generalized coordinate
R	aerodynamic rolling moment, lb. ft.
R_e	Reynolds number based on total length, $\dfrac{CV}{v}$
r	corner radius, ft.
r_f	final drive ratio between transmission and rear wheel
r_i	i_{th} gear ratio
r_p	primary input gear ratio between engine and transmission
s	specific fuel consumption, gal./hp./sec.)
T	kinetic energy, lb. ft.
t	front wheel trail, ft.; time, sec.
U	potential energy, lb. ft.
V	forward speed, ft./sec.
V_c	cornering speed, ft./sec.
W	motorcycle weight, lb.
Y	aerodynamic side force, lb.
Z	vertical reaction force at tire-ground contact point, lb.
α	wind angle (Fig. 21), radians or degrees
γ	effective front wheel steer angle (Fig. 21), radians
$\triangle$	incremental quantity
δ	steering angle about axis AZ, radians
ϵ	steering head angle (Fig. 19), radians
η	transmission efficiency
θ	corner angle, degrees
λ	gear ratio between engine flywheel and rear wheel
μ	fuel consumption, ft./gal.
v	kinematic viscosity of air at STP, 1.567×10^{-4} ft.^{2}/sec.
ρ	air density at STP, 2.38×10^{-3} slugs/ft.^{3}
σ	tire relaxation length, ft.
ϕ	engine rotational displacement; motorcycle roll angle, radians
ψ	motorcycle yaw angle, radians

Subscripts and Superscripts

a	aerodynamic
sa	steady aerodynamic
ua	unsteady aerodynamic
r	rear wheel or rear frame
f	front wheel or frame
e	engine
t	tire property
Y	along AY
ψ	about AZ
ϕ	about AX
δ	about steering axis

Abbreviations

PS	partially streamlined fairing
FS	fully streamlined fairing
CG	centre of gravity
ET	elapsed time, sec
cp	centre of pressure

1. INTRODUCTION

Over much of its life span the motorcycle has been developed by a process of "empirical selection", whereby a design was formulated based on previous experience with little recourse to mathematical analysis. Although a mathematical analysis of the two-wheeled, single track vehicle was first published just before the beginning of this century[1], it was only recently that advanced formulations of the dynamics, incorporating adequate tire characteristics, were postulated. The work of Sharp[2], Ellis and Hayhoe[3], and Roland[4] is particularly noteworthy, providing considerable insight into single track vehicle stability and handling. However the two cases[2,3] which treated motorcycles did not include the influence of aerodynamic forces! By contrast, the effect of aerodynamics on both passenger and racing cars has received much attention resulting in significant improvements in handling and performance.

It may be readily shown that aerodynamics has a greater effect on motorcycle performance than on automobile performance due to the relative magnitude of tire and aerodynamic forces. Current passenger cars have average weights and frontal areas of approximately 4000 lb. and 25 ft.^{2} respectively, giving a weight to area ratio of 160 lb./ft.^{2}. The average motorcycle weight is about 550 lb. and with a frontal area of approximately 7.5 ft.^{2} (rider sitting) has a weight to area ratio of 73 lb./ft.^{2}. Since tire forces are proportional to weight, and aerodynamic forces can be related to frontal area, one can see that at the same speed the ratio of aerodynamic forces to tire forces will be greater for the motorcycle than for the automobile. In light of this finding it is surprising that more emphasis has not been placed on motorcycle aerodynamics.

The current program, initiated in July 1973 at the request of CAN-AM Motorcycles, a division of Bombardier Ltd., was first concerned with the design of low drag fairings to be used on a 125 c.c. motorcycle in the partially and fully streamlined classes at Bonneville the following August. CAN-AM had felt that the fairing used on the motorcycle the previous year, an off-the-shelf racing fairing, was not the optimum and wished to develop one with lower drag. That the work performed was successful was attested to when the motorcycle shattered the previous year's partially streamlined class record of 110.5 m.p.h. with a two way average of 136.5 m.p.h., running on alcohol. Unfortunately, this same motorcycle and fairing, with the addition of a full tail cone 2.5 ft. long became dynamically unstable at about 80 m.p.h. and was unrideable by 95 m.p.h. It was the occurrence of this event which gave impetus to the stability investigation. At the same time, analytical investigations into acceleration performance and fuel economy, as affected by aerodynamic drag, were undertaken with the hope of improving the performance of road motorcycles as well as racing machines.

It is hoped that the following discussion of the results of both the wind tunnel tests and the various analyses will provide a greater insight into the influence of aerodynamics on the performance and stability of a motorcycle and will indicate the potential benefits which may accrue when advantage is taken of a favourable aerodynamic configuration.

2. MEAN AERODYNAMIC FORCES

At the outset it would seem appropriate to consider the nature of the mean aerodynamic forces acting on motorcycles. The force measurements were made in a 6 ft. × 9 ft. working section wind tunnel (Fig. 1) whose maximum speed capability is 300 ft./sec.

The motorcycles were mounted on a 10-in. wide, 5-ft. long steel plate which was attached to the wind tunnel's six-component balance and lay flush with the top of the wind tunnel's turntable (Fig. 2). The rear axle was attached to two vertical struts and the front wheels rested on a small wheel lying flush with the top of the mounting plate. This small wheel was driven by a 1 h.p. electric motor and could spin the the motorcycle front wheel at a rotational speed equivalent to 124 m.p.h. Provision was made for pitch angle variations.

The removal of the ground plane boundary layer provides a reasonable wind tunnel simulation of a vehicle moving through the air over a fixed ground. A boundary layer "scraper" consisting of two 2-1/2 in. high plates (Fig. 3) mounted in a "V", pointing upstream ahead of the motorcycle, was used to remove the wind tunnel floor's boundary layer[5]. Use of this simple and effective device avoids the complexity of the more common separate ground board.

FIG. 1   Views of the Test Section Showing the CAN-AM 175 MX and Rider

FIG. 2   Mounting Plate and Turntable

FIG. 3   Boundary Layer Scraper

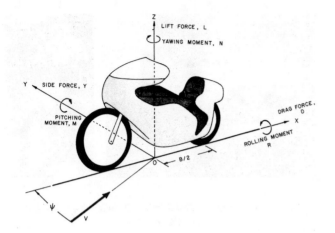

FIG. 4 Body Axes Coordinate System

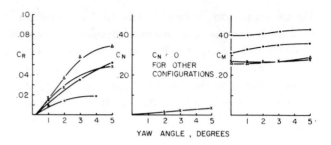

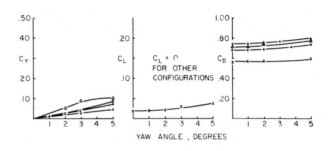

FIG. 5 Steady Aerodynamic Forces on Road Motorcycles

Three components of aerodynamic force (lift, drag, side force) and three aerodynamic moments (yaw, pitch, roll) were measured over a range of wind speeds and yaw angles. The forces and moments were measured by a balance fixed below the wind tunnel floor and were then transformed to a coordinate system fixed in the body. The origin of this coordinate system was at ground level, midway between the front and rear axles.

The detailed definition of the forces and moments in this system are shown in Figure 4. The forces and moments were non-dimensionalized in the standard manner as defined in the nomenclature. The aerodynamic data were corrected for both solid and wake blockage.

Measurements were made for a wide range of motorcycle-rider configurations including:

(i)   motocross machines
(ii) road machines with one and two riders in different positions
(iii) road machines with windshields and fairings
(iv) faired road racing machines
(v)   partially streamlined and fully streamlined record machines.

The data from these vehicles fall into two groups, one for road machines, the other for racing and record machines.

The force data for four different road bike configurations with riders are shown in Figure 5 for a range of yaw angles at a speed of 50 ft./sec. The lift coefficients for these vehicles are close to zero and the drag coefficients are high, ranging from 0.56 to 0.75 at zero yaw angle. The pitching moment coefficients are also high, primarily due to the drag vector acting above the ground. The slopes of the side force coefficient curves are low compared to those for highly streamlined motorcycles resulting in low slopes for the yawing moment and rolling moment curves.

The aerodynamic data for three full-scale, streamlined record machines with riders are shown in Figure 6 for a range of yaw angles at 140 m.p.h. When compared to the results in Figure 5 these machines are typified by reduced drag and pitching moments, moderate lift coefficients, high slopes of the curves for side force coefficient (especially for the machines with disk wheel fairings) and high slopes for the yawing moment and rolling moment coefficient curves. The high positive yawing moments in the presence of moderate length tails is probably a result of the forward movement of the lateral centre of pressure on the streamlined bodies. Some data measured in the 14 in. × 14 in. wind tunnel for a 1:10 scale model of a fully enclosed streamliner at 300 ft./sec. (Re = 2 × 10^6) are also included in this figure.

Rotation of the front wheel at road speed had no significant effect on the forces or moments except for a small reduction in lift coefficient. The reduction in lift agrees with observations made on other vehicles tested with rotating wheels[6].

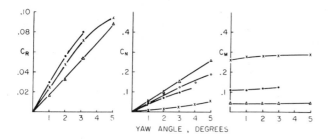

FIG. 7 Visualization of the Large Separated Wake Behind a Partially Streamlined Motorcycle, Re = 10^4

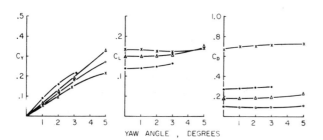

FIG. 6 Steady Aerodynamic Forces on Racing Motorcycles

The forces on the unstreamlined and partially streamlined motorcycles showed no change with increasing Reynolds number (increasing velocity) except for a tendency for drag to rise slightly. The fully enclosed streamliner, on the other hand, showed a large drag reduction with increasing Reynolds number.

No significant variation in the aerodynamic forces was found over a pitch angle range of 4 degrees for the partially and fully streamlined machines.

3. DRAG REDUCTION

The single most important aerodynamic parameter affecting motorcycle performance is the drag force, which may be expressed as

$$D_a = \tfrac{1}{2}\rho V^2 (C_D \cdot A) \qquad (3.1)$$

The drag coefficient is a measure of the nature of the flow around the motorcycle, and is typically 0.70 to 0.75 for the case of a single rider sitting upright on an unstreamlined machine. In comparison, most contemporary automobiles have drag coefficients in the range 0.40 - 0.45. As a result, the motorcycle may have a total aerodynamic drag which is 50 percent of that for a full size car, 60 percent of that for a compact car and 70 percent of that for a small car.

The high drag coefficients measured for the standard road motorcycle are primarily due to the large separated wake resulting from the bluff shape of the rider-machine combination and secondly from the cumulative effect of various small, high drag, exposed components of the motorcycle. This wake region is clearly shown in Figure 7, where a dye trace is used in the N.A.E.'s 10 in. × 13 in. test section water tunnel to visualize the flow around and behind a partially streamlined motorcycle.

There are only two ways to reduce this drag; one is to reduce the frontal area, as many riders do by leaning forward, the other is to change the shape of the vehicle and its components. The particular approach required depends upon whether the motorcycle is to be raced or ridden on the street.

A road motorcycle is generally configured for two people, and this requirement plus that of adequate freedom to monitor traffic beside and behind necessitates an upright rider position, allowing little possibility for frontal area reduction. On the other hand it is possible to provide a fairing and windshield which reduce the drag coefficient and at the same time improve rider comfort. However, the presence of a fairing per se does not guarantee drag reduction. In fact, based on reports in the literature, these fairings are designed primarily for comfort and appearance and often lead to an increase in fuel consumption and a reduction in performance. Wind tunnel tests on a prototype CAN-AM road motorcycle were used to develop several fairing designs which

(a) Tall Windshield,   (b) Low Windshield,

Upright Rider   Leaning Rider

FIG. 8 Prototype CAN-AM Road Fairings

MOTORCYCLE CONFIGURATION	NUMBER OF RIDERS	RIDER UPRIGHT		RIDER LEANING	
		C_D	A	C_D	A
No fairing Upright rider	1	.705	7.20	678	6.25
No fairing Upright rider	2	.755	7.50	726	6.50
Fairing + Tall Windshield	1	594	7.20	581	6.25
Fairing + Short Windshield	1	691	7.20	560	6.25
Fairing + Short Windshield	2	.674	7.50	.620	6.50

TABLE 1 Measured Drag Coefficients for Several Prototype CAN-AM Road Motorcycles

(a) CAN-AM 1972 PS Fairing   (b) Yamaha Fairing

FIG. 9 Partial Streamlined Motorcycles

FIG. 10 CAN-AM 1973 PS Bonneville Fairing

would shelter the rider and reduce drag. Figure 8 shows the motorcycle with tall and short windshields on a common fairing and also shows the upright and leaning rider positions employed. Table 1 summarizes the drag measurements, all taken at 70 m.p.h.

A more extreme rider position is acceptable for a racing machine, permitting a considerable reduction in frontal area. A value of 4.5 - 5.0 ft.^{2} would be typical of many racing motorcycles today. At the same time, better shaped and more extensive fairings — within the confines of the racing regulations — are possible. Figure 9 shows two racing fairings typical of those commonly used in the "partially streamlined" classes at Bonneville and on road racing motorcycles. One is that used by CAN-AM at its first Bonneville trials in 1972, while the other is the fairing provided by Yamaha for its road racing 350 c.c. motorcycles. The drag coefficient of the CAN-AM fairing is 0.608 while that of the Yamaha fairing is 0.450 based on A = 4.5 ft.^{2}. The high drag on the first CAN-AM fairing was due to the fairing being too narrow. The flow from the fairing struck the rider's shoulders instead of passing smoothly down his sides, leading to increased pressure drag. Figure 10 shows the fairing developed at N.A.E. for the 1973 Bonneville trials. Although it is similar to both the other fairings in appearance, it has a much lower drag coefficient of 0.274 based on the same frontal area. This low drag value was achieved by changing the shapes of the vehicle and its components. The main effort was aimed at reducing the wake size and thus decreasing the associated pressure drag, the most significant source of drag. The approach used was based on an attempt to integrate the rider with the fairing, making his body as nearly continuous with the fairing surface as possible. Careful reading of the American Motorcycle Association Regulations showed that some body panels were permitted behind the rider. The seat was greatly enlarged and the fairing panels as well as a belly pan were extended behind and under the rider. Careful fitting of these additions to the rider, whose torso had been lowered, permitted the flow to stay attached to the rider-fairing combination to the rear of the motorcycle. The drag of the basic fairing with the rider in place but without the seat, rear fairing or other hardware shown in Figure 9, and with the handlebars angled back was C_D = 0.372. The additions of the rear panels and seat lowered this to C_D = 0.326. With the main fairing working well, attention was then concentrated on cleaning up exposed hardware. A point often overlooked is that the drag coefficient of a circular cylinder (handlebars, forks, spokes, etc.) is 1.20 at subcritical Reynolds numbers; at this high value of drag coefficient it does not require a large frontal area to contribute significantly to the total drag. The handlebars were angled back placing them within the fairing, the lower portions of both forks were faired with simple fillets, and the spoke wheels were covered with disk fairings. The disk

TABLE 2 Summary of Drag Reduction

MOTORCYCLE CONFIGURATION	C_D	$C_D A$
Can-Am 1972 PS	.608	2.736
Can-Am 1973 PS Basic Fairing	.372	1.674
As Above + Seat and Rear Fairing	.326	1.467
As Above + Disk Fairings	.297	1.337
As Above + Fork Fairings	.274	1.233

With Canopy

Without Canopy

(a) Interim CAN-AM Fairing   (b) Prototype 1:10 Scale Fully Enclosed Streamliners

FIG. 11 Fully Streamlined Motorcycles

fairings provided a drag reduction of $\Delta C_D = 0.029$ and the fork fairings provided a further reduction of $\Delta C_D = 0.023$ to give the final drag coefficient of 0.274. Table 2 summarizes the drag coefficients measured.

Figure 11 shows three motorcycle configurations designed to run in the fully streamlined class at Bonneville. The full scale prototype shown represents a development of the partially streamlined motorcycle discussed above. A full nose and tail cone have been added providing an interim "full streamliner". This motorcycle has a drag coefficient of 0.190 based on a frontal area of 4.0 ft.^{2}.

The full-scale models were usually wool tufted to help identify regions of separated flow. These tufts were very useful in fine tuning the rider-fairing interfaces.

The two 1:10 scale models were preliminary models of a more extreme configuration where the rider lies on his back, slung between the wheels with the motor behind his seat back. Both models had the same drag coefficient of 0.10 based on frontal areas of 3.5 ft.^{2} and 3.0 ft.^{2} for the cases with canopy and without canopy, respectively. The measurements were made at a Reynolds number of 2×10^6, well past the critical Reynolds number for this configuration, and so should provide a reasonable estimate of the full-scale drag.

Figure 12 shows three kinds of flow visualization employed to study the flow over this model. The dye trace in water was taken at a Reynolds number of 10^4 and shows the expected early laminar separation. The use of aluminum particles in water illuminated with a strobe lamp allows higher water speeds. The photograph shown was taken at a Reynolds number of 5×10^5 and only a small separated region is seen at the extreme aft end of the model. Both of these studies were carried out in the N.A.E.'s water tunnel. The third photograph shows a china clay (mixture of chalk dust and kerosene) visualization performed

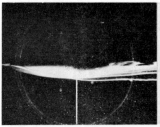

(a) Fluorescent Dye in Water, Re = 10^4

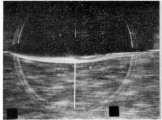
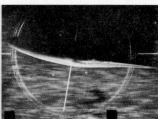

(b) Aluminum Particles in Water, Re = 10^5

(c) China Clay in Air, Re = 2×10^6

FIG. 12 Flow Visualization Techniques (Flow from Left to Right)

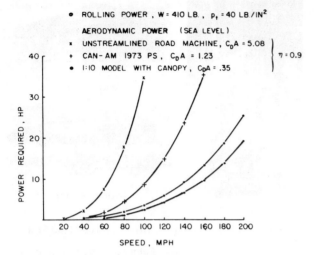

FIG. 13 Power Consumed Overcoming Aerodynamic and
Rolling Resistance

TABLE 3 Motorcycle Parameters

MOTORCYCLE CONFIGURATION	C_D	A (FT²)	W (LB)	C_DA (FT²)
Unstreamlined Road Machine Rider Upright	.705	7.2	410	5.08
Road Machine + Tall Windshield Rider Upright	.594	7.2	435	4.28
Road Machine + Low Windshield Rider Leaning	.560	6.25	435	3.50
Can–Am 1972 PS	.608	4.5	350	2.70
Yamaha Fairing	.450	4.5	350	2.03
Can–Am 1973 PS	.274	4.5	360	1.23
Can–Am Interim Streamliner	.19	4.0	375	.76
Full Streamliner, Canopy	.10	3.5	450	.35
Full Streamliner, No Canopy	.10	3.0	450	.30

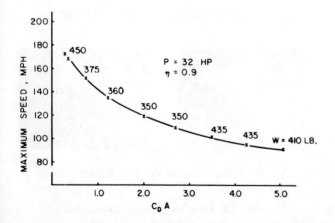

FIG. 14 Variation of Maximum Speed with Aerodynamic Drag

during the measurements in the N.A.E.'s 14 in. × 14 in. wind tunnel at a Reynolds number of 2×10^6. In this case no flow separation was observed.

4. SPEED PERFORMANCE

Once the aerodynamic drag of a vehicle is known and assuming that the rolling resistance can be estimated, it becomes possible to compute the maximum speed which that vehicle can attain[7] for a given engine power.

The power required to propel a motorcycle at V ft./sec. may be expressed as

$$P = (D_r + D_a) V/550\eta \quad \text{h.p.} \qquad (4.1)$$

The aerodynamic drag is given by equation (3.1) and the rolling resistance of the motorcycle is given by

$$D_r = [a_1 + a_2 V^2]W \qquad (4.2)$$

Equation (4.2) was based on an equation given by Hoerner[8]. This expression provides the greatest uncertainty in the analysis and would best be replaced with measured data for the correct tire-surface combination. The constants in equation (4.2), fitting some current automobile tire data, were established to be

$$a_1 = .0085 + .255/p_t, \ a_2 = 2.771 \times 10^{-5}/p_t; \text{ for } V < 150 \text{ ft./sec.}$$

$$a_1 = .255/p_t, \ a_2 = 5.1 \times 10^{-5}/p_t; \text{ for } V > 150 \text{ ft./sec.} \qquad (4.3)$$

The power consumed by a 410 lb. motorcycle overcoming rolling resistance is shown in Figure 13 for a tire pressure of 40 lb./in.². The power required to overcome aerodynamic drag is also shown for the cases of $C_D A = 5.08$ (unfaired CAN-AM road machine) and $C_D A = 1.23$ (CAN-AM 1973 PS Bonneville machine) and $C_D A = 0.35$ (1:10 model with canopy). The last case emphasizes the need for a low weight for highly streamlined motorcycles as rolling power can be greater than aerodynamic power.

Substituting (3.1) and (4.2) in (4.1) leads to the complete expression for the engine power required in the form

$$P = \left\{ a_1 W + \left[a_2 W + \frac{\rho C_D A}{2} \right] V^2 \right\} \frac{V}{550\eta} \qquad (4.4)$$

Equation (4.4) was used to calculate the maximum speeds for the motorcycles discussed in the previous section. Table 3 outlines the parameters of the motorcycles investigated. The solutions were obtained using a simple iteration and are presented as a function of $C_D A$ in Figure 14. The calculations were performed at sea level for a tire pressure of 40 lb./in.², a transmission efficiency of $\eta = 0.90$, weights appropriate to each machine and an engine power of 32.0 h.p.

The same calculation was also performed for the CAN-AM 1972 PS and 1973 PS motorcycles, which have set world records in the 125 cc partially streamlined gas and fuel classes at Bonneville. Table 4 summarizes these results in comparison to the achieved speeds for engine powers derated to the 4300 ft. altitude of the Bonneville Salt Flats. The tire pressure was 60 lb./in.^{2} and the transmission efficiency was 0.90.

The speeds calculated for the 1973 runs were about 7 percent higher than achieved. This could result in part from a low estimate of rolling resistance as the track was rough (due to rain), and in part from the difficulty in selecting the best gears caused by an inoperative tachometer.

MOTORCYCLE CONFIGURATION	CLASS	C_D	POWER (HP)	$V_{CALC.}$ (MPH)	$V_{MEAS.}$ (MPH)
1972 PS	125 APS – AG	.608	25.9	109.8	111.6
1973 PS	125 APS – AG	.274	27.6	138.6	128.5
1973 PS	125 APS – AF	.274	32.0	145.5	136.5

TABLE 4 Comparison of Calculated and Observed Performance

5. ACCELERATION PERFORMANCE

Another aspect of performance which is at least as important as top speed, for road and road racing motorcycles, is the acceleration capability of the machine. Any improvements in acceleration will reduce the hazards of passing and entering freeways, and will improve the lap times of racing vehicles. A single-degree-of-freedom equation of longitudinal motion has been used to investigate the effect of changes in aerodynamic drag on acceleration.

The longitudinal forces acting on an accelerating motorcycle are ($\dot{x} = dx/dt$ etc.)

$$F_x = m\ddot{x} = F_e - D_a - D_r \qquad (5.1)$$

D_a and D_r are given by (3.1) and (4.2) while the propulsive force supplied by the engine is

$$F_e = (\eta P)\frac{550}{\dot{x}} \qquad (5.2)$$

The substitution of (3.1), (4.2) and (5.2) in (5.1), with some rearranging provides an equation for the acceleration of the motorcycle:

$$\ddot{x} = \frac{550\eta P}{m\dot{x}} - \frac{\rho}{2m}C_D A\dot{x}^2 - \left(a_1 + a_2\dot{x}^2\right)\frac{W}{m} \qquad (5.3)$$

This equation is more conveniently expressed in terms of the engine rotational acceleration, $\ddot{\phi}$, and the rotational speed, $\dot{\phi}$. While the motorcycle engine rotates ϕ revolutions, the motorcycle travels a distance x feet which depends upon wheel diameter D, primary gear ratio r_p, final drive ratio r_t, and transmission ratio r_i.

$$x = \left(\frac{\pi\,d_r}{r_t\,r_p}\right)\left(\frac{\phi}{r_i}\right) \qquad (5.4)$$

Substituting the appropriate time derivatives of (5.4) in (5.3) provides the required equation of motion.

$$\ddot{\phi} = \left(\frac{550\eta P}{m}\right)\left(\frac{r_i\,r_f\,r_p}{\pi\,d_r}\right)^2\dot{\phi}^{-1} - \frac{\rho\,C_D A}{2m}\left(\frac{\pi\,d_r}{r_i\,r_f\,r_p}\right)\dot{\phi}^2$$

$$-\left[a_1\left(\frac{r_i\,r_f\,r_p}{\pi\,d_r}\right) + a_2\left(\frac{\pi\,d_r}{r_i\,r_f\,r_p}\right)\dot{\phi}^2\right]g \qquad (5.5)$$

This equation was solved using a Runge-Kutta iteration routine. The gear shifting was carried out numerically by one of two selection procedures with shifting either occurring at a preset engine speed which could vary from gear to gear, or as prescribed by an optimization routine. In the latter case, the current gear and the next higher gear were compared point by point until the acceleration in the higher gear exceeded that in the lower gear at which time a gear shift was carried out. The engine power was determined by linear interpolation in a table of power versus engine speed data obtained from steady state dynamometer measurements.

Although no pitch degree of freedom was included, some of the effects of weight transfer under acceleration were included by assuming that 80 percent of the motorcycles weight acted on the rear wheel. A coefficient of friction of 1.0 was used and if the thrust force generated by the engine exceeded the force capability of the tire, then the longitudinal force was restricted to .8 mg, providing a simple representation of wheel slip. This technique was felt to be adequate for most road motorcycles although it might not be as good for very highly powered machines. In such cases, a more complex formulation, such as that by Pershing[9] would be required.

The motorcycles were started by assuming an initial engine speed and then using the constant power level corresponding to that speed until the motorcycle velocity had increased to a value which matched that engine speed. From this point onward the motorcycle accelerated along its power curve, through each successive gear, to a preset limit of speed or distance.

MOTORCYCLE CONFIGURATION	ELAPSED TIME (SEC)		SPEED (MPH)		% ERROR	
	CALCULATED	OBSERVED	CALCULATED	OBSERVED	TIME	SPEED
Can-Am 175 Enduro	16.0	16.2	77.6	77.3	-1.2	0.4
Honda MT 125 Enduro	20.8	21.1	59.9	57.6	-1.4	4.0
Honda MT 250 Enduro	17.8	17.9	70.9	69.8	-0.6	1.6
Honda CB 200	18.4	18.3	68.3	69.2	0.5	-1.3
Honda CB 360 G	15.7	15.4	81.6	82.9	1.9	-1.6
Honda CB 450 K7	14.9	14.4	85.3	89.3	3.5	-4.5
Triumph TR5 MX	13.9	14.6	85.8	85.8	-4.8	0
Suzuki T500	15.2	14.7	85.0	89.3	3.4	-4.8
Montessa 250	17.8	17.8	68.8	72.5	0	-5.1

TABLE 5 Computed ¼ Mile Acceleration Performance

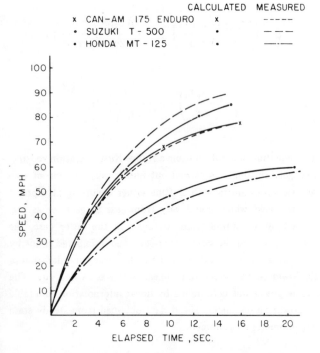

CALCULATED   MEASURED

x CAN-AM 175 ENDURO   x   -----
• SUZUKI T-500   •   ---
• HONDA MT-125   •   —-—

FIG. 15 Quarter-Mile Acceleration Performance

MOTORCYCLE CONFIGURATION	0-30 (MPH)	30-50 (MPH)	50-70 (MPH)	70-90 (MPH)	90-105 (MPH)	1/4 MILE E.T. (SEC)	1/4 MILE SPEED (MPH)
Unstreamlined Road Machine – Rider Upright	5.2	3.1	3.4	12.0	–	17.7	85.0
Road Machine + Tall Windshield – Rider Upright	5.5	3.2	3.1	8.2	–	17.9	86.9
Road Machine + Low Windshield – Rider Leaning	5.5	3.1	3.0	6.3	–	17.7	89.9
Can-Am 1972 PS	3.6	1.8	2.2	4.0	8.7	14.7	99.9
Yamaha Fairing	3.6	1.7	2.1	3.6	4.3	14.6	102.9
Can-Am 1973 PS	3.7	1.8	2.1	3.2	3.1	14.5	105.8

TABLE 6 Effect of Configuration on Acceleration Performance

Provision was also made for tire growth with speed increase. This was done as it was hoped that the analysis could be used to select gear ratios for Bonneville. Since the power bands of the record engines are very narrow, changes in the effective gear ratio due to tire growth becomes important. The initial investigations used a function which changed the diameter as the square of velocity, giving an increase of 10 percent at 200 m.p.h.

The mathematical model outlined above was verified in comparison with the 1/4 mile acceleration times of 11 of the motorcycles tested between August 1973 and April 1974 by CYCLE magazine, a monthly periodical published by the Ziff-Davis Publishing Co. The road reports included the gear ratios, tire sizes, test weight and a measured power curve for each motorcycle tested. The engine powers were measured on a chassis dynamometer so a value of $\eta = 1.0$ was used. Table 5 summarizes these results and gives the percent error relative to the measurement.

The average error magnitude was 2.2 percent for elapsed time and 3.0 percent for velocity. The results are very good when one considers that the initial conditions, shifting times, motorcycle frontal areas and rider positions were not known exactly. Figure 15 shows velocity as a function of time for three sample cases. The plotted symbols indicate the computed shift points.

The acceleration analysis was then applied to the first 6 motorcycles listed in Table 3 using the parameters given there, with each motorcycle geared the same. The maximum engine power was 32.0 h.p. The resultant acceleration times over several speed ranges are shown in Table 6.

For the road machine it is evident that the weight increase due to the fairing leads to a slight deterioration of low speed performance but an increase in high speed performance which is progressively larger over 40 m.p.h. A fairing of the type used on the CAN-AM 1973 Bonneville motorcycle provides a considerable increase in acceleration at road racing speeds in comparison to the two more conventional fairing configurations.

In order to better define the improvement in performance possible for a road racing motorcycle with different fairings, the acceleration analysis was used in conjunction with a control program which would "drive" the motorcycle around any given track. The track was defined using a series of straight lines and circular arcs. Cornering and braking were simulated using constant acceleration rates. Thus the cornering speed was specified by

$$V_c = \sqrt{a_c\, r} \quad \text{ft./sec.} \qquad (5.6)$$

The braking point before each corner was found by iterating the motorcycles progress such that: at velocity V on the straight, and a distance x from the approaching corner, the braking distance given by

$$d = Vt + \frac{1}{2} a_b t^2 \qquad (5.7)$$

just equalled x, where the time t, required to decelerate from V to V_c is

$$t = \frac{(V_c - V)}{a_b} \qquad (5.8)$$

This procedure was applied to a test track consisting of five corners and having a length of 1.65 miles, as shown in Figure 16, for each of the last three motorcycles in Table 6. The cornering acceleration was assumed to be 0.85 g = 27.34 ft./sec.^{2} and the braking acceleration was assumed to be −0.90 g = −28.94 ft./sec.^{2}. The results are compared in Table 7 and it is clear that significant reductions in lap times are possible through drag reduction. The increases would be even greater on a higher speed course.

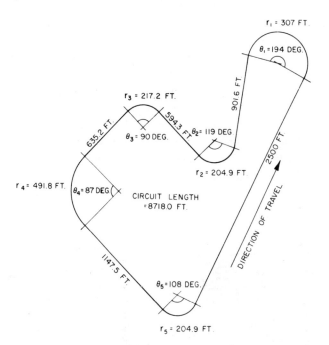

FIG. 16   Hypothetical Road Racing Circuit

MOTORCYCLE CONFIGURATION	LAP TIME (SEC)	AVERAGE SPEED (MPH)
Can – Am 1972 PS	80.3	74.1
Yamaha Fairing	79.5	74.8
Can – Am 1973 PS	78.8	75.4

TABLE 7   Effect of Drag Reduction on Lap Times

6. FUEL CONSUMPTION IMPROVEMENTS THROUGH DRAG REDUCTION

Aerodynamic drag, as well as having an effect on acceleration and top speed, also can have a considerable effect on fuel consumption. In light of the present fuel shortages and associated higher prices, any reduction in fuel consumption would be valuable. The following analysis[10] gives an indication of the changes in fuel consumption to be expected due to changes in aerodynamic drag.

The power required at any speed is given by (4.4). The amount of fuel consumed per second at a speed V ft./sec. is

$$f = sP \text{ gal./sec.} \qquad (6.1)$$

and the fuel consumption in ft./gal. is given by

$$\mu = V/sP \text{ ft./gal.} \qquad (6.2)$$

Rearranging (6.2) and substituting for P from (4.4) gives

$$\left\{ a_1 W + \left[a_2 W + \frac{\rho C_D A}{2} \right] V^2 \right\} \frac{V}{550\eta} - \frac{V}{s\mu} = 0 \qquad (6.3)$$

Differentiating (6.3) holding all variables fixed except $C_D A$, μ and W, after some manipulation. leads to

$$\frac{\Delta\mu}{\mu} = - \frac{WC_D A}{\eta P} \left\{ 9.09 \times 10^{-4} \left(\frac{\rho V^3}{W} \right) \frac{\Delta(C_D A)}{C_D A} \right.$$

$$\left. + \left(\frac{a_1 V + a_2 V^2}{550 C_D A} \right) \left(\frac{\Delta W}{W} \right) \right\} \qquad (6.4)$$

where the differential quantities have been replaced by small increments in fuel consumption, aerodynamic drag and weight (due to the fairing).

Using equation (6.4) the fractional change in fuel consumption due to an incremental change $\Delta C_D A$ may be calculated as a function of vehicle velocity. The following two examples are taken from the drag reduction data presented in Section 3.

The reference case is the standard road motorcycle with upright rider for which $(C_D A)_0 = 5.08$. It will be compared to the same vehicle with tall windshield and upright rider, $(\Delta C_D A/C_D A)_1 = -0.157$, and the case with low windshield and leaning rider, $(\Delta C_D A/C_D A)_2 = -0.311$. A weight increment of 25 lb. was used to represent the additional weight of the fairing and windshield, $(\Delta W/W) = +0.061$. Thus we have

$$\left(\frac{\Delta\mu}{\mu}\right)_1 = \frac{1}{P}\left[1.731\times 10^{-6}V^3 - 1.733\times 10^{-5}V^2\right.$$

$$\left. - 6.764\times 10^{-4}V\right] \qquad (6.5)$$

$$\left(\frac{\nabla\mu}{\mu}\right)_2 = \frac{1}{P}\left[3.418\times 10^{-6}V^3 - 1.733\times 10^{-5}V^2\right.$$

$$\left. - 6.764\times 10^{-4}V\right] \qquad (6.6)$$

These equations were evaluated from 10 ft./sec. to 150 ft./sec. and the results are plotted in Figure 17. Case 1 gives a fuel consumption reduction of 5.7 percent at 44 ft./sec. and 11.2 percent at 88 ft./sec. while case 2 gives 15.5 percent and 24.2 percent reductions respectively. It is interesting to note that the incremental reduction in fuel consumption appears to asymptote to a value near the fractional reduction in drag.

Although the increments in drag reduction are not "small", as was assumed in the development, they are small enough that the results are valid.

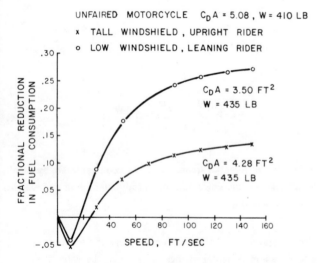

FIG. 17   Changes in Fuel Consumption with Drag Reduction for Two Road Motorcycles

7. ANALYSIS OF MOTORCYCLE STABILITY

The occurrence of an aerodynamically excited instability on the long-tailed CAN-AM Bonneville motorcycle (Fig. 18) in 1973 and the history of similar occurrences on other Bonneville machines emphasized the requirement for a better understanding of motorcycle stability. It was felt that a mathematical model of the motorcycle dynamics, including adequate representation of tire and aerodynamic forces, would be very useful in aiding the design of future record machines. The same analysis would also apply to investigations of road motorcycle handling. A literature search revealed the excellent analysis performed by Sharp[2]. This analysis provides an adequate number of degrees-of-freedom and incorporates a comprehensive treatment of tire behaviour. Sharp's equations of motion were extended to include both steady and unsteady aerodynamic forces.

The motorcycle was assumed to consist of two rigid frames hinged at the steering axis, having thin, rigid wheels rolling without longitudinal slip on a flat road surface at constant forward speed. The motorcycle was free to yaw, roll, sideslip and steer the front wheel. Only small perturbations from straight line running were considered. The tire side force coefficients were linearly related to the tire loads and sideslip and camber angles. Allowance was made for the lag between the steering of pneumatic tired wheels and the build-up of the side forces toward steady state values. The pneumatic trail, leading to a self-aligning torque generated by the tires, was excluded and the front tire drag force was considered small compared to the side force. The rider was considered to be attached rigidly to the rear frame, providing no control inputs. Work by Weir[11] on the dynamics of the motorcycle-rider system suggests that such a "free control" model of motorcycle dynamics is acceptable. The rider was observed to have little influence on the high speed weave mode stability. His primary task was that of balancing the motorcycle. Quasi-steady, linear aerodynamics were assumed to apply.

FIG. 18   CAN-AM 1972 Bonneville Motorcycle with Long Tail

A schematic representation of the motorcycle is shown in Figure 19. The point A is the intersection of the ground plane with the vertical transverse plane containing the rear frame mass centre and the longitudinal plane of symmetry. A is the origin of a right-handed, orthogonal axis system AXYZ which moves with the vehicle. AX is aligned horizontally, fixed in the longitudinal plane of symmetry, and pointing forward. AY is horizontal and to the right and AZ is vertical downwards. The coordinates of A, relative to an inertial reference frame $0X_0Y_0Z_0$ whose origin is in the ground surface, are (x_0, y_0). The angle ψ, between AX and $0X_0$, is the yaw angle of the motorcycle (Fig. 20). The roll angle, ϕ, is defined as the rotation of the motorcycle plane of symmetry about the AX axis. The steer angle, δ, is the angle of rotation of the plane of symmetry of the front frame relative to that of the rear frame, about the steer axis.

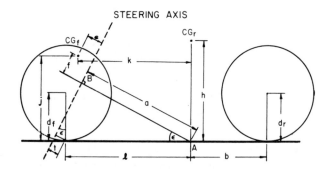

FIG. 19   Schematic of Motorcycle Geometry

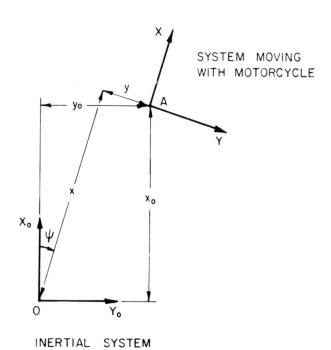

FIG. 20   Motorcycle Coordinate Systems

A second reference frame $BX_1Y_1Z_1$ is required for the front frame. B is located at the position shown in Figure 19. BZ_1 is directed downward along the steering axis, BX_1 is directed forward in the wheel plane of symmetry and BY_1 is directed to the right.

The equations of motion were developed by Sharp using an application of Lagrange's equation.

$$\frac{d}{dt}\left(\frac{\partial T}{\partial \dot{q}}\right) - \frac{\partial T}{\partial q} + \frac{\partial U}{\partial q} = Q_q \qquad (7.1)$$

The generalized forces, Q_q, contain both the tire forces and the aerodynamic forces, expressed in terms of the vehicle motion parameters. The following linearized equations of motion were found.

(i)   Lateral (sideslip) equation

$$(m_f + m_r)(\ddot{y} + V\dot{\psi}) + m_f k \ddot{\psi} + (m_f j + m_r h)\ddot{\phi}$$

$$+ m_f e \ddot{\delta} = Q_Y^t + Q_Y^a \qquad (7.2)$$

(ii)   Yaw equation

$$m_f k \ddot{y} + (m_f ek + I_{fz}\cos\epsilon)\ddot{\delta} + (m_f k^2 + I_{rz} + I_{fx}\sin^2\epsilon$$

$$+ I_{fz}\cos^2\epsilon)\ddot{\psi} + \left\{m_f jk - C_{rxz} + (I_{fz} - I_{fx})\sin\epsilon\,\cos\epsilon\right\}\ddot{\phi}$$

$$-\left(\frac{i_{fy}}{d_f} + \frac{i_{ry} + \lambda i}{d_r}\right)V\dot{\phi} + m_f kV\dot{\psi} - \frac{i_{fy}}{d_f}\sin\epsilon\,V\dot{\delta}$$

$$= Q_\psi^t + Q_\psi^a \qquad (7.3)$$

(iii)   Roll equation

$$(m_f j + m_r h)\ddot{y} + (m_f ej + I_{fz}\sin\epsilon)\ddot{\delta} + (m_f j^2 + m_r h^2 + I_{rx}$$

$$+ I_{fx}\cos^2\epsilon + I_{fz}\sin^2\epsilon)\ddot{\phi} + \left\{m_f jk - C_{rxz}\right.$$

$$+ (I_{fz} - I_{fx})\sin\epsilon\,\cos\epsilon\left.\right\}\ddot{\psi} + \frac{i_{fy}}{d_f}\cos\epsilon\,V\dot{\delta}$$

$$+ \left(m_f j + m_r h + \frac{i_{fy}}{d_f} + \frac{i_{ry} + \lambda i}{d_r}\right)V\dot{\psi} - m_f eg\,\delta$$

$$- (m_f j + m_r h)\,g\,\phi = Q_\phi^t + Q_\phi^a \qquad (7.4)$$

177

(iv)   Steering equation

$$m_f e \ddot{y} + (I_{fz} + m_f e^2)\,\ddot{\delta} + (m_f ej + I_{fz}\sin\epsilon)\,\ddot{\phi} + (m_f ek + I_{fz}\cos\epsilon)\,\ddot{\psi}$$

$$- \frac{i_{fy}}{d_f}\cos\epsilon\, V\,\dot{\phi} + \left(m_f e + \frac{i_{fy}}{d_f}\sin\epsilon\right)V\,\dot{\psi} - m_f eg\sin\epsilon\,\delta$$

$$- m_f eg\,\phi = Q_\delta^t - K\dot{\delta} + Q_\delta^a \qquad (7.5)$$

The tire generated generalized forces are

$$Q_Y^t \simeq Y_f + Y_r \qquad (7.6)$$

$$Q_\psi^t \simeq \ell Y_f - b Y_r \qquad (7.7)$$

$$Q_\phi^t \simeq -t Z_f\,\delta \qquad (7.8)$$

$$\phi_\delta^t \simeq -K\delta - t Z_f\sin\epsilon\,\delta - t Y_f - t Z_f\,\phi \qquad (7.8)$$

The instantaneous tire side forces, Y_f and Y_r, expressed in terms of the motorcycle motion parameters, are obtained from the following two equations which are solved simultaneously with the equations of motion, (7.2) to (7.5).

$$\left(\frac{\sigma_f}{V}\right)\dot{Y}_f + Y_f = C_{f_1}\,m_f g\,\left(\delta\cos\epsilon - \frac{\dot{y} + \ell\dot{\psi} - t\dot{\delta}}{V}\right)$$

$$+ C_{f_2}\,m_f g\,(\phi + \delta\sin\epsilon) \qquad (7.9)$$

$$\left(\frac{\sigma_r}{V}\right)\dot{Y}_r + Y_r = C_{r_1}\,m_r g\left(\frac{b\dot{\psi} - \dot{y}}{V}\right) + C_{r_2}\,m_r g\,\phi \qquad (7.10)$$

These equations represent an exponential change in tire force with time following a change in sideslip or camber angle, introducing a lag between tire steering and tire response. Characteristic times for this response are given by σ_r/V and σ_f/V. σ_f and σ_r are of the order of the radius[12] of the wheel or less.

The parameter values for the 1973 partially streamlined CAN-AM motorcycle are listed below in Table 8.

m_f = 1.34 slugs	$d_f = d_r$ = 1.0 ft.	I_{rx} = 13.8 slug ft.^{2}
m_r = 9.54 slugs	t = .292 ft.	I_{rz} = 9.3 " "
B = 4.375 ft.	$\sigma_f = \sigma_r$ = .5 ft.	C_{rxz}= 0.77 " "
b = 1.676 ft.	ϵ = .492 rad. (28°)	I_{fx} = 0.58 " "
a = 2.55 ft.	K = 6.0 lb.ft. / (rad./sec.)	I_{fz} = 0.21 " "
e = .217 ft.	$C_{f1} = C_{r1}$ = 11.12	i_{fy} = 0.40 " "
f = −.167 ft.	$C_{f2} = C_{r2}$= 0.934	$i_{ry}+\lambda_y$= 0.60 " "
h = 2.00 ft.	Z_f = − 157.5 lb.	

TABLE 8   Motorcycle Parameters

8. GENERALIZED AERODYNAMIC FORCES

As a motorcycle moves through still air the relative velocity vector between both the front and rear motorcycle frames and the air fluctuates with the motorcycle motion about its equilibrium, straight-line path. These fluctuating, induced wind angles lead to fluctuating aerodynamic forces and moments on the motorcycle. It will be assumed that the aerodynamic forces and moments at any instantaneous wind vector angle will have the steady state values measured for the same motorcycle orientation. This "quasi-steady" assumption requires that the disturbance velocities leading to the induced wind angles are small compared to the forward velocity of the motorcycle. In light of the small disturbance nature of the analysis this requirement will be readily met. Further, the small disturbance assumption allows the use of linearized aerodynamics where a general aerodynamic coefficient may be written

$$C_F = C_{F_0} + \sum_i \left(\frac{\partial C_F}{\partial q_i}\right) q_i + \sum_i \left(\frac{\partial C_F}{\partial \dot{q}_i}\right)\dot{q}_i \qquad (8.1)$$

and C_{F_0} is the equilibrium value of the aerodynamic coefficient (usually zero for lateral forces and moments).

The aerodynamic derivatives in equation (8.1) can be divided into two classes, steady and unsteady. The steady derivatives are those obtained from steady force measurements as outlined in Section 2. The unsteady derivatives are measured for an oscillating model, or they may be estimated, under certain conditions, from steady aerodynamic force data.

The steady aerodynamic forces will be derived first. Figure 21 indicates the angles induced at the front and rear frames due to motorcycle motion. The body axis coordinate system used is identical to the AXYZ system used for the motorcycle dynamics. It was assumed for small roll angles, that, the aerodynamic forces would be those measured at zero roll angle. Thus a simple resolution of forces through the roll angle will give the required horizontal components. The forces and moments on the front frame were not measured directly but were deduced from the differences between sets of measurements with the front frame steered at various angles relative to the rear frame. It was possible to estimate the side force due to the front frame and find its centre of pressure. The moments about the required axes due to this side force could then be calculated.

The wind angles relative to the front and rear frames are

$$\alpha_f = -\tan^{-1}\left[(\dot{y} + \ell\dot{\psi})/V\right] + \gamma \qquad (8.2)$$

and

$$\alpha_r = -\tan^{-1}\left[\dot{y}/V\right] \qquad (8.3)$$

It was assumed in arriving at equation (8.3) that the effective lateral velocity of the front wheel due to yaw rate was that of the wheel centre.

With the motorcycle near its upright equilibrium position, γ may be written in terms of the steering head angle and the steering angle as

$$\gamma = \delta \cos \epsilon \qquad (8.4)$$

Using these angles and the appropriate slopes of the steady aerodynamic force and moment curves, one obtains the following steady aerodynamic components of the generalized forces.

(i) Side force along AY

$$Q_Y^{sa} = Q_{Y_f}^{sa} + Q_{Y_r}^{sa}$$

$$= \frac{\rho A V^2}{2} \left[\left(\frac{\partial C_{Y_r}}{\partial \alpha} \right) \alpha_r + \left(\frac{\partial C_{Y_f}}{\partial \alpha} \right) \alpha_f \right] \cos \phi, \qquad \text{or}$$

$$Q_Y^{sa} = \frac{\rho A V^2}{2} \left[\left(\frac{\partial C_{Y_r}}{\partial \alpha} \right) \alpha_r + \left(\frac{\partial C_{Y_f}}{\partial \alpha} \right) \alpha_f \right] \qquad (8.5)$$

(ii) Yawing moment about AZ

$$Q_\psi^{sa} = Q_{\psi_f}^{sa} + Q_{\psi_r}^{sa}$$

$$= \frac{\rho A V^2}{2} \left[B \left(\frac{\partial C_{N_r}}{\partial \alpha} \right) \alpha_r + \ell_1 \left(\frac{\partial C_{Y_f}}{\partial \alpha} \right) \alpha_r \right] \qquad (8.6)$$

The yawing moment component due to the front frame has been represented by the side force of the front frame acting a distance ℓ_1 ahead of the main frame centre of gravity.

(iii) Rolling moment about AX

$$Q_\phi^{sa} = Q_{\phi_f}^{sa} + Q_{\phi_r}^{sa}$$

$$= \frac{\rho A V^2}{2} \left[B \left(\frac{\partial C_{R_r}}{\partial \alpha} \right) \alpha_r + \ell_2 \left(\frac{\partial C_{Y_f}}{\partial \alpha} \right) \alpha_f \right] \qquad (8.7)$$

ℓ_2 is the height of the front frame centre of pressure.

(iv) Yawing moment about the steering axis BZ_1

$$Q_\delta^{sa} = \frac{\rho A V^2}{2} \left[\ell_3 \left(\frac{\partial C_{Y_f}}{\partial \alpha} \right) \alpha_f \right] \qquad (8.8)$$

ℓ_3 is the perpendicular distance from the front frame centre of pressure to the steering axis.

The last term, equation (8.8) was the reason for the separation of the aerodynamic forces into front and rear frame components. It was expected that the rear frame aerodynamic forces would be stabilizing, (i.e. damping forces) but it was not clear whether the moment about the steering axis due to the front frame side force would be, especially when the disk fairings were fitted to the wheels.

The following derivatives were obtained for the rear frame of the long-tailed Bonneville motorcycle near zero degrees yaw angle.

$$\left(\frac{\partial C_{Y_r}}{\partial \alpha} \right) = 2.68 \text{ rad}^{-1}; \quad \left(\frac{\partial C_{N_r}}{\partial \alpha} \right) = 1.27 \text{ rad}^{-1};$$

$$\left(\frac{\partial C_{R_r}}{\partial \alpha} \right) = 1.41 \text{ rad}^{-1}.$$

The front frame forces were obtained for both the spoked front wheel and the disk front wheel.

$$\left(\frac{\partial C_{Y_f}}{\partial \alpha} \right)_{\text{spoke}} = 0.21 \text{ rad}^{-1}; \quad \left(\frac{\partial C_{Y_f}}{\partial \alpha} \right)_{\text{disk}} = 0.92 \text{ rad}^{-1}.$$

The location of the centres of pressure of the front and rear frames were found to be

$$\ell_1 = 2.92 \text{ ft.}; \quad \ell_2 = 1.5 \text{ ft.}; \quad \ell_3 = 0.27 \text{ ft.}$$

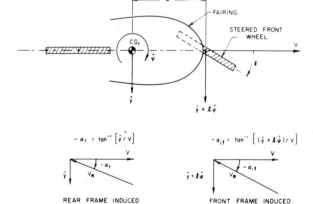

FIG. 21 Definition of Induced Wind Angles

179

Although the equations of motion allow no pitch or vertical degrees of freedom, the aerodynamic lift force and pitching moment affect the vertical reaction force at each wheel contact point, thus modifying the tire forces. At a sufficiently high speed it would be possible to completely unload the front wheel leading to a loss of control. Assuming that the drag vector acts through the centroid of frontal area, the centre of pressure of the lift force was found to be 3.24 ft. ahead of the rear axle. The change of reaction force at the front and rear wheel contact points becomes

$$\Delta Z_f = \frac{\rho A V^2}{2} \left[\left(\frac{3.24}{B}\right) C_L + C_M \right] \qquad (8.9)$$

$$\Delta Z_r = \frac{A V^2}{2} \left[\left(\frac{B - 3.24}{B}\right) C_L - C_M \right] \qquad (8.10)$$

These equations were used to modify the vertical tire reaction forces. The speed at which the front wheel of the long-tailed streamliner would just lift is given by

$$V = \left[\left(\frac{2 Z_f}{\rho A}\right) \left(\frac{3.24}{B} C_L + C_M\right)^{-1} \right]^{\frac{1}{2}} \qquad (8.11)$$

For a C_L and C_M of 0.12 and with the front wheel supporting a weight of 157.5 lb. this speed would be 375 ft./sec. (256 m.p.h.). At a speed of 150 m.p.h. the front wheel contact force would be reduced by 54.4 lb., 34.5 percent of the total at rest.

It was felt that the instability encountered was a result of unsteady aerodynamic forces due to the presence of the extended tail. Comparison of the steady force data for the 1973 Bonneville motorcycle with and without the tail provided no clue as to the excitation since both sets of forces were similar. In fact the long-tailed version should have been superior in a cross wind due to the reduced slope of its side force coefficient curve and the attendant reduced yawing moments.

No unsteady derivatives had been measured so a technique outlined by Etkin[13] was used to estimate the unsteady side force on the rear frame, and its centre of pressure, due to a yaw rate at zero yaw angle. Once these quantities were found the unsteady rolling moment and yawing moment due to yaw rate would also be known. The technique used consisted of replacement of the motorcycle shape by an equivalent cambered shape with the same thickness distribution, at the yaw angle required. The steady force and moment changes due to the camber may be used to find the unsteady forces and moments on the yawing body.

As the motorcycle yaws with a velocity $\dot{\psi}$ rad./sec. about the AZ axis each point on the body has a velocity component of $\dot{\psi} x$ where x is the distance from A, along AX, to the point considered. The mean camber line of the equivalent cambered shape which would have the same velocity distribution normal to its surface is

$$\frac{z}{C} = \left(\frac{x^2}{2 V C}\right) \dot{\psi} \qquad (8.12)$$

Reference to a handbook of two-dimensional airfoil data[14] shows that the NACA 65_4-021 airfoil has a thickness distribution similar to that of the motorcycle fairing. The least cambered airfoil in this series, the 65_4-221 was used as the base from which the unsteady forces were computed. The lift and pitching moment coefficients were referenced to frontal area and adjusted for aspect ratio. Table 9 gives the modified characteristics of this airfoil at zero angle of attack. The negative value of $cp_{c/4}$ indicates that the centre of pressure is located behind the quarter chord point. The reduction of the lift and pitching moment coefficients of the modified airfoil data by the ratio of the maximum camber given by (8.12) to the camber for the airfoil gives the unsteady side force and pitching moment coefficients for the streamlined motorcycle. The unsteady derivatives for a yaw rate of 0.5 rad./sec. are shown in Figure 22 for CG positions 0.5 ft. ahead of, and behind, the nominal position. In the first case the unsteady yawing moment is stabilizing and the side force and rolling moment are reduced compared to the case for the rearward CG. This change is due to the centre of pressure, in the first instance, being located behind the assumed CG, while in the second case, it is ahead of the CG. The unsteady aerodynamic forces on the motorcycle due to yaw rate are

(i)   Side force along AY

$$Q_Y^{ua} = \frac{\rho A V^2}{2} \left[\left(\frac{\partial C_Y}{\partial \dot{\psi}}\right) \dot{\psi} \right] \qquad (8.13)$$

(ii)   Yawing moment about AZ

$$Q_\psi^{ua} = \frac{\rho A V^2}{2} \left[\ell_4 \left(\frac{\partial C_Y}{\partial \dot{\psi}}\right) \dot{\psi} \right] \qquad (8.14)$$

(iii)   Rolling moment about AX

$$Q_\phi^{ua} = \frac{\rho A V^2}{2} \left[\ell_2 \left(\frac{\partial C_Y}{\partial \dot{\psi}}\right) \dot{\psi} \right] \qquad (8.15)$$

AIRFOIL	c(%C)	C_L	$C_{M_{C/4}}$	c.p.$_{C/4}$ (FT)	ℓ_c
65_4–221	1.10	0.107	−0.020	−1.45	3.39

TABLE 9   Cambered Airfoil Characteristics Corrected for Aspect Ratio

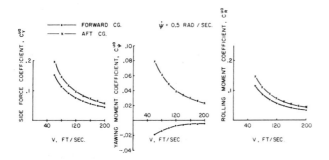

FIG. 22   Estimated Unsteady Aerodynamic Forces on the Long-Tailed CAN-AM Bonneville Motorcycle

No attempt was made to estimate other dynamic derivatives or cross-derivatives. The use of two-dimensional airfoil data to represent the unsteady forces on a fully streamlined motorcycle, which is more realistically a very low aspect ratio wing, will not yield quantitatively accurate results. However, it is hoped that the qualitative results, the presence or lack of an instability and the nature of the instability, should provide some insight into the cause of the unstable behaviour of the Bonneville machine.

The appropriate summations of the steady aerodynamic forces (equations (8.5) to (8.8)), the unsteady aerodynamic forces (equations (8.12) to (8.15)) and the tire forces provide the generalized forces required in the equations of motion. The resulting equations were reduced to a set of ten coupled, first order differential equations whose eigenvalues were found numerically.

9. RESULTS OF STABILITY ANALYSIS

As a prelude to the discussion of the effects of aerodynamic forces on stability it would be appropriate to discuss the type of dynamic behaviour predicted by the analysis and its relation to known motorcycle behaviour.

Examination of the equations of motion shows that two of the coordinates are cyclic. Of the remaining eight roots all but five (two complex conjugate pairs and one real root) are highly damped. These lightly damped roots represent three modes referred to by Sharp as; the "wobble" mode, an oscillation of the front frame about the steering axis having a natural fre-quency of about 10 hz; the "weave" mode, an oscillation of the main frame about its equilibrium position in yaw, roll and sideslip at 0.10-4.0 hz depending on speed; the non-oscillatory "capsize" mode, a divergence where the motorcycle falls over onto its side. This latter mode is usually easily controlled by the rider's use of his weight and steering torque to balance the motorcycle. Generally the wobble mode is highly stable at low speed with a possible instability at high speed. The weave mode may be unstable at low speed, below 20 ft./sec., well damped at intermediate speeds and less well damped or unstable at high speed. The low speed weave oscillation is often observed as a motorcycle accelerates slowly from rest, particularly when a passenger is carried.

While there is no direct experimental verification of the validity of this theory it does appear to predict many characteristics of motorcycle stability which are well known. It is generally recognized that a lower, more forward rear frame centre of gravity improves stability and this was found to be the case. It was also found that moving the rear wheel back, increasing trail and increasing the steering head angle all lead to increased stability. However, if several motorcycle parameters are changed together the results do not always fall into the expected patterns. In one case a reduction in steering head angle, while leading to a less well-damped wobble mode of oscillation, showed an increase in weave mode damping at high speed.

Figure 23 summarizes the effect of the aerodynamic forces previously outlined on stability. Both the weave and wobble mode damping terms are shown as functions of forward speed. The motorcycle properties were those tabulated for the 1973 CAN-AM partially streamlined motorcycle. The roots for the reference case are given by the heavy curves. This motorcycle was not equipped with a steering damper and had shown no tendency toward a wobble instability. The damping value chosen for the steering equation was an approximation of the damping at rest. The weave mode is also adequately damped, as was the case for the partially streamlined Bonneville machine. At high speed the inclusion of the full steady aerodynamic treatment made a small change in the damping values, while at low speed the effects were insignificant. The weave mode damping was slightly increased while that of the wobble mode was slightly decreased. It is interesting to note that opposite changes in damping usually occurred for these two modes with any parameter change. That is, a change which increased weave mode damping usually lowered the wobble mode damping and vice versa. Although not shown here, removal of the front frame forces resulted in behaviour which was virtually identical with that for the case of the full aerodynamic forces. Thus it would appear that the separation of forces or separate measurement of front and rear frame forces is unnecessary.

181

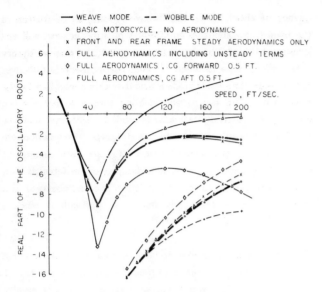

— WEAVE MODE — — WOBBLE MODE
o BASIC MOTORCYCLE, NO AERODYNAMICS
x FRONT AND REAR FRAME STEADY AERODYNAMICS ONLY
△ FULL AERODYNAMICS INCLUDING UNSTEADY TERMS
◇ FULL AERODYNAMICS, CG FORWARD 0.5 FT.
+ FULL AERODYNAMICS, CG AFT 0.5 FT.

FIG. 23   Motorcycle Stability

While the steady aerodynamic forces have little influence on stability, the unsteady aerodynamic forces estimated for the long-tailed CAN-AM Bonneville machine have a strong influence. The inclusion of the unsteady forces with the CG at its estimated nominal position lead to greatly reduced weave mode damping and nearly unchanged wobble mode damping. A 0.5 ft. rearward move of the CG leads, in the presence of the unsteady forces, to a strong weave mode instability commencing at 97.5 ft./sec. (66 m.p.h.). When the CG was moved back just 0.25 ft. the onset speed increased to 120 ft./sec. (82 m.p.h.). When the CG was moved 0.5 ft. forward of the nominal position the weave mode was strongly stabilized. In these cases only part of the observed changes in damping relative to the base case were due to the unsteady forces and moments. An indication of the change due to the CG shift alone is given in Table 10 which compares the real parts of the weave mode roots (proportional to damping) with and without the unsteady aerodynamic forces.

The parameter of most importance would appear to be the location of the unsteady side force centre of pressure. Use of a sufficiently long tail should guarantee that the centre of pressure will fall <u>behind</u> the CG providing a stabilizing influence.

SPEED (FT/SEC)	CG FORWARD 0.5 FT		CG AFT 0.5 FT	
	UNSTEADY AERO	NO UNSTEADY AERO	UNSTEADY AERO	NO UNSTEADY AERO
80	− 6.99	− 6.38	− 1.49	− 2.27
120	− 5.43	− 4.35	1.26	− 0.38
160	− 6.05	− 4.26	2.69	− 0.19
200	− 7.82	− 4.64	3.75	− 0.63

TABLE 10   Comparison of the Real Parts of the Weave Mode Roots with and without Unsteady Aerodynamics

The Bonneville streamliner, when run at a later date with the front disk wheel fairing removed, was found to be stable, but lightly damped. The removal of the disk fairing would tend to shift the centre of pressure aft, just stabilizing the motorcycle. This observation appears to agree with the analytical result.

There are, of course, other possible sources of handling problems including chassis stiffness effects and the response to side winds. The current analysis could be readily extended to consider the latter case. A simple modification to the steady aerodynamic force terms would allow the inclusion of gust generated forces. The equations could then be solved using a Runge-Kutta iteration and the time history of motorcycle response to an arbitrary wind gust could be obtained. One could also investigate the effect of control inputs in the same manner. It would be necessary to include a simple "rider" or "controller" whose task would be to stabilize the capsize mode only.

10. CONCLUSIONS

Clearly, aerodynamic forces play a significant role in the performance of high speed motorcycles and, depending upon the motorcycle configuration, may have a great influence on stability.

The reduction of drag through the use of properly designed, simple, fairings results in large performance gains at all but the lowest speeds. Road motorcycles equipped with fairings will have fuel mileage increases of the order of 15 percent or more at highway speeds. Passing times due to improved acceleration will be reduced by about 10 percent at highway speeds, reducing passing risk. With a fairing in use it would be possible to re-gear the motorcycle to allow the same acceleration as an unfaired motorcycle at highway speeds while having a lower cruising engine speed and higher top speed capability. The fairing also has several non-performance advantages. It increases rider comfort and safety by affording some protection from aerodynamic loads, weather and airborne debris. The fairing, if lined with a sound absorber, would reduce the noise level of the motorcycle both to the rider and external to the machine.

The performance benefits which accrue for road-racing and Bonneville record machines are even greater. Since a more extreme rider position is acceptable, the more extensive, smaller, fairings which are possible may lead to very low drag values. An approach to the streamlining of a partially streamlined motorcycle which integrates the rider and fairing leads to drag coefficients which are 70 percent of the values for the type of fairings currently used. This improvement provides increased top speed, higher rates of acceleration, reduced fuel consumption and the possibility of considerably reduced lap times on a road-racing course.

The mathematical model of motorcycle stability outlined appears to predict motorcycle behaviour which is qualitatively like that observed. The steady state aerodynamic forces were shown to exert a stabilizing influence on the motorcycle's weave mode stability. It would appear to be unnecessary to separate the aerodynamic forces into those on the front and rear frames. Estimated unsteady aerodynamic forces, postulated as applying to a long-tailed streamlined motorcycle, or to fully enclosed streamliners, predicted a weave mode instability similar to that encountered by one machine at Bonneville. It is felt that these unsteady forces may have caused some of the handling problems encountered by other machines at Bonneville. The problem will be avoided if the motorcycle tail is made sufficiently long that the centre of pressure of the unsteady lateral force lies behind the motorcycle's rear frame centre of gravity.

The wind tunnel has shown itself to be an economic and very useful tool in improving the general performance of a wide range of motorcycles. In fact, to obtain the optimum performance from any given configuration, the use of a wind tunnel should be considered mandatory.

REFERENCES

(1) Whipple, F.J.W., "The Stability of the Motion of the Bicycle", Q.J. Math. 1899.

(2) Sharp, R.S., "The Stability and Control of Motorcycles". J. Mech. Eng. Science, 1971.

(3) Ellis, J.R., Hayhoe, G.F., "The Steady State and Transient Handling Characteristics of a Motorcycle", Second Int. Conf. on Auto Safety, 1973.

(4) Roland, R.D., "A Computer Simulation of Bicycle Dynamics". ASCE Symposium on Mechanics and Sport. November 1973.

(5) Dunsby, J.A., Wardlaw, R.L., Marsden, D.J., "An Experimental Investigation of Some Methods of Reducing the Boundary Layer Thickness on the Working Section of No. 3 Low Speed Wind Tunnel with Particular Reference to Half-Model Testing", Lab Memo AE-106, NAE, Ottawa, Canada, 1958.

(6) Bettes, W.H., "Aerodynamic Testing of High Performance Land Borne Vehicles — A Criterial Review", Proceeding of the AIAA Symposium on the Aerodynamics of Sports and Competition Automobiles, Los Angeles, Ca., 1968.

(7) Cooper, K.R., "The Wind Tunnel Development of a Low Drag, Partially Streamlined Motorcycle", DME/NAE Quarterly Bulletin No. 1973 (4), NRC, Ottawa, Canada.

(8) Hoerner, S.F., "Fluid Dynamic Drag". Published by the Author.

(9) Pershing, B., "Dragster Aerodynamics — Streamlining Versus Weight", Proceedings of the AIAA Symposium on the Aerodynamics of Sports and Competition Automobiles", Los Angeles, 1968.

(10) Stafford, L.G., Russel, J.B., "Aerodynamic Design. Part 1: The Fundamental Principles", Journal of Automotive Engineering.

(11) Weir, D., "Motorcycle Handling Dynamics and Rider Control and the Effect of Design Configuration on Response and Performance", University of California, Los Angeles, 1972.

(12) Ellis, J.R., "Vehicle Dynamics", London Business Books Ltd., London, England.

(13) Etkin, B., "Dynamics of Flight, Stability and Control", John Wiley and Sons Inc.

(14) Abbot, I.H., Von Doenhoff, A.E., "Theory of Wing Sections", Dover Publications, Inc., New York.

DISCUSSION

JON McKIBBEN: What is your opinion regarding the levels of roll and yaw stability for the Bonneville streamlined motorcycle as compared to the four-wheel vehicle where the classic approach is to use a large vertical tail to get an aft center of pressure? Specifically, do you have analyses to show the relative effects of roll and yaw due to sidewinds?

COOPER: The case I presented of a bike with the tailcone on showed that if the center of gravity was not sufficiently far forward, there are problems with certain of the stability derivatives. In terms of response to the wind, I don't feel that you want a lot of weathercock stability, that is, you should try to use as small a vertical tail as possible. To initiate a right turn on a motorcycle you have to initially steer left. Following this line of reasoning, if a sidewind from the right hits a motorcycle with weathercock stability, it will cause the motorcycle to turn right into the wind. But the aerodynamic rolling moment and the lateral acceleration due to path curvature will cause the motorcycle to lean left getting you into real trouble. I think what you want is a careful balance of aerodynamic roll and yaw moment such that the wind vector will tend to force the motorcycle out of the wind but this tendency will be balanced by the lateral acceleration produced by the curvature of the path which will roll the motorcycle into the sidewind. From these arguments it's clear that you don't want to follow the dictates of aircraft or of four-wheel cars. You must consider the aero surfaces and the chassis together because a surface vehicle has tires which are doing things at the same time the aerodynamic forces are acting. There are also other effects such as gyroscopic forces which complicate the problem for motorcycles.

AUD. QUESTION: For road machines with the rider sitting erect, at what speed would aerodynamic effects become significant and what areas of streamlining or partial streamlining would you concentrate on to get good handling?

COOPER: When a vehicle is disturbed and it oscillates along its track, the steady aerodynamic forces acting on it are stabilizing. But when a sidewind acts on the vehicle, then you have to consider the yawing moments and sideforces. However, it turns out that for road motorcycles with or without fairings, there is little or no yawing moment. That is, the force vector acts nearly at the center of gravity of the motorcycle producing a sideforce but little or no moment. As a result, the response characteristics due to a sidewind are not too bad and from this standpoint the fairing design does not appear to be critical.

THE DYNAMICS AND AERODYNAMICS
OF JUMP MOTORCYCLES

Douglas J. Malewicki
Manager, Advanced Research and Development
L. M. Cox Manufacturing Co., Inc.
Santa Ana, California

Abstract

Long distance daredevil motorcycle jumpers have gradually extended their aerodynamic journeys into a realm where experience and instinctive judgement
alone no longer fully suffice. The jumpers who do not start taking advantage of
technology and the readily available analytical tools of aerodynamics, math, and
physics are foregoing cheap insurance for some rather disastrous consequences.
This paper represents the first attempt to investigate critical jump trajectory
parameters; in flight stability and control forces; takeoff and landing ramp
design problems; and jump motorcycle design limitations. Recommendations
for today's jumpers are explained, and advanced motorcycle designs that meet
the requirements for safe, super-long jumps are discussed.

1. INTRODUCTION

1.1 DEFINITION OF THE JUMP MANEUVER

The maneuver of interest involves a person driving his motorcycle at speeds which sometimes
approach 100 miles per hour straight onto a shallow inclined ramp. This launches the rider and
his machine into the air usually over a specific
number of side-by-side parked cars. The object,
of course, is to successfully clear the distance
one has been boasting about in earlier widespread
publicity. The maneuver is ideally concluded with
a smooth safe landing as seen in the sequence of
Figure 1.

In the instances where the jumper has managed to
remain fully intact, he can then enjoy both the
adulation of the paying spectators and the quite
substantial income earned for his feat. The non-
ideal landing, on the other hand, can be painfully
disastrous!

Hopefully, this paper will give today's jumpers
additional safety through a better understanding of
the physical phenomena involved. Also, it is

Figure 1. Bob Gill Enters Ramp, Launches Into the Air, Clears Cars and Lands Safely.

hoped that some of the more blatant design omissions will be corrected.

1.2 HISTORICAL PERSPECTIVE

Most people think ramp-to-ramp jumping is a recent invention of man. Figures 2 and 3 show some remarkably similar activity occurring in 1905.

Figure 2. Michaels - The Original Ramp-to-Ramp Jumper.

Figure 3. Newspaper Clipping from the Year, 1905 Photos from the Collection of Ky Michaelson.

As you can see, Mr. Michaels converted potential energy into kinetic energy for his motive power. While speeds and distances were not very great, the hazards remained.

Mr. Michaels is the grand-uncle of Ky Michaelson of Minnesota. Ky is presently heavily involved in Hydrogen Peroxide rocket cars and his machines hold numerous speed and acceleration records. According to Ky, the man who built most of Harry Houdini's equipment also built the ramp for Ky's grand-uncle.

In the mid-60's, Robert Craig "Evel" Knievel reinvented and popularized this ramp-to-ramp daredevil stunt. In addition to cars, Evel jumps trucks, fountains and even pits of rattlesnakes with mountain lions tied at the end of the ramp. A movie has been made of his life and even gyro stabilized toy dolls that duplicate his jumping feats in miniature have been produced. It is interesting to note that on several of his indoor jumps where acceleration distances were limited, Evel has used a Michaels type downhill starting ramp.

1.3 TODAY'S JUMPERS

The 1970's now see a proliferation of professional jumpers. The most famous of these were interviewed for this paper to gain practical insight into the jumpers' problems. Table I presents a summary of their statistics. Their portraits and some action shots are shown in Figures 4 through 6.

Note that Bob Gill of Florida is unique in that he alone does not use any landing ramp whatsoever! Also note that most jumpers blend their ramps with a van roof as shown in Figure 7 and count cars that are under the ramp as long as the rear wheel touches down beyond these cars.

Using cars as a unit of measurement for these leaps is quite prevalent. This is interesting, especially when one realizes the possible variations that exist in car widths shown in Table II.

Apparently the general public is not very accuracy-oriented and perhaps even quite gullible. One example, I remember, was a jumper proudly

186

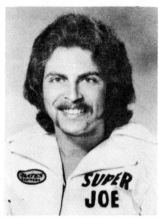

Evel Knievel   Debbie Lawler   Bob Gill   Super Joe Einhorn

Figure 4. The Professional Motorcycle Jumpers.

Figure 5. Jumpers in Action

Right - Super Joe Einhorn in Midair.

Middle - Debbie Lawler Off the Ramp.

Right Bottom - Blackwell and Davis in Their 22 Car Double Jump.

Figure 6. Below - Bob Gill in Flight.

Table I
Statistics of Current Professional Jumpers

Item	Evel Knievel	Super Joe Einhorn	Bob Gill	Debbie Lawler	Rex Blackwell
First Jump for $	1966	1971	1970	1972	1972
Number of Jumps for $	300 (est.)	52	140	13	35
Longest Jump	129 ft (19 cars)	144 ft (20 cars)	171 ft (22 cars)	120 ft (15 cars)	138 ft (20 cars)
Number of Accidents	41	13	3	1	1
Present Age	35 yrs	26 yrs	28 yrs	21 yrs	20 yrs
Weight	180 lb	185 lb	165 lb	120 lb	165 lb
Type of Motorcycle	Harley XR-750	Triumph 650 cc	Kawasaki 350 cc F-9	Suzuki 250 cc	BSA 500 cc
Take-off Ramp					
Length	48 ft	32 ft	Classified	48 ft	48 ft
Height	7 ft	7.5 ft	Adjustable	7 ft	7 ft
Launch Angle	8.4 deg	10 deg	Adjustable	8.4 deg	8.4 deg
Transition?	No	Yes (16 ft)	Contoured	Yes (8 ft)	Yes (8 ft)
Any Trajectory Analysis?	No	Trial and Error	Computer - But No Wind Effects	Manager	Trial and Error
Landing Ramp Length	Blended and Over Cars	55 ft	None	60 ft	60 ft
Landing Ramp Height		6.5 ft		6 ft	6 ft

announcing in early promotional interviews that his "record jump attempt will not be over any of those **++#!!# dinky foreign cars." So after you pay to get in you find a string of American Dodge Colts between and under the ramps. It's an exciting show nevertheless - so no one really complains.

Is motorcycle jumping a legitimate sport? If so, we are viewing a sport with some technical prob-

lems. Even if it's not a real sport, the people still exist and are delving into high technology. How do you do it intelligently and where does it all lead?

Today it is not uncommon to see neighborhood youngsters on their pedal bikes jumping home-made ramps, and doing balanced wheelies. Ten years ago this activity was virtually unknown. Does that mean we can expect an Olympic motor-

Figure 7. Evel Knievel's 19-Car Record Jump at Ontario Motor Speedway, February 1972.

Table II
Car Width Variation

Car	Width	20 Car Widths
Honda Civic	59.25 Inches	98.7 ft
VW Beetle	61.0 Inches	101.5 ft
Cadillac	79.8 Inches	132.9 ft

cycle jumping distance event similar to ski jumping by the mid-80's? Time will tell. Hopefully
the following analysis will lay some groundwork
to make it all a bit safer.

2. PERFORMANCE ANALYSIS

2.1 THE JUMP TRAJECTORY

Most of the jumpers interviewed have a large "X"
painted in the middle of their 60-foot long by 7-foot
wide landing ramps. Their general feeling is that
the landing and run-out will be fine if they touch
down within 5 feet fore or aft of the "X". Ideally,
the motorcycle attitude is at a 20 to 30 degree
nose up angle with the rear wheel hitting first.

Grossly undershooting the ramp does not seem to
be any problem. However, just catching the forward lip of the ramp and destroying rear tires has
occurred. Overshooting the ramp entirely, on the
other hand, seems quite prevalent. The impact is
much harder to deal with and injuries often occur.
To date there is no recorded instance of anyone
missing the ramp sideways.

In order to systematically study the effects of
winds, weight variations, ramp exit speed variations, ramp angle variations, etc., a point mass
trajectory computer program was written. All
Fortran programming, debugging and computer
plotting of trajectories was done by my long-time
friend, Bruce Williams of Costa Mesa.

First, a review of the basic aerodynamic drag
formula is given in Figure 8.

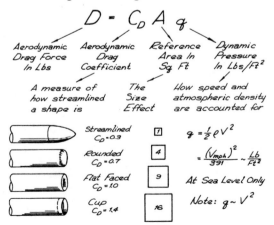

Figure 8. Aerodynamic Drag.

The free body diagram and equations of motion are
presented in Figure 9.

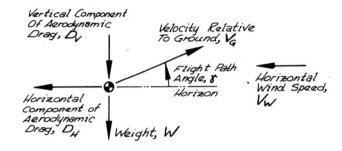

FREE BODY DIAGRAM

RESOLUTION OF RELATIVE WIND AND DRAG

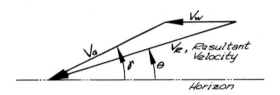

$$V_R = \sqrt{(V_G \sin \gamma)^2 + (V_G \cos \gamma + V_W)^2}$$

$$\theta = Tan^{-1}\left(\frac{V_G \sin \gamma}{V_G \cos \gamma + V_W}\right)$$

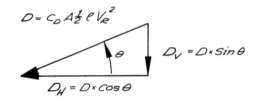

$$D = C_D A \frac{1}{2} \rho V_R^2$$

$$D_V = D \times \sin \theta$$

$$D_H = D \times \cos \theta$$

NEWTONS LAW

$$\begin{bmatrix} \text{Sumation of Forces} \\ \text{Acting on the Body} \end{bmatrix} = \begin{bmatrix} \text{Mass of} \\ \text{Body} \end{bmatrix} \times \begin{bmatrix} \text{Acceleration} \\ \text{of Body} \end{bmatrix}$$

$$\Sigma F = m \times a$$

At Any Specific Instant of Time

$$\begin{bmatrix} \text{Vertical Component of} \\ \text{Acceleration in g's} \end{bmatrix} = a_V = \Sigma \frac{F_V}{W} = \frac{-D_V - W}{W}$$

$$\begin{bmatrix} \text{Horizontal Component of} \\ \text{Acceleration in g's} \end{bmatrix} = a_H = \Sigma \frac{F_H}{W} = -\frac{D_H}{W}$$

Figure 9. Forces Acting on a Jump Motorcycle.

Range and height are numerically computed using the following relationships.

For the time interval, Δt:

New velocity relative to the ground

Horizontal component, $V_{H_{New}}$

$$V_{H_{New}} = V_{H_{old}} + a_H \times g \times \Delta t$$

Vertical component, $V_{V_{New}}$

$$V_{V_{New}} = V_{V_{old}} + a_V \times g \times \Delta t$$

New flight path angle, γ_{New}

$$\gamma_{New} = Tan^{-1} \left(V_{V_{New}} / V_{H_{New}} \right)$$

Average speed in interval, Δt, V_{Avg}

$$V_{Avg} = \left(V_{New} + V_{old} \right) / 2$$

New range, R_{New}

$$R_{New} = R_{old} + V_{H_{Avg}} \times \Delta t$$

New height, H_{New}

$$H_{New} = H_{old} + V_{V_{Avg}} \times \Delta t$$

Horizontal head and tail winds as a variable are included. For program simplification the bike was assumed to maintain a constant angle-of-attack to the relative wind vector. Thus, a constant drag coefficient could be used. Also, any lift was assumed negligible. The nominal conditions for this study were:

Weight of Man - Motorcycle = 500 lb
Ramp Exit Height = 7 ft
Ramp Launch Angle = 8.4 deg
Ramp Exit Speed = 80 mph
No Winds

With the program results we can better understand what variables most seriously perturb the nominally desired jump distance (accuracy of landing right on the "X").

In order to study the effects of aerodynamic drag on the trajectories, we need to estimate the drag area, $C_D A$, of the motorcycle with man as it flies through the air. The drag area of the flying motorcycle was estimated from data given in Reference 1 as shown in Figure 10.

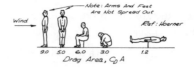

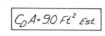

Figure 10. Flying Motorcycle Drag Estimation.

The nominal trajectory results in a landing on the ground 1.38 seconds after takeoff at a point 150 ft beyond the 7-foot high ramp. For our comparisons, we will use the horizontal ground surface rather than the middle of a landing ramp for our range variation studies. This eliminates having to move the ramp back and forth mathematically for exact center landings. It also keeps all perturbed trajectories on the same impact potential energy plane for subsequent analysis of that problem.

Figure 11 shows range variations with weight changes. This would roughly cover the extremes from little Debbie Lawler on her 250 CC Suzuki to one of the heavier jumpers on his big Harley. As you can see, a 20% change in weight only affects range by 1.3%. Note, however, that the variation of the vertical component of Kinetic Energy (to be absorbed by the motorcycle shock absorbers) at the instant of impact increases exactly as weight increases.

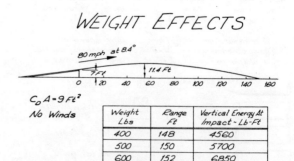

Figure 11. Effect of Weight on Trajectory.

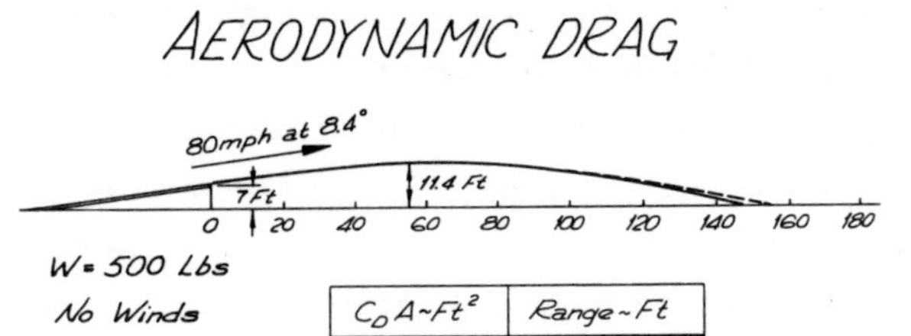

AERODYNAMIC DRAG

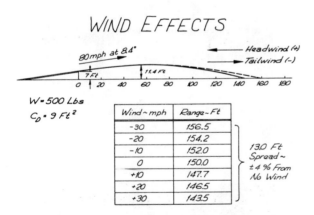

Figure 12. Effect of Aerodyamic Drag on Trajectory.

Figure 12 helps to show that a precise estimate of the aerodynamic drag area is not too important. If the motorcycle were so streamlined that drag was negligible ($C_DA = 0$) the range would only increase by 8 feet. Alternatively, a 33% increase in drag area from 9 to 12 square feet only reduces range by 2.5 feet or 1.6%.

Figure 13 shows the effect on jump distance of head and tail winds. The extreme case of fighting a 30 mph headwind only reduces the nominal range by 4%.

WIND EFFECTS

Figure 13. Effect of Wind on Trajectory.

The primary reason for this surprising result is that the time aloft is only 1.38 seconds. With the full 30 mph headwind, the horizontal component of aerodynamic drag is 278 lb which gives 0.55 g's of horizontal deceleration. Alternately, with a full 30 mph tailwind, the horizontal component of aerodynamic drag is only 58 lb which means only 0.12 g's of deceleration. A crude steady state estimate shows the no drag range of 159 feet would be reduced by 17 feet (or 142-foot jump) in the extreme

headwind case, while the extreme tailwind condition produces a 3-foot reduction (or a 150-foot jump). The differences in deceleration level are large, but the time they act is so short that the end differences in range would be inconsequential in any realistic wind conditions.

If the above crude analysis had been performed prior to writing and debugging the computer program, we would have discovered that the program was not needed. Use of the simple drag free projectile equations taught in high school physics will yield quite useful jump distance data. Of course, as speeds, distances, and times aloft are increased, aerodynamics will have to become a part of any useful analysis.

CROSSWIND EFFECTS

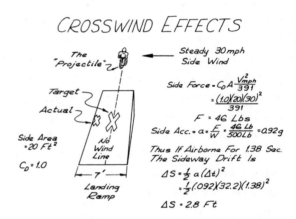

Figure 14. Effect of Crosswind on Trajectory.

Figure 14 is an estimate of how far off course an extreme 30 mph crosswind would carry the rider. It looks quite critical, but in reality, most jumpers wouldn't perform in such bad crosswinds. It is also reasonable to assume they would instinctively compensate by aiming off center into a crosswind.

Next, we want to look at the effect of ramp angle variations as shown in Figure 15. If the takeoff ramp happens to be set one degree lower than normal, the desired range can quickly be reduced by 10 feet. Precision ramp angle settings are quite important. In the case of a fixed non-adjustable ramp, it merely means that the actual ramp angle must initially be precisely determined in order to take advantage of any mathematical analysis.

Some readers may ask the question why the jumpers, who are supposedly intent on maximizing

RAMP ANGLE EFFECTS

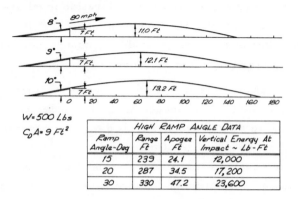

W=500 Lbs
$C_DA=9 Ft^2$

HIGH RAMP ANGLE DATA			
Ramp Angle~Deg	Range Ft	Apogee Ft	Vertical Energy At Impact ~ Lb-Ft
15	239	24.1	12,000
20	287	34.5	17,200
30	330	47.2	23,600

Figure 15. Effect of Ramp Angle on Trajectory.

their range, merely don't increase their launch angle closer to an optimum 45 degrees. The table in Figure 15 shows that increasing the angle of launch does increase range fantastically. However, it also increases the landing impact energy quickly to a value where it becomes physically impossible to absorb it. The simple analogy is to visualize the bike and man being dropped from an 11-foot high cliff. Then imagine what would happen if dropped from a 47-foot high cliff. You don't really need any equations to describe the horrible crunch that would result.

SPEED SENSITIVITY

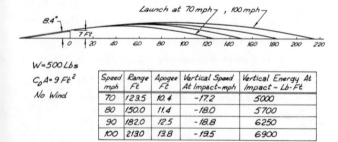

W=500 Lbs
$C_DA=9 Ft^2$
No Wind

Speed mph	Range Ft	Apogee Ft	Vertical Speed At Impact~mph	Vertical Energy At Impact ~ Lb-Ft
70	123.5	10.4	-17.2	5000
80	150.0	11.4	-18.0	5700
90	182.0	12.5	-18.8	6250
100	213.0	13.8	-19.5	6900

Figure 16. Effect of Launch Speed on Trajectory.

Lastly, Figure 16 shows how sensitive range is to launch speed variations. Leaving the ramp at a speed that is 10 mph or 12% too high, results in a range that is 32 feet or 21% longer than desired. Super precise control of speed turns out to be especially significant. This perhaps explains why the jumpers comment that they, on occasion, take their eyes off the ramp to glance at the speedometer when as close as 20 feet to the ramp. It

also explains why they make many high speed runs past the side of their ramps prior to the actual jump. They want to sharpen their feel for the sound of the engine at the selected speed so they won't have to bother looking down at the speedometer just when things are getting critical. The sequence of shots in Figure 17 shows an overly-long landing due to incorrect takeoff speed.

Figure 17. The Consequences of Excess Launch Speed. Top, Super Joe Einhorn in Fight. Second Frame, Rear Tire Hits Far End of Ramp Landing 30 Feet Beyond "X" Due to 10 MPH Excess Speed at Take-off. Third Frame, Impact Put a 3 Foot Hole in Ramp Destroying Tire. Severe Jolt Throws Super Joe From Bike. Above, Einhorn Contacts Ground.

Figure 18. Night Photo of Rex Blackwell and Gary Davis Crossover Jump.

The ballistic nature of the jumpers' trajectory is vividly displayed in Figure 18.

The photo also suggests an inexpensive method for obtaining experimental verification of any computer math model. A time exposure using one-tenth of a second strobe light flashes, in conjunction with lights on the spinning wheels, measured wind data, and dimensions of the motorcycle would allow complete definition of velocity, range and altitude versus time.

2.2 STABILITY AND CONTROL

A man riding a motorcycle through the air is not an aerodynamically stable configuration. It would tumble given a sufficient time for the destabilizing pressures to act. Fortunately, at today's jump distances, the time aloft is short.

This section analyzes the various in-flight control forces available to the jumper to compensate for any destabilizing forces. Pitch and roll moments of inertia are estimated on the low side, while command forces are approximated on the high side. Thus, maximum possible vehicle control motions can be estimated.

It should be noted that the jumpers unanimously state that once airborne, they can't really react fast enough to affect any changes. They concentrate on a clean takeoff at the proper speed and merely hang on as passengers for the remainder of the flight.

Figure 19 shows the pitch moment of inertia estimates for the man/motorcycle combination and for a separate 20-pound wheel. Figure 20 shows the roll moments of inertia estimate for the man/motorcycle combination.

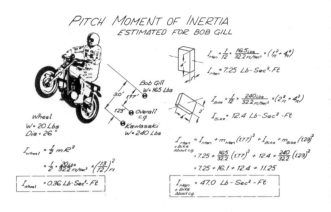

Figure 19. Pitch Moment of Inertia.

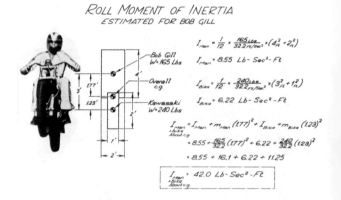

Figure 20. Roll Moment of Inertia.

Figure 21 is an estimate for the net pitch up moment due to aerodynamic pressure forces that could be expected to act on the man and bike. The moment produces an angular pitch up acceleration that could increase the attitude of the bike by 125 degrees in 1.4 seconds. This would put the bike on its back! In reality, one would expect the moment about the center of gravity would change as attitude shifted.

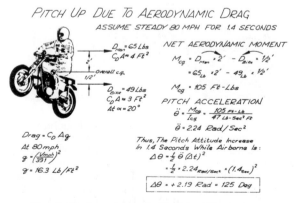

Figure 21. Aerodynamic Pitching Moment.

The sequence of Figure 22 shows extreme pitch ups which could be due to aerodynamic causes or improper use of throttle.

Figure 22. Effect of Pitch Attitude at Touchdown. Top, Evel Knievel Approaches Ramp at Very High Angle, Las Vegas Ceasars Palace, 1968. Second Frame, Severe Jolt Whips Bike Down Hard, Rips Control Bar From Evel's Hands. Thrid Frame, Driver Thrown Over Bike. Above, Driver and Bike tangle. The Launch Speed on This Jump Was Approximately 10 MPH Too Slow. Touchdown Was About 30 Feet Short of the Desired "X".

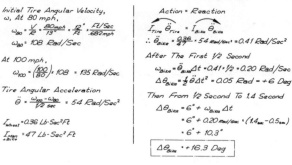

Figure 23. Pitch-Up Due To Throttle Action.

Figure 23 is an estimate of the pitch attitude that could result from a short burst of throttle once airborne. Essentially the action of spinning up the tire in one direction causes an opposite reaction on the entire bike with man in the opposite direction in proportion to the relative moment of inertia ratio. Of course, the opposite reaction (a pitch down) would occur if the brakes were applied at the same rate instead. Now, if the driver senses an excess pitch up due to aerodynamic forces, he can apply the brakes in mid-air to cancel or at least retard the aerodynamic upset. Recently, we have conducted some preliminary experiments in the desert on some very short jumps to evaluate this control force. The right toe brake for the rear wheel is hard to use as your body is in free fall with nothing to react against. The throttle, however, is extremely powerful in increasing pitch attitude. Application of full front brake would work, but it would have

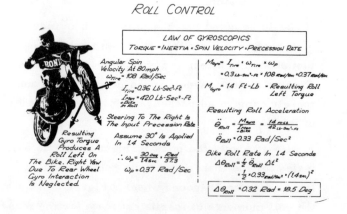

Figure 24. Gyroscopic Roll Control.

194

to be released before impact. Our jumps were too short to risk evaluating that.

Figure 24 gives an idea of the inflight roll correction one can obtain by precessing the front wheel. In actual practice, the bikes appear to maintain a perfect vertical attitude throughout the jump. This is probably due to instinctive control by the rider after experiencing the effect many, many times and learning how to hold a vertical attitude. It is recommended that the pitch control modes described previously be experimented on short jumps. As the jumpers develop confidence in the machine's response, they can then take advantage of this learning process when in trouble on a long jump.

2.3 LANDING IMPACT CONSIDERATIONS

Figure 25 vividly shows why touching down on the landing ramp at a shallow angle should be much better than landing flat without a ramp. The energy to be absorbed by the shocks on a perfect mid-ramp landing is one-fifth of the energy to be absorbed on a flat landing. This is due to the

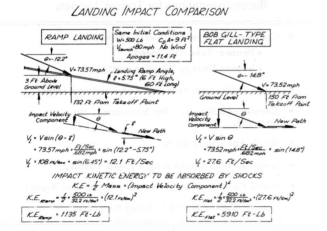

Figure 25. Landing Impact Comparison.

height difference, (3 feet of drop height energy has been eliminated) and the greatly reduced component of velocity perpendicular to the landing surface. In terms of pure distance, not using a landing ramp is advantageous. 150 feet is attained from the same initial launch conditions that yield only 138 feet with a perfect ramp landing.

Figure 26 carries the landing impact considerations further. Imagine being on a motorcycle that

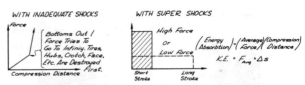

IMPACT ENERGY ABSORPTION

Figure 26. Impact Energy Absorbtion.

is dropped from an 11.4-foot high bridge. As soon as the wheels touch ground, the shock absorbers begin to reduce the vertical velocity. Once their energy absorption limit is reached, the driver feels a severe jolt through the mass of his body as it decelerates to zero vertical velocity in an instant. Now, mentally superimpose the horizontal velocity of 70 mph into the situation and you can easily visualize why the impact jolt can result in a subsequent loss of control.

New design shocks are needed with longer strokes. All of the impact energy must be capable of being absorbed while maximum vertical deceleration forces are kept at some level that the driver's body can withstand. Figure 26 shows how a longer stroke shock absorber, operating at lower average forces, can greatly reduce the deceleration levels the person feels. The idea, of course, is to spend a longer time absorbing the energy.

Figure 27 shows a sequence from one of Bob Gill's flat landings. The severity of the body jolting is most dramatic when watching the actual 200 frames per second movies. The enigma is Bob Gill's far superior safety record - only 3 minor injuries in 140 jumps. How can this be when a ramp landing buys you an 80% reduction in impact forces? It may have something to do with rebound of the shock absorbers occurring almost in conjunction with the big jolt. Then about a quarter-of-a-second later, a secondary impact into the flat ground surface, almost as severe as the first, occurs. Does the quarter-of-a-second from the first jolt allow enough time for a mental evaluation of any impact related control problems, let alone corrections?

Figure 27. Flat Landing. Top, Bob Gill Jumps 120 Foot Canyon. Second Frame, Bike at 50° Pitch Attitude. Control Bar is Tight Against Bob's Body. Third Frame, Rear Wheel Touches Down First. Impact Causes bike to Pitch Forward. Above, Shock Absorbers Bottom Out. Bob's Body Compresses.

Figure 28 shows that the answer to the secondary impact problem is a properly designed contoured exit section. Simply don't allow a second jolt to occur! Spread the angular change in the velocity vector over a large distance. Same idea as using a long stroke shock absorber. A smooth 2g pull-up design should be adequate.

A summary of useful improvements that jumpers should incorporate is shown in Table III.

Figure 28. Second Impact.

Table III
Recommendations for Todays Jumpers

- Complete Analysis of Each Trajectory.
  - Proper Take-Off Speed.
  - Impact Energy Requirements.
- Fully Contoured Take-Off and Landing Ramps.
- Engineered Shocks - No Bottoming, No Rebound.
- Shock Absorbing Seat.
- Body-to-Bike Cushioning - Rigid Foams.
- Speed Control Device or Audio Tone, Not Visual.
- Longer Take-Off and Landing Runways.

3. THE SUPER LONG JUMP

Some jumpers, never content with their past achievements, have strong desires to jump over more impressive objects such as shown in Figure 29. One way to go about it is shown in Figure 30. The problem is cost, not technological limitations! With enough dollars, one could buy and launch a Saturn V with a couple of Honda wheels attached and claim the modified motorcycle record of jumping the moon.

Figure 29. The Grand Canyon, Arizona, USA.

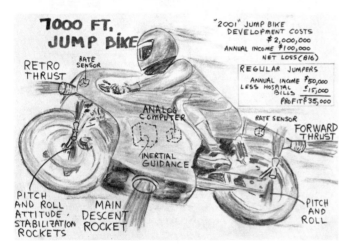

Figure 30. The 700 Foot Jump Bike.

3.1 THE EVEL KNIEVEL SKYCYCLE PROJECT

Figure 31 shows the modified motorcycle in which Evel Knievel was claiming he would jump the 3/4-mile site at the Grand Canyon on Labor Day of 1968.

I first saw it on display on Phoenix in August of 1968. Stable? No Way! Adequate thrust? No Way! Those are turbonique monopropellant rockets producing a maximum of 400 lb thrust each. At the time, the high pressure lines which should run to a nitrogen tank, the thermolene monopropellant tank, and an oxygen tank ran right to the motorcycle gas tank. Efficient lift from flat plate wings mounted at a well beyond stall angle-of-attack of 45 degrees? No Way! Lots of

additional drag? Yes! Claims of leaving the ramp at 300 mph to make the 3/4-mile distance were checked. If you launched at an optimum 45 degrees and didn't have any drag, yes, you could barely make it. Leave off the "wings" to reduce drag-area to 9 square feet and at 300 mph you still have 1450 pounds of drag to contend with! Also, how were the two mere 400-pound thrust rockets supposed to get the bike up to 300 mph in the first place?

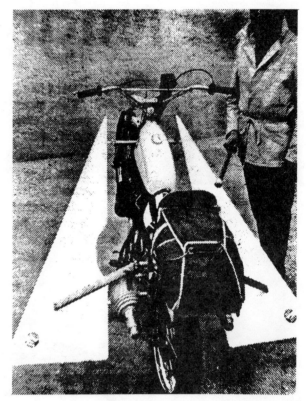

Figure 31. Evel Knievel's Original Rocket Powered Winged Grand Canyon Jump Bike.

A three-page letter of technical questions yielded an interview with the famous daredevil, Knievel. Shortly thereafter, a functioning rocket powered model was built, launched, and successfully re-covered by parachute in conjunction with Evel's 1968 jump at Phoenix's BeeLine Dragway. Unfor-tunately, Evel wasn't there to see it! He broke a leg practicing that afternoon. His very nervous stand-in overcompensated and landed very hard on the asphalt beyond the ramp. The jolt, when the shocks bottomed out, decelerated his body so hard that his chin took 28 stitches where it im-pacted against the unpadded structure.

197

Word of the successful rocket model flight, of course, got back to Evel and details for a hopefully sound 3/4-mile rocket-powered bike were underway. Figure 32 shows the concept poised for launch. Figure 33 shows it in the air. Note that it has two wheels so it qualifies as a motorcycle in much the way the fully-enclosed Bonneville Land Speed Record streamliners are still identified as motorcycles.

Figure 32. Aerodynamically Stable Streamlined Rocket Powered Motorcycle Concept.

Figure 33. Fins Provide In-Flight Stability.

Purchasing a suitable rocket propulsion unit from any reputable aerospace company for such a "weird" project turned out to be impossible. A steam rocket was specially built by Robert Truax of Maryland. The basic drawing for the vehicle with this unique propulsion system is shown in Figure 34. Figure 35 shows one of the final qualification tests of the steam rocket at the Perkins Test Center in Sacramento. It develops 1333 pounds of thrust, for 6 seconds, for a total impulse of 8000 pounds-seconds. Specific impulse of such engines is low, only 40 seconds. Two hundred pounds of superheated water are expelled in 6 seconds. This is one-tenth the total impulse

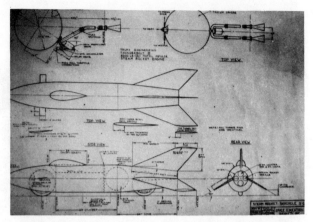

Figure 34. Skycycle General Arrangement Drawing.

Figure 35. Static Test of 1333 Pound Thrust Steam Rocket.

per pound of propellant that a Liquid Hydrogen-Liquid Oxygen rocket engine produces. Steam rocket fuel, however, is quite inexpensive, is non-toxic (even drinkable) and presents no handling, storage, or shipping problems.
Where do you get the best water in the world? Yes, Evel actually obtained the Olympia Brewing Company of Tumwater, Washington as one of the major sponsors for the appropriately named "Skycycle".

Figure 36 shows the titanium pressure vessel of the steam rocket (with added insulation to retain the heat energy) installed into the frame along with other structural details.

Figure 37 gives the complete sequence of events proposed for the vehicle's flight (i.e., the motorcycle jump). Note that the steam rocket's Total Impulse represents only one-third of the total

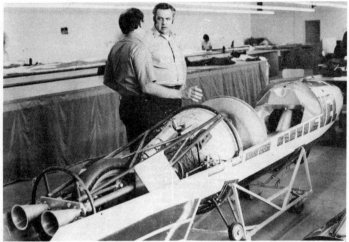

Figure 36. Structural Details of Skycycle.

Top Left, Insulated Steam Rocket. Retractable Wheels Keep Vehicle Upright at Low Speeds.

Left, Frame Details. Twin Exhaust Go Around Tire.

Above, Vehicle in Early Phase of Contruction. Russ Wheeler Shown With Author Constructed Parachute Recovery System.

CANYON JUMP – SEQUENCE OF EVENTS

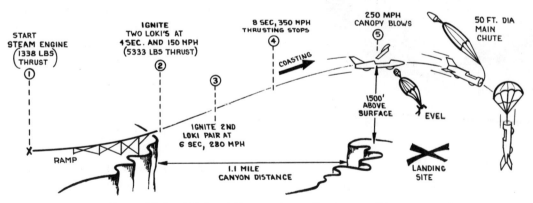

Figure 37. Evel Knievel Canyon Jump Sequence of Events.

power required to achieve peak altitude some 500 feet beyond the far rim of the canyon. The computer program for these trajectories (which properly accounted for thrust and weight loss) and a special program to develop a ramp contour which would give a constant 2g pullup on the bike and man were also written by Bruce Williams.

The 1.1-mile distance shown in Figure 37 is image, not real! Topological maps say it's only 1580 feet across where the real jump would take place. Also note the launch angle is not an optimum 45 degrees because of a cost constraint. If the driver didn't insist on personally controlling something, we could have set him up a much shorter launch ramp under high g's at a more optimum 45 degrees. An inert passenger can't add to technical problems. Note that chutes are used; the jumper does not intend to land on a ramp at 300 mph on the other side.

Figure 38 shows a rear view of.the near completed vehicle. The fins are quite large. Using the methods of Reference 2, the static stability margin computes out to be 1.25d where d is the major diameter of the body. All pitch and yaw motions in free flight occur about the vehicle's center-of-gravity. The resultant of all lift force pressures distributed over the body (at small angles-of-attack) is called the center of pressure. In this case, the center of pressure is 1.25 major body diameters behind the center-of-gravity. The static stability margin is a bit on the high side because the vehicle is not long and slender like an archer's arrow, but instead, is short and fat. This short coupling presents a more critical dynamic stability problem.

Figure 39. Two Views of Skycycle Showing Clean Design. Top, Minimum Frontal Area is Limited By Steam Rocket Tank Diameter. Above, Parabolic Nosecone Section.

Figure 38. Skycycle Prior to Painting.

The vehicle is designed to leave the ramp at 150 mph. At this speed, and above, the airflow over the fins provides adequate aerodynamic steering correction forces for quick, smooth, pitch and yaw responses. At much slower speeds, self stable response becomes mushy.

Figure 39 shows two front views of the Skycycle, so streamlining can be appreciated. The top speed of 350 mph is only seen for an instant and one

could really power his way through for the distance with more thrust. Good aerodynamics, however, costs less than a more powerful engine with more heavy fuel and its supporting structure. All the extra mass would then have to be brought down by a larger, more complicated, parachute system.

Figure 40 shows the Skycycle at its unveiling to the public at the Snake River Canyon jumpsite in May 1972. This was also the first public firing of the steam rocket. At this time, the parachute recovery system and the solid propellant extender motors were not installed.

Figure 41 shows one of the three test models fired from the launch side lip of the Snake River Canyon the afternoon of the unveiling. According to the computer, a 28-degree launch should have brought the model exactly to the landing side corner lip of the canyon. A short landing would tell us our drag

Figure 40. Skycycle Debute. Snake River Canyon, 1972.

Left, Preparation for First Public Test Firing. Note Tether Cable Between Exhausts.

Above, Entering Cockpit. External Turbine Heater in Background.

Bottom Left, First Public Firing. Skycycle Tether in Place.

estimates were low; a long landing would tell us our drag estimates were high. The chute popped out an estimated 50 feet above the far corner lip and it landed some 20 feet down on the almost sheer face. Hooray for 1% accuracy!

The second test model contained a high-speed Super 8 color rearward-looking movie camera and was launched at 45 degrees. The chute never ejected and it was destroyed. The third launch was also at 45 degrees, but we left the spare camera off. All worked fine and the chute ejected near apogee, well past the far rim.

That was May 1972. For numerous, interesting reasons, I was no longer involved with the Sky-cycle project after July 1972. In November of

Figure 41. Skycycle Subscale Test Model.

Top, 18 Inch Long Model Poised for Shallow 28 Degree Launch.

Above, Lift-Off From Lip of Snake River Canyon, Twin Falls, Idaho.

Figure 42. 5-4-3-2-1-CRASH!

1973, the vehicle met its demise in the bottom of the canyon as shown in Figure 42. It was a short launch on steam only. It left the ramp at considerably slower speed than required for aerodynamic stability, tumbled twice; became stable once it picked up sufficient speed on the way down and impacted in the middle of the Snake River - never to be seen again. Inadequate ground acceleration distance; inadequate Total Impulse; no rider; no parachutes!

3.2 SUPER JOE EINHORN ROCKET MOTORCYCLE

In September 1972, a design for a bigger and better rocket powered jump motorcycle, as shown by the rendering of Figure 43 and model of Figure 44, was underway for Super Joe Einhorn of San Pablo, California.

Bill Fredericks, who designed and built the rocket powered dragster "Courage of Australia", was

Figure 44. Proposal Model.

chosen as builder for the Super Joe Rocket. On one of its first runs in 1971, the Courage, shown in Figure 45, turned 311 mph in the quarter mile on 75% rocket thrust. Numerous discussions with Bill led to what is really a two-wheeled, lengthened version of Courage, that is aerodynamically stable so it can fly through the air ballistically like an arrow, and is recoverable by parachute.

Figure 46 shows some of the preliminary drawings which were used in the formal money raising presentations. Investor interest was good enough to get started on construction. The machine got as far along as shown in Figure 47. Unfortunately, it sagged after the first $9,000 was spent. The striking fact is that cost is always the too real limitation; not technical feasibility.

3.3 THE "FOR-REAL" FLYING MOTORCYCLE

Such frustration requires an entertaining, exhilirating mental break for a few months. The author bought and super-cautiously learned how to fly a hang glider. Lift-to-drag ratio is abominable, but portability and cost far outweigh that problem.

Figure 43. Rendering of 30 Foot Long Jump Motorcycle.

Figure 45. Courage of Australia.

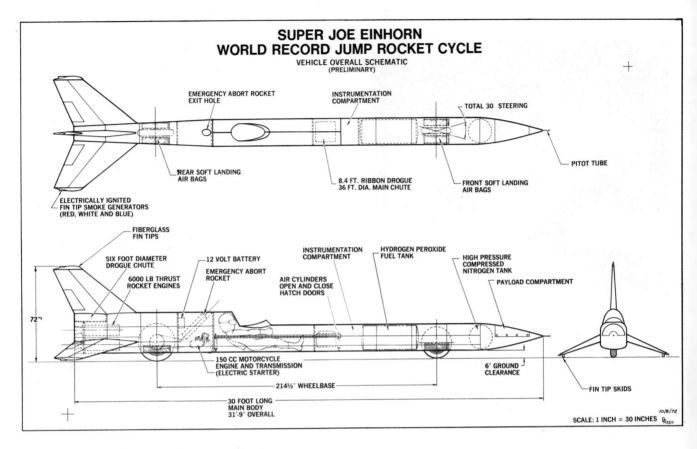

SUPER JOE EINHORN
WORLD RECORD JUMP ROCKET CYCLE
VEHICLE OVERALL SCHEMATIC
(PRELIMINARY)

EMERGENCY ABORT ROCKET
EXIT HOLE

INSTRUMENTATION
COMPARTMENT

TOTAL 30 STEERING

PITOT TUBE

REAR SOFT LANDING
AIR BAGS

8.4 FT. RIBBON DROGUE
36 FT. DIA. MAIN CHUTE

FRONT SOFT LANDING
AIR BAGS

ELECTRICALLY IGNITED
FIN TIP SMOKE GENERATORS
(RED, WHITE AND BLUE)

FIBERGLASS
FIN TIPS

SIX FOOT DIAMETER
DROGUE CHUTE

6000 LB THRUST
ROCKET ENGINES

12 VOLT BATTERY

EMERGENCY ABORT
ROCKET

INSTRUMENTATION
COMPARTMENT

HYDROGEN PEROXIDE
FUEL TANK

HIGH PRESSURE
COMPRESSED
NITROGEN TANK

PAYLOAD COMPARTMENT

AIR CYLINDERS
OPEN AND CLOSE
HATCH DOORS

72"

150 CC MOTORCYCLE
ENGINE AND TRANSMISSION
(ELECTRIC STARTER)

214½" WHEELBASE

6" GROUND
CLEARANCE

FIN TIP SKIDS

30 FOOT LONG
MAIN BODY
31'-9" OVERALL

10/8/72

SCALE: 1 INCH = 30 INCHES

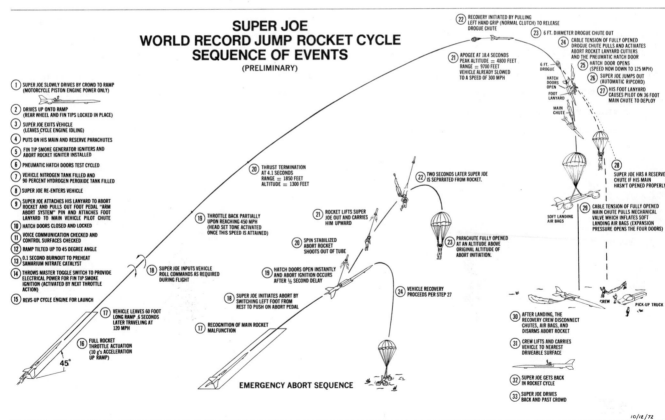

SUPER JOE
WORLD RECORD JUMP ROCKET CYCLE
SEQUENCE OF EVENTS
(PRELIMINARY)

1. SUPER JOE SLOWLY DRIVES BY CROWD TO RAMP (MOTORCYCLE PISTON ENGINE POWER ONLY)
2. DRIVES UP ONTO RAMP (REAR WHEEL AND FIN TIPS LOCKED IN PLACE)
3. SUPER JOE EXITS VEHICLE (LEAVES CYCLE ENGINE IDLING)
4. PUTS ON HIS MAIN AND RESERVE PARACHUTES
5. FIN TIP SMOKE GENERATOR IGNITERS AND ABORT ROCKET IGNITER INSTALLED
6. PNEUMATIC HATCH DOORS TEST CYCLED
7. VEHICLE NITROGEN TANK FILLED AND 90 PERCENT HYDROGEN PEROXIDE TANK FILLED
8. SUPER JOE RE-ENTERS VEHICLE
9. SUPER JOE ATTACHES HIS LANYARD TO ABORT ROCKET AND PULLS OUT FOOT PEDAL "ARM ABORT SYSTEM" PIN AND ATTACHES FOOT LANYARD TO MAIN VEHICLE PILOT CHUTE
10. HATCH DOORS CLOSED AND LOCKED
11. VOICE COMMUNICATION CHECKED AND CONTROL SURFACES CHECKED
12. RAMP TILTED UP TO 45 DEGREE ANGLE
13. 0.1 SECOND BURNOUT TO PREHEAT SAMARIUM NITRATE CATALYST
14. THROWS MASTER TOGGLE SWITCH TO PROVIDE ELECTRICAL POWER FOR FIN TIP SMOKE IGNITION (ACTIVATED BY NEXT THROTTLE ACTION)
15. REVS-UP CYCLE ENGINE FOR LAUNCH
16. FULL ROCKET THROTTLE ACTUATION (10 g's ACCELERATION UP RAMP)
17. VEHICLE LEAVES 60 FOOT LONG RAMP .6 SECONDS LATER TRAVELING AT 120 MPH

45°

18. SUPER JOE INPUTS VEHICLE ROLL COMMANDS AS REQUIRED DURING FLIGHT
19. THROTTLE BACK PARTIALLY UPON REACHING 450 MPH (HEAD SET TONE ACTIVATED ONCE THIS SPEED IS ATTAINED)
20. THRUST TERMINATION AT 4.1 SECONDS RANGE = 1850 FEET ALTITUDE = 1300 FEET
21. APOGEE AT 18.4 SECONDS PEAK ALTITUDE = 4800 FEET RANGE = 9700 FEET VEHICLE ALREADY SLOWED TO A SPEED OF 300 MPH
22. RECOVERY INITIATED BY PULLING LEFT HAND GRIP (NORMAL CLUTCH) TO RELEASE DROGUE CHUTE
23. 6 FT. DIAMETER DROGUE CHUTE OUT
24. CABLE TENSION OF FULLY OPENED DROGUE CHUTE PULLS AND ACTIVATES ABORT ROCKET LANYARD CUTTERS AND THE PNEUMATIC HATCH DOOR
25. HATCH DOOR OPENS (SPEED NOW DOWN TO 125 MPH)
26. SUPER JOE JUMPS OUT (AUTOMATIC RIPCORD)
27. HIS FOOT LANYARD CAUSES PILOT ON 36 FOOT MAIN CHUTE TO DEPLOY
28. SUPER JOE HAS A RESERVE CHUTE IF HIS MAIN HASN'T OPENED PROPERLY
29. CABLE TENSION OF FULLY OPENED MAIN CHUTE PULLS MECHANICAL VALVE WHICH INFLATES SOFT LANDING AIR BAGS (EXPANSION PRESSURE OPENS THE FOUR DOORS)

6 FT. DROGUE

HATCH DOORS OPEN

FOOT LANYARD

MAIN CHUTE

SOFT LANDING AIR BAGS

EMERGENCY ABORT SEQUENCE

17. RECOGNITION OF MAIN ROCKET MALFUNCTION
18. SUPER JOE INITIATES ABORT BY SWITCHING LEFT FOOT FROM REST TO PUSH ON ABORT PEDAL
19. HATCH DOORS OPEN INSTANTLY AND ABORT IGNITION OCCURS AFTER ½ SECOND DELAY
20. SPIN STABILIZED ABORT ROCKET SHOOTS OUT OF TUBE
21. ROCKET LIFTS SUPER JOE OUT AND CARRIES HIM UPWARD
22. TWO SECONDS LATER SUPER JOE IS SEPARATED FROM ROCKET.
23. PARACHUTE FULLY OPENED AT AN ALTITUDE ABOVE ORIGINAL ALTITUDE OF ABORT INITIATION.
24. VEHICLE RECOVERY PROCEEDS PER STEP 27

CREW

PICK-UP TRUCK

30. AFTER LANDING, THE RECOVERY CREW DISCONNECT CHUTES, AIR BAGS, AND DISARMS ABORT ROCKET
31. CREW LIFTS AND CARRIES VEHICLE TO NEAREST DRIVEABLE SURFACE
32. SUPER JOE GETS BACK IN ROCKET CYCLE
33. SUPER JOE DRIVES BACK AND PAST CROWD

10/12/72

Figure 46. Super Joe Rocket Cycle Briefing Charts.

203

Figure 47. 30 Foot Long Shell on Tubular Frame.

Soon, the now relaxed brain starts churning out technical ideas. Investigations of real motorcycle's power-to-weight ensues, followed by discussion with motorcycle manufacturer's R&D special project groups.

With the properly selected motocross machine, one can bolt a hang glider to it. Next, the rear wheel chain is extended so it can run past the sprocket up to some newly added aft motorcycle structure which supports a gear box and three-foot diameter shrouded propeller. Rough calculations show ridiculously short takeoff and landing

distances, a 300-foot per minute climb capability and a top cruise speed in the low 40 to 50 mph range.

Why bother with a 1580-foot span canyon when a no-wind 100-mile range falls out of the calculations? Carry an extra fuel tank and go from LA to Frisco non-stop! Anyone for formation motorcycle flights to Cataline Island for Sunday breakfast? How about the Barstow-to-Vegas cycle race without getting cooked by the sun and vibrated to pieces by the route terrain? Be the only motorcyclist in your neighborhood who doesn't get rained on!

The concept is simple and cheap enough. Approaching the first sponsor yielded a less grandiose, but financed project with mass production possibilities which we call the "Jump Extender". Never, never discuss the steps involved in FAA certification of a new airplane design to a potential sponsor.

The Jump Extender, as seen in Figure 48, is a small, 12-foot kite mounted to a motorcycle, in this case, a loaned Honda Special Projects 250cc Elsinore. Bob Wills of Sports Kites, Santa Ana, built the special kite and volunteered to be test pilot as part of the package. Bob is an experienced motocross racer, a trick motorcyclist and just happens to be the acknowledged top hang

Figure 48. The Jump Extender Piloted By Bob Wills, Motorcycle Jump Distance World Record Holder.

Figure 49. Test Pilot, Bob Wills at Top With Honda Elsinore. Packaged Kite Weighs 25 Pounds.

glider person in the world. Excellent combination of talents for testing an unknown thing that could be either a killer or a fun toy.

The results of April 28, 1974 testing showed we had a fun toy on our hands. As shown in Figure 49, the 250cc machine achieved 115 feet from a 20-inch high ramp at a speed of 45 mph. Regular cycles only achieved 40 feet from the same range and were launching at speeds of 60 to 70 mph. They definitely hit hard, whereas the bike with jump extender landed softly and never once bottomed out the shocks.

A second day of testing occurred June 1, 1974, with a lowered kite and changed balance point for better flare control. After starting out gradually and going through a series of about 80 ever longer jumps, Bob Wills ended up breaking Knievel's 129-foot record 18 times; Super Joe's 144-foot record 14 times; and Bob Gill's 171-foot record 4 times.

Figure 50. The End or Beginning? Note use of Body English to Steer Vehicle and Keep it Properly Aligned in Crosswinds.

Wills passed the 200-foot mark twice before the sun set on us. See Figure 50 for an idea of how high the bike was getting on the long jumps. All the landings were still super soft! The machine was extremely stable and never got crossed up or fell over once. The ramp was only 26-1/2 inches high! Bob, of course, wanted to get into the motorcycle car jumping business as of the second day of testing.

4. CONCLUSIONS

The following conclusions are obtained from a review of the technological aspects of the jump motorcycle.

(1) Conventional Jump Motorcycles

    (a) Analysis of the complete trajectory, and particularly the takeoff speed and impact dynamics, is necessary for safe operation.

    (b) For the short jumps currently performed, aerodynamics is of secondary importance.

    (c) Efficient shock absorbing systems, i.e., long stroke shock absorbers, energy absorbing seats, etc., are necessary for rider safety.

(2) Super Long Jump Vehicles
Jumps of a mile and more can be safely made with properly designed "motorcycle" vehicles based on well established engineering principles. The real limitations in such projects are financial, not technological.

(3) Jump Extender Motorcycle
By the addition of a delta hang glider-type wing to a motorcycle, a system is obtained which can perform extended jumps, is very docile, and economical, and, with the addition of a propeller, has the potential for sustained low speed cruising flight.

ACKNOWLEDGEMENTS

I wish to thank the Jumpers for both their time and enjoyable conversations; Bruce Williams for his programming efforts; David Ross for his photographic shooting, developing and printing contributions; Beth Lehman for her hours of typing, and lastly, Symposium Chairman, Bernard Pershing for his many valuable suggestions and guidance throughout this project.

REFERENCES

(1) Hoener, Sighard F., "Fluid Dynamic Drag," 148 Busteed Dr., Midland Park, New Jersey, 1965.

(2) Crone, Richard, "Rocketry," Goddard Space Flight Center, Greenbelt, Maryland, 1970.

(3) Any High School or Freshman College Level Physics Text.

MOTORCYCLE STREAMLINER DESIGN
OR
LOW DRAG IS THE EASY PART

Jon S. McKibben
President
McKibben Engineering Company
Irvine, California

Abstract

The Honda Hawk is a streamlined motorcycle which was designed to capture the Land Speed Record in its category. In two years of development on the Bonneville Salt Flats it set the fastest one-way officially timed speed record for motorcycles at 286.7 mph and an AMA class record of 232.7 mph before destroying itself in a spectacular high speed crash. The lessons learned in the design, development and operation of the Hawk are presented. The design considerations which are the foundation of high performance vehicle programs are listed and explained and their priorities are established so that they may serve as a sound basis for future motorcycle streamliner designs. In particular, it is shown that crashworthiness, stability and control, and operational consistency are fundamental preliminary design considerations and must be given priority even at the expense of vehicle performances.

1. INTRODUCTION

Bonneville's seemingly endless expanse of smooth white salt tantalizes racing machine designers like no other competitive arena in the world. Nowhere have more bizarre vehicles lined up alongside head-in-the-sand hardware with greater frequency. At the salt flats, one can go really fast.

In May 1971, the Reaction Dynamics people in Milwaukee, Wisconsin convinced American Honda that now was the time to construct an LSR motorcycle. This writer was contracted with early in the project, to provide engineering assistance where required, and to ride the machine to speeds never before reached by a two-wheeled vehicle. The final product, the Honda Hawk, is shown at speed on the Bonneville Salt Flats in Figure 1.

Great speeds were attained; a measured mile at 286.7 mph, still the fastest one-way officially timed speed ever recorded with a streamlined motorcycle, and an AMA class record of 232.7 mph was set. Yet little in the way of dramatic new technology was produced during those two years of heartbreak and hard work. Rather, a new appreciation was gained for the problems inherent in record-setting on the salt flats.

This then is a discussion of proper design priorities. Design considerations are listed and explained and their priorities established so that they may serve as a sound basis for future motorcycle streamliner designs. These opinions are rooted in experience, seasoned with occasional flashes of tremendous motor vehicle performance, and garnished with survival of one of the most spectacular crashes ever to occur at Bonneville, a 275-mph flight and landing that demolished a magnificent racing machine, but failed to seriously injure the rider.

Figure 1. Honda Hawk at Over 250 mph. Black Roostertail from Course Centerline.

2. PRELIMINARY DESIGN

Upon initiation of a design effort intended to produce a streamlined motorcycle, the designer must define certain gross parameters. In this, the conceptual design phase, decisions must be made regarding:

(1) Basic vehicle configuration.

(2) Drivetrain layout.

(3) Tire/wheel type.

(4) Rider/driver orientation.

(5) Performance envelope.

At this stage, it is unnecessary to define priorities for these gross parameters; it is only necessary to consider all of the parameters in a realistic manner. That is, if the performance envelope is estimated to contain a speed requirement of 0-300 mph, it is mandatory that the overall configuration not be so restrictive that only a low-output power train can be installed. Also, the designer must not restrict himself to a vehicle configuration incapable of carrying tires rated for such speeds.

Assuming that a conceptual design is formulated which embodies the gross parameters listed above, it is now necessary to establish priorities for the multitude of design compromises which lay between concept and functioning vehicle. For example, having decided that the machine is to be a two-wheeled streamliner carrying two 750 cc motorcycle engines, that the rider will be carried in a rearward reclining position near the middle of the machine, that the vehicle will roll on 3.50-19 tires, and will be designed to reach a top speed of at least 300 mph, the real task of designing a practical, usable machine begins.

Before entering into detailed discussions of design priorities, it is important to note that the subject here is a streamlined motorcycle. It is clear from many of the machines built in the past that their designers have applied four-wheel vehicle technology and experience to a two-wheel vehicle. While some of the same logic and design philosophy applies to both, two-wheelers have their own peculiar problems. The point is that streamlined cars and streamlined motorcycles are different kinds of machines. Mechanically, dynamically and aerodynamically, they have distinct differences. A designer ignoring these differences, or unaware of them is doomed to failure. More to the point, the rider of the machine may also be doomed.

3. DESIGN PHILOSOPHY

In establishing priorities for the design elements, both philosophy and technology interact. Consideration of human life is the first major element of philosophy, and dictates that rider safety hold the highest priority in the total design effort. The final run of the Honda Hawk terminated in a severe crash from an initial speed of about 275 mph. That this writer walked away from that crash without injury speaks more strongly than any words regarding the extraordinary safety and crashworthiness of the Hawk's structure. That another streamliner rider was killed in a 60-80 mph crash also speaks strongly, this time regarding the tragic consequences of a design with defects in the critical safety systems.

Often, vehicles are designed in an environment totally free of racing experience; others are designed solely on the basis of racing experience,

without taking advantage of available engineering technology. Both design philosophies have a place in streamliner design. Experience in racing tells a designer that such mundane parameters as mechanical maintenance, reliability and accessibility make the difference between performance potential on paper, and a successful assault on a racing goal, while good technology can highlight areas where greater performance could be attained without loss of other desirable qualities.

One fact becomes obvious in reviewing past streamliner designs. The highest priority has been placed on minimizing aerodynamic drag. Frontal area and form clearly were the dominant elements in the vehicle's design format. Subordinate to these factors were the unexciting parameters of stability, rider environment and mechanical layout. Reviewing the four fastest motorcycles in history, one is struck by the realization that this aerodynamically-based design philosophy is wrong. All four of these machines possess serious defects in their original design, and in every case it appears that these defects were generated by an overwhelming desire to reduce aerodynamic drag regardless of the resultant compromises. When raced, a combination of structural inadequacies, rider control complications, and deficient mechanical components combined to prevent these machines from reaching their speed potential. What really was gained by emphasizing the low-drag shape?

4. TECHNOLOGICAL PRIORITIES

If there is a key word in establishing technological priorities for streamliner design, that word is consistency. Winning designs have been those which offered consistent competitive performance. And, total system consistency demands individual element consistency.

While a streamlined motorcycle may seem a simple machine, the mechanical complexities are imposing. Because of speeds required, one is forced to rely on complex and highly stressed powertrains. Suspension systems, simple in concept, become complicated because of system rigidity requirements. Auxiliary control and safety systems, including parachutes, control linkages, electrical subassemblies, fire extinguishing systems and performance monitoring equipment, add to design integration and to the overall vehicle reliability assurance tasks.

Bulk, weight and simplicity considerations demand that redundancy be minimized. It is neither reasonable nor intelligent to double or triple each system to prevent machine failure due to subsystem manfunction. The designer must produce individual subsystem configurations which are as inherently reliable as possible. Then, to have a chance of making the runs necessary for checkout and record attempts, each system must be designed for easy inspection, maintenance or replacement with minimal labor.

The problems which can occur in competition are amazing. For example, the Honda Hawk incorporated engine speed limiters (ignition interrupt type) to prevent overspeeding when the rider was engaged in keeping the machine on the course during acceleration through the gears. The ignition systems had been extensively tested on a dynamometer during engine development. When hard running began on the salt flats some sick-running engines were pulled from the machine, and it was discovered that all the valves were bent. Obviously, the engines had been run at well over intended speed. The speed limiter system, so reliable during warm dynamometer room testing, proved completely inoperative at the 30-40 °F ambient temperatures encountered at the Bonneville Salt Flats during the month of November.

In this discussion, the term consistency has been used rather than reliability because reliability usually has a connotation of non-failure. Since it is evident from any form of racing that failures are bound to occur, the object then becomes one of maintaining the consistent operation necessary for racing success. Consistency means lack of failure, to be sure, but it also contains an element

of fault diagnosis, repairability and minimization of down-time. The object is to keep running as frequently as possible. When the course is available, and environmental conditions acceptable, the machine must always be ready to race.

Consistency of operation, that is consistent performance of the man-machine system, is also of great importance. A machine cannot deliver consistent performance unless the operator is able to consistently exercise the machine. Rider performance is, to a large extent, dependent on the design of the machine itself. Assuming that the rider has physiological and psychological capabilities equal to the task of running at record speeds, he still must be given a control system, and machine response properties, that best complement his talents. If, for example, gear changing is such an awkward and difficult task that each run is a game of "guess which gear we get this time?", it is unlikely that the rider will be able to concentrate on the primary task of pushing the machine to its limits of speed through the desired course. Similarly, a rider who has trouble seeing and finding the course could hardly be expected to operate the controls of the machine in optimum fashion each and every run.

Each step of machine operation must be considered by the designer, and each made as foolproof as possible. Almost a week of time was lost during initial runs with the Hawk trying to get the machine started and launched. A change from roller starting and drive away to towrope starting at low speeds solved the difficulties. Had these problems been eliminated on the drawing board, a land speed record may well have been set the first year.

Combining overall philosophical and technological themes, priority assessment must be predicated upon safety and consistency. Each design parameter has at least an indirect effect on these qualities. However, some parameters are more important than others and therefore each must be given a ranking consistent with their impact on the safety and consistency of the final design.

5. DESIGN PARAMETER RANKING

Parameter rankings predicated on the foregoing rationale are listed as follows:

I. Crashworthiness
    A. Structural Integrity
    B. Occupant Restraint
    C. Support Systems

II. Stability and Control
    A. Rider Vision
    B. Control Layout and Function
    C. Chassis Rigidity
    D. Steering and Suspension Geometry
    E. Aerodynamic Influences

III. Mechanical Systems Operational Consistency
    A. Drivetrain
    B. Auxiliary Systems

IV. Maximum Performance Potential
    A. Power Available
    B. Power Required

5.1 CRASHWORTHINESS

Structural Crashworthiness refers to the ability of a vehicle to withstand a crash without injuring occupants of that vehicle. More specifically, it relates to the ability of a given structure to protect occupants through resistance to penetration of occupant space and through controlled dissipation of acceleration-producing impact forces. Streamliner designers today are able to draw upon the work conducted by safety research engineer to define the effectiveness of various occupant injury prevention systems, and to define the injury thresholds of humans for optimization of safety systems design.

Unlike the highway vehicle designer, the streamliner designer has a very limited crash environment which he must consider. At Bonneville, the likelihood of a collision with another vehicle, or with a fixed object on the surface is remote. Essentially, the streamliner will only crash into the flat surface of the salt, or onto the course itself. Also, unlike the typical ignorant highway motorist, the streamliner rider will be utilizing restraint systems, he will be seated in a predetermined position and location, and he will, in general, be making optimum use of available safety systems. Further, the configuration of the streamliner will dictate that the rider is closely confined by the interior structure. Thus, the difficult problem of dissipating high relative velocity impacts between occupant and vehicle interior disappears.

At Bonneville, crashworthiness comes down to a rather simply defined goal: prevent distortion and penetration of the rider compartment and keep the rider in a non-injurious posture. Controlled crush of structural elements in front, sides and rear of the machine is of minimal importance due to the improbability of high-speed impacts with fixed objects with attendant concentrated, short-term acceleration peaks. A Bonneville crash invariably is a long-duration event. The machine slides, flies or tumbles for a very long time before dissipating all of its initial velocity. This is different from an automobile crash where a vehicle must, on occasion, dissipate speed of 30 or 40 mph against an immovable object in a period of one-tenth of a second.

The extended time of a Bonneville crash, while eliminating acceleration and energy dissipation problems, creates other important demands. It is mandatory that the rider remain completely confined and protected by his surrounding structure. More than one streamliner rider has been severely injured by escaping, at least partially, from his protective compartment. Total rider confinement and protection must be maintained through an unpredictable variety of motions, and through a series of moderate, multi-directional impacts.

Stated succinctly, crashworthiness requirements dictate that distortion and penetration of the rider compartment be prevented at all times, rider ejection from the compartment, either complete or partial, be avoided, and the velocity of the compartment itself be dissipated in the gentlest, most controlled manner practical.

5.1.1 Occupant Restraint

When the worst occurs at Bonneville, it comes in the form of flight from the course surface. As discovered with the Hawk, two-wheelers do fly and come back to earth with a fierce impact. The rider is best protected by a restraint system which distributes impact forces over as much of his body as possible. Also, it is important that the interior compartment be laid out so as to prevent contact between the restrained rider and projections. Research indicates that a properly restrained human, in reasonable seated position relative to direction of impact forces, can withstand 40g acceleration without serious injury. It is nearly impossible for a Bonneville streamliner to incur a 40g impact with the course surface, regardless of the unplanned excursions above the salt. Recognizing this, the designer should strive to restrain the rider as tightly and solidly as possible within the compartment. The rider should be made to experience, as nearly as possible, the gross acceleration levels of the machine structure. These accelerations will, almost certainly, be within the tolerance envelope. In contrast, a rider who is not locked solidly to the structure may generate accelerations which are vastly higher than those incurred by the structure. These higher accelerations come from impacts between the rider and the machine, rather than between the machine and the salt.

The Hawk employed a nine-point belt-type restraint system. In addition to a lap belt around the pelvis, a double shoulder harness system was used where a pair of shoulder straps went over the rider's shoulders and down to anchors behind the rider's back. An additional pair of belts continued upward from the shoulders and fastened to anchors a few inches above the top plane of the rider's shoulders. To keep the lap belt securely down over the pelvis, and thereby transmit lap belt loads to the strong pelvic bone structure rather than the soft abdominal area, a crotch strap and two under-leg straps were used. These did not carry body restraining loads, but rather prevented the lap belt from riding upward during impacts to the forward portions of the vehicle structure.

The total restraint system fitted to the Hawk was, by design, effective in restraining the rider in a predetermined position through all conceivable combinations of top, side and frontal impacts. During the 275 mph flight and crash of the Hawk, the system performed brilliantly. The addition of arm straps, which loosely connected the rider's arms to the lap belt, prevented violent thrashing of the arms and would have prevented arm ejection through the top hatch had the hatch come open. It did not, but the reduction in arm thrashing and bruising was most welcome to this writer.

As previously mentioned, a rider was killed in a streamlined motorcycle while crashing onto the salt during a run at about 60-80 mph. It appears that the rider entry hatch was lost, the rider slipped out of at least a portion of his shoulder harness system, and his head was crushed between the streamliner shell and the salt surface as the machine rolled. This tragic occurrence could have been prevented through good safety systems design, both in machine crashworthiness and in restraint system design.

5.1.2 Support Systems and Cockpit Controls

Parachutes constitute one of the more important auxiliary safety systems of a Bonneville streamlined motorcycle. They are not used, though, as necessary service brakes. Rather, parachutes control the orientation of the machine relative to its trajectory and, in so doing, are a critical part of the crashworthiness system. A motorcycle streamliner is a long, slender form which in a crash, will roll across the surface of the salt like a pencil down an inclined board. Violent roll motions could cause rider injuries. Internal organs can be injured through accelerations within the rider's torso cavity. Thrashing of extremities, arms and legs, within the compartment could cause serious injuries even if the extremities remain within the compartment. "Football" tumbling almost certainly will accompany violent rolling, at random intervals.

Securely attached parachutes, providing a constant drag on the rear of the machine throughout a crash, will keep the machine aligned on the course. As long as the longitudinal axis of a motorcycle streamliner is aligned with its direction of travel, the likelihood of tumbling is dramatically reduced. The machine will simply slide on one side or the other until it stops, dissipating velocity through harmless friction. Having survived about 14 such crashes, some at speeds well above 200 mph, this writer can attest to the relatively gentle, non-injurious nature of such a crash.

Tight containment of the rider demands that another auxiliary system, fire extinguishing equipment, be designed for complete prevention of fire and excessive heat in the rider compartment. In racing automobiles, Freon-charged automatic extinguishing systems are employed. These may easily be adapted to streamliners, and are very effective when operated by combined automatic and manual controls.

The Honda Hawk utilized a Freon-spray system with primary dispersion nozzles installed in the engine and rider compartments. On the 275 mph crash of the Hawk, the tail-mounted fuel tank was ruptured and the alcohol fuel ignited during the crash landing and skid. Manual actuation of the fire extinguishing system promptly and completely banked the flames, and heat never was a problem. Additional fire and heat protection was afforded by a Diest four-layer Beta glass fire suit worn by the rider of the Hawk on every run.

Control placement and actuation of rider operated auxiliary safety systems is a critical parameter in itself. The designer must always bear in mind that the rider will be occupied full-time, and with intense concentration, by the task of accelerating and steering the vehicle at extraordinary speeds. Improperly placed controls for parachutes or fire extinguishing systems can cause a crash, rather than prevent one. Any design scheme which minimizes the concentration required to perform secondary control functions will enhance the success of the machine, both in competitive speed and in overall safety and consistency.

Up to the limit of cluttering the primary control zone, all auxiliary system controls should be placed so that rider actuation may be accomplished

with minimal motion of extremities, and without taking eyes far from the normal riding vision zone. In the Hawk, the fire extinguishing control was a large red pushbutton, positioned just above and to the right of the right handlebar grip. This location permitted easy identification of the control, and simple activation without perturbing the steer attitude of the vehicle.

Parachute controls on the Hawk were similarly well thought out. The high-speed parachute, first to be deployed in the event of high-speed control difficulties, was actuated by the right-hand lever normally used for front wheel braking on a road motorcycle. Thus, the parachute could be deployed without taking the right hand off the handlebar, and without losing steering control of the machine.

It is assumed, of course, that the rider will take advantage of the best available personal safety items. A top-grade, full coverage helmet, fire-proof gloves and boot covers, and the best available fire suit are mandatory. The capabilities and limitations of such personal equipment should be recognized by the designer so that the vehicle will best complement the equipment used.

In summary, then, a streamliner must be designed first and foremost for rider safety. Injury prevention may best be accomplished by designing the machine's structure for complete integrity, through the most severe crash imaginable at Bonneville, and for firm containment of the rider in a non-injurious posture. Ejection of any part of the rider's body must be prevented through the range of rolls and tumbles that accompany a Bonneville crash at high speed. Auxiliary safety systems, including parachutes and fire extinguishing equipment, must be readily actuated by the rider without undue attention to the task, and must be reliable and effective in controlling machine attitude, trajectory and fire.

5.2   STABILITY AND CONTROL

No topic in motor racing is subject to more diverse opinion and folklore than is streamliner stability and control. It would be presumptuous to state that this writer has all of the answers to this complex question. However, after riding a motorcycle streamliner to speeds well above those attained by any other person in history, and having a strong education and professional background in vehicle dynamics, it seems appropriate to present certain views and opinions which, if not totally comprehensive of the subject, may at least reduce the false starts made by a future designer of such vehicles.

5.2.1 The Auto-Aerodynamic System

A streamlined motorcycle is not an aircraft. Nor, in the limited sense, is it a road motorcycle. The streamliner, due to its configuration and operating envelope lies somewhere between these vehicle categories. Yet previous designers often have attempted to define the stability and control parameters of motorcycle streamliners either in purely aerodynamic or purely chassis dynamics contexts. Such an approach is an invitation to disaster. It reflects a void in the overall technical competence of the designer. A streamliner is a ground vehicle, one which rolls on, and is guided and propelled by, pneumatic tires. But, at maximum speeds, the streamliner is heavily affected by aerodynamic loadings and is perhaps dominated in its response characteristics by the aerodynamic forces acting on the machine's exterior. Recognizing this complex interaction is the first step in analyzing the stability and control properties of a streamliner and in attempting to design a machine which will have optimum characteristics.

5.2.2 Rider Vision

There is one element of major importance that has, in the past, been too frequently left out of the machine design phase. That element is the rider. The rider is at the controls and must see where he is going and what is happening to the vehicle. For example, roll attitude is judged by the tilt of the horizon; without a sufficient lateral view of the course, the rider may progressively lean onto the side of the shell without ever being aware of his impending doom. The writer had the

misfortune of attempting to ride a machine which was designed in a nearly sterile atmosphere of aerodynamic purity. The Hawk, in its orignal form, had a shape which looked like an exercise in ultimate drag reduction. The slippery form was achieved at the cost of almost total lack of rider visibility. The prospect of steering a machine at nearly 300 mph down a course that can't even be seen was cause for many sleepless nights.

Where reduction of frontal area and optimization of overall form conflict with rider visibility, the latter must be given priority. Far too many crashes have occurred at Bonneville due to lack of sufficient rider vision, and consequently, lack of rider information feedback. Any aerodynamicist worth his salt can develop a reasonable low drag form around a machine which affords the rider clear vision, sufficient room to operate controls in an efficient manner, and has adequate structure for rigidity and safety.

5.2.3 Chassis Rigidity

The designer must next consider the problems of vehicle stability and response. Immediately he becomes aware of the need for absolute structural rigidity to maintain whatever geometric relationships are designed into the structure and suspension system of the machine. The machine's exterior must also be designed with sufficient rigidity to maintain form under high aerodynamic loading.

Forces exerted on suspension components in a streamliner are enormous. Bonneville's salt surface is anything but smooth, varying year to year, from rough to terrible. At speeds of 300 mph, tires inflated to 150 psi transmit severe shocks to suspension and chassis members. Also, gyroscopic forces generated by heavy tire/wheel assemblies reach high levels, and while these gyroscopic forces tend to give the machine its inherent stability, they can, given perturbations from their design vertical and/or lateral orientation, induce strong destabilizing couples which may propagate into a dreaded speed wobble. Once the bug gyroscopes are bounced into an oscillation, aided by the undamped springy support from flexible suspension system or chassis members, an uncontrollable wobbling of the entire machine can develop with alarming rapidity.

Streamliner chassis rigidity must be very high in bending and in torsion. Too often a streamliner is designed with insufficient attention paid to keeping front and rear wheels aligned on the same vertical axis. When subjected to torsional stresses between the axle locations, the frame twists and instability occurs. At maximum speeds, this instability may grow to the point where the rider no longer is able to hold or control the steering.

A note of caution is appropriate here, and that concerns the apparent fervor of some streamliner designers to minimize the total weight of the machine. Certainly a streamliner can accelerate more rapidly if it is light in weight. However, with about five miles in which to attain maximum speed, and in view of the power available in modern motorcycle engines, it is illogical and tragically foolish to attempt to reduce vehicle weight at the expense of chassis integrity. The Hawk weighed approximately 1700 lb. This is, by about a factor of two, the heaviest motorcycle ever run in speed record competition. Yet, the Hawk was able to accelerate to almost 300 mph in a four-mile distance. Even higher speeds could have been attained through rather simple and moderate engine tuning and optimization of gear ratios.

A breakdown of weights for the Hawk shows that the powertrain weighed about 600 lb, the outer removable body shell components, accessories, wheels and suspension components, and controls added approximately another 900 lb, and the major chassis structure contributed roughly 200-250 lb. How much weight could have been saved by trimming the double-wall monocoque structure to marginal stiffness and rigidity? Surely the savings would have been insignificant to the speed potential of the machine. And, where in doubt, the most positive method of ensuring structural integrity is to make the part thicker, larger and stronger.

5.2.4 Suspension and Steering Geometry

Suspension Geometry. When the subject of suspension and steering geometry is broached, here is where the opinions begin to flow. Probably any of the various systems tried in the past could be made to work in a streamliner, given sufficient geometric analysis and proper structural design. However, of the types of front suspensions seen on streamliners which have attained relatively high speeds, the center-pivot hub system seems to have overwhelming advantages. First, this type of steering allows the construction of a link-type, very rigid front suspension. Suspension at the front of the streamlined motorcycle can be essentially identical to that used on the rear end of both streamliners and modern road machines. That is, a pair of suspension arms leading from a pivot tube backward or forward along each side of the tire/wheel assembly, and connected to an axle shaft passing through the center of the wheel.

There are geometric deficiencies in such a system. It is true that, given practical lengths for the suspension links, the wheelbase of the machine will change slightly as the wheels move up and down in jounce and rebound. Also, it is somewhat difficult to construct the link arms with high rigidity. However, the rear suspension system installed on the 1972 edition of the Honda Hawk, designed and built by Dix Erickson of American Honda, is an outstanding example of the rigidity which is possible with a link-type, or swinging arm, suspension. The Hawk's rear suspension, shown in Figures 2 and 3, incorporates a very large diameter cross tube above the actual arm pivot tube. This large crosstube adds immensely to the rigidity of the swinging arm assembly, both in total bending, and in preventing individual arms on either side of the wheel from moving relative to each other and thereby letting the wheel tilt from the machine's vertical axis.

The swinging arm system, used front and rear, permits employment of conventional coil springs and shock absorbers. Since a motorcycle stream-

Figure 2. Right Side View of Hawk Rear Swing Arm Suspension Unit.

Figure 3. Rear View of Hawk Rear Swing Arm Suspension Unit.

liner weighs in the range of modern racing cars, springs, dampers and technology are available to give the streamliner designer whatever he desires in the way of suspension rates.

Damping System. Motorcycle suspension geometry (not steering geometry) is simplicity itself. One should attempt to minimize wheelbase change, and keep the wheels vertically, laterally, and longitudinally aligned throughout the range of predicted dynamic motion and forces. Jounce and rebound may be limited to approximately two inches in either direction, controlled by springs and dampers matched to the weight of the machine. Damping is somewhat more complicated, and will not be thoroughly discussed here except to note that the surface of the Bonneville Salt Flats is random in roughness. That is, one does not find the kind of periodic "washboard" disturbances which exist on many dirt or even paved surfaces. Thus, the suspension system may be tuned for a "white noise" input, rather than trying to prevent resonance by a disturbance of known frequency content.

The bumps in the salt surface tend to be very frequent. These small magnitude, high frequency disturbances may tend to "pump down" a damper which is too heavily biased toward rebound damping. The damper will be compressed in jounce by a small bump. Then, before the damper can extend back to original length, it may be bumped again in jounce and compressed further. Carried to sufficient extremes, this pumping action can

cause the damper to bottom, lending the machine an essentially rigid suspension. This is obviously undesirable, and dictates that shock absorbers be capable of accepting myriad small bumps occurring at very high frequencies, yielding to these bumps rather softly yet extending after each bump to keep the suspension system near the design height throughout the run.

During the Hawk project, it was found that suppliers of high quality racing shock absorbers are quite willing to discuss our application problems. If the streamliner designer is able to intelligently outline his particular application and problems, the shock absorber suppliers can provide valuable information as to unit selection and/or modification of available units. Space prohibits a more scholarly dissertation on spring and shock absorber selection, but it is believed that this is one of the more easily solved problems facing the streamliner designer.

Steering Geometry. The choice of steering geometry is extremely critical. If the designer chooses a center-pivot hub system, the system probably will be constructed so as to be completely adjustable for rake, or caster setting. Typically, rake and trail will be mutually dependent. That is, altering the rake angle (or caster angle) will simultaneously alter the trail setting. Figure 3 illustrates the geometric relationships for a common center-pivot-hub steering system. While the center-pivot systems used in other streamliners had incorporated the wheel steering axis into the geometric centerline of the wheel, a conventional motorcycle invariably includes some forward offset of the wheel axle centerline from the steering post axis. In a conventional motorcycle, the forks are set forward of the steering head assembly, and the handlebars (or steering bars) are typically at or behind the steering head axis.

The center-pivot hub designed for the Hawk by Dix Erickson of American Honda is certainly the strongest and most precisely controlled design ever used on a streamliner. It was designed with the steering axis, or kingpin centerline set rearward of the geometric center of the wheel hub and steering arm. The effect was to give a geometric offset relatively close to that of a conventional motorcycle. An additional kingpin gore was machined at the hub and steering arm geometric centerline in case the offset system proved troublesome for the rider. The Hawk's center-pivot steering system with forward-offset kingpin axis proved superbly controllable at low and high speeds alike. Of course, a number of runs were necessary to establish the best combination of rake and trail settings for decent low-speed controllability along with high-speed stability.

It was discovered during early runs that rake, or caster, settings of less than 35 degrees would generally result in a speed wobble, or weave, in the 200-260 mph range. While such settings were confortable for low-speed operation and permitted large steering inputs to correct potential low-speed fallovers, the subsequent high-speed weaves were totally unacceptable and produced more than one loss of course direction at speeds well over 200 mph.

William Otto, a physicist who recently has done some basic research and computations regarding motorcycle stability and geometry optimization, ran some simplified hand calculations on the Hawk to attempt to locate an apparent optimum setting for rake and trail for high-speed stability. Bill's calculations, outlined in Appendix A, showed "knees" in the stability curves at about 50 degrees

of caster. This tremendously large caster angle prompted grave doubts in the minds of the Hawk crew and rider as to low-speed controllability. As a result, early runs during the 1972 phase of the Hawk record attempts were conducted with caster set at a more conservative 35 degrees.

Violent weaving during shutdown from about 270 mph on the first full-throttle 1972 run prompted resetting of the front wheel caster angle to 53 degrees. Subsequent running was limited to just one high-speed pass. However, low-speed handling during that run was excellent, dispelling doubts as to the controllability of a streamliner with extreme caster angles at speeds below 150 mph.

It is of interest to note that other streamliner racers have generally set caster in the 30-35 degree range. Such settings have proven acceptable for their low-speed runs. However, rider comments lead to the belief that, in the very few instances when speeds of more than 250 mph had been reached, the high-speed stability of these machines was less than solid. It has been noted by these riders that on some runs the machines had a tendency to shake and possibly weave in response to minor perturbations of the wheels due to uneven salt surface or slight wind gusts. Very likely, increasing the caster angle settings would improve high-speed stability without damaging low-speed controllability to an unacceptable degree.

Much more can be written on steering geometry but it is probably sufficient to note here that much of the foregoing has been devoted to a review of what has been done, and what seems to work. But, and this is a big but, it is absolutely not sufficient, or remotely intelligent, to start out with a new machine design and rely on steering geometry parameters arrived at on a different machine, possibly operating in different speed ranges. With today's analytical tools and stability models, it would be foolish not to use these technical aids in establishing the basic alignment and geometry characteristics of a new streamliner.

Considering the high cost of producing a serious land speed record machine, even on minimal operating budgets, another few thousand dollars for stability analysis and consultation with experienced and competent technical advisors is a trivial expense. Yet, in terms of dramatically enhancing the probability of success, this investment easily could be the most important of the whole venture.

5.3 MECHANICAL SYSTEMS OPERATIONAL CONSISTENCY

Amazingly, a high percentage of record-pretenders have apparently ignored vital portions of the mechanical systems design phase of their projects. Predictable phenomena such as engines blown through overstress and overtuning have been relatively infrequent. Instead, components like transmissions, final drive chains and coupling belts, wheel bearings, suspension members and control elements have littered the course (truly) at Bonneville.

Yet the analysis of a Bonneville streamliner is relatively simple. Unlike the brutal launches of a drag race, starts at Bonneville can be relatively gentle, and clutches and gearboxes can be nursed through the gears with care without costing too much in terms of ultimate speed. However, there is the length of the run, and the very long time under full power. And here is where a machine's mechanical Achilles heel shows up.

Of primary concern is the heat of highly loaded systems operating within a confined, poorly-ventilated environment. Motorcycle streamliners have competed at Bonneville with cooling vents that wouldn't be acceptable for exhausting a pot-belly stove. Ducts are installed which cause tremendous drag, and then funnel air into the top of an engine compartment where it blows over the top of the engine, misses the clutch and transmission completely, and then blows out the tail of the shell barely warmer than when it entered.

The design of final drive chains capable of transmitting the tremendous power of current engines has long been the most difficult mechanical design problem facing the designer. Past designs have featured final drive chains of various types and sizes, all running as on a typical road machine, without the benefit of any type of continuous lubrication. Practice has been to lube the chain before a run, and check it afterward.

The Hawk used the relatively recent HyVo chain system from Morse Chain Division of Borg Warner. The HyVo chain was lubricated with some incredibly expensive molybdenum paste applied before each run, with a paint brush. During the first year's runs, on rough salt with no rear suspension, the final drive chain failed with distressing regularity. Part of the problem was the Hawk crew's unfamiliarity with proper tension or slack setting; part of the problem was caused by the very rough course imparting a series of hammer-like shock loads to the chain under full power. Installing Dix Erickson's rear suspension system, with much-improved chain geometry and center distance control, resulted in the abbreviated second-year running being completed with no problems whatsoever from the chain or sprockets.

With the increasing number of shaft-drive motorcycles for road use, it may be that shaft-drive streamliners will become more popular. However, it must be remembered that gear ratios for Bonneville machines are far different from those of road motorcycles. In the Hawk, for example, first gear would carry to approximately 125 mph, and the shift from fourth to fifth was made at more than 250 mph. Considering that the rear tire on the Hawk was a rather ordinary 19-inch motorcycle size, it is obvious that gear ratios were extraordinarily tall (numerically low).

Perhaps mechanical systems consistency is the wrong term to use in conjunction with ignition units. But this is another area where the streamliner designer must be constantly alert for potential malfunctions. A perfectly good run was lost during the second year's operation of the Hawk due to insertion of a low-value fuse in the ignition circuit. Earlier massive ignition failures were the result of mounting high-radiating ignition unit boxes too close together producing interference.

As a summary, mechanical systems on a Bonne-ville streamliner must be designed as simply as possible. Components should be carefully analyzed for steady-state operational loads, then redesigned to accommodate the surface roughness, repeated shock loads, and occasional spills that are sure to occur. Finally, all systems should be easy to maintain and check, and should be so designed as to be able to withstand sustained maximum-performance operation for a period of at least 20 miles without requiring rebuilt or major adjustment. Remember, to set an inter-national speed record at Bonneville it is neces-sary to complete the second pass through the speed clocks within an hour of the first. No real changes, or significant repairs, are possible within that time period. As to final drive com-ponents, rules specifically prohibit alteration of final drive units between runs, an obvious pre-caution against some enterprising racer using upwind and downwind gear ratios during the same record attempt.

5.4 MAXIMUM PERFORMANCE POTENTIAL

Only after having designed a safe, controllable, reliable and consistently operating machine can the designer direct his full attention to the matter of producing speed. Here the aerodynamicist, the hot-dog engine builder and the true racers can finally exercise their creativity and talents. But, and this is the most important "but" in the entire design exercise, all of the aforementioned ele-ments must be given priority.

Nearly anyone can design a machine that can travel very fast, at least on paper. The require-ments reduce to the following parameters:

    (1)   Power Available
    (2)   Power Required

The game is to provide more available power than is required to attain the desired speeds.

5.4.1 Power Available

Power available refers to that power produced by the engine system which is fed into the rear tire

to work against the salt. Only power made avail-able for driving the machine is of consequence to the designer. Power consumed by the transmis-sion and final drive system, and power which cannot be converted into driving thrust are of no value in the speed equation.

Powerplant. Viewing today's dazzling array of available high-performance motorcycle engines, it is obvious that there is no problem making at least 250, and possibly as much as 400, basic engine horsepower. Current road racing engines from Yamaha, Suzuki and Kawasaki all seem to be capable of generating 125-140 bhp from 750cc displacement. Coupling two of these into a streamliner would provide enough power to reach speeds of up to 300 mph, assuming a creditable job of designing the remainder of the machine. The pair of 750cc Honda engines used in the Hawk were capable of a relatively easy 300 bhp total, and proved to be more than adequate for 300-plus mph speeds when functioning at optimum levels.

Predicated upon streamliner experience of recent years, it appears most practical to employ engines of reasonably mild tune, at least initially, and then to increase engine output and corresponding stress levels until the record is achieved, or until engine failures consistently occur. The Hawk is a per-fect example of this approach in that the engines utilized turbocharger boost to produce horsepower from essentially stock road machine hardware. Running at low boost levels, the Hawk engines were as reliable as freight trains. Raising boost level (a very simple operation involving adjustment of the waste gate relief pressure) raised power out-put to whatever level desired and/or tolerable by the engine components.

Highly stressed normally aspirated engines running on exotic fuels, whether two-stroke or four-cycle engines, tend to be very sensitive to atmospheric conditions, inherently overheat to a catastrophic level if slightly off-tune, and at high engine speeds, tend to overheat and disintegrate under Bonne-ville's long-duration maximum output running. Thus, such engines should be avoided by the streamliner designer unless he has such vast experience and tuning talents that he, like Don Vesco, is able to consistently extract high power with minimal problems.

Generally, engine weight and overall bulk are relatively unimportant for streamliners assuming that gains in durability are realized through using a larger and/or heavier engine. Usually, the rider of a Bonneville machine will define the overall streamliner shell bulk and, to a major extent, the minimum possible frontal area. The engines, given reasonably clever air and engine plumbing, typically can be fitted inside the rider's frontal profile without significantly expanding the machine cross-sectional area.

International rules permit the use of a maximum of two motorcycle engines, with maximum total displacement of 3000cc. With the exception of Harley-Davidson, no current motorcycle manufacturer makes engines that likely would be expandable to come near the maximum displacement value. As a result, it is very probable that history has seen the last of the Bonneville Land Speed Record motorcycles in the highest speed class using a single engine.

Drivetrain. Recognizing that future machines almost certainly will use two engines, each with 750cc or more displacement, the designer should choose his powerplants with an eye toward coupling these in a reasonably efficient manner. Several mechanical systems have been employed, including roller chains, HyVo chains, and toothed timing belts. Drivelines have incorporated a single transmission for the pair of engines, and the Hawk used two complete engine/transmission units coupled at the output shafts.

An untouched area offering great potential for streamliner advancement is the use of a simplified automatic transmission with torque converter. Preliminary design work indicates that such a system could materially reduce rider difficulties, and could substantially improve control of the machine through smoothness of power delivery and expansion of initially available low-speed

driving torque. Given good, strong, flexible engines, an LSR motorcycle might be able to make do with only two forward speeds plus an efficient, high-stall speed torque converter tailored to the engine unit's torque curve. Three speeds forward are probably the absolute maximum that would be required even for the highest speed machines. The torque converter could serve as a shock isolator for the driveline, and might be of assistance in preventing some of the driveline destruction that has been seen in past designs.

Mechanical efficiency is the guideline for coupling and final drive units. Data from Morse chain on the HyVo units used on the Hawk indicate mechanical efficiencies as high as 98-99% for properly lubricated HyVo chains. What the actual efficiency of the coupling and final drive chains was at Bonneville, given the between-run hand lubrication job, is a good question but it did appear that the HyVo units consumed very little power. Other forms of automotive drive units have been shown to be as little as 88-90% efficient, resulting in a potential loss of more than 25 bhp in the ranges under consideration for an open-class LSR machine. Such losses must be considered by the designer as they make the difference between a record and a near miss.

Rear Wheel Assembly. Hawk experience indicates that LSR motorcycles may have reached the limit of tire performance for available high-speed units. Only Dunlop is apparently still in the supply business for LSR motorcycle tires, Goodyear having allegedly scrapped the molds for their long-successful 3.59-19 units which were fitted to the last few contenders at Bonneville.

With increasing power and performance, the motorcycle streamliner designer may have to look toward the LSR automobile suppliers for usable tires. More traction will be required, while maintaining the degree of banking and turn control peculiar to a two-wheeled vehicle. More traction probably means a broader contact patch between tire and salt, yet designers will continue to attempt to design machines with minimal frontal area and minimum possible overall height. The obvious solution is a tire of very low profile with a broad, flat contact surface. How such tires will work on a banking two-wheeler is, at this point, generally unknown. Previous LSR motorcycle tires employed basically round sections, which give a nearly constant camber thrust pattern as the tire is banked. Broader tires of lower profile will tend to produce different bank versus contact point center relationships, as the tire is leaned over onto a rather sharp shoulder which is far displaced from the geometric vertical centerline of the tire.

Available power for driving the machine is limited to the power which can be efficiently transmitted to the salt by the tire. It is believed that the Hawk crashed during a 275-mph run because the rear tire broke loose on relatively wet, slippery salt. The full 300 bhp potential of the Hawk was too much for the narrow 3.50-19 tire to apply against the salt without wheelspin. With wheelspin comes a loss in tire directional stability and tracking, and an attendant loss in total machine directional control. Thus, rear tire traction is critical not only for maximum speed, but for maximum security during an extremely high speed race.

5.4.2 Power Required

Power required is composed of several factors. The most obvious is the power necessary to push the streamliner bulk down the course and through the air. Rolling resistance and aerodynamic loads are the keys here. Added to these elements is the power required to overcome mechanical losses between the engines and the salt surface. These losses have been discussed in the previous section.

Rolling resistance has been shown to be roughly proportional to the mass of a given machine, and is heavily dependent upon the type of tires used. Thus, wider contact patch automobile tires may be a mixed blessing to a streamliner motorcycle, in that the increase in tractive potential may, in part, be consumed in overcoming increased rolling resistance. Similarly using large and heavy

engines will increase the power consumed in overcoming rolling resistance. As an example, the 1700-lb Honda Hawk undoubtedly offered far more rolling resistance at 280-mph than Don Vesco's 800-lb Yamaha machine. The Hawk engines admittedly were more powerful by a substantial margin but a great deal of that power advantage was required just to overcome rolling resistance and to accelerate the greater mass.

Someone once described Bonneville record running as the "World's Longest Drag Race." This is certainly an apt description of the engineering problems at Bonneville, since it is necessary not only to be capable of very high top speeds, but to be able to closely approach these speeds within the limited course length. Depending upon the year, anything from 3.5 to 6 miles might be available for acceleration into the top speed traps. Seldom would more than 4 miles be available at more than one end of the course, so that top average speed through the timing trap will be predicated mainly upon the maximum speed which can be attained on the shortest approach course. The designer must always consider the speed that is reasonably attainable in, say, 4 miles of acceleration. How much power is required to initially accelerate the machine's bulk, how much to continuously overcome the total rolling resistance of tires and chassis, and how much is demanded by the aerodynamic drag on the machine which tends to become important during the over-200 mph portion of a given run?

Appendix B displays an analytically-derived performance profile of the original Honda Hawk concept. Note the word concept, since the final machine had several significant variables that make this performance analysis somewhat fictitious. Surprisingly, several of the major variances between concept and final machine cancelled each other in terms of performance, and the plot shown in Appendix B is not unreasonable in terms of machine capabilities as actually raced.

Aerodynamic drag initially estimated for the Hawk was predicated upon an almost perfectly clean,

Figure 4. Hawk Rider Jon McKibben Checks Out Interior Compartment. Note Side Cooling Air Vents, Top Turbocharger Air Intake, Compactness of Rider Compartment With Adequate Head Clearance.

bullet-nosed shape with tail fin. External shell surface openings were limited to those through which the front and rear wheels extended, a small NACA duct above the engine compartment for turbocharger air intake, and a pair of large NACA ducts on each side of the machine for cooling air intake. The flat-sided tail section was left open at the rear to provide escape for cooling air and random air let in through wheel openings. Some of these details are clearly shown in Figure 4. Rider ventilation depended upon air entering around the front wheel and this proved to be adequate for running even at maximum Bonneville temperatures approaching 100 °F.

During development runs it was found that the Hawk's bullet nose required extensive modification to allow even minimal rider visibility. The measured 286.7 mph run was made with the compound curved plexiglass nose bubble chopped through and a thick plate of flat plexiglass glued and taped into the upper surface, extending to the side of the bubble so as to form a blockish protuberance jutting up from the curved side and top surfaces of the bubble. Although it afforded minimal visibility area, the plate was free from the psychodelic distortion patterns of the original bubble which produced a full-circle 360-degree horizon line when viewed from the rider compartment. How much the "bandaged" nose cost the Hawk in increased drag is unknown. Yet, the machine attained tremendous speeds with this configuration, so the drag may not have been as drastic as might superficially appear. It is inferred from this experience that the nose shape of a motorcycle streamliner is a trivial design consideration when weighed against other parameters such as frontal area and rider vision.

Reid Railton, brilliant designer of Bonneville LSR machines, stated years ago that the proper approach to streamliner design is to wrap the mechanical components as tightly as possible within a shell of absolute minimal frontal area, then round the corners and the nose and tail as much as practical. The result will have less drag, and be more free from aerodynamic problems, than a dramatically clean form which is much larger and smoother.

The Hawk is an example of the "clean form" school of aerodynamic design. Frontal area was substantially greater than absolutely necessary, but the purity of the compound-curved nose proved impractical due to restrictions it imposed on rider vision.

Perhaps the best example of the "minimum frontal area" school of motorcycle streamliner design is Don Vesco's Yamaha machine. Don's scooter is incredibly small in cross-section, and is forced to use bubbles for tire clearance and a protruding canopy and headrest fairing for rider clearance. Don's machine is so low that he has no direct forward vision over the front tire bubble fairing, a condition that Don would be the first to admit is very undesirable. Without his vast experience in

running at Bonneville, Don might well be unable to control his machine because of this vision handicap, and no newcomer to the salt should even consider attempting to operate a similarly-comprised machine.

From experience with the Hawk, and from viewing the performance of Don Vesco's machine (which is mechanically far below the performance capability of the Hawk), this writer tends to strongly favor the minimum frontal area design approach. The use of a canopy is the only reasonable way to give adequate forward and peripheral rider vision. The nose window approach, used on Cal Rayborn's Harley Davidson and on the Hawk, is impractical and never, to this writer's knowledge, has been successfully employed. Both Rayborn and this writer suffered the traumatic experience of travelling at super speeds with vision to the outside world nearly cut off. This is dangerous and foolish and must be avoided in future streamliner packaging concepts. A cleverly-designed canopy can produce a machine with far greater rider accommodation, better vision, and less total drag than a necessarily larger bullet form.

Aerodynamic cleanliness of future machines will be facilitated by the abundance of liquid-cooled high-performance motorcycle engines now available. Preliminary calculations indicate that adequate cooling can be provided for Bonneville competition without any need for air ducted into the motorcycle. Evaporation can be employed to handle thermal overload of a simple tank system. Vesco has already shown that such an approach is practical, though his particular installation could be improved through employment of a properly coolant heat exchanger/evaporator.

In considering high speed directional stability, classical aerodynamic theory demands that the center of pressure be located behind the neutral steer line (basically the center of gravity of a ground vehicle). To do this, it is often necessary to add side area in the form of a tail fin to a streamlined motorcycle. The Hawk had a tremendous tail fin extending far above the already tall body shell. Side winds, even the 2-4 mph variety considered tolerable for Bonneville running, rolled the machine away from the direction of the wind. Rolling a motorcycle causes it to turn in the direction of lean. The net effect on the Hawk was to amplify the effect of any slight side wind to the point where extreme steering input forces and displacements were required. Typically, the machine would travel thousands of feet down the course in a straight line while heeled over like a sailboat in a gale.

It is the opinion of this writer that the unique requirements of motorcycle dynamics necessitate a streamliner shape of minimum side area, well rounded contours and minimum possible height. If an aerodynamicist presents a convincing argument for rearward displacement of the center of pressure, this is best accomplished through addition of an extension to the tail of the machine, running straight back from the general side contours and tapering down, not up, as it goes back.

What, then, is the job of the streamliner aerodynamicist? Primarily, the task is to create a clean form which has minimum frontal area, provides excellent rider visibility of the course, permits incorporation of ultrastrong structure around and over the rider compartment, and to ensure that the resulting form is free from undesirable stability influences which might corrupt the handling of a basically sound chassis. Viewing the data in Appendix B, it is clear that aerodynamic drag is an important consideration in attaining record speeds, both because of power requirements from the drivetrain, and because of the limited tire propulsion forces on the salt surface of Bonneville at high speeds.

6. SUMMARY

The whole topic of streamliner design can be summarized by considering the need to make the machine (1) as safe as possible, (2) as stable and controllable as possible, (3) as reliable and consistent as possible, and finally, (4) as fast as possible. Taken in that order, the overall design requirements can be met through logical, realistic engineering to ensure that from the very outset of the project the final machine will have a very good chance of performing well.

Will a new streamliner so conceived break speed records? Probably, and surely the design will reach its maximum performance levels with minimal hazard to its rider, and with the least practical trouble to its crew. Since there are no guarantees at Bonneville as to salt conditions which will allow the machine to run fast and smooth, there are no guarantees that any machine, no matter how well engineered, will ever display its maximum potential. But an intelligent, well executed design which is safe and has mechanical integrity will go far toward equalizing problems with Mother Nature. When the salt is ready, a well-designed machine will also be ready. And, given a stable platform, with good vision, and safe surroundings, the streamliner rider will have full opportunity to show his talent and courage. Hopefully, the basic machine will handle so well as to make the rider's job of secondary importance to the project's ultimate success. Even more important, should problems occur and the machine be crashed onto the salt's unforgiving surface, a good machine will give that rider a chance to return and try again to defeat the ghosts of speed that lurk deep in Bonneville's salt cellars.

APPENDIX A

PRELIMINARY STABILITY ANALYSIS OF THE HONDA HAWK PERFORMED BY WILLIAM OTTO

A-1. INTRODUCTION

This appendix contains a sample of some of the mathematical model input parameters and stability optimization computations performed on the Honda Hawk after initial completion. Subsequent to this preliminary analysis, Mr. Otto's model was improved, expanded, and automated for computer simulation. The model concept and use of optimization curves (as opposed to quantitative stability parameters or force magnitudes) has been found useful and is considered a proper approach to motorcycle streamliner preliminary design analysis and parametric definition of system elements.

A-2. ANALYTIC MODEL

A set of linearized equations was derived which describes the dynamic behavior of a two-wheeled vehicle. The present analytic model is more complete than most models which have appeared in the published literature, and can be reduced to the same or equivalent forms by elimination of appropriate variables. The model has been checked and found to be reasonably accurate in its description of vehicle response under various conditions. Additionally, correlations with published test results and with the results of some rudimentary tests performed by the author have shown the predictions to be well within experimental accuracy. It should be noted that since this is a nonlinear problem, there may be some additional effects which are obscured in the process of linearization.

A-3. NUMERICAL RESULTS

The parameters which describe the Hawk are shown in Figure A-1 and listed in Table A-I. Numerical results were obtained for three rake angles, 30, 45, and 60 degrees. The Routh-Hurwitz stability criteria were used to determine the stability boundaries. Only two functions showed any appreciable variation, or tendency to become negative. They are plotted in Figure A-2 and are labelled Δ_2' and Δ_1.

It is difficult to assign a physical meaning to any of the Routh-Hurwitz criteria, since they do not represent actual solutions of the differential equations. Rather, they are the necessary and sufficient conditions that the exponentials which are the actual solutions have real negative parts.

Table A-I
Basic Input Parameters for Stability Analysis of the Honda Hawk.

Item	Symbol	Values
Wheelbase	l	160.0 in.
Front Wheel - C.G. Distance	l_2	102.25 in.
Rear Wheel - C.G. Distance	a_2	57.75 in.
Front Tire Rolling Radius	b_f	13.0, 12.4, 11.0 in.
Rear Tire Rolling Radius	b_r	13.0, 12.4, 11.0 in.
C.G. Height Above Ground	h_1	13.0 in.
Aerodynamic Center Height Above Ground	h_2	11.5 in.
Steering Neck Offset	l_1	0.0, 1.5 in.
Front Wheel Trail	a_1	6.50, 9.19, 11.25 in.
Full Suspension Travel	l_3	2.50 in.
Rake Angle	α	30, 45, 60 deg
Total Vehicle Weight	W	1677 lb
Front Tire Normal Force	W_f	605 lb
Rear Tire Normal Force	W_r	1072 lb
Sprung Mass	m_2	4.22 lb-sec^2/in.
Front Wheel Mass	m_1	0.12 lb-sec^2/in.
Inertias of Sprung Mass	I_{x_2}	25,345 lb-in.^{2}-sec^2/ft
	I_{y_2}	262,565 lb-in.^{2}-sec^2/ft
	I_{x_2}	252,565 lb-in.^{2}-sec^2/ft
Inertia of Front Wheel	I'_{y_1}	97.0 lb-in.^{2}-sec^2/ft
Inertia of Rear Wheel	I'_{y_2}	97.0 lb-in.^{2}-sec^2/ft

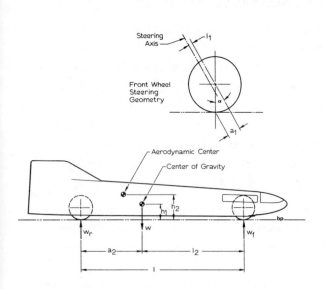

Figure A-1. Honda Hawk Physical Parameters.

This means that any oscillation resulting from a disturbance will die out. In order to obtain the physical behavior of the system, it is necessary to obtain an actual solution. Nevertheless, we can determine well enough the physical meaning of negative values of the two criteria of interest here.

The first of these, Δ_2', is a function of vehicle velocity. Curves of Δ_2' for two steering neck offsets are shown in Figure A-2a as a function of rake angle. As Δ_2' becomes larger, the Routh-Hurwitz criterion becomes positive at a lower velocity, and the vehicle will be stable at a lower velocity. At a 45-degree rake angle with no steering neck offset, the speed at which the criterion becomes positive is 8 ft/sec or approximately 5.5 mph. This does not mean that the vehicle will necessarily feel stable. On the contrary, any disturbance will cause the vehicle to go into wide sweeping turns in order to maintain an erect position and will appear to be out of control to the rider. The cycle will be technically stable, but will steer a rather poor course when disturbed. If the rider attempts to correct the course changes without using some secondary stability correction mechanism such as body shift, his "correction" will usually decrease the centrifugal acceleration generated by the turn.

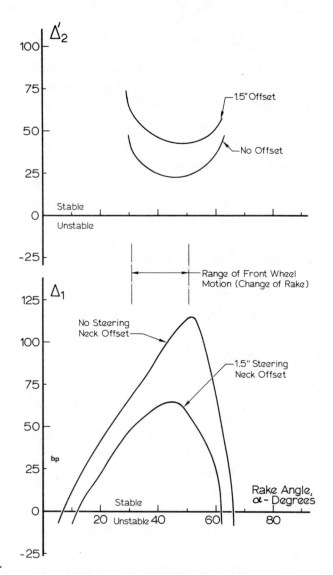

Figure A-2 Hawk Stability Coefficient Versus Rake and Offset.

This in turn will cause the initial disturbance to go uncorrected which will usually cause the cycle to fall over. A better set of criteria would include a limitation on course changes, but this is beyond the scope of a linear model.

The second criterion, Δ_1, is primarily a function of vehicle geometry and mass characteristics. Two curves of Δ_1 corresponding to the conditions for Δ_2' are shown in Figure A-2b. Note that the vehicle is unstable at both small and large rake angles. This term is generally a function of rake and trail, although in the Hawk these two variables are coupled. In a high speed turn with a large bank angle, trail will decrease and a cycle which is otherwise stable will drop into an unstable region of Δ_1. The Hawk should not experience this phenomenon since it will generally be moving in a straight line.

There is an effect which was not included in the model, but which could cause a rapid change of effective trail at low speeds. With a broad flat tire, very small bank angles will cause large changes in the center of pressure of the contact patch. This in turn will be acted upon by the rolling resistance of the tire/pavement combination, and the result will be a very sudden increase in the torque on the steering assembly tending to turn the steering assembly into the direction of lean. This will have the same effect as a large trail, and can be compared to the effects of a negative trail, since to a degree, the larger the steering angle, the greater will be the destabilizing torque. A round tire was assumed in the model, since the tire will be round at high speeds, and since the flat tire causes a trail parameter which is a function of the lean angle and therefore causes a nonlinearity.

A.4. DISCUSSION OF RESULTS

The numerical results indicate that an optimum rake angle would be approximately 45 degrees with the steering neck offset not set at zero. This gives a rather broad region in which the steering characteristics of the vehicle will reamin essentially constant. Flexing of the front suspension will cause little change in steering characteristics at that setting, and the value of the Hurwitz criterion at that angle is near maximum, thus the stability is also near maximum.

The effect of rake angle on the stability of a cycle is complicated. Nevertheless, an attempt will be made here to provide some physical understanding. One may separate all the torques acting on the steering assembly into those acting about the vertical axis and those acting about the horizontal axis. These torques have components about the steering axis and normal to it which are functions of the rake angle. The vertical torques are slip angle aligning torques, that is, torques caused by trail and the weight of the vehicle, drag torques

both aerodynamic and road, and gyro torque due to the angular rate about the horizontal axis. Horizontal torques are principally those caused by gravity acting on the offset center of mass of the steering assembly, and gyro torques due to the angular rate of the turn. Small rake angles will cause the vertical torques to dominate and large rake angles will cause the horizontal torques to dominate. Generally, for stable operation of the cycle, components of both are required. It is possible to obtain a stable set-up using zero rake.

In the Hawk, because the rider cannot shift his weight sufficiently, all corrections of aerodynamic or mass balance disturbances must be accomplished by turning the vehicle. This will result in the vehicle hunting around its mean path. The hunting frequency is low, in the neighborhood of less than one cycle per second, the value being determined by the correction rate of the rider. Left to its own devices, the vehicle will wander, but will be stable in the sense that it will not fall over. In the event of strong wander tendencies, it would probably be a good idea to install a trim tab that could be adjusted through a very limited range by the rider.

APPENDIX B
PRELIMINARY PERFORMANCE ESTIMATES FOR HONDA HAWK

Figure B-1 is a display of computer-predicted performance for the Honda Hawk. It is based on aerodynamic drag factors determined from supplementary computer analysis and engine output curves conservatively estimated for the Hawk power train using simplified calculations of turbocharger effectiveness and engine characteristics. These performance predictions were proven by actual runs at Bonneville to be reasonbly accurate. However, available power appeared to be substantially higher than originally anticipated and vehicle weight was much higher than initially estimated, ultimately reaching 1700 lb, rather than the 1000-lb figure indicated on the performance plots.

Adjusting the plots for the actual machine weight, and for the additional power produced by the Hawk engines, it was found that acceleration performance was close to original predictions. It should be noted that the gearing indicated on the performance plots was not employed during runs. Due to a rather short available course higher numerical gear ratios were employed, favoring acceleration in lieu of theoretical maximum top speed.

EFFECTS OF REALISTIC TIRE ROLLING RESISTANCE
UPON THE DETERMINATION OF AERODYNAMIC DRAG
FROM ROAD-VEHICLE COAST-DOWN TESTS*

Bain Dayman, Jr.
Jet Propulsion Laboratory
Pasadena, California

Abstract

An analytical numerical study was made of the effects of assuming a constant rolling resistance when inferring aerodynamic resistance from coast-down tests of road-vehicles when, in fact, the actual rolling resistance varies with velocity.

The error in the inferred aerodynamic resistance can be quite high for conventional bias tires, up to about 35%, and as high as 15% even for radial tires. Dividing the total coast-down velocity history into a number of smaller velocity ranges does not necessarily decrease the error in the inferred aerodynamic resistance. By assuming a rolling resistance that varies with velocity (say V^4), not only are the errors in the determination of aerodynamic resistance substantially reduced, but a reasonable approximation of the rolling resistance is obtained from the coast-down history of road vehicles.

NOMENCLATURE

A = Frontal area of vehicle.

C_D = Aerodynamic drag coefficient = $\dfrac{D}{\frac{1}{2}\rho(V-U)^2 A}$

C_{RR} = Rolling resistance coefficient of tires = $\dfrac{RR}{mg}$

$C_{0,1,2,3}$ = Coefficients in cubic equation used to match rolling resistances of tires shown in Figure 1 (see Equation 3).

$C_{R0,V}$ = Coefficients in exponential equation used for assumed rolling resistance of tires (see Equation 4).

D = Aerodynamic drag = $\frac{1}{2}\rho(V-U)^2 C_D A$

g = Gravitational force.

L = Aerodynamic Lift.

m = Mass of vehicle.

Δm = Correction to mass of vehicle to account for addition of rotational kinetic energy to translational kinetic energy.

$\overline{m}$ = $m + \Delta m$.

N = Exponent on V in Equation 4.

RMS = Least root-mean-square deviation in time (sec.) at the 10 mph velocity increments of Table I for curve-fitting coast-down history.

RR = Rolling resistance of all four tires.

S = Distance vehicle traveled during coast down.

t = Time from initiation of coast down.

*This paper presents the work of one phase of the research carried out at the Jet Propulsion Laboratory, California Institute of Technology, under NASA Contract NAS7-100.

229

U   = Wind velocity. Positive in direction of vehicle travel.

V   = Velocity of vehicle during coast down.

W   = Weight of vehicle = mg.

β = $\dfrac{\overline{m}}{m}$

ρ = Air density.

θ = Grade of road. Positive for vehicle going uphill.

1. INTRODUCTION

Coast-down tests have been used for quite some time in order to obtain aerodynamic drag of road-vehicles. Although this may seem to be an ideal way to infer the aerodynamic drag since the actual road-vehicle is in its natural environment, it is not straightforward as it is necessary to separate the aerodynamic resistance from the rolling resistance (the tires being the primary source). In order to separate out the rolling resistance, it is convenient to assume it to be independent of velocity[1,2,3] or else incorporate some assumed or measured value of rolling resistance.[4,5]

This paper discusses the effects upon the inferred aerodynamic drag coefficient that are introduced by the assumption of a constant rolling resistance. This is accomplished by generating hypothetical coast-down histories using realistic tire rolling resistances and then applying the constant rolling resistance assumption to infer the aerodynamic drag. Finally, a non-linear rolling-resistance approach is examined to see if these effects can be decreased.

2. HYPOTHETICAL COAST-DOWN HISTORIES

2.1 FORMULATION

Hypothetical coast-down histories for a number of typical cases were computer-generated using rolling resistances that varied realistically with velocity. The aerodynamic drag coefficient was taken to be constant (a reasonable assumption for velocities above 10 mph). The usual F = ma

approach was followed, yielding:

$$-\overline{m}\frac{dV}{dt} = (mg\cos\theta - L)C_{RR} + mg\sin\theta + \tfrac{1}{2}\rho(V-U)^2 C_D A \qquad (1)$$

where $\overline{m} = m + \Delta m$. In order to account for the rotational kinetic energy, the mass of the vehicle (m) is increased by the increment Δm. The first term on the right-hand side of the equation is the rolling resistance force where the vehicle weight (mg) is decreased by the aerodynamic lift (L); the second term accounts for the effect of an uphill grade; the third term is the aerodynamic drag force with a tailwind. For the usual small grade, $\cos\theta \sim 1$ and $\sin\theta \sim \theta$. By letting $\beta = 1 + \Delta m/m$, we get:

$$dt = -\frac{m\beta}{(mg-L)C_{RR} + mg\theta + \tfrac{1}{2}\rho(V-U)^2 C_D A}\, dV \qquad (2)$$

For a typical vehicle the lift is of the order of the aerodynamic drag, and the aerodynamic drag coefficient is of the order of $\tfrac{1}{2}$.

Equation (2) was integrated numerically using a computer with increments of dV equal to 0.1 mph*

2.2 CALCULATED HISTORIES

Since the effects of grade and wind are not being considered in this paper, θ and U were set to zero. The rolling resistance was taken to be that of various types of tires.[6,7] Nothing was included to account for the rotational resistance of the drive train when the road vehicle is coasting in neutral. This is a reasonable assumption for the purposes of this paper for two reasons: (1) the major part of the rolling resistance is due to the tires; (2) the tire rolling resistances in References 6 and 7 are greater than they would be on a road because the data were obtained on a drum which caused the tires to be over-flexed due to the drum's small radius of curvature.

The effects of three typical types of tire rolling resistances were investigated: conventional bias, belted bias, and radial. The rolling resistance

*The coast-down histories are not sensitive to values of dV below 1 mph.

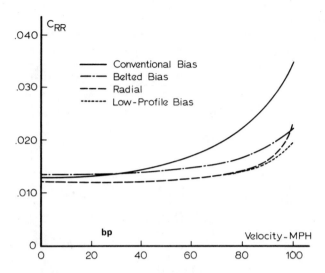

Figure 1. Rolling Resistance Coefficients of Various Tire Types.

of low profile bias tires is quite similar to that of the radial.[6,7] The curves for these tires are shown in Figure 1. For convenience in computing the hypothetical coast-down histories, these curves were approximated by the cubic equation:

$$C_{RR} = C_0 + C_1\left(\frac{V}{100}\right) + C_2\left(\frac{V}{100}\right)^2 + C_3\left(\frac{V}{100}\right)^3 \qquad (3)$$

where the values for the constants are:

Tire	Conventional	Belted	Radial
C_0	.0124	.0130	.0120
C_1	.0047	.0110	.00575
C_2	-.018	-.030	-.020
C_3	.035	.029	.022
Table I	A	B, D, E, F and III	C

for the following cases:

Vehicle	Standard Car	Standard Car	Camper	Standard Car
Wt. (lb)	4000	4000	5000	4000
Area (ft^2)	22.5	22.5	35.0	22.5
C_D	0.45	0.35	0.75	0.45
Tires	All 3	Belted	Belted	Belted
L/D	0	0	0	1*
Tables I and II	A, B, C	D	E	F

*Included only to demonstrate the effect of aerodynamic lift on the coast-down history.

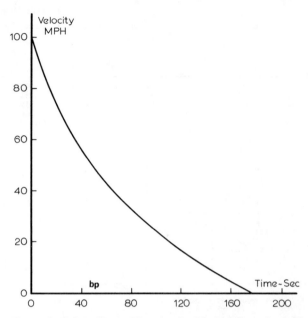

Figure 2. Coast-Down History of a Typical Standard-Size Car With Belted Bias Tires.

In all cases standard atmosphere density was used (ρ = 0.00238 slug/ft^3) and β = 1.05 was assumed in order to exaggerate the effect of rotational kinetic energy (a more realistic value for normal road vehicles would be about 1.025). The velocity-time-distance coast-down histories from 100 mph presented in Table I are considered to be fairly realistic and are taken as the baseline

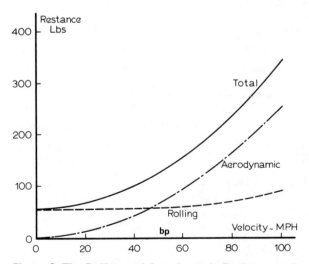

Figure 3. Tire Rolling and Aerodynamic Resistance of a Typical Standard-Size Car With Belted Bias Tires.

Table I
Vehicle Coast-Down History

A. STANDARD-SIZE CAR WITH CONVENTIONAL BIAS TIRES

V (mph)	t (sec)	S (ft)	D (lbs)	RR (lbs)
100	0.000	0.0000	259.18	136.40
95	2.551	3.6464+02*	233.91	122.51
90	5.387	7.4915+02	209.94	110.26
85	8.548	1.1546+03	187.26	99.54
80	12.083	1.5821+03	165.88	90.24
75	16.047	2.0324+03	145.79	82.26
70	20.505	2.5061+03	127.00	75.50
65	25.532	3.0035+03	109.51	69.85
60	31.215	3.5240+03	93.31	65.20
55	37.651	4.0662+03	78.40	61.45
50	44.949	4.6276+03	64.80	58.50
45	53.227	5.2036+03	52.48	56.24
40	62.607	5.7877+03	41.47	54.56
35	73.211	6.3701+03	31.75	53.36
30	85.143	6.9380+03	23.33	52.54
25	98.475	7.4749+03	16.20	51.99
20	113.230	7.9609+03	10.37	51.60
15	129.354	8.3740+03	5.83	51.27
10	146.711	8.6915+03	2.59	50.90
5	165.073	8.8930+03	0.65	50.38
0	184.140	8.9626+03	0.00	49.60

B. STANDARD-SIZE CAR WITH BELTED BIAS TIRES

V (mph)	t (sec)	S (ft)	D (lbs)	RR (lbs)
100	0.000	0.0000	259.18	92.00
95	2.863	4.0918+02	233.91	84.96
90	6.019	8.3717+02	209.94	78.96
85	9.506	1.2845+03	187.26	73.94
80	13.367	1.7514+03	165.88	69.79
75	17.651	2.2381+03	145.79	66.44
70	22.412	2.7440+03	127.00	63.79
65	27.712	3.2684+03	109.51	61.76
60	33.620	3.8096+03	93.31	60.26
55	40.212	4.3650+03	78.40	59.20
50	47.568	4.9310+03	64.80	58.50
45	55.776	5.5022+03	52.48	58.07
40	64.923	6.0718+03	41.47	57.82
35	75.094	6.6306+03	31.75	57.67
30	86.366	7.1672+03	23.33	57.53
25	98.799	7.6679+03	16.20	57.31
20	112.428	8.1170+03	10.37	56.93
15	127.255	8.4968+03	5.83	56.29
10	143.240	8.7892+03	2.59	55.32
5	160.296	8.9762+03	0.65	53.91
0	178.295	9.0416+03	0.00	52.00

C. STANDARD-SIZE CAR WITH RADIAL TIRES

V (mph)	t (sec)	S (ft)	D (lbs)	RR (lbs)
100	0.000	0.0000	259.18	79.00
95	2.973	4.2493+02	233.91	73.10
90	6.252	8.6957+02	209.94	68.05
85	9.878	1.3347+03	187.26	63.79
80	13.898	1.8209+03	165.88	60.26
75	18.367	2.3286+03	145.79	57.38
70	23.348	2.8579+03	127.00	55.08
65	28.912	3.4084+03	109.51	53.32
60	35.141	3.9789+03	93.31	52.01
55	42.126	4.5675+03	78.40	51.09
50	49.968	5.1707+03	64.80	50.50
45	58.776	5.7838+03	52.48	50.17
40	68.665	6.3995+03	41.47	50.03
35	79.746	7.0082+03	31.75	50.02
30	92.119	7.5971+03	23.33	50.08
25	105.859	8.1505+03	16.20	50.12
20	121.000	8.6493+03	10.37	50.10
15	137.513	9.0723+03	5.83	49.95
10	155.290	9.3975+03	2.59	49.59
5	174.143	9.6043+03	0.65	48.96
0	193.799	9.6760+03	0.00	48.00

D. LOW-DRAG STANDARD-SIZE CAR WITH BELTED BIAS TIRES

V (mph)	t (sec)	S (ft)	D (lbs)	RR (lbs)
100	0.000	0.0000	201.59	92.00
95	3.422	4.8918+02	181.93	84.96
90	7.190	1.0001+03	163.28	78.96
85	11.343	1.5329+03	145.65	73.94
80	15.929	2.0874+03	129.02	69.79
75	20.996	2.6630+03	113.39	66.44
70	26.599	3.2585+03	98.78	63.79
65	32.798	3.8719+03	85.17	61.76
60	39.657	4.5002+03	72.57	60.26
55	47.241	5.1393+03	60.98	59.20
50	55.617	5.7838+03	50.40	58.50
45	64.852	6.4266+03	40.82	58.07
40	75.006	7.0589+03	32.25	57.82
35	86.132	7.6703+03	24.69	57.67
30	98.271	8.2483+03	18.14	57.53
25	111.448	8.7791+03	12.60	57.31
20	125.667	9.2477+03	8.06	56.93
15	140.910	9.6383+03	4.54	56.29
10	157.140	9.9353+03	2.02	55.32
5	174.297	1.0123+04	0.50	53.91
0	192.312	1.0189+04	0.00	52.00

E. TYPICAL CAMPER WITH BELTED BIAS TIRES

V (mph)	t (sec)	S (ft)	D (lbs)	RR (lbs)
100	0.000	0.0000	671.95	115.00
95	1.599	2.2853+02	606.44	106.19
90	3.368	4.6838+02	544.28	98.71
85	5.332	7.2032+02	485.49	92.42
80	7.522	9.8514+02	430.05	87.24
75	9.973	1.2637+03	377.98	83.05
70	12.731	1.5567+03	329.26	79.74
65	15.847	1.8649+03	283.90	77.20
60	19.385	2.1890+03	241.90	75.32
55	23.423	2.5291+03	203.27	74.00
50	28.055	2.8854+03	167.99	73.13
45	33.394	3.2569+03	136.07	72.59
40	39.579	3.6419+03	107.51	72.28
35	46.769	4.0367+03	82.32	72.09
30	55.150	4.4354+03	60.48	71.92
25	64.922	4.8286+03	42.00	71.64
20	76.281	5.2024+03	26.88	71.16
15	89.383	5.5376+03	15.12	70.36
10	104.284	5.8097+03	6.72	69.15
5	120.869	5.9912+03	1.68	67.39
0	138.792	6.0563+03	0.00	65.00

F. STANDARD-SIZE CAR WITH BELTED BIAS TIRES (L/D = 1)

V (mph)	t (sec)	S (ft)	D (lbs)	RR (lbs)
100	0.000	0.0000	259.18	86.04
95	2.909	4.1581+02	233.91	79.99
90	6.113	8.5031+02	209.94	74.82
85	9.649	1.3039+03	187.26	70.48
80	13.560	1.7769+03	165.88	66.90
75	17.895	2.2694+03	145.79	64.02
70	22.710	2.7810+03	127.00	61.76
65	28.065	3.3108+03	109.51	60.07
60	34.030	3.8572+03	93.31	58.85
55	40.680	4.4176+03	78.40	58.04
50	48.096	4.9881+03	64.80	57.55
45	56.365	5.5636+03	52.48	57.31
40	65.571	6.1369+03	41.47	57.22
35	75.800	6.6988+03	31.75	57.22
30	87.124	7.2379+03	23.33	57.20
25	99.603	7.7405+03	16.20	57.08
20	113.269	8.1908+03	10.37	56.78
15	128.123	8.5713+03	5.83	56.21
10	144.123	8.8640+03	2.59	55.28
5	161.185	9.0511+03	0.65	53.91
0	179.185	9.1165+03	0.00	52.00

data for comparative purposes in this paper. For background information, the calculated magnitudes of the aerodynamic and rolling resistances are listed. The coast-down history for the case of Table I.B is plotted in Figure 2 while the magnitudes of the aerodynamic and rolling resistances are plotted in Figure 3. Note that the two resistive forces are equal in the 45-50 mph range, a typical situation.

3. DETERMINATION OF AERODYNAMIC DRAG AND ROLLING RESISTANCE

3.1 METHOD

Since the technique described in Reference 1 allows for subjective judgment, the solution is not unique, and hence is not considered convenient to use. The technique described in References 2 and 3 (it, too, assumes rolling resistance as well as the aerodynamic drag coefficient to be constant) is a convenient one to use since it yields unique solutions. However, when the rolling resistance deviates from being independent of velocity, it loses accuracy in the determination of aerodynamic drag. In order to improve upon the general accuracy in the determination of the aerodynamic drag coefficients from road-vehicle coast-down velocity histories, some reasonable multi-term function of the velocity (but having no V^2 term) can be used which has the characteristic shape of the rolling resistance expected for the

*Exponent on base-10, i.e., 364.64.

Table II
Solutions to Coast-Down History of Table I

A. STANDARD-SIZE CAR WITH CONVENTIONAL BIAS TIRES

Velocity Range (mph)	$C_{RR} = C_{R_O}$			$C_{RR} = C_{R_O} + C_{R_V} \cdot (\frac{V}{100})^4$			
	C_D	C_{R_O}	RMS	C_D	C_{R_O}	C_{R_V}	RMS
100-10	.547	.0121	.513	.468	.0127	.0197	.018
80-10	.527	.0123	.285	.470	.0127	.0200	.045
60-10	.505	.0126	.105	.474	.0127	.0158	.030
100-50	.613	.0079	.065	.489	.0122	.0165	.003
80-40	.568	.0105	.050	.473	.0126	.0193	.001
90-60	.618	.0072	.012	.484	.0123	.0174	.001
70-40	.555	.0110	.022	.472	.0126	.0197	.002
50-20	.502	.0125	.026	.465	.0128	.0202	.006
Avg.	.529	.0108		.474	.0126		

$C_{D_{Actual}} = 0.45$ $C_{R_{O_{Actual}}} = 0.0124$

B. STANDARD-SIZE CAR WITH BELTED BIAS TIRES

Velocity Range (mph)	$C_{RR} = C_{R_O}$			$C_{RR} = C_{R_O} + C_{R_V} \cdot (\frac{V}{100})^4$			
	C_D	C_{R_O}	RMS	C_D	C_{R_O}	C_{R_V}	RMS
100-10	.485	.0139	.214	.455	.0141	.0070	.074
80-10	.474	.0140	.076	.454	.0141	.0068	.078
60-10	.468	.0141	.054	.455	.0141	.0066	.081
100-50	.517	.0117	.051	.432	.0146	.0111	.003
80-40	.487	.0134	.031	.437	.0145	.0100	.004
90-60	.518	.0113	.010	.449	.0139	.0090	.002
70-40	.477	.0137	.013	.447	.0143	.0075	.004
50-20	.460	.0142	.004	.451	.0143	.0052	.008
Avg.	.486	.0133		.447	.0142		

$C_{D_{Actual}} = 0.45$ $C_{R_{O_{Actual}}} = 0.013$

C. STANDARD-SIZE CAR WITH RADIAL TIRES

Velocity Range (mph)	$C_{RR} = C_{R_O}$			$C_{RR} = C_{R_O} + C_{R_V} \cdot (\frac{V}{100})^4$			
	C_D	C_{R_O}	RMS	C_D	C_{R_O}	C_{R_V}	RMS
100-10	.475	.0122	.272	.436	.0126	.0091	.035
80-10	.464	.0124	.121	.437	.0126	.0090	.039
60-10	.455	.0125	.025	.439	.0126	.0079	.040
100-50	.507	.0101	.047	.445	.0122	.0081	.007
80-40	.481	.0116	.032	.438	.0125	.0088	.005
90-60	.509	.0097	.008	.438	.0119	.0091	.001
70-40	.473	.0119	.013	.433	.0127	.0097	.001
50-20	.450	.0125	.008	.439	.0126	.0070	.001
Avg.	.477	.0117		.438	.0125		

$C_{D_{Actual}} = 0.45$ $C_{R_{O_{Actual}}} = 0.012$

D. LOW-DRAG STANDARD-SIZE CAR WITH BELTED BIAS TIRES

Velocity Range (mph)	$C_{RR} = C_{R_O}$			$C_{RR} = C_{R_O} + C_{R_V} \cdot (\frac{V}{100})^4$			
	C_D	C_{R_O}	RMS	C_D	C_{R_O}	C_{R_V}	RMS
100-10	.386	.0138	.284	.351	.0142	.0079	.085
80-10	.374	.0140	.098	.361	.0141	.0041	.069
60-10	.367	.0141	.059	.373	.0140	-.0029	.048
100-50	.417	.0116	.070	.339	.0143	.0102	.006
80-40	.387	.0133	.042	.332	.0146	.0110	.002
90-60	.418	.0113	.013	.345	.0141	.0095	.002
70-40	.378	.0137	.016	.330	.0146	.0115	.001
50-20	.360	.0142	.004	.352	.0143	.0044	.009
Avg.	.386	.0133		.348	.0143		

$C_{D_{Actual}} = 0.35$ $C_{R_{O_{Actual}}} = 0.013$

E. TYPICAL CAMPER WITH BELTED BIAS TIRES

Velocity Range (mph)	$C_{RR} = C_{R_O}$			$C_{RR} = C_{R_O} + C_{R_V} \cdot (\frac{V}{100})^4$			
	C_D	C_{R_O}	RMS	C_D	C_{R_O}	C_{R_V}	RMS
100-10	.776	.0139	.079	.757	.0141	.0060	.042
80-10	.768	.0140	.035	.761	.0141	.0038	.040
60-10	.766	.0140	.037	.761	.0141	.0044	.048
100-50	.802	.0118	.017	.740	.0144	.0103	.002
80-40	.778	.0134	.012	.741	.0144	.0038	.040
90-60	.805	.0112	.003	.749	.0139	.0090	.001
70-40	.771	.0137	.005	.742	.0144	.0089	.001
50-20	.759	.0142	.002	.755	.0143	.0024	.003
Avg.	.778	.0133		.751	.0142		

$C_{D_{Actual}} = 0.75$ $C_{R_{O_{Actual}}} = 0.013$

particular vehicle being investigated. This arbitrary function of V should be chosen such that only two coefficients are required in order to define it: one for the level at V = 0; the other as a vertical (or even a horizontal) scale factor. Then the total number of coefficients which must be solved for will be increased just to three from the two of References 1-3, minimizing the severity of the data requirements for the actual coast-down history test procedures.

For illustration in this paper, the effect of a variation of the rolling resistance with velocity in the form:

$$C_{RR} = C_{R_O} + C_{R_V} \cdot (\frac{V}{100})^N \qquad (4)$$

was investigated. Equation (2) was numerically integrated for combinations of appropriate values of C_D, C_{R_O}, C_{R_V} and N. The resulting velocity-time histories were then compared with the appropriate hypothetical case that was generated as described in Section 2. The combination of these four constants which yielded the best fit (least RMS deviation from the discrete times for velocity increments of 10 mph for each coast-down history shown in Table I) was determined.

3.2 RESULTS

For the characteristics of the rolling resistances (Figure 1) used in the hypothetical coast-down histories of Table I, values of N = 3, 4, 5, or 6 each give reasonable solutions, i.e., the inferred aerodynamic and rolling resistances are reasonably close to those of the hypothetical cases. Therefore, for convenience, N was fixed at 4, thereby decreasing the number of coefficients to solve for down to the suggested three. Solutions for the hypothetical coast-down histories in Table I are tabulated in Table II. Figure 4 shows one manner of plotting the data of Table II.A in order to demonstrate the effect of the velocity range upon the inferred aerodynamic drag coefficient for the constant rolling resistance solution; the effect of the span of the velocity range is minor while the mid-point of the velocity range dominates the effect of velocity upon C_D. Even for a velocity

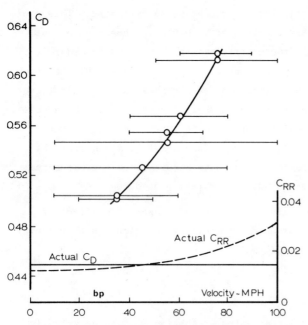

Figure 4. Aerodynamic Resistance Coefficients Inferred from Hypothetical Coast-Down History With Rolling Resistance Assumed Constant. Standard-Size Car With Conventional Bias Tires.

range midpoint as low as 35 mph the error in C_D is about 12% for the conventional bias tire.

For N = 0, a rolling resistance solution independent of velocity would be obtained since $C_{RR} = C_{R_O} + C_{R_V}$, hence is virtually the same as setting $C_{R_V} = 0$. As suggested in Ref. 8, by setting N = 1, quite good solutions can be obtained for a limited velocity range where a sloping straight line fairly well approximates the rolling resistance curve.* The advantage of this linear, but not constant, rolling-resistance approach is that it can utilize the analytical method of Ref. 2. But, this technique has a drawback; the values of C_{R_O} and C_{R_V} are both strongly dependent upon the velocity range being investigated. For N = 4, these values are relatively weak functions of the velocity range. Setting N = 2 results in an indeterminant solution.

The solution assuming constant values for both C_D and C_{RR} actually implies that C_{RR} varies with the square of the velocity; but this variation is included in the value for C_D since the aerodynamic

drag force varies with velocity squared and the two cannot be separated without some additional information. That is why the constant C_D and C_{RR} solutions shown in Table II yield C_D's which are higher than the C_D's of the hypothetical histories.

Solutions for a low-drag car as well as a camper-type vehicle are included in order to demonstrate the effect of varying the aerodynamic drag while keeping the rolling resistance coefficient constant. The increased weight of the camper over the standard car does not significantly detract from the effect of an increase in the aerodynamic resistance relative to the rolling resistance.

The cases analyzed in this paper are for the coast-down histories for vehicles having no aerodynamic lift. Although there is an effect of lift upon the coast-down history (as seen by comparing Table I.F with I.B), if the correct form for the lift is included in the drag-determination process, then the presence of lift will have little effect upon the accuracy of the solution. This same principle applies to all other characteristics such as grade, wind, β, weight, and air density. However, if the presence of lift that does occur during the coast-down history is ignored in the solution for the aerodynamic resistance, then an error will occur in the solution. For the standard car (Table I.F) the aerodynamic drag coefficient comes out about 1½% lower when the lift is ignored during the solution process than when the correct factor for lift is included in the solution process. This is due to the increase in the rolling resistance since the weight of the vehicle was not reduced by the lift.

4. DISCUSSION

As can be seen from the RMS values in Table II, the assumption of a rolling resistance that varies exponentially with velocity generally yields solutions which better fit the actual data (smaller RMS deviations) than does the assumption of a constant rolling resistance. This is especially so

---

*For N = 1, negative values of C_{R_V} can be the optimum solution for small ranges of velocity when the rolling resistance is rapidly increasing with velocity. For example, for the conditions in Table II.B in the 90-60 mph velocity range $C_{R_O} = -0.005$, $C_{R_V} = 0.033$, $C_D = 0.462$, RMS = 0.02.

234

when the rolling resistance is a strong function
of velocity, such as for the conventional bias tire
case at all velocities, and even for the radial
tires at the upper velocity regimes. However, the
constant rolling resistance solutions are better
for the radial tires at the lower velocity ranges
where rolling resistance is nearly independent of
the velocity. On the other hand, the exponential-
rolling-resistance solutions are less affected by
the type of tire and are relatively independent of
the velocity range included in the data reduction.

In terms of C_D, the constant rolling-resistance
solution is improved as the relative value of the
aerodynamic drag to the rolling resistance is
increased. As an example, see Table II.E for the
camper. On the other hand, the percentage error
in the solution increases when the opposite occurs
as shown in Table II.D for the low-drag standard
car. However, the solution assuming an exponen-
tially-varying rolling resistance is essentially
unaffected by the relative values of the aerodynamic and rolling resistances. This can be seen
by comparing the average C_D's in Tables II.B, D,
and E.

It is important to note that the constant-rolling-
resistance solution is not necessarily improved by
dividing the entire coast-down velocity range into
several smaller velocity ranges. It just turns
out that the least RMS fit results in the rolling
resistance being about equal to or less than the
hypothetical value at zero velocity rather than
being an average of the hypothetical rolling resistance within the smaller velocity range. In
the case of the conventional bias tires, although
the RMS deviation is decreased, the value of both
the aerodynamic drag and rolling resistance coefficients are worse at 90-60 mph velocity range
than for the entire 100-10 mph velocity range.
The exponential rolling-resistance solutions are
relatively insensitive to the velocity range seg-
ments chosen.

A summary of the aerodynamic drag coefficients in
Tables II.A, B, and C (the standard car with the
three types of tires) is shown in Figure 5. These

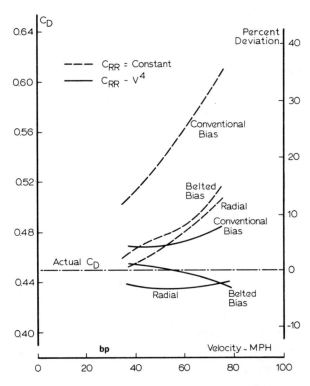

Figure 5. Values of Aerodynamic Drag Coefficient
Determined from Hypothetical Coast-Down Histories for
a Typical Standard-Size Car With Various Types of Tires.

curves, composites of figures similar to Figure 4,
demonstrate the sensitivity (and inaccuracy) of
the C_D data to the midpoint of the velocity range
when the solution is based upon constant rolling
resistance. On the other hand, the assumption of
a rolling resistance that varies with the fourth
power of velocity yields C_D's which are far less
sensitive to the type of tire and the inaccuracies
are less than for the constant rolling resistance
solution, being around 5% high for the conventional
bias tires and well within 3% of the correct value
for both the belted bias and radial tires (the
inferred C_D for the radial tires comes out to be
around 3% low).

For all of the exponential rolling-resistance
solutions, inferred rolling resistances are fairly
close to the actual rolling resistance of the
hypothetical coast-down histories. An example of
this for the standard-size car with belted-bias
tires is shown in Table III and in Figure 6. It
is quite clear that at the higher velocity ranges
where the aerodynamic resistance dominates, the

Velocity Range (mph)	Velocity (mph)	Rolling Resistance Coefficient (C_{RR})	
		Actual*	Inferred**
100–10	100	.0230	.0211
	80	.0174	.0170
	60	.0151	.0150
	40	.0145	.0143
	20	.0142	.0141
100–50	100	.0230	.0241
	90	.0197	.0207
	80	.0174	.0183
	70	.0159	.0166
	60	.0151	.0155
	50	.0146	.0148
60–10	60	.0151	.0153
	40	.0145	.0144
	20	.0142	.0142
90–60	90	.0197	.0188
	80	.0174	.0169
	70	.0159	.0155
	60	.0151	.0146
50–20	50	.0146	.0146
	40	.0145	.0144
	30	.0144	.0143
	20	.0142	.0143

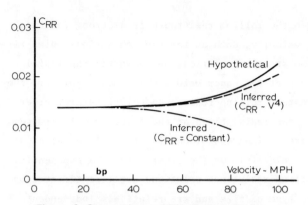

Figure 6. Comparison of Tire Rolling Resistance
Coefficients Inferred from Coast-Down History to
Hypothetical Value. Standard-Size Car With Belted Bias
Tires.

assumption of a constant rolling resistance results in the worst determination of the tire
rolling resistance as well as the aerodynamic
resistance.

5. CONCLUSIONS

The convenience of using the constant rolling resistance and aerodynamic drag coefficients approach
described in References 2 and 3 for determining
aerodynamic drag from road-vehicle coast-down
tests is offset by the limited conditions under
which accurate aerodynamic drag data can be inferred from coast-down histories of road-vehicles.
If conventional bias tires are used at normal inflation pressures, there are no velocity ranges
where reasonably accurate aerodynamic drag data
can be inferred when the rolling resistance is
assumed to be constant. In fact, breaking up the
overall velocity range covered into increments,
such as 90–60 mph, could result in even a poorer
determination of the aerodynamic resistance. If
radial tires are used, reasonably accurate deter-
minations of aerodynamic resistance are possible
at the lower velocity ranges (below 60 mph) with

the constant rolling resistance assumption. . .
but this places greater restrictions on the test
procedures. However, using the C_D data shown in
Table II, adjustments can be applied to the data
obtained in the manner of References 2 and 3 in
order to produce more accurate results. The use
of such correction factors does imply a reasonable
knowledge of the characteristics of the rolling
resistance and its general magnitude relative to
the aerodynamic resistance.

The use of a rolling resistance which varies exponentially with velocity considerably improves the
determination of aerodynamic resistance from coast-
down histories. Furthermore, this approximation
yields reasonably accurate values of the rolling
resistance as it varies with velocity. This technique, too, has limitations. If the rolling resistance varies with the square of the velocity,
then the C_{R_V} rolling resistance coefficient will
be combined with the aerodynamic drag coefficient
(C_D), and there is no way to separate the two
without further information.[4] The less the
rolling resistance curve approximates a velocity-
squared dependence, the better the approach involving Equation (4) will work in determining each
the aerodynamic and the rolling resistances from
coast-down data. But it is necessary that the
actual shape of the rolling resistance as a
function of velocity can be reasonably well
approximated by Equation (4) with N ≥ 3. This

*From Table I.B (put into coefficient form)
**From Table II.B (for $C_{RR} = C_{R_0} + C_{R_V} \cdot (\frac{V}{100})^4$)

236

condition is met by the rolling resistances assumed for this paper.

The rolling resistance of an actual road-vehicle includes the drive train with an automatic transmission if it is not physically decoupled from the drive shaft. Further analytical studies utilizing typical drive-train resistances would be helpful in quantifying the possible effects. However, experience in using this "V^4" technique in determining aerodynamic and rolling resistances from coast-down tests of actual vehicles does not indicate any problems (such as what might be caused by the drive train) beyond those already encountered during the analytical investigation described in this paper.

In summary, the assumption of a constant rolling resistance when inferring aerodynamic resistance from coast-down time-velocity histories will result in C_D's that are high by about 20-25%* for a standard car with conventional bias tires, 5-10% with belted bias tires, and around 5%* with radial tires. Little, if any, feeling for the realistic rolling resistance can be obtained using this assumption. By assuming a rolling resistance that varies exponentially with velocity, these errors will decrease to about 5% for the conventional bias tires and even less for the other tires. Furthermore, a fairly good determination of the rolling resistance as a function of velocity can be made.

The exponentially varying rolling resistance example shown in this paper demonstrates the advantage of using a variable rolling resistance which can fairly well approximate the actual case over the use of an assumed constant rolling resistance. In actual practice, a more complicated function than V^N:

$$C_{RR} = C_{R_O} + C_{R_V} \cdot fnc(V)$$

should be used in order to further improve upon the accuracy of the determination of both the aerodynamic and rolling resistances from coast-down histories, where $fnc(V)$ can be some appropriate multi-term function (but having no V^2 term) which has the characteristic shape of the rolling resistance expected for the particular vehicle being investigated for aerodynamic resistance. The solution process for this would be identical to the one described where $C_{RR} = C_{R_O} + C_{R_V} \left(\frac{V}{100}\right)^N$ in that the optimum combination of the three variables (C_D, C_{R_O}, C_{R_V}) giving the least RMS is to be determined.

REFERENCES

(1) Larrabee, E. E., "Measuring Car Drag," Road and Track Magazine, Vol. 12, No. 6, pp. 24-28.

(2) White, R. A. and Korst, H. H., "The Determination of Vehicle Drag Contributions from Coast-Down Tests," SAE Paper 720099, 1972.

(3) Korst, H. H. and White, R. A., "Aerodynamic and Rolling Resistances of Vehicles as Obtained from Coast-Down Experiments," 2nd International Conference on Vehicle Mechanics, Paris, September, 1971.

(4) White, R. A. and Korst, H. H., "A Generalized Method for Determining Drag Coefficient or Rolling Resistances from Coast-Down Tests," prepared for BHRA (England) Meeting, January, 1973 (meeting not held but proceedings were published).

(5) Bez, U., "Messung des Luftwinderstandes von Kraftfahrzeugen durch Auslaufversuche," Research Report, Dip. Engr. Thesis, Tech. Univ. at Stuttgart, January 1972, and Porsche Research Rept.

(6) Curtiss, W. W., "Low Power Loss Tires," SAE Automotive Engineering Congress, Detroit, Michigan, January 1969, Paper No. 710576.

(7) Walter, J. D., "Energy Losses in Tires", Caltech Seminar Series: Energy Consumption in Private Transportation, Pasadena, December, 1973.

(8) Kaiser, K., (DOT-TSC) private communication, January, 1974.

*For the practical velocity ranges.

237

AUD. QUESTION: When you talk about rolling resistance, aren't you really talking about transmission losses?

DAYMAN: Yes, all the losses are included. For this particular study we let the tire represent the entire source of loss. In the real case, the non-tire losses are considerably smaller in magnitude than the tire rolling resistance so letting the tires represent the entire loss as we did here is quite reasonable. Ideally, you would like to know what all the losses are so that you could represent them functionally and further improve the accuracy of the analysis.

HENRY JEX: If the aerodynamic drag is a small fraction of the rolling resistance, the curvature of the speed versus time curve is small and a very small change in the assumption of rolling resistance will reflect itself in a radical change in drag coefficient. This problem would be even worse for race cars which have low drag coefficients intrinsically. To reduce the data for low drag cars runs should be made at the highest possible speeds where the aerodynamic drag is a larger fraction of the decelerating force.

DAYMAN: My concern regarding race cars is that the tire rolling resistance may be a V^2 type function. The closer it is to a V^2 function, the more difficult it is to obtain a good solution for the drag coefficient and if it is identically a V^2 function, you cannot obtain a solution.

RESEARCH IN AERODYNAMIC DRAG REDUCTION
OF TRUCKS*

P. B. S. Lissaman
Director, Aerosciences
AeroVironment, Inc., Pasadena, CA

Abstract

A summary of AeroVironment Inc. research programs in Truck Drag Reduction is given. These programs have involved analytical studies, wind tunnel testing, full scale field tests, full scale road test, and operational testing. A number of different test methods and instrumentation techniques have been perfected which operate simply and reliably, and give precision of higher than 2% under windless conditions.

A discussion of the basic elements of bluff body drag, as it relates to truck air resistance is given. The concept of a dragless forebody is introduced. It is shown that this dragless state can nearly be achieved with a lip-like device on the front face of the van. The shielding effect of one body ahead of another is described, and the deleterious effects of crossflow in the gap between the bodies is discussed. In particular, it is shown that some add-on devices are particularly susceptible to crosswind flows and lose effectiveness at a few degrees of yaw.

Drag savings for simple add-on devices are reported. For tractor/trailer combinations 20% aerodynamic drag reductions have been achieved, while for single-chassis units up to 35% have been achieved. Fuel savings depend upon payload, speed, etc., but can be as much as 60% of the aerodynamic drag savings.

1. INTRODUCTION

In the past the aerodynamic drag of road vehicles has not been considered to be of great importance. This is not surprising in view of the fact that the first role of the power in the vehicle, namely to move the payload of the vehicle from point to point was of all-consuming significance. It is interesting to observe that even in the case of aircraft it was only about 20 years after the first flights of the Wright Brothers that much thought was given to the aerodynamic drag of the airplane. Today, in times of scarce energy resources and of high cruising highway speeds and larger vehicles, designers have come to pay more attention to aerodynamic drag of vehicles. It is a matter of interest that the aerodynamic drag of road vehicles consumes about 7% of the entire energy consumed in the United States. This energy base includes not only petroleum, but coal and natural gas.

Recently much work has been done on the aerodynamics of race cars, particularly with respect to producing lift or downward forces to assist in control and traction of such vehicles. The aerodynamic drag of the automobile is also of importance and interest, although it can be noted here that the drag coefficients of standard 1975-type automobiles are not exceptionally large. They

* Portions of this work were supported by a Grant from RANN Program of the National Science Foundation.

are of the order of about 0.50 based on frontal area. Although significant reductions in this drag coefficient are possible it is fair to say that a reasonably competent job of streamlining has been done on these vehicles.

With large trucks, however, it is another matter. Here we find, because of the bulky box-like structure of the van of the truck, a much larger proportion of the engine power is consumed in aerodynamic drag. This proportion varies according to payload, truck geometry, and road speed but in general is between 30 and 50% of the engine power. The drag coefficients of trucks are of the order of 1.0 based on frontal area. This is comparable to the drag of the square, flat plate, and thus would not be considered excessive in terms of what might be expected from such a body. It has long been known that, using aerodynamic principles, the body of a truck could be effectively streamlined to bring this drag coefficient down, possibly by a factor of 3. However, to date most of these attempts at streamlining had envisaged fairing on the traditional line of aircraft contouring, that is, a rounded front end and a tapering, pointed tail. Certainly, a teardrop with a wheel on each corner would be a fine low-drag vehicle, but at the same time it must be pointed out that this is very ineffective from the operational aspect -- both from the point of view of capacity, that is payload storage, and from the point of view of wheel base and overhangs.

One of the dominant factors entering into the streamlining of vehicles is the ubiquitous crosswind. Those trained in aerospace technology are inclined to think of the drag, and the main operating conditions of the vehicle, as being in a state of zero sideslip. Of course, in the case of road vehicles this is very seldom the case since roads do not always go in the direction of the wind. Thus, from the start, streamlining of road vehicles must be considered in the light of streamlining of a vehicle which will be continually subject to sideslip or yawed conditions. Not only must a low drag under conditions of

zero yaw be achieved, but also the drag must be acceptable for sideslip angles of up to 7°. This point is very important in considering the effectiveness of various streamlining devices. Some devices may have exceptionally low drag at zero sideslip, but severe drag increases at 2 or 3 degrees of yaw. In general, such a streamlining mechanism will be less effective than a streamlined vehicle with low drag in the range of 0°-7° of sideslip.

It is also interesting and important to remark that, especially in the case of large trucks, drag reductions with such vehicles can confer additional side benefits in the interaction between these vehicles and other road vehicles. It has long been known that passing of a large truck by a smaller vehicle, particularly in crosswind conditions, can produce hazardous effects on the small vehicle. While it is not certain that this will be the case, it appears highly likely that the streamlining of a larger vehicle will in general terms reduce the induced aerodynamic effects on nearby vehicles. This reduction in induced airflows will add to the safety of the passing vehicles. Many other benefits, over and above direct savings in fuel, occur on a streamlined vehicle, particularly a streamlined truck. For example, not only is the driving power reduced but presumably also the engine and drive train maintenance and wear. Simultaneously, the reduction in drag of a large truck-like shape may result in considerable reduction in the buffeting of such a vehicle due to flow separations. This reduction in buffeting can considerably reduce vibration and vibration-induced stresses throughout the vehicle, as well as lowering vibration-induced stresses on the driver himself, thus minimizing driver fatigue and increasing man/machine controllability.

2. VEHICLE DRAG RESEARCH AT AEROVIRONMENT

2.1 PRELIMINARY WORK

AeroVironment Inc., of Pasadena, California, has been actively involved in vehicle drag reduction for the past two years. This program has been principally aimed at the reduction of the drag of large highway trucks. However, in the course of this research many other vehicles have been tested. Figure 1 shows a small European light-weight automobile (Karman Ghia) which has been extensively work by AeroVironment to increase its streamlining. This vehicle was used for road testing, and for testing of the precision of instrumentation in estimating drag and methods of drag testing (Ref. 1). Initially, a number of tow tests were attempted with the vehicle. Although these tests were carried out under rather crude conditions and the methods could undoubtedly be improved, it appeared to us that tow testing would not be suitable to determine the resistance of the vehicle because of the large unsteady loads involved in the tow cable system. There were also the difficulties of operating on public highways while towing another vehicle and in addition, problems of avoiding the wake of the two vehicle became very serious.

Figure 1. Streamlined Test Vehicle.

A series of simply instrumented coast-down experiments were conducted. These were surprisingly successful. The car was run up to speed and allowed to decelerate in neutral on a relatively untraveled strip of highway. The car speedometer itself was used as the principal speed measuring instrument and a stopwatch used to clock the vehicle as it passed through various speeds, that is from 60 to 55 to 50 to 45, etc. Quite good correlation was obtained in these experiments. As an additional check a simple drag brake was installed on the car, (Figure 2).

Figure 2. Drag Plate Installation.

This brake added approximately 20% to the aerodynamic drag of the vehicle and the effect on deceleration of this device was quite easily observed with the simple instrumentation used in this testing. It was noted that one of the principal difficulties in this type of testing was obtaining a perfectly level roadway, and that the effects of the wind seemed to be present and were very difficult to remove. However, it was felt that even with these very elementary techniques one could obtain precision to within about 5%. This led us to believe that, with proper instrumentation and with a fully level surface, we could conduct very precise measurements of vehicle drag using the standard coast-down technique.

2.2 NATIONAL SCIENCE FOUNDATION PROGRAM

Following these experiments a large semi-trailer/tractor rig was instrumented for a series of tests conducted under a grant from the National Science Foundation. These tests had three goals. First was to establish and prove methods of testing vehicles for aerodynamic drag; second was to determine the drag coefficients of the vehicle, and the effect of drag on crosswind; and third, to test a variety of proprietary and experimental add-on aerodynamic devices intended to reduce drag. Since many of these add-on devices could be expected to change the drag by about 10% or less, it was obvious that fairly high precision instrumentation was required.

Thus a comprehensive instrumentation package was designed for the vehicle. The sensors consisted of a propeller anemometer and wind vane mounted on a probe ahead of the vehicle and a specially constructed fifth wheel attached to the rear of the trailer. These devices made it possible to measure ground speed, air speed, and relative wind direction with high precision. The data was then processed through two channels. One channel was a standard strip chart recorder giving an analog trace of the three signals, the other a processor which stored digital data on tape. Aboard the tractor was carried a Hewlett Packard 9820B computer and plotter which acted as a processor, computer, and a programmer, which received the data and at the end of each run would process the data in any form required with a graphical printout. The vehicle was also instrumented for airflow. The left side of the vehicle was fitted with a large number of tufts to show flow direction, while the right side was fitted with 25 static pressure orifices in strategic positions. These orifices were tapped into the interior of the trailer where a multi-tube manometer bank was mounted. The manometer

Table I
Equipment List

1967 White Freightliner truck

1968 Timpte 40' aluminum dry freight trailer (13'6" high)

AV developed 5th wheel system for ground speed and acceleration

R. M. Young propeller anemometer for air speed

AV developed anemometer for air direction

AV developed filter system to interface 5th-wheel and anemometers to recorder and computer system

Hewlett Packard 9821A computer

Hewlett Packard 9862A plotter

Hewlett Packard 3485A scanner

Hewlett Packard 3480B digital voltmeter

Soltec B-261 3-channel recorder

Manometer tube bank for pressure measurements

Tufts taped to the outside of the vehicle for flow visualization

Wilmore 300 watt and 500 watt inverters for A.C. power

readings were recorded photographically by an observer inside the trailer. Instruments are listed in Table I.

Excellent performance was obtained from this instrumentation package. Field conditions were very extreme, involving large changes in ambient temperatures, severe shock and vibration, a dirty, dusty environment, and poorly controlled electrical power sources.

It was felt that it would be necessary to obtain a flat, level piece of ground in which the vehicle could travel in any direction to exploit or amplify wind effects. For this reason, El Mirage Dry Lake (California) was selected, and special permission from the Bureau of Land Management was obtained to conduct the tests on specified days. A large number of tests were conducted during the periods March to July 1974. During these tests, which consisted of coast-down test-

Figure 3. Baseline Tractor/Trailer Vehicle.

Figure 4. Full Fairing Vehicle.

ing, crosswind testing, airflow photography, and pressure recording, a number of different vehicle configurations were tried. First, the basic vehicle itself was tested and variations on the gap between the trailer and the tractor tried (Fig. 3). Next a large full fairing device, which fitted fully over the tractor and faired the tractor smoothly into the trailer was tested (Fig. 4). This device had special hinged plates on the side to enable the tractor to jackknife and was fully street legal. Finally, a variety of special add-on devices, both tractor and trailer mounted, were tested.

Testing on the desert was conducted at different periods during the 24-hour day to take advantage of the calms at night and early morning and also of the strong winds, which frequently gust up to 30 mph during the noon period in the Mojave Desert. Although all standard control procedures were used, it was found that the tests were not, in fact, repeatable to within 2%. After an exhaustive analysis of the data and after many different techniques of analysis were employed it was determined that this 2 to 3% variance in the data of nominally identical testing conditions was in fact a true indication of events. By this it is implied that the effect of the gusty winds and the effects of the irregular lake surface over which the course was run were actually affecting the vehicle, and while instrumentation was sufficient to record this with great accuracy, the tests were not actually being conducted under properly identical ambient conditions. Results of the tests and data reduction procedures and the analysis of this data are described in Ref. 2.

Following the desert tests two other test procedures were used. The first procedure has been named hill rolling. In this method the vehicle is freely rolled down a long hill of uniform slope and its terminal velocity measured. An add-on aerodynamic device is then attached to the vehicle and the test repeated so that the new terminal velocity can be determined. It was found that this method of testing, although comparative, is ex-

tremely accurate, and very simple to conduct providing one has accurate speed measuring equipment. More details of this method are given in Ref. 3. The final test method was for fuel consumption under controlled conditions. Here the vehicle was driven over a measured freeway course of about 270 miles in length, consisting of three identical 90 mile laps. Results of this test program are fully reported in Ref. 2, and for semi-trailer/tractors can be summarized as follows: it was found that the full fairing gave substantial aerodynamic drag reductions, of the order of 23%, resulting in fuel savings of about 18% under regular highway driving conditions. The other add-on devices, smaller and simpler and more practical, gave aerodynamic drag reductions between 20 and 8%, depending upon tractor type, gap, and nature of front edges of the trailers.

2.3 FURTHER AV RESEARCH ON SINGLE CHASSIS UNITS

Following the desert tests a device developed by AeroVironment -- the lip (Figure 5) -- was fitted on a standard single-chassis truck (Figure 6) for testing under the AV corporate program. This truck was compared with an identical unmodified truck in hill rolling tests. Fuel consumption of both vehicles, under both long-range and "instantaneous" conditions, was measured. "Instantaneous", short duration (30 sec) tests used a burette tube spliced into the fuel system, to meter fuel flow. It was found that the lip gave very substantial reduction in the aerodynamic drag of the vehicle. Conditions of strong crosswinds were specifically sought out and the two vehicles were tested under crosswinds of the order of 20 mph. It was found again here that the lip was extremely effective, and in many cases the vehicle fitted with the aerodynamic lip was able to maintain 55 mph highway speed, while the unmodified vehicle did not have enough power to reach this speed. General results showed about 35% reduction in aero drag coefficient, with 23% fuel saving under regular driving conditions.

Figure 5. Lip Fairing Device.

2.4 WIND TUNNEL TEST PROGRAM

A series of tests on a 1/24th scale semi-trailer/
tractor rig were conducted in the 10' GALCIT
wind tunnel at the California Institute of Technology as a further element in the corporate program. The model was identical to the full-scale
vehicle used in the AeroVironment desert and
road tests. In the wind tunnel standard aerodynamic tests were conducted and a number of add-
on devices, both tractor- and trailer-mounted,
were examined. It was found that the results of
the wind tunnel did not correlate favorably with
those obtained in direct field testing. After
studying the flow patterns in the wind tunnel it
was determined that the flow field was not the
same as that occurring on the full-scale vehicle.
In particular, the important flow impingement

Figure 6. Matched Single Chassis Vehicle.

point on the forward face of the trailer was significantly different in the wind tunnel from what had
been measured to be on the full-scale vehicle. In
the wind tunnel, this flow impingement point was
higher on the trailer face than on the full-scale
vehicle, and because of this, add-on devices
designed to minimize the effect of the sharp edge
of the top edge of the trailer, while very effective
in the field, did not show up well in the wind tunnel. Also, presumably because of this effect,
tractor-mounted devices, which are intended to
deflect the flow before it impinges on the trailer,
did not exhibit the same performance in the wind
tunnel as they did in the road testing. The Reynolds Number of testing was 0.47 million based
on the square root of the frontal area of the model, and the tunnel speed was 125 mph corresponding to a q of 40.0 psf. No special precautions
were taken about the ground plane in the test except that the standard GALCIT ground plane, used
extensively for automobile testing was used. It is
believed that the flow on the upper portions of the
model is affected by the flow down through the
gap between the tractor and the trailer and out
along the bottom of the trailer. For this reason
the ground plane can affect the flow on the upper
surfaces of the tractor. It is believed that this
is an important effect which must be carefully
examined by other investigators before using
tunnel data to infer full-scale data. It was decided that for the small effects which were being

sought, that is, the effects of the order of 10%, that the wind tunnel, at least at this scale and under the conditions under which we tested, could give quite deceptive results.

3. SOME FUNDAMENTAL ELEMENTS OF BLUFF BODY DRAG

In order to clarify some of the ideas about truck aerodynamic resistance we discuss here some of the basic elements of bluff body drag, starting from the simplest element of all -- a single, rectangular box in a uniform flow space, from here we go onto discuss the effects of the addition of a separate forward body, and the addition of a ground plane, and try to develop inferences on what can be done towards reducing the drag of trucks without substantial changes in the shape of the vehicle itself.

3.1 SINGLE BLUFF BODY

If we consider a single rectangular shape of square cross section normal to the wind and of length approximately four times the height we perceive that this behaves essentially as a sharp-edged bluff body. In order to simplify matters let us first consider this without the inference of ground plane so that the flow is symmetrical in the crosswind directions of the body. We observe first that the forward face of the body contains a stagnation region around the center, and from this region the flow accelerates to a relatively high speed before separating at the edges of the forward face. From here the separation streamline will be curved in a streamline direction until approximately parallel to the main stream, and will presumably eventually reattach to the body sides, due to the influence of turbulent entrainment. It appears that a body length ratio of 4 or 5 to 1 is about sufficient to establish that the flow behaves as though this were a semi-infinite body, that is, on the side faces of the block the pressure will presumably reach an approximately steady-state with no further downstream changes on the truck sides. More significantly, conditions at the front are unaffected by those at the

rear. At the base of the body there is a general separation region and the pressure here is apparently mainly a function of the flow Reynolds Number. Experimental results record pressure coefficients in this region of the order of -0.20 to -0.30. Presumably the separation bubble closes some distance downstream in the wake. Returning now to the front face we perceive that the average pressure on the front face may be expected to be lower than unity because of the relatively low pressures near the edge of the box. No theoretical calculations for this have been made, although it is believed that present methods of turbulent boundary layer calculation and numerical computer techniques could yield some interesting analytical results for this problem, particularly if it is regarded as the forebody* of an infinite body.

If we now attempt to sum the drag components of the body we come up with the result that, based on the frontal area of the body, the drag contribution of the forward face may be of the order of .60, the drag contribution of the rear face may be of the order of .30, and the drag contribution of the side surfaces might be expected to be negligible. This seems to be an important and interesting point, since if the side surfaces are totally immersed in a separated flow, than any skin friction which might occur there will be necessarily of very small magnitude. Some indication of this magnitude can be inferred by assuming initially that the flow is attached on these faces. Then, assuming a skin friction drag coefficient of the order of .003 and a surface of approximately 16 times that of the frontal area, we note that the drag contribution of the sides could only be of the order of about .05. This number is very much smaller than the forward and rear face drag and in any event the number calculated here is probably considerably lower than what actually occurs on the faces, because of the separated flow. It is interesting here to observe that it is recorded that external posts on the sides of a

---

*For conciseness, we will use "forebody" for the front end of a single body, "foreward body" for the upstream body of a pair of shapes.

truck do, in fact, increase the drag of the vehicle. If the flow is totally separated this is surprising. We infer from this that if these results quoted here are in fact correct, then the flow must reattach some along the rear of the side faces and it is only the reattached flow which can be affected by the protrusions of the side posts.

In spite of the interesting experimental work described in Ref. 4, very little is known about the details of the flow over a body of box-like shape. In view of the relative simplicity and basic quality of the geometry it would be extremely interesting to conduct wind tunnel experiments, supported by analysis, continuing the work of Ref. 4.

However, if we stick to the assumptions that we have made above we see that it may be expected that a rectangular sharp-edged body of the type described would have a drag coefficient of the order of about 0.90. We note that this is about the number reported in the tests conducted by MIRA (Ref. 4), in which a shape of this type was tested. We should note the Reynolds Number of the test was appreciably lower than that which actually occurs on large trucks.

3.2 THE CONCEPT OF A DRAGLESS FOREBODY

A well known theorem of classical fluid mechanics (D'Alembert's Paradox) states that there is no drag on a closed body or a semi-infinite shape in a uniform incompressible flow. A consequence of this is that the total ideal pressure force on the front face of such a body will be zero. Now, it is known that if the viscous boundary layer is relatively thin and unseparated, then the real pressure field will be very similar to the ideal. Thus one is led to the conclusion that, provided separation can be avoided near the front face, one can approach the potential pressure distribution and thus achieve a nearly dragless forebody. This has been demonstrated experimentally (but not commented on) in Ref. 4, where it is shown that, provided the edges of the box are rounded to a radius of 30% of the width,

*Patent applied for.

the total drag coefficient is about .30 while the base contribution is about .20. Evidently, the rounded edges have eliminated separation on the forward part of the body and the forebody is virtually dragless.

It was this concept which led to the development of the AeroVironment Lip.* The principle was to achieve attached flow all over the front portion of the body without having to remove structure, as would be required to round the edge. Flow and pressure tests showed that this approach was very successful and the effect of reduced aerodynamic drag was proven in the hill rolling and fuel consumption tests.

3.3 EFFECT OF THE GROUND PLANE

The experiments of Ref. 4 show that the ground clearance does not appear to have much effect for sharp-edged boxes; for well rounded edges it appears that provided the ground clearance/height ratio is above 1/6 that the free drag is much the same as the drag in ground effect. This indicates that for trailer body heights of this magnitude the ground clearance may not be very important. This is in distinction to automobiles, and certainly race cars, where the ground effects seem to be significant.

3.4 EFFECT OF A SEPARATE FORWARD BODY

If the trailer box is shielded by a separate rectangular forward body (the tractor) an interesting effect occurs. It seems that while the drag of the forward body is large, the rear body is immersed in a wake of low dynamic pressure, so that the net drag of the system may be smaller than that of the rear element alone, provided the forward body is of smaller frontal area than the latter.

Evidently there is a coupling here between the size of the forward body and its position, as well as its shape. It may be advantageous to increase the forward body size to increase the shielding, while still reducing the system drag. This effect can be achieved by mounting an impervious plate on the tractor. Obviously the size and position of such a plate must be optimal. Such devices were tested by AV (Ref 2) and drag coefficient reductions of up to 17% measured.

However, a plate on the lower part of the tractor added to the drag. For this test, an air dam (effectively a downward extension of the front bumper) was added to the tractor. It was found that this increased the drag, as was expected, since the underbody of the tractor extends below the trailer, thus overshielding the lower trailer edge even in the unmodified configuration.

3.5 EFFECT OF TRACTOR/TRAILER GAP

It has been noted above that the windwise placement of a foreward body is certainly significant in defining the shielded area relative to the rear body. If the flow is not symmetrical in crosswind directions, then a further perturbation occurs causing flow through the gap separating the two bodies. Evidently this always occurs in flows with yaw (or crosswind components); however, it is noted that it also occurs if the tractor/trailer combination is not symmetrical in the vertical plane parallel to motion. In other words, if the central axis of the tractor is not aligned with that of the trailer there will be vertical gap flows. Consequently, there are always vertical velocity components in the gap, creating gap flows and losses even in unyawed motion. Apparently this is a major drag element in the two-body combination, since whether the gap flow is vertical downwards, or crosswise, there are large momentum losses. In the unyawed case, it appears that the "step" (difference in height between trailer roof and tractor roof) causes a portion of the upper surface flow over the tractor to be directed downwards into the gap. This mass then flows rearward under the trailer after considerable losses in head. In the yawed case a similar situation occurs in the lateral direction. The magnitude of the additional drag is quite large. For example, the AV wind tunnel tests described previously indicate that the drag coefficient of the unmodified tractor/trailer rig is about 0.83 at zero yaw and 1.08 at 6° of yaw, about a 30% increase. Part of this is due simply to the yawed flow about each body; however, it is

apparent that the gap increases the drag. For example, Ref. 4 shows a sharp-edged box has a drag change from 0.85 to 0.94 for 6° of yaw, about 10% increase. We attempt to estimate the gap effect by calculating the amount of trailer face unshielded by the crossflow. Assuming flow separating at 6° from the rear windward corner of the tractor, we find that this exposes extra trailer face of about 3.5 ft^2 for 50" gap and 100" tractor height. Assuming a nominal total drag area of about 100 ft^2, one would expect the increase in drag to be less than 5%, making the crude assumption that the increase is due to increased area at a drag coefficient of unity. There still appears to be about 15% of drag unaccounted for, presumably due to complicated flows in the gap. It is of interest to observe here that Ref. 4 shows the increase in drag with sideslip for a rounded body to be quite small, thus it might be expected that avoiding separation at the vertical front corners of the trailer, either by rounding or lipping, would be effective.

Considering now the effects of crosswind on plates attached to the tractor roof we observe that similar but more exaggerated effects may be expected. Good road test data is lacking here; however, wind tunnel tests conducted by AV showed that with tractor mounted planar shield type devices, the increase in drag with yaw is quite severe, amounting to about 40% increase at 6°. Now, it must be noted that, as stated in a previous section, it is believed that the wind tunnel tests are not exactly comparable with full-scale results; however, the large degradation with crosswind of solid planar tractor mounted devices has been observed also in road test and operational testing.

The yaw degradation of performance of solid shielding plates is a matter of considerable importance in which there is very little published data. It appears that the placement of such elements is very critical, and when properly positioned they create conditions minimizing the downward flow through the gap, thus having a more profound effect than the simple shielding of the trailer step. If this is the case, then the "triggering effect" (a small perturbation inducing a much larger one) can possibly easily be "detuned", which presumably is why the effectiveness is lost in the crosswind. It appears likely that vorticity and turbulence of rather large scale is shed in the wake of such a plate. In support of this, large airflow fluctuations were observed in AV full scale testing of impervious tractor mounted plates, as well as distinct buffeting of the plate itself. Possibly the large scale vortex system has a very narrow range of stable geometrical configurations.

3.6 SUMMARY OF DRAG ELEMENTS OF A TRUCK BODY

Although the above paragraphs represent insufficiently documented phenomena it appears that the following conclusions can be drawn.

1. The theoretical ideal of a dragless forebody can be achieved by preventing separation on the forward face. This can be accomplished quite practically by a forward protruding lip.

2. The base pressure appears to stabilize at modest underpressures of two or three tenths of dynamic pressure and further reduction of this can apparently only be achieved by some form of flow aspiration.

3. Providing there is no gap, that is on a single chassis type truck, a very significant drag reduction can be obtained by making the forebody dragless, and this reduction is maintained in a yawed flow.

4. For two-body vehicles, like a tractor/trailer rig, both edge treatment of the trailer (e.g., a lip type device) and deflectors on the tractor (e.g., a shield type device) can be quite effective at zero yaw. In yawed flows the tractor mounted deflector devices are not very effective. In addition, in yawed flow, quite significant drag increases are caused by the gap between the tractor and trailer. The mechanics of this flow is very poorly understood.

4. CONCLUSIONS

This report has described the various AeroVironment Truck Drag Reduction programs. Research has included analytical studies, wind tunnel testing, full scale field test, full scale road test, and operational testing. A number of different testing techniques have been perfected which operate simply and reliably and give precision of higher than 2% under windless conditions.

While drag reductions depend very much on exact configuration of equipment, significant savings have been achieved and validated on the two major truck types, using simple add-on devices. For tractor/trailer rigs maximum drag coefficient savings of the order of 20% have been achieved, while for single-chassis truck units 35% savings have been measured.

An understanding of the fluid dynamical mechanisms of truck aero drag has been obtained, and the ideal dragless forebody can be almost achieved in real conditions. Gap flows represent a significant drag producing factor and are not fully understood.

In all truck drag research the effects of yaw, caused by crosswind, is extremely important, and causes large drag increase. It appears that some add-on drag reducing devices are extremely sensitive to yaw, and lose effectiveness at a few degrees of sideslip. Other devices maintain good performance under yawed conditions.

A number of pay-off areas for basic and applied research are identified. These particularly involve the gap flow and the yawed condition.

REFERENCES

(1)   Bate, E. R., Jr. "An Assessment of Full Scale Vehicle Drag Measurements", AeroVironment Inc. Report M 361, November, 1973.

(2)   Lissaman, P. B. S., and J. H. Lambie, "Reduction of the Aerodynamic Drag of Large Highway Trucks", Proceedings of the RANN/DOT Conference on Reduction of the Aerodynamic Drag of Trucks, NSF RANN Document Center, October, 1974.

(3)   Lambie, J. H., "Techniques for Road Testing Under Controlled Conditions", Proceedings of the RANN/DOT Conference on Reduction of the Aerodynamic Drag of Trucks, NSF RANN Document Center, October, 1974.

(4)   Carr, G. W., "The Aerodynamics of Basic Shapes for Road Vehicles", Motor Industry Research Association, Britain, Report No. 1968/2, November, 1967.

DRAG REDUCTION OF TRUCKS WITH S^3 AIRVANES

Jeffrey W. Kirsch
Systems, Science and Software
La Jolla, California 92037

Abstract

S^3 Airvanes are airfoils which, installed in close proximity to the leading edges of a bluff ground vehicle, eliminate flow separation and reduce the pressure drag on the vehicle front face. A 1/20 scale wind tunnel program and road tests utilizing small and heavy duty trucks were performed to evaluate the effectiveness of the S^3 Airvanes in reducing air drag and improving energy efficiency of cargo vehicles. Through use of the airvanes a 38 percent drag reduction was obtained in the tunnel tests and it was found that the optimum location of the airvanes could be qualitatively determined from model tuft studies. Equilibrium rolling velocity tests on a full scale pick-up truck/box van indicated that the S^3 Airvanes yielded a 35 percent reduction in air drag. An 8000-mile freeway test program utilizing the pick-up truck and a heavy duty truck with various S^3 airvane configurations demonstrated increases in fuel economy from 9.2 to 26.5 percent.

1. INTRODUCTION

The wide variety of body shapes and truck configurations that typify the nation's trucking fleet present a formidable obstacle to the development of a clear-cut set of aerodynamic design criteria. Figure 1 is a series of schematic illustrations that demonstrate the different aerodynamic concepts to achieve drag reduction. First is to simply streamline the vehicle, by eliminating sharp corners and fairing the various flow transition regions. A second approach is to affix fairings to unstreamlined designs. The third and perhaps most popular concept is the utilization of flow deflectors, mounted on the tractor cab, to divert the brunt of the air flow over and around the top edges of the trailer.

Each of these three design approaches works; that is, they do reduce the air drag of commercial vehicles. However, there are problems associated with each concept. Streamlining often results in reduced payload capacity. Collapsible or permanent fairings may be difficult to adapt from one configuration to another. Air deflectors must be "tuned" to insure that the main air flow does, indeed, avoid the front trailer edges.

In an internally funded research program, Systems, Science and Software (S^3) has been investigating the feasibility of a different approach, the airvane concept. The fundamental idea is to reduce the air drag associated with sharp or bluff edges exposed to high velocity air flows. The basic concept is as follows: Air flow impacting on a bluff surface, radially diverges from the stagnation point. As this outflow approaches the windward edges it separates from the surface because, unless there is sufficient curvature, the flow cannot negotiate the bluff edge geometry. The bluff face causes the air flow to react as if a significantly larger body was responsible for the

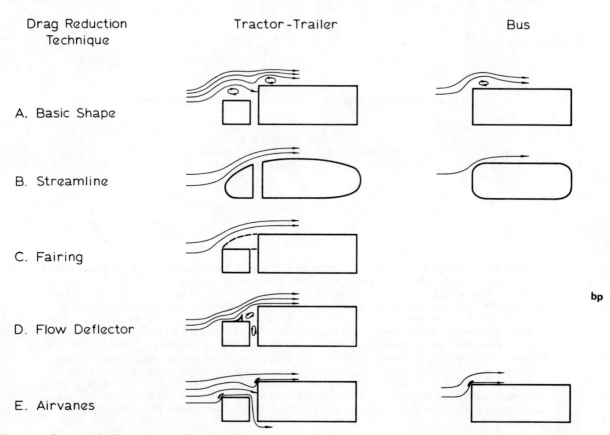

Drag Reduction Technique	Tractor-Trailer	Bus
A. Basic Shape		
B. Streamline		
C. Fairing		
D. Flow Deflector		
E. Airvanes		

bp

Figure 1. Schematic Illustrations of Various Techniques to Reduce the Air Drag of Truck and Bus Configurations.

displacement of air from the vehicle's path. This results in excessive pressure drag on the front face.

Positioning an airvane at the edge, as shown in Fig. 2, forces a portion of the interior flow to turn the corner. Under optimal conditions, the interior air flow that exits the slot between the vane and the leeward side of the edge attaches to the wall and smoothly merges with the exterior flow (which in turn is attached to the outer surface of the vane). The net result is that pressure on the windward face is reduced and an aerodynamic force is produced on the vane. At the rear corners, airvanes may be used to induce some degree of base pressure recovery.

The first phase of our research on the airvane concept was a wind tunnel program conducted at Cal Tech's Merrill wind tunnel in 1971. Using a 1/20 scale tractor-trailer model, we were able to

show that airvanes have significant drag reduction potential when placed in optimal positions relative to the various front edges of the trailer model. Front mounted airvanes reduced the drag of the trailer by 38 percent for wind speeds between 40 and 120 mph. With a streamlined cab in position, there was a 30 percent drag reduction. Rear mounted airvanes provided an additional 3-6 percent drag reduction, but were found to be prone to interference effects. This work was reported in an SAE paper of June 1973.[1]

Presented in this paper are the results of a road test program that demonstrate the applicability of the S^3 airvane concept to the leading edges of full scale vehicles. This research has resulted in patent applications for S^3 airvane design criteria,[2,3] and was crucial to S^3 being awarded a grant from the National Science Foundation to determine the degree to which S^3 airvanes are

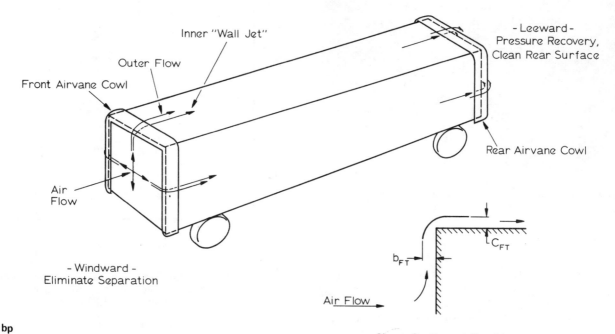

Figure 2. Schematic of Airvane Configurations for (Sharp-Edged) Basic Box Shape. Inset Shows Cross-Sectional Detail of Top Front Airvane.

capable of improving the fuel economy of heavy duty trucking rigs. The latter program will involve additional wind tunnel studies and full scale testing of S^3 airvanes and airdams (or spoilers) to reduce truck air drag.

2. PREVIOUS WIND TUNNEL RESULTS

The most significant results of the earlier wind tunnel study were the determination of the design criteria for optimum airvane efficiency and the observation that flow patterns indicated by tufts on the leeward surfaces were strongly correlated with airvane efficiency. This can be seen in Figs. 3 through 5. Separated flow regions downstream of the leading edges that extend for approximately one-third of the trailer model's length are associated with the unmodified vehicle (Fig. 3). The outer flow reattaches, and smooth flow is established on the last third of the trailer.

Figure 3. Flow Visualization Using Tufts and 1/20 Scale Wind Tunnel Model. Headwind of 112 MPH.

Figure 4. Flow Visualization Test. 1/20 Scale Model With Top, Front Mounted Airvane in Near-Optimum Position.

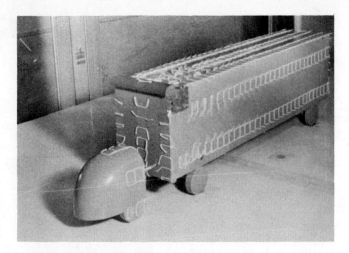

Figure 5. Flow Visualization Test. 1/20 Scale Model With Top, Front Mounted Airvane in Off-Optimum Position.

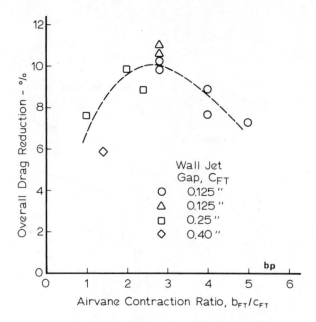

Figure 6. Overall Drag Reduction as a Function of Top Front Vane Contraction Ratio, b_{FT}/c_{FT}. Reynolds Number = 1.82 x 106.

Positioning of the top mounted airvane at a near-optimum location leads to elimination of the separated flow region (Fig. 4). Note the tuft located on the exterior of the vane indicates attached flow.

The airvane at an off-optimum position produces a flow pattern intermediate between the two extremes (Fig. 5).

These changes in the flow pattern downstream of the top edge are reflected in the drag reduction data associated with different airvane positions relative to the top front edge. These positions determine a contraction ratio, b/c (see Fig. 2 for b,c definition), which is used to correlate the drag reduction data, as shown in Fig. 6. These results demonstrate that optimal drag reduction by airvanes is sensitive to the relative position of the airvanes, and that an optimal location exists for a given airvane design.

It should also be noted that positive lift increments comparable to about half the measured reduction in air drag were measured when the airvanes were in position. Although pressure measurements on the front trailer face and direct force readings on the airvane were not obtained, it seems reasonable to conclude that the extra lift is at least partially due to that acting directly on the airvane.* Such a lift force is the vertical component of the aerodynamic force acting on the vane that would also contain a thrust component of similar magnitude. Hence, the drag reduction associated with airvanes is most likely due to a combination of reduced pressure loading on the front surface and the development of a net thrust on the airvane.

3. ROAD TEST PROGRAM

A road test program to evaluate the airvane concept was conducted by S^3 from July 1973 to March 1974. It consisted of three different types of tests. Over 8,000 miles of fuel economy road tests were recorded. Until test results from the current NSF program are reported, these data are our primary evidence for the fuel economy improvements that can be realized by reducing air drag with S^3 airvanes.

In addition to fuel economy tests, tufts affixed to the test vehicles were used to determine the effectiveness of airvane geometries. Relative changes in the drag coefficient were obtained in a

---

*Carr,[4] in his wind tunnel study of box aerodynamics, reports slight positive lift increments when the front edges are rounded and the box is in ground proximity. Thus, a portion of the lift increase on the airvaned model is due to modifications to flow about the model configuration.

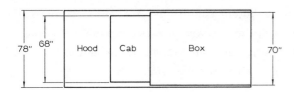

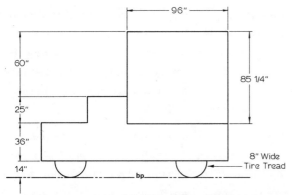

Figure 7. Schematic of 1961 Chevy Pick-Up and Box-Van Test Vehicle.

Figure 8. Three-Quarter View of 1961 Pick-Up Truck/Box Van Test Vehicle. Plexiglas Window on Right Side of Box Van is Visible, as is the Near Surface Flow Pattern Indicated by Tufts. Road Speed is 50 MPH.

series of tests that measured the equilibrium velocity of the test vehicle rolling down a grade for the different airvane configurations.

3.1 TEST VEHICLES

The primary test vehicle (~7,000 miles of fuel economy testing) was a 1961 Chevy Apache 10 pick-up truck that was specially fitted with a box-shaped van located in the truck bed (Figs. 7, 8). The van presents a 70 in. x 60 in. frontal surface to the relative wind (doubling the frontal area of the truck). A relatively small percentage of the fuel economy tests were conducted with the van frontal surface extended six inches over the cab so that curved and beveled side corners could be evaluated.

The van was fitted with side and top, plexiglas windows, four feet long, that were placed four inches downstream of the windward edge. Black, acrilan tufts were affixed to the truck surfaces. They could be readily observed by both observers within and outside the truck van.

Each of the three front edges was fitted with air-vanes that could be moved longitudinally and locked

in position to allow study of airvane position effects. Two airvane geometries were evaluated, to be referred to as the nominal and small airvanes, respectively.[*] They were fabricated from rolled steel sheet.

Halfway through the program, the truck was equipped with a Floscan totalizer[5] that instantaneously monitors fuel flow to the nearest tenth of a gallon. This is a device that counts the digital signal from a matched, rotating impeller type flow transducer connected in the fuel line. Tire pressures were maintained at 42 psig ±1 psig throughout the test program.

Prior to initiating the test program, the truck was lubricated and tuned, and the odometer was calibrated. It was determined that peak horsepower developed by the six-cylinder, 235-cubic inch truck engine (measured on a dynamometer) was 70 HP delivered to the rear wheels at 60 mph. This is 85 percent of the original engine BHP rating (assuming a 75 percent drive train efficiency). (Two-thirds of the way through the program, standard maintenance service was performed on the vehicle.)

In addition to the pick-up truck, a limited number of tests was conducted with a new 22-ft, 23,000-GVW van truck.[**] The C-700 Ford was equipped

[*]Exact dimensions and drawings of the S³ airvanes are withheld pending the outcome of two patent applications submitted by S³.

[**]Courtesy of the PhD Corporation, San Diego, California.

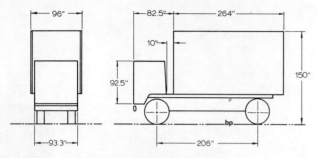

VEHICLE SPECIFICATIONS

C-700 Ford 2 Ton 22' Van
Current Model (1974)
Power Steering, Power Brakes
Radio and Heater
5 Speed, 2 Speed Transmission
361 CID Heavy Duty V8 Engine
206" Wheelbase

1,500 Lbs Capacity Hydraulic
Lift Gate
9:00 · 20 Tires
23,000 Lbs G.V.W.
Payload Capacity: 12,000 Lbs
Width: 8', Height: 8' 6", Length: 22'
Weight: 12,000 Lbs

Figure 9. Schematic and Vehicle Specifications of Heavy Duty Truck Used in Fuel Economy Tests to Evaluate S³ Airvane Mounted on Top, Front Edge of Van.

with a 361 C.I.D. heavy duty V-8 engine, and the unladen weight was 11,000 pounds. Tire pressure was maintained at 75 psig for all tests. On this particular truck the van box was displaced 10 inches aft of the truck cab and had three-inch beleveled, vertical side edges. A schematic of the truck is given in Fig. 9.

3.2 FLOW VISUALIZATION EXPERIMENTS

The flow visualization tests were conducted under zero or low wind conditions. The truck was driven at 50 mph and observers within the van, or in other vehicles traveling in close vicinity to the test vehicle, observed the overall flow pattern and obtained numerous 35 mm still photographs of the tufts' positions (at shutter speeds of

1/250 or 1/125 seconds). It was also noted that, under turbulent conditions, the tufts' rapid oscillations led to a characteristic random clicking noise within the van caused by the individual tufts lashing against the van surfaces.

The flow patterns observed in these tests are reminiscent of the wind tunnel results. Figure 8 is an exterior 3/4 shot of the unmodified vehicle. Note the wholesale separation downstream of the leading edge is dominated by a circulatory flow pattern. This is more clearly illustrated in Fig. 10, where the side wall tuft distribution is shown in more detail.

An interior shot of the tufts on the top plexiglas panel (Fig. 11) illustrates the type of separation observed aft of the roof edge. Here the flow reversal is more two-dimensional in the sense that the near surface flow is dominated by a more uniform, reversed flow.

As one might expect, the positioning of airvanes at the windward edges lead to dramatic changes in the flow patterns. Figure 12 shows the 3/4 view of the modified truck. Note that the side flow is much more uniform, all tufts indicating relatively smooth, attached flow. In these configurations the drumming/clicking noises of the tufts on the vehicle walls is eliminated. Another characteristic feature of airvane-modified truck flows is that the stagnation zone location is not changed from the unmodified configuration.

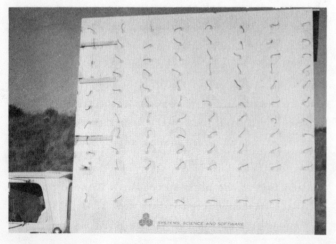

Figure 10. Close-Up View of Left Side of Test Vehicle. Note Separated Flow Pattern Downstream of Left Verticle Edge. Road Speed is 50 MPH.

Figure 11. Tuft Pattern on Center Roof Plexiglas Panel Without Airvane in Position. Note that Tufts Indicate Reverse Flow, as Observed in Wind Tunnel Experiments, Figure 3. Road Speed is 50 MPH.

Figure 12. Three-Quarter View of Test Vehicle With S³ Airvanes in Position at Three Front Edges of Box Van. Attached Flow Pattern Indicated by Tufts.

Figure 13. Close-Up View of Left Side of Test Vehicle With S³ Airvanes in Position. Note Attached Flow Pattern Downstream of Left Vertical Side Edge.

A close-up view of the vehicle side wall is shown in Fig. 13.

As in the case of the wind tunnel model, it was observed that it was more difficult to achieve smooth, attached flow on the top roof surface with airvanes than at the side surfaces. This may be related to the stabilizing influence of attached flow on the lower boundary of the side walls.

Photographs of the tuft patterns on the top plexiglas panel indicate that optimal locations of the airvane can be determined. Figure 14 shows the tufts' distribution for the smaller airvane placed with the leading edge too close to the truck roof corner. The first row of tufts indicates the "wall jet" flow out of the vane is not smoothly attached to the surface, and attachment of the main exterior flow occurs at/or beyond the fifth row.

This situation is improved by increasing the front overhang of the airvane, as shown in Fig. 15. The attachment of the inner and outer flows is definite, although considerable irregularity in the flow pattern is an indication that the smaller airvane may not be adequate to achieve maximum drag reduction.

Tests with the larger airvanes indicated that the flow on the roof surface could be further smoothed, as shown in Fig. 16. The larger airvane was set at the nominal configuration when this photograph was taken. Placing the larger airvane at an off-optimal location (in this case, moving the leading

Figure 14. Tuft Pattern, Center Roof Panel, With Small S³ Airvane in Off-Design Position. The Tufts Indicate Incomplete Attachment of Air Flow. Note Flow Reversal in Third and Fourth Rows of Tufts. Road Speed is 50 MPH.

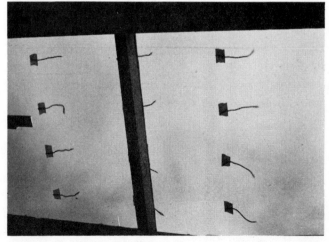

Figure 15. Tuft Pattern, Center Roof Panel, With Small S³ Airvane in Design Position. The Tufts Still Indicate Imcomplete Flow Attachment on Vehicle Roof.

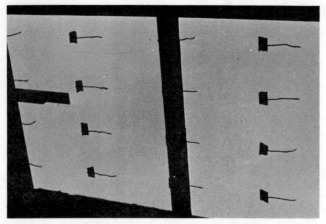

Figure 16. Tuft Pattern, Center Roof Panel With Nominal S3 Airvane in Design Position. Tufts Indicate Attached Air Flow. Road Speed is 50 MPH.

Figure 17. Tuft Pattern, Center Roof Panel, With Nominal S3 Airvane in Off-Design Position. Tufts Indicate Perturbed Attachment Flow Pattern.

edge closer to the roof corner) leads to a more turbulent attachment, illustrated by the tufts' pattern in Fig. 17.

3.3 ROLLING VELOCITY TESTS

The equilibrium or terminal velocity of a vehicle rolling down an incline is reached when the gravitational force is balanced by the rolling resistance and air drag acting on the vehicle, i.e.,

$$D + R = W \sin \alpha \qquad (1)$$

where

D = air drag
R = rolling resistance
W = vehicle weight
α = grade angle

This is illustrated in Fig. 18.

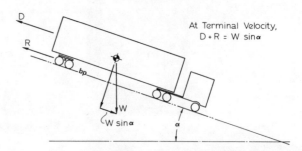

Figure 18. Schematic Illustration of Terminal Velocity Tests.

When the drag and rolling resistance are written in coefficient form, i.e.,

$$D = C_D \left\{ \frac{1}{2} \rho V_a^2 \right\} A \qquad (2)$$

$$R = C_R \left\{ W \cos \alpha \right\}^* \qquad (3)$$

where

C_D = air drag coefficient
ρ = air density
V_a = relative air velocity
A = cross-sectional area of vehicle
C_R = rolling resistance coefficient

the equations reduce to

$$C_D = \frac{W}{V_a^2} \left\{ \frac{2}{\rho A} \right\} (\sin \alpha - C_R \cos \alpha) \qquad (4)$$

Thus, if W, ρ, A, α, and C_R are fixed at constant values, the relative change in vehicle drag coefficient from configuration 1 to configuration 2 is given by

$$C_{D_2} = C_{D_1} \left(\frac{V_{a_1}^2}{V_{a_2}^2} \right) \qquad (5)$$

In our tests, we employed a 5 percent grade section of Pacific Coast Highway that passes through the Torrey Pines State Reserve. Although very near the ocean, the road was partially shielded from the prevailing sea breeze and early morning tests with low wind speeds were possible. However, even small gusts perturb such a test, and the accuracy of these experiments is strongly

---

*For simplicity, C_R is assumed to be independent of the rolling velocity.

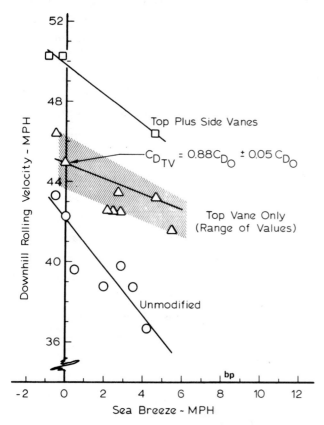

Figure 19. Downhill Rolling Velocity as a Function of Sea Breeze for Various Configurations.

Labels in figure:
Downhill Rolling Velocity - MPH
Top Plus Side Vanes
$C_{D_{TV}} = 0.88 C_{D_O} \pm 0.05 C_{D_O}$
Top Vane Only (Range of Values)
Unmodified
bp
Sea Breeze - MPH

dependent on exact measurements of relative air velocity. These were not measured in our tests, as we recorded only the road velocity. Figure 19 is a composite plot of typical results with this simple technique. For each configuration, there is a large spread in the recorded terminal velocities, which are plotted as a function of the sea breeze (measured at the bottom of the grade). The data spread of ± 5 percent is large enough to mask the effects of airvane optimization. Therefore, no serious attempts were made to exploit this technique.[*]

Nevertheless, these experiments are useful in showing that our qualitative results from the tufts visualization study were qualitatively corroborated by our terminal velocity observations. The top

vane provided approximately 12 percent reduction in drag coefficient, and all three airvanes yielded a 28 percent drag reduction. These numbers are clearly in good agreement with wind tunnel results.

To compute C_D for the unmodified vehicle in zero cross-winds, let us assume that $C_R \approx 0.01$. Substituting the vital parameters into Eq. (4) yields a value for C_D of 0.71. This gives a maximum level grade velocity for the truck of about 55 mph; an upper limit that the unmodified truck could not maintain over the freeway test course.

3.4 FUEL ECONOMY TESTS

It is evident from the flow visualization and terminal velocity studies, that airvanes are appropriate for full scale road vehicles, i.e., they should reduce the power requirements of vehicles and thereby cut down the fuel consumption for vehicles driven at equal road speeds. Three separate test series, each involving various front mounted vane configurations, were made with the pick-up truck/box van test vehicle. Because the air drag of this vehicle accounts for approximately 80 percent to 85 percent of the total resistance acting on the truck, this vehicle was an ideal test bed to evaluate the impact of aerodynamic devices on fuel economy. It is not, of course, a heavy duty truck. To demonstrate that the design criteria generated in the wind tunnel and road test program were applicable to full size trucks, a series of fuel economy tests was also conducted with the 22-ft, bob-tail truck (Fig. 9).

Each road test in the study was conducted over an identical 58.8 mile Interstate 5 freeway course under actual traffic conditions. The road grades are moderate (3 percent or less) for this section of I-5.[**] The first three test series were conducted at a nominal road speed of 50 mph. The heavy duty truck tests were conducted at 55 mph. Cross-winds are measured at the start, middle,

[*]Of course, improvements in instrumentation to measure V_a would then require more accurate assessment of quantities affecting ρ and C_R, which was beyond the scope of the present program.

[**]The trades have been categorized as follows: 38% of the test course has a grade less than 1%, 35% of the test course has a grade between 1% and 2.5%, and 26.8% has a grade from 2.5% to 3%. A small section of the course, 0.2% (or 0.1 mile), as a grade of 5%.

and end points of each run so that some measure of their influence on S^3 airvane performance could be ascertained. In general, the majority of cross-wind results presented in this paper are for the dominant westerly sea breeze, perpendicular to the roadway direction over most of the course.

Test Series 1. Thirty-three mileage runs were made with the basic test vehicle in three configurations:

(1) S^3 airvanes at front top and side edges of van

(2) S^3 airvanes at front top edge only

(3) Square edges - unmodified vehicle

The fuel economy measurements, in mpg, are plotted as a function of cross-wind speed in Fig. 20. It is readily apparent that S^3 airvanes are extremely effective in reducing the power/fuel requirements to move a box through the air medium. The top vane alone yields an average 10.5 percent increase in fuel economy (mpg), while the side vanes give an additional 16 percent improvement. An interesting result is that the top vane

maintains its efficiency under high cross-winds whereas the side air vanes work better at low cross-winds. (This has been remedied in subsequent S^3 airvane designs.) If we assume that the rolling friction and air drag coefficients for the unmodified configuration are 0.01 and 0.71, respectively, the calculated air drag reduction with the top vane is 12.2 percent and for all three vanes, 27 percent.

Translating these results into fuel savings for full scale trucks is best accomplished by using the fuel economy figures in gpm. In Table 1, savings are given for S^3 test vehicle, at a cross-wind of 3 mph, and a full size truck with 60 percent additional exposed cross-sectional area. Note that the top vane could save 750 gallons of fuel per 50,000 miles. Since fuel consumption for a typical truck is 0.2 gpm to 0.25 gpm, this represents a 6 percent to 7 percent fuel savings for gasoline fueled engines. *

Table I
S^3 Airvane Fuel Savings

Item	Fuel Consumption, gpm	Fuel Savings, gpm	
		Measured	Anticipated
Configuration	S^3 Test Vehicle	S^3 Test Vehicle	Full Size Trucks
Unmodified	0.0905	------	------
Top Vane Only	0.0813	0.0092	0.0147
Top Plus Side Vanes	0.0706	0.0199	0.0318

Test Series 2, 3. The second and third test series evaluated the following configurations:

(1) Front side edges beveled with a 6 in., 45 deg cut

(a) Top vane only

(b) Side plus top vanes

(c) Without vanes

(2) Front side edges fitted with 2 in. radius of curvature

(a) With side vanes only

(b) With side vanes plus edge spoilers

(c) Without vanes

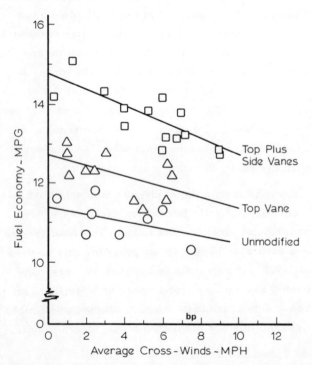

Figure 20. Fuel Economy Variation with Cross-Wind for Unmodified and Modified Configurations of the S^3 Test Vehicle. Road Speed is 50 MPH.

*Diesel efficiency is higher than gasoline/spark engines, hence the fuel savings in gpm will be slightly lower (from 0.01 gpm to 0.013 gpm).

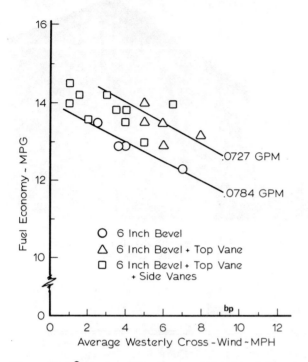

Figure 21. S³ Airvane Effectiveness With 6 Inch Bevel on Vertical Edges of S³ Test Vehicle. Road Speed is 50 MPH.

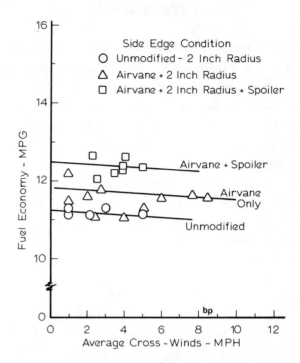

Figure 22. Effectiveness of S³ Airvanes With Rounded Edges. Road Speed is 50 MPH.

As shown in Fig. 21, the top vane provided a 7.2 percent fuel economy improvement to the beveled edge front; however, the side vanes did not measurably affect the fuel mileage. Since fuel economy with only the top vane and the bevel edges was comparable to that measured for top plus side vanes with square edges configuration, it could be argued that the bevel plus top vane configuration was sufficient to reduce drag to a minimum, and that addition of side vanes may even be expected to incur a drag penalty. That this penalty was not observed is encouraging. Optimal airvane configurations may exist such that additional drag reduction can be achieved for highly beveled corners.

The 2 in. radius configuration fuel economy results (plotted in Fig. 22 as a function of wind speed) provided a great deal of insight on an important technical point about airvane design. The small degree of curvature on the sides did not provide a significant savings, even with side mounted airvanes in place. However, by adding a sharp edge "spoiler" to the front radii, the drag reduction was greatly enhanced and fuel economy went up 1.5 mpg.

These results indicate that the airvane works not only by establishing attached flow downstream of the edges, but also by generating a net aerodynamic force that has a component opposite in direction to the pressure drag on the bluff vehicle.

Heavy Duty Truck Tests. A series of nine road tests (540 miles) was made with the 22-ft van "bob-tail" truck to ascertain if the S³ airvane results obtained with the pick-up truck test vehicle were attainable with larger vehicles. The nominal top vane design was scaled to an 8-ft wide truck and installed at the top front roof edge, as shown in Fig. 23. Test results are tabulated in Table 2. Although wind conditions were such as to preclude comparisons of fuel economy versus wind velocity, the average fuel savings was 0.014 gpm with the top mounted S³ airvane for cross-winds less than 5 mph. While more data are required to pin down the exact fuel savings potential of S³ airvanes for various truck configurations, these preliminary findings give every indication that S³ airvanes are capable of significantly reducing the air drag of bluff surfaces exposed to the wind.

261

4. FUTURE RESEARCH

S^3 is currently conducting a research program with a grant from the National Science Foundation to further determine the feasibility of S^3 airvanes as truck air drag reduction devices. It will consist of fuel economy road tests with large trucks and tractor/trailer configurations to be conducted in conjunction with wind tunnel studies of the aerodynamics of truck vehicles. In addition to the S^3 airvanes, new airvane configurations and airdams (or spoilers) located so as to deflect high velocity flow from the front wheel axle assemblies will be evaluated.

Figure 23. S^3 Airvane Installed on Top, Front Roof of Heavy Duty Truck Van.

Table II
Fuel Economy Test Results - Heavy Duty Truck

Run	Config.	Date	Winds (mph)	Time, hr	Fuel, gal	gpm
1	Unmod.	2/13/74	2.84, W	1.15	11.15	0.187
2	Unmod.	2/14/74	1.2, NE	1.13	10.78	0.181
3	Unmod.	2/24/74	1.5, W	1.10	10.45	0.176
4	Unmod.	2/25/74	5.5, WNW	1.12	10.40	0.175
				Unmodified, Average = 0.180 gpm		
5	Top Vane	2/12/74	0.75, NE	1.12	9.58	0.161
6	Top Vane	2/12/74	1.2, W	1.10	9.60	0.161
7	Top Vane	2/14/74	4.5, W	1.10	10.63	0.179
8	Top Vane	2/28/74	4.4, E-W (gusty)	1.13	9.58	0.161
9	Top Vane	2/28/74	4.5, NNW	1.12	9.98	0.168
			Top Vane Configuration, Average = 0.166 gpm			

ACKNOWLEDGEMENTS

The author wishes to take this opportunity to thank Messrs. R. Broce, E. Day, and A. Good for their meaningful contributions to the conduct of this research program. Their assistance, and the financial support of Systems, Science and Software (S^3) made this paper possible.

REFERENCES

(1) Kirsch, J.W., S.K. Garg, and W.H. Bettes, "Drag Reduction of Bluff Vehicles with Airvanes," SAE Paper No. 730686, Presented at Combined Commercial Vehicle Engineering and Operations and Powerplant Meetings, Chicago, Ill., June 18-22, 1973.

(2) Kirsch, J.W., and S.K. Garg, "Airvane Device for Bluff Vehicles and the Like," Patent Application No. 456,470.

(3) Kirsch, J.W., and E.A. Day, "Air Guide Kit and Improved Airvane Therefor," Patent Application No. 456,469.

(4) Carr, G.W., "The Aerodynamics of Basic Shapes for Road Vehicles, Part 1, Simple Rectangular Bodies," Motor Industry Research Association, Great Britain, Report No. 1968/2.

(5) Floscan Totalizer, Floscan Instrument Company, 3016 N.E. Blakely Street, Seattle, Washington 98105.

DISCUSSION

AUD. QUESTION: What was the coefficient of drag of your test vehicle before you started to modify it and what was it after modification?

KIRSCH: The drag coefficient of the basic vehicle was about 0.7. That's a believable number since it corresponds to a required horsepower of 70 at 50 mph. The modifications gave us a reduction in drag of 12 to 27 percent.

FIELDS: What kind of drag reduction did you get from vanes installed on the back of the truck?

KIRSCH: We didn't evaluate vanes at the back because our wind tunnel results indicated that it would take too much finessing with the configuration to achieve the 3 to 5 percent improvement that they are capable of providing. I am not belittling that kind of improvement; 5 percent is a significant number in trucking operations. The details of the rear vane work are reported in SAE Paper No. 730686.

HENRY JEX: You mentioned that half of the drag reduction you obtained is due to a reduction of forces on the front, a Townend ring effect. To what do you attribute the rest of the drag reduction?

KIRSCH: The major reduction in drag is associated with the elimination of separation on the sides. The flow is no longer looking at a big box; because separation has been eliminated, the flow thinks it is working on a smaller box.

Richard Scherrer, Session Chairman and Peter Bryant

Bernard Pershing, Meeting Chairman

Lynn Yakel

J. J. Cornish III

Jon McKibben

Pershing and Douglas Malewicki

Glen Brown

Kevin Cooper, Roger Hawks
and E. Eugene Larrabee

Discussions During The Break

Henry Jex, Walter Korff and William Bettes

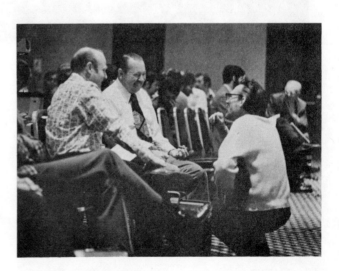

Alex Tremulis, Jon McKibben and
Henry Jex Viewing Alex's Display of
Experimental Automobile Models

Dean Batchelor

Peter Lissaman and Jeffrey Kirsch

Pershing and Eugene Olsen
of Ford Motor Co.